THE CAREER OF ARTHUR HAMILTON GORDON

Sir Arthur Gordon, *circa* 1870

The Career of

ARTHUR HAMILTON GORDON

First Lord Stanmore

1829-1912

J. K. CHAPMAN

UNIVERSITY OF TORONTO PRESS

PREFACE

❦

A CENTURY AGO, Arthur Hamilton Gordon began a distinguished thirty-year career as a colonial governor. In October 1861, the aristocratic youngest son of the fourth Earl of Aberdeen took office as lieutenant-governor of New Brunswick in Fredericton, the quiet provincial capital, where this study of his life has been written. Honest, gentlemanly Gordon soon came to hold the democratic New Brunswickers in low esteem. Those who took part in politics were mostly corrupt and ill-educated. Most well-established, educated men refused to enter political life. Gordon found that he lacked constitutional power to make a useful contribution to provincial life. Frustrated and bitter, he swore that he would never again reign over a colony having responsible government. He broke his vow only once, late in his career, when he became governor of New Zealand. That experience did nothing to raise his opinion of self-governing colonials.

In so far as Gordon's New Brunswick and New Zealand administrations have hitherto been studied, they have generally been considered unsuccessful. Too many scholars have based their judgment upon incomplete information. Others have had their vision clouded by colonial nationalism. Few have established valid criteria for judging a governor's success under responsible government. Should the laurel wreath be given only to the governor who looked upon his office as a sinecure and whose only activity consisted in keeping on the good side of his ministers? Should it not, with greater justice, go to the governor who sought, even unavailingly, to influence his ministers away from ill-judged actions and to persuade them to take a higher view of the public welfare than party advantage? During the first generation or more of responsible government, governors could prevent mischief only if their ministers' hearts were not set upon it, and only in rare and exceptional circumstances could they persuade their ministers to do positive good. Gordon never stopped trying.

Although Arthur Gordon's strong proconsular predilections ill fitted him for self-governing colonies, they served him well in Crown colonies where he spent most of his career. Trinidad, Mauritius (although here the governor's power was inhibited by an unofficial majority in the council), Fiji, and Ceylon all offered Gordon great scope for his undoubted administrative talents and many opportunities for promoting public welfare. In those colonies and in the offices of high commissioner and consul-general for the Western Pacific, which he held for over six years, he exercised his power to the full and conferred positive and lasting benefits upon those colonies and islands.

Rarely did nineteenth-century governors have as long and varied careers in the colonial service as Gordon. More rarely still did they preserve their private papers. Gordon believed justifiably that he had shown ability, versatility, and inventiveness, and that he had demonstrated how a dedicated governor could better the lives of countless people. Often pessimistic, he feared his work would go unrecognized or be forgotten. Although he gained some recognition during his lifetime, he got less than he thought he deserved. Nearly always egotistical, he preserved his extensive correspondence to assure his biographer ample information. Upon that collection (now in the British Museum[1]) and upon the Colonial Office records in the Public Record Office, this book is largely based.

Sir Arthur Gordon was the outstanding governor of his generation as Sir George Grey and Sir Frederick Lugard were of the generation before and after. All three were men of thought and action. All were innovators. All left their marks upon the colonies they governed and upon British colonial policy. Together their careers spanned the middle and late years of the nineteenth and the early years of the twentieth centuries. Gordon was a friend of both Grey and Lugard, and was the connecting link between them; as his policies owed something to Grey's experiences in Cape Colony and New Zealand, so, too, was Lugard partly indebted to Gordon for his successful policies in West Africa. Authoritative studies of the careers of Grey[2] and Lugard[3] have recently appeared and have added appreciably to our understanding of the governor's rôle in British colonial administration. Nevertheless, a shortage of biographies of

[1]Most of Gordon's New Brunswick correspondence is lodged in the Bonar Law–Bennett Library at the University of New Brunswick.

[2]J. Rutherford, *Sir George Grey, K.C.B., 1812–1898, A Study in Colonial Government* (London, 1961).

[3]M. Perham, *Lugard* (2 vols., London, 1956, 1960).

colonial governors continues to preclude a definitive assessment of that rôle. The primary and limited purpose of the present biography is to bring such an assessment a step closer to realization.

This book is a study of Gordon and his work. It is neither an examination of British colonial policy nor a history of the colonies in which Gordon served. I hope, however, that it will throw new light upon certain aspects of colonial policy and upon the history of those colonies and that it will establish Gordon in his rightful place as one of the great governors of the Second British Empire.

I owe thanks to many persons and organizations for their help. I must express my deep sense of obligation to Gordon's son, the late Baron Stanmore, who gave me full access to his father's papers and who accepted my suggestion that they be lodged in the British Museum. I gratefully acknowledge the co-operation of the British Museum's Manuscript Division, especially that of Mr. Philip Blake-Hill. I would note, too, the cheerful efficiency of the Public Record Office staff under often badly overcrowded conditions.

Among the scholars to whom I am indebted for suggestions and encouragement are Professor Gerald S. Graham, Rhodes Professor of Imperial History, King's College, University of London; Professor Paul Knaplund, Professor Emeritus of History, University of Wisconsin; my colleagues at the University of New Brunswick, Professors A. G. Bailey, W. S. MacNutt, D. M. Young and D. W. L. Earl; and, finally, Professor Alec Lucas of the Department of English, McGill University. Professor Lucas was kind enough to read the manuscript and suggest stylistic changes.

Few research projects are now undertaken without financial assistance. My research has been made possible by the generosity of Rt. Hon. Lord Beaverbrook, the Institute of Historical Research at the University of London, the Social Science Research Council of Canada, and the Canada Council. This work has been published with the help of a grant from the Social Science Research Council, using funds provided by the Canada Council, and with assistance from the Publications Fund of the University of Toronto Press.

Throughout the ten years during which I have intermittently been preparing this book my wife has given cheerfully of her time and energy as typist. To her I lovingly dedicate it.

J. K. CHAPMAN

University of New Brunswick
Fredericton, N.B.

CONTENTS

❧

ILLUSTRATIONS

❧

THE CAREER OF ARTHUR HAMILTON GORDON

I

EARLY LIFE OF ARTHUR HAMILTON GORDON

⚜

ARTHUR HAMILTON GORDON was thirty-one when he received his first appointment as a colonial governor. His tastes and habits, his early training and associations, had given him "a broader and more statesman-like way of looking at things than most Governors possess. . . ."[1] He had excellent natural abilities and a strong desire to use them for good. He had good political connections and a passion for power and fame. He had great energy and a strong will. All combined to make him one of the most distinguished administrators in the British Empire during the latter half of the nineteenth century.

Arthur Gordon was born 26 November 1829, at Argyll House in London, the youngest of the four sons of the fourth Earl of Aberdeen and his second wife. At that time, Lord Aberdeen was foreign secretary in Wellington's cabinet and was destined to succeed Sir Robert Peel as leader of the Peelite faction and, in 1852, to become prime minister. On the death, in 1829, of the last of the daughters of his first marriage, Lord Aberdeen transferred to his infant son the affection he had given them.[2] The death of Arthur's mother in 1833 and of his only sister in 1834, and his own delicate health, further focused his father's love and attention upon him.

Until he was fifteen he was Lord Aberdeen's almost constant companion, and during this time, spent partly in London and partly at Haddo House, the ancestral home of the Aberdeens, he lived a sheltered and even pampered life. Considered too delicate for public school, he was educated at home.

[1]Arthur Gordon to Roundell Palmer, Earl of Selborne (private), 13 April 1883, quoting Lord Granville, Stanmore Papers, 49218.
[2]Lady Frances Balfour, *The Life of George, Fourth Earl of Aberdeen*, II, 6.

His early harbourage behind the paternal breakwater and an uneven education left Arthur Gordon with personality defects which he never completely overcame. It is true that he might not have survived without the special tenderness shown him by his father, but that tenderness and his own loving and gentle disposition led him to "desire full returns of confidence and affection," an attitude which later brought him much pain and anxiety.[3] In 1846, Lady Henrietta Frances de Grey chided him for his morbidly sensitive and romantic attachment to her nephew, Goderich,[4] and offered him the following analysis and advice:

You have been a Hot House plant read beyond your years, and inheriting from your Father deep feelings, without a Mother or unmarried sister to lavish those feelings upon and therefore you exaggerate them to yourself and trifles prey upon you. . . . Don't be morbid, try and take things more as you find them—do not think too much about yourself, your feelings etc., etc., watch others whom you respect and admire, endeavour to imitate them—do not analyse motives of others. . . . Endeavour to form your ideas as to what your future life is to be, and do not dream life away—but steadily pursue your course, with a view to attaining distinction in it. Let religion in everything guide your conduct.[5]

At seventeen Gordon was probably less self-confident and self-reliant than he would have been had he attended a public school; yet a public school might have warped and hurt him. He was still impulsive and showed a tendency to avoid difficult subjects. These faults had not been corrected "by the necessity either extraneous or self-imposed of doing certain things at certain times."[6] He neglected Latin and Greek and lagged far behind those of his own age in mathematics. But he had a keen interest in history and law, and raised as he was in an atmosphere of politics, in almost daily contact with Lord Aberdeen's cabinet colleagues, he had a knowledge and judgment of contemporary affairs quite beyond his years.[7] There were, however, disadvantages in this political precocity. One of his tutors put it this way: "By quickness of apprehension and memory he has laid hold of large truths and conceptions without any real effort of thought in acquiring them. He has got treasures without paying the labour price for them."[8]

[3]H. V. Elliott to Lord Aberdeen, 25 Sept. 1845, Stanmore Papers, 49224. Elliott was curate of St. Mary's, Brighton.

[4]George Frederick Samuel Robinson, Viscount Goderich, succeeded his father as Earl of Ripon and his uncle as Earl de Grey, and was created Marquis of Ripon in 1871.

[5]Henrietta Frances de Grey to Gordon, 23 July [1846], Stanmore Papers, 49233.

[6]James Garbett to Lord Aberdeen, 5 June 1847, Stanmore Papers, 49224. James Garbett was rector at Clayton, near Brighton, and was Gordon's tutor in 1846 and 1847.

[7]Elliott to Aberdeen, 25 Sept. 1845, Stanmore Papers, 49224.

[8]Garbett to Aberdeen, 5 June 1847, Stanmore Papers, 49224.

Arthur Gordon's leisured and secluded youth came to end with a year of fairly concentrated study especially in Latin, Greek, and mathematics under James Garbett, who, in his rectory near Brighton, usually prepared several boys for university. Gordon passed his entrance examinations with credit and entered Trinity College, Cambridge, in the autumn of 1847. Here he was independent for the first time and, given his serious nature, he formulated, as was perhaps inevitable, a set of rules to replace the parental hand as a guide to life. He would, he vowed, attend morning prayers always, take Holy Communion at St. Giles as frequently as possible, follow the New Testament lessons in Greek, refuse invitations to supper, and exercise great discretion respecting breakfast parties. He would never return to a wine party after chapel unless at some intimate friend's and he would avoid all immoral society. He would always read from nine until two and in the evening from nine until eleven. He vowed to fast humbly every Friday, and also on Wednesday during Lent. He would attend no parties on fast-days or during Lent, or on the Lord's Day. Finally he would do his duty quietly and humbly, never setting himself up as superior to others or speaking ill of others.[9] Gordon must have honoured the rules he imposed upon himself, judging by the testimony of William Carus, senior dean of Trinity College. Late in 1849, Carus wrote to Gordon:

I cannot take leave of you this Xmas, (whilst also bidding farewell to the office I have so long held) without an expression of my very sincere regard for you, after the exemplary manner in which you have uniformly fulfilled the whole of your college duties.

The pattern which you have given to all around you, more especially in a regular and devout attendance at Chapel has I doubt not been influential for good. I should not do justice to my own feelings and I should fail also in the discharge of a duty, which is really owing to you, if I did not offer you this slight token of my high esteem.[10]

Gordon led an active and busy life at Cambridge. He swam and walked. He taught at St. Giles school. He became president of the Cambridge Union in 1848–49 (which enabled him partly to overcome his shyness and to become a fairly accomplished speaker). He studied hard, as his reading list in history[11] during the autumn term of 1848 demonstrates. It included Thierry's *Conquest*, Ranke's *Popes*, Dunham's *Germany*, *Martyrs' Letters*, Palmer's *Ecclesiastical History*, Wilberforce's *American Church*, Macaulay's *England*, two volumes of Thirlwall's *Greece*, and part of Lorenzo de Medici. Nor was this all. He read much of Chaucer and Shakespeare and a good deal in divinity.

[9]Gordon's diary, [Sept., 1847?], Stanmore Papers, 49233, f. 147.
[10]William Carus to Gordon, 17 Dec. 1849, Stanmore Papers, 49233, f. 239.
[11]Gordon's diary, 15 Dec. 1848, Stanmore Papers, 49253, f. 41.

The last included Wordsworth's *Letters to Goudon*,[12] Mill's[13] *Lent Sermons*, and the first part of Hooker.[14] At this time Gordon considered taking the newly established honours tripos, but on the advice of his father did not.

Despite a degree of satisfaction with his studies and much happiness in the friendships he had formed, especially with Henry Bradshaw (later Cambridge University librarian) and Alfred Barry (later primate of Australia), Gordon was discontented. He had not as yet decided upon a career. As early as 1845, before his sixteenth birthday, his father had asked him what profession he wished to follow. He had replied, after some deliberation, that, while the life of a country clergyman was undoubtedly the most peacefully happy, he did not think he ought to enter the Church because he felt insufficiently desirous and worthy. He rejected the army as "an idle and unprofitable way of spending one's life." He did not have a penchant for the law, which, however, was doubtless an important profession "in this lawyer-ridden country." He disliked diplomacy and his dislike increased daily: "It seems to me," he wrote, "that even supposing one attains the highest ranks one is always in a false position, obliged to enforce instructions from home which perhaps one does not agree with by arguments of which one perhaps sees the fallacy—and one is always dependant and if one fails one gets the blame, if one succeeds most likely the minister at home gets the credit."[15] He would, he said, try to distinguish himself in whatever profession his father chose for him; but before that choice was made he had some comments and a suggestion to offer:

I feel . . . an excessive desire to be eminent. I believe it is wrong and . . . I have tried to subdue it but in vain, and though I feel that it can never make me happy I still most *earnestly* desire greatness and power.

Now in England among such a crowd of people and so many younger sons I feel that my chance is a small one—even if I were to get into Parliament (which you seem to think not impossible) I should probably not be listened to—or if I was I should never be able to make a party. . . .

My idea—one that has occupied me for nearly 3 years . . . is this. To emigrate to Canada. I prefer Canada because . . . Canada is our most important [colony] . . . at present and will be so for some time to come. Emigration is now generally thought of as a last resource to people who have ruined themselves at home but I do not see why it should be so. If a good number of younger sons who vegetate in England were to go out there it might be useful as forming a sort of aristocracy which is so much

[12]Christopher Wordsworth (1807–85) published *Letters to Goudon* in 1847.
[13]William Hodge Mill (1792–1853).
[14]Richard Hooker (1554?–1600), *The Lawes of Ecclesiasticall Politie*.
[15]Gordon to Aberdeen, 28 July 1845, Stanmore Papers, 49224.

wanted there. . . . Though not able to do so in England I might perhaps lead a *Canadian* parliament.[16]

The desire for useful work, eminence, power, and public recognition, delineated in this youthful but remarkably thoughtful letter, are themes which were to recur again and again throughout Arthur Gordon's life. In this letter he also reveals a desire for the career which he was ultimately to follow, although he lost sight of it for more than a dozen years and was to give it a somewhat different form when he did take it up.

Although Lord Aberdeen wanted Arthur to choose a career for himself, his own preference was at first the Church "as it would afford the prospect of a useful life and a secure haven against the dangers and troubles of this world."[17] Arthur, however, showed no inclination for the Church until he went up to Cambridge; and then only after long deliberation did he decide upon it as his calling. His diary entry for 25 November 1848 states:

Almost all around me are quietly preparing themselves to be useful in some station to which they are already destined but I am still uncertain and doubtful and this suspense gives an indecision to all I do or purpose. Tomorrow I shall enter on my twentieth year. May it not be wasted—as my nineteenth *has*—may it lead to some decision.[18]

Some two weeks later he wrote:

To tea with Barry . . . and talked long and earnestly on our future prospects. How many men who are now forgotten or who are known for evil have left this college with aims as noble as our own and how do we know that we too shall not fall away when we look round and see statesman after statesman failing in his efforts, and these too, men whose genius we cannot hope to rival, what can we expect to do. Shall we oppose ourselves to the current of the world and sink in the attempt? Shall we turn and head it? Or shall we in some distant corner of the globe attempt to *re-create* what we cannot restore?[19]

Sometime during the early months of 1849 both Gordon and Barry decided to enter the Church. Lord Aberdeen, who had noted a growing self-sufficiency and a disposition to arrogance in his son, did not believe a clergyman ought to have such characteristics. Nor did he believe that Arthur had made his decision of his own free will. He accused him of having been influenced by Barry. Gordon denied this however, and

[16]*Ibid.*
[17]Aberdeen to Elliott, 15 Sept. 1845, Stanmore Papers, 49224.
[18]Gordon's diary, 25 Nov. 1848, Stanmore Papers, 49253.
[19]*Ibid.*, 11 Dec. 1848.

asserted that he had made up his mind before Barry.[20] Aberdeen visited Cambridge in the spring of 1849 and, either to test the strength of Arthur's decision or to dissuade him from it, offered him a seat in Parliament. Gordon confided to his diary that his father would apparently accept

but one decision though I believe he imagines he is leaving me to chuse. I know were I to say "parliament" he would consider the matter decided. Though I persist in repeating "orders" he will not so consider it. I confess that for a quarter of an hour or so after such propositions [viz., Parliament] are made I feel a glow of ambition and excitement but I do not think these transient feelings should weight much against the steady decision of my reason and inclination.[21]

For the next three years Gordon held to his intention to enter the Church. In the meantime he took his Master of Arts degree (1851), became an examiner for Radley School, and interested himself in Trinity College, Glenalmond.

Lord Aberdeen was prepared to acquiesce in his son's choice although none too happily. He told Arthur on the latter's twenty-first birthday that he believed he had chosen well and had done so after full deliberation but "the difficulties of your calling will be increased by the aspect of the times; and perhaps there is something in your character and tendencies not very well calculated to overcome them."[22] He felt that Gordon had become too much influenced by the Oxford Movement with its emphasis upon external order and ceremonial. Aberdeen's own "taste, sympathy, and inclination" were favourable to those "observances and notions," but he did not regard them as the essence of religion and strove through good advice to moderate their impression upon his son. "I think," he wrote late in 1851, "there is danger of your attaching too much importance to that which is not essential. . . . My advice . . . is, Be moderate; be charitable; and however uncompromising in essential matters avoid all heat and contest in those which are non essential."[23] Earlier he had ridiculed Arthur's practice of dating his letters "All Saints" or "St. Simon and St. Jude," etc. "This is affectation, or it is superstition; and in either case you will do well to avoid it. . . . Your date is Ultra Tractarian. I heard that the present Archbishop in answer to such a correspondent, when Bishop of Chester, dated his letter 'Monday (Washing Day)'."[24] Aberdeen's advice perhaps led Gordon to be more

[20]*Ibid.*, 29 May 1849, Stanmore Papers, 49254, f. 148.
[21]*Ibid.*, [23 May] 1849, f. 50.
[22]Aberdeen to Gordon, 26 Nov. 1850, Stanmore Papers, 49224.
[23]*Ibid.*, 26 Nov. 1851.
[24]*Ibid.*, 4 Nov. 1848.

tolerant of those who did not share his High Church views, but it did not persuade him to abandon the practice of dating his letters by Saints' days.

After taking his degree at Cambridge, Gordon began studying for holy orders at Wells. He found it a disagreeable experience since his "proud ambitious heart still throbbed with a strong and burning desire for power and rule."[25] In a letter to Henry Bradshaw, in the summer of 1852, he revealed the questions that tortured him. His disclosure took the form of a conversation between his Ego and Alter Ego.

Alter Ego: "Thou wouldst have *thy will* the law to others & . . . it is most bitter *to thee* to renounce the attempt. And is not the calling [holy orders] a low, narrow, ignoble one?"

Ego: "*No No*, the noblest, the highest."

A.E.: ". . . Let me ask thee what thou thinkest of the majority of thy future black coated brethren?—they are not prejudiced,—narrow minded, utterly incapable of broad views . . . ? Oh no!"

E.: "The majority are not the standard by which to judge; what for instance are the majority of members of parliament?"

A.E.: "Apes, dolts—who *you* would speedily distance; the incapability of your associates there would be agreeable as in clerical life it would be dismal."

E.: "*Dubio*—to be misconstrued and misunderstood—I think of Burke."

A.E.: "Well, I fancy you will be misunderstood and misconstrued enough in orders . . . ; moreover *you* are not Burke."

E.: "*That* I know very well. Why then should I try a sphere which even Burke's abilities failed to render a suitable one for a temperament in which alone I resemble him?"

A.E.: "Never mind that. . . . Dost thou not feel that thou canst and will rule?"

E.: "Alas, Alas. *I do*."

A.E.: ". . . Thou who talkest so much of duty, is not public life the station naturally appointed for thee? Why run away?"

E.: "The vexations—the temptations."

A.E.: "The vexations properly borne may be your appointed 'cross' & as to temptations there are as many & as subtle temptations in orders as in office."

E.: "Art thou a devil tempting me or an angel bidding me return to the path marked out for me?"

A.E.: ". . . I am neither. I am but thyself bidding thee know thyself."[26]

But at this point Ego would listen no longer "and the cawing of the rooks, the humming of the bees, & the merry peal of bells from S. Cuthbert's tower"[27] drowned Alter Ego's voice; but only temporarily.

[25]Gordon to Bradshaw, Whit-Sunday 1852, Stanmore Papers, 49272.
[26]*Ibid.*
[27]*Ibid.*

Although his inner conflict continued, he remained at Wells until December, when Lord Aberdeen became prime minister and called him to become his private secretary. Even then he did not wholly give up the idea of a clerical life. In 1853, he wrote Bradshaw saying: ". . . My misgivings have now settled into the conviction that I have done wisely in resolving to take orders—and yet I have just ordered a smart new uniform . . . which I certainly cannot preach in."[28] But as Gordon became more concerned with political life and with acting as go-between in the movement for the revival of Convocation, he dropped the idea of entering the Church and we hear no more of it.

The moving spirit behind the agitation of the younger High-Churchmen to restore Convocation, which, though elected, had been silenced for 130 years, was Samuel ("Soapy Sam") Wilberforce, Bishop of Oxford. Wilberforce found in Arthur Gordon a strong supporter and one who, as private secretary to and son of the Prime Minister, was in a uniquely favourable position to act as a liaison between Wilberforce and the government. Gordon fulfilled this rôle admirably. Aberdeen himself sympathized with the movement, but was hampered by the rank and file of his Whig and Radical following who did not. He was reluctant to move at all, but Wilberforce, Gladstone, and Gordon persuaded him at least to allow Convocation liberty of speech. He did not, however, give it the legislative powers which the leaders of the movement desired. In the course of their collaboration Gordon and Wilberforce established a friendship which was to last until the Bishop's death in 1873.

Arthur Gordon's religious friendships were not confined to the High Church party. Among the friends he made during this period were H. E. Manning and Charles Kingsley. The former perhaps influenced Gordon, in his gubernatorial career, to accord a high degree of tolerance to Roman Catholics. Kingsley's Christian Socialism found a close parallel in the concern which Gordon was to demonstrate for the welfare of the labouring classes in the colonies he was to govern.

The term "private secretary" scarcely conveys an adequate idea of the relationship between Gordon and Lord Aberdeen. From 1852 until the Earl's death neither of them received a letter which the other did not see. The confidence and responsibility which his father bestowed upon him worried Gordon, and there were times when he wished to consult others whose judgment on political affairs he respected. Nevertheless he enjoyed being at the centre of English politics and it was natural that he should now finally decide to enter public life. His opportunity came in the summer of 1854, when Francis Lawley, a popular

[28]*Ibid.*, Whit-Sunday 1853.

follower of Gladstone, gave up the Beverley constituency in Yorkshire. Gordon, with his father's consent and Gladstone's support, decided to offer himself for the seat.

He hoped to be returned unopposed since he was determined to spend no money to influence the electors and he feared that if an unscrupulous adversary appeared he would be beaten. Beverley was a safe Whig-Liberal seat, and the Tories did not fight the by-election. However, a young man named Hastings (Gordon, who had known him at Cambridge, called him "a goose"), appeared as his opponent. Gordon did not think Hastings would bribe lavishly, but he was afraid that the Tories in Beverley, who were "most venomous" against Lord Aberdeen, might vote for Hastings. In his election speech Gordon supported free trade, an extension of the franchise, and the Crimean War. He wished the last could have been avoided, but thought it a just war. He was afraid that Gladstone, whom he wished to take as his guide in politics, would think the speech too liberal, but Gladstone read a copy of it with satisfaction. Gordon won the election without difficulty but realized that most of the credit belonged to Lawley who had accompanied him everywhere "through tan yards & forges, shaking all the black grimy fellows by the hand, as if he were standing for a fresh election himself."[29]

Arthur Gordon remained in the Commons only until the general election of 1857. He was, of course, a Peelite (although in 1856 he called himself a Radical)[30] and supported first his father's government and, after February 1855, that of Lord Aberdeen's successor, Lord Palmerston. The Peelites agreed with the liberal-conservatism of Palmerston's domestic policies but were more critical of the demagogic character of his foreign policy. They withdrew their support over the Chinese question, and his government fell. In the general election that followed, Palmerston's policy proved the more popular and Gordon, with many another Peelite, lost his seat.

Although he had found his position in the House of Commons much reduced after his father's retirement, he had nevertheless enjoyed himself. He regarded his defeat as a calamity and a crisis in his career. It was undoubtedly a turning-point. Had he retained his seat he would have continued in politics and, with his administrative ability and the help of powerful friends, may have become a cabinet minister under Gladstone.[31]

---

[29]Gordon to Gladstone, 29 July 1854, Gladstone Papers, 44319.

[30]Roundell Palmer, Earl of Selborne, *Memorials*: Part I, *Family and Personal 1766–1865*, II, 311.

[31]Gordon was a better leader than follower and since Gladstone asked unquestioning obedience of those he led it is likely that Gordon would have quarrelled with him.

He was now at loose ends and free to accept an invitation to be private secretary to Gladstone upon his appointment, in 1858, as special high commissioner to the Ionian Islands. This mission was to reawaken Gordon's youthful interest in colonies and to lead him a step closer to his life's work.

Gordon had known Gladstone for nearly twenty years and by the late 1850's they were close friends. Although Gladstone's mission to Ionia was important it was not urgent. The journey to Corfu was leisurely, broken by calls upon King Leopold of the Belgians, the Emperor and Empress of the Austro-Hungarian Empire, and the King and Queen of Greece. But Gordon's appointment was not simply the paid vacation that both he and Lord Aberdeen had anticipated, because once arrived Gladstone tackled his job with typical energy and he proved a hard and exacting task-master. On one occasion he informed Gordon that he should not read letters from his father during working hours since his time belonged to the public. Gordon's reply was rude.

Gordon did not, like Lord Aberdeen, wholly disapprove of Gladstone's policy in the Ionians, but he was highly critical of his chief's methods. He objected to Gladstone's "kissing the pudgy hands of every bishop he could get hold of . . . ,"[32] to his somewhat cavalier treatment of the resident High Commissioner, Sir John Young,[33] to his unquestioning confidence in the leaders of the popular party,[34] and to the verbosity and circumlocutory character of his dispatches.[35] Being, as he later phrased it, a "querulous and captious critic" of his friends[36] he expressed his feelings to Gladstone. Mrs. Gladstone told him he ought to resign; but he was enjoying the "delicious climate" and companions of his own age, and therefore found it easy to obey his father's explicit order not to resign in any circumstances.[37]

The mission ended early in the spring of 1859, but Gordon's relations with the Gladstones were cool until late in 1860. Then Gordon wrote a long letter to Gladstone, not withdrawing his criticisms, but apologizing for not having resigned. "I did not act towards you as I ought to have

[32]Gordon to Aberdeen, 27 Dec. 1858, Aberdeen Papers, 43226.

[33]*Ibid.* Sir John Young, later Lord Lisgar, was shortly to become governor-general of New South Wales, and in 1868, of Canada.

[34]Gordon to Aberdeen, 4 Dec. 1858, Aberdeen Papers, 43226.

[35]Gordon to Ottiwell Waterfield, 2 Dec. 1858, Stanmore Papers, 49249. Waterfield, a college friend of Gordon's, had become a master at Eton and was later to be headmaster at Skeen. He was also a well-to-do company director.

[36]Gordon to Gladstone, 26 July 1874, Gladstone Papers, 44320.

[37]Gordon to Gladstone, 12 Nov. 1860, Gladstone Papers, 44319; Aberdeen to Gordon, 25 Jan. 1859, Aberdeen Papers, 43226. Aberdeen wished to avoid a public impression that there was a rift between himself and Gladstone.

done, or as I should like a subordinate of my own to act towards me."[38] Gladstone received this letter with "unfeigned pleasure" and forgot Gordon's shabby behaviour towards him.[39] Their old intimacy was resumed, in so far as Gladstone's ministerial duties and Gordon's long absences from England permitted, but there are indications that Gordon's confidence in Gladstone's practical statesmanship which had been shaken in Ionia did not wholly revive, and that Gladstone never fully trusted Gordon to follow him unhesitatingly.

At the close of the mission to the Ionian Islands Gordon described it as "a political drama alternately tragical and comic, not unmixed with occasional scenes of the broadest farce, but always picturesque."[40] He did not regret having participated in it. It had given him an increased knowledge of the world and of himself. He returned from Corfu determined to enter the colonial service, sure that a governor's career would suit him better than any other.[41] He approached the Secretary of State for the Colonies, the Duke of Newcastle, who had been Aberdeen's secretary of state for war and the colonies and whom he knew well. Newcastle could not at first offer him any appointment but, by December 1859, gave Gordon to understand that he might be able to give him the governorship of British Guiana when it fell vacant some months hence.[42] Gordon had to be content with this. In any case he would have been unable to accept an appointment during 1860 because Lord Aberdeen, whose health was gradually failing, required his constant attention.

No father and son could have been more bound by mutual affection than Lord Aberdeen and his youngest son. This was to sustain Gordon during the difficult last year of his father's life. For weeks on end, except for very short periods, Gordon could scarcely leave the house by himself. He had to drive with his father around Regent's Park three times every afternoon and read to him for hours every evening. "Oh weary weary days, oh tedious months, oh wasting profitless years!"[43] he exclaimed in his diary the day before his thirtieth birthday. Yet when Lord Aberdeen died in December 1860, Gordon experienced no sense of freedom, only grief. "If ever the blessing of the first commandment with promise were sure to fall on any it is on you,"[44] Bishop Wilberforce wrote to

[38]Gordon to Gladstone, 12 Nov. 1860, Gladstone Papers, 44319.
[39]Gladstone to Gordon, 15 Nov. 1860, Gladstone Papers, 44319.
[40]Gordon to Waterfield, 7 March 1859, Stanmore Papers, 49249.
[41]Gordon to Wilberforce, 16 Dec. 1859, Stanmore Papers, 49214.
[42]Ibid.
[43]Gordon's diary, 25 Nov. 1859, Stanmore Papers, 49257.
[44]Wilberforce to Gordon, 14 Dec. 1860, quoted in Reginald D. Wilberforce, Life of the Right Reverend Samuel Wilberforce . . ., II, 464.

Gordon on receiving news of Lord Aberdeen's death. It was a just tribute.

A few weeks after his father's death, Gordon, accompanied by Harry Moody,[45] went to Egypt to see his eldest brother, who had now become the fifth Earl of Aberdeen, on family business. He had obtained permission from the Duke of Newcastle to make this journey since he was now free to take up a colonial appointment. He returned to England in July 1861, by way of Turkey and the Balkans. On his way back Gordon heard that Lieutenant-Governor Walker of British Guiana had been appointed governor[46] of the colony. Gordon was much disappointed. He was aware that Newcastle had objections to appointing an inexperienced man as governor to a difficult and important colony like British Guiana. Yet he had had a half-promise of it, had studied its curious constitution, and had looked to it as satisfactory in size and extent.[47] "Of course," he wrote to Wilberforce, "beggars have no right to be choosers and I must I suppose take with gratitude what is offered, but . . . it will not be without a sigh that I shall reconcile myself to an insignificant post in a pestilential climate."[48]

The Duke of Newcastle strengthened the policy begun by Earl Grey of appointing as colonial governors men who were willing to make governing a career.[49] This policy required a new recruit to the profession to begin in one of the minor colonies. As he acquired experience and seniority his succeeding appointments would be to more important colonies with higher salaries. Outstanding work would tend to hasten promotion. It was unlikely then that Newcastle could appoint Gordon to a very important colony. When Gordon saw him in July 1861, Newcastle was prepared to offer him either New Brunswick or Antigua. Gordon asked for Trinidad; he was told that it would not be vacant for a year and advised to accept what was offered since Newcastle might not long be secretary of state. He was given a week to decide. He supposed, he told Bishop Wilberforce gloomily, that he must make up his mind "to encounter the Arctic winter" of New Brunswick.[50] This he did.

Arthur Hamilton Gordon had no need, financially, to accept any

---

[45]Moody was to become Gordon's aide-de-camp in New Brunswick.
[46]Actually Walker was only appointed acting governor and early in 1862 Sir Francis Hincks was appointed governor of British Guiana.
[47]Gordon to Wilberforce, 22 Feb. 1861, Stanmore Papers, 49214.
[48]Ibid.
[49]Henry L. Hall, The Colonial Office, 57.
[50]Gordon to Wilberforce, 9 July 1861, Stanmore Papers, 49214.

employment at all. His father had left him property[51] that produced an income of some £2,000 annually, a very comfortable living. But Gordon had a strong desire to serve his country and win pre-eminence in the process. Parliament seemed at least temporarily closed to him. He could have stood for Aberdeenshire in 1861 and might have been elected. He had lived much of his life there and (being in the habit of walking about the country-side and stopping to chat with the farmers) was on easy terms with the local people. He was also the popular commandant of the First Aberdeenshire Rifle Volunteers, having been commissioned in February 1860 by Lord Aberdeen, the lord-lieutenant of the county. However, he refused to stand for election partly because of his prospects of becoming a colonial governor, and partly to avoid a quarrel with his brother, Colonel (later General) Alexander Gordon, who wanted the seat for himself.[52] Despite a requisition, signed by a large number of voters, urging him to stand he maintained his refusal. A few months later he was appointed to New Brunswick.

After farewell visits to the Gladstones and to Guizot,[53] Gordon sailed for America on 5 October 1861. Accompanying him were Harry Moody, his aide-de-camp, and David Wilson,[54] his private secretary.

[51]The unentailed lands of Pitrichie.
[52]Alexander Gordon was not elected. The seat was won by Bannerman, a Liberal.
[53]Guizot through his friendship with Aberdeen had also become a friend of Gordon's.
[54]The son of the Dean of Aberdeen.

II

NEW BRUNSWICK, 1861–1866
Gordon's First Governorship

❧

LANDING AT HALIFAX in mid-October, Arthur Gordon spent a day or two with the Lieutenant-Governor of Nova Scotia then left for New Brunswick by train. His predecessor, Sir John H. T. Manners Sutton, met him at the town of Sussex and gave him a brief account of public affairs and officials in the province. He continued his journey on the same day by train to Saint John where he boarded the river-steamer for Fredericton, the capital.

If first impressions affect one's future happiness in a place, Gordon's five-year term in New Brunswick should have been joyous indeed. The new Lieutenant-Governor was a sensitive man with an instinct for beauty and a keen appreciation of nature. New Brunswick possesses great natural charm, and nowhere, perhaps, is autumn more extravagant. Colour is piled upon colour—the gold and brown of elm and oak, the crimson and scarlet of maple and sumac, the dark green of fir and pine, the blue of river and sky—all subtly blended and softened by the smoke-haze of Indian summer. Gordon was agreeably surprised and pleasantly stirred. " 'The lot has fallen unto me in a fair ground,' " he quoted. "I had expected stunted vegetation, wild rock, and evident traces of the long cold winter on every object. I find a rich and varied landscape with no outward sign of the rigorous frost now rapidly approaching."[1]

His initially favourable impression strengthened as the months passed.

[1]Gordon to Palmer, 27 Oct. 1861, Stanmore Papers. Except for the Palmer correspondence, the Stanmore Papers covering Gordon's New Brunswick career are filed in the Bonar Law–Bennett Library of the University of New Brunswick and bear no volume numbers. References to these letters will carry the letters (N.B.) to distinguish them from the major collection filed in the British Museum.

Each season claimed his attention and won his admiration, and he soon became a confirmed lover of New Brunswick. His official duties allowed him ample time for travelling, hunting, and fishing. He visited the settled portions of the province, on horseback or foot. He paddled rivers and streams, some explored previously only by Indians. On snowshoes he hunted elk (caribou) and moose, and he slept in the open when the frost cracked in the forest like rifle shots. He was on easy terms with the farmers, back-woodsmen, and Indians. The last liked his silences and at night round their campfires confided their legends to him.[2] He travelled hundreds of miles by sleigh in the winter, "lightly skimming over the rock-hard snow roads,—over the frozen lakes,—over the ice bound rivers,—up over the mountains,—away through the dark still forests. . . . Out on the clear keen air . . . [rang] the tinkle of the sleigh bells, as . . . [he was] whirled along under the still sunlight or the frosty starlight, or . . . through blinding drifts of storm."[3] He exulted in his tremendous appetite and in the toughness of his body which tingled with "life and vigour" such as he had never before known. He was thankful that it had been given him "to experience such exquisite pleasure from a ripple on the river, or the reflection of a cloudlet, or the arrangement and colouring of a tuft of glowing autumn leaves." "How very much they lose," he exclaimed, "who have not the eye to see or the heart to interpret and store up such things."[4] As he sat in the Cathedral and watched the light falling through the windows, saw the goodly choir and spacious nave filled with familiar faces, and as he listened to the voice of the bishop or the well-remembered music, Arthur Gordon began to feel that he had found a home in New Brunswick.

Yet for all these pleasures, he was lonely. He liked being "*regulus quidam*," but he was embarrassed always to be called "sir" by grey-headed judges and generals, and he found it "a bore" to have no equals with whom to associate.[5] Only Chief Justice Sir James Carter had sufficient status to be eligible for close friendship without provoking jealousies among the provincials.

Gordon quickly became attached to the governor's residence, the first house in which he had resided as master. Unfortunately it lacked a mistress. Shortly before Gordon sailed for New Brunswick, he thought he had found "all that any man should desire in a life's companion" in

[2]See Gordon's own account of his back-country travels, "Wilderness Journeys in New Brunswick."

[3]Gordon to William Wood, 12 Feb. 186[?], Stanmore Papers (N.B.). Wood, a college friend, was sub-warden, later warden, of Radley College.

[4]Gordon to Palmer, 8 Nov. 1863, Stanmore Papers, 49217.

[5]*Ibid.*, 1 Jan. 1863.

Agnes Gladstone, but she professed to feel only strong friendship for him.[6] Wanting a wife and appreciative of attractive and intelligent women, he found himself, so he confessed, "gauche and incoherent" in their company. It seemed to him a great puzzle how to persuade a woman to fall in love with him. He would not marry simply for the sake of being married, and he could not bring himself to marry a New Brunswick girl since "these colonists are after all essentially foreigners."[7]

In 1862, when Moody, his aide-de-camp, proposed to marry Judge Parker's daughter, Gordon was mildly critical. But later the same year when Wilson, his private secretary, also fell in love with a "Bluenose lady," he was "anything but amused." "To have one through-the-nose-speaking, ill educated, unmannered native girl a member of my habitual familiar society is bad enough," he wrote, "but two! How the two would fight, and how, between them, everything that passed here would become private property . . . !"[8] Although he soon came to like Mrs. Moody, and to consider her "one of the very nicest ladies here," he still thought Moody would have done better to have looked out for a wife at home.[9]

Gordon himself remained a reluctant bachelor until 1865 when he married Rachel, the eldest daughter of Sir John Shaw-Lefevre. Thus, for the greater part of his governorship of New Brunswick, he was thrown back upon the young men in his official retinue for companionship. Before taking up his appointment, he had had visions of a staff attached to him by the "strongest ties of affection" based upon his consideration for and kindness to them. He found, however, that his "awkwardnesses and unamiabilities" precluded a return of the friendship and affection which he desired to give.[10] Nevertheless, his relationships with his staff were cordial if not affectionate and its members served him well. His marriage brought a happiness to his personal life marred only by the several miscarriages suffered by his wife during their first years together.

Arthur Gordon's public life in New Brunswick was to be much less happy and satisfying than his private life. Before he finished it, he came to wish he had never seen the colony. His aristocratic background, his shy and diffident manner, his honesty, ambition, and philanthropy, all tended to fit him to govern primitive Crown colonies rather than more advanced and sensitive colonies practising responsible government. His

[6]Gordon to Gladstone, 5 Oct. 1861, Stanmore Papers (N.B.).

[7]Gordon to Waterfield, 27 Jan. 1863, and Gordon to Wilberforce, 19 July 1863, Stanmore Papers (N.B.); Gordon to Palmer, 8 Nov. 1863.

[8]Gordon to Waterfield, 11 Nov. 1862, Stanmore Papers (N.B.).

[9]Gordon to Wilberforce, 19 July 1863, Stanmore Papers (N.B.).

[10]Gordon to Barry, 22 June 1862, Stanmore Papers (N.B.).

"force and reality of character, . . . power of intellectual discernment, . . . habit of sound and independent judgment, and . . . invariable preference for what was just and pure and true over everything artificial, hollow or low in tone and aim . . ."[11] were qualities unlikely to endear him to the toughened politicians of New Brunswick.

In that frontier colony political integrity had little meaning and, within its narrow confines, statesmanship was almost unachievable. Since the founding of the province in 1784, bribery, corruption, and waste had reigned almost without a break and, in recent years, the rot had worsened. Personal and political morality were unrelated attributes, and a most flagrant brand of Jacksonian democracy prevailed. "Strong" governors were no longer viewed with favour—if indeed, they ever had been. It was unlikely that the local "bosses" who managed politics would willingly concede much power to a governor whose efforts to bring about honesty and respectability in government would, if successful, threaten the sources of their authority and prevent their exploitation of the provincial treasury and the natural resources of the colony.

In such circumstances it was inevitable that there would be clashes between Gordon and his constitutional advisers. Only a governor who would allow his council to carry him unresisting over the stony administrative terrain of self-governing New Brunswick could avoid barking his shins. Gordon did not intend to be the passive occupant of a sedan chair and, if his constitutional powers were not extensive, they did exist. Furthermore, the governor could still exert considerable influence.

In these early years of responsible government, the governor retained the right to be kept informed and to be consulted by his ministers before they came to final decisions. He could offer his opinions which, however, the ministers might reject if they desired. He could still communicate directly with individual ministers. He was as yet the sole medium of official correspondence between the colonial and Imperial governments and his ministers had no right to see confidential dispatches or to know their subject matter. Neither of Gordon's predecessors (Sir Edmund Head and Sir John Manners Sutton) in New Brunswick under responsible government had admitted their inability to refuse ministerial advice.[12] Gordon was unlikely to concede that right. Nor would he be disposed to surrender to his council control of the provincial militia of which, by separate commission, he was commander-in-chief.

Several sources of influence were available to the governor of New Brunswick. He represented the Imperial government (technically, the

[11]Selborne, *Memorials*: Part I, II, 261.
[12]See p. 41, fn. 84, for a case in point.

Crown), the source of defence against foreign attack and of the financial power through which the province might indirectly acquire funds for the construction of railways. Railways and defence were to become subjects of intense interest to New Brunswickers during Gordon's administration. The governor also represented the dignified element in the British constitution, albeit without the built-in powers of the monarch based on continuity and honours giving. New Brunswick responded with greater enthusiasm to the appeal of the Crown than the other colonies of British North America. It was the "Loyalist Province." True, its once predominant Loyalist element had now been diluted by an influx of lower class settlers from the United Kingdom, especially from Ireland, and by a burgeoning Acadian-French population. True, also, that political control had fallen into the hands of middle class money-grubbers to whom any other loyalty than loyalty to the dollar was at best skin deep. Nevertheless, Gordon, both as the Queen's representative and as the son of one of her prime ministers could be sure of the sympathy and understanding of the Loyalist-descended, educated, landed, and professional element. He would find some support also among those subsistence farmers, woods-workers, and labourers who were descended from the rank and file of the Loyalist regiments. Although normally the politicians could buy the votes of this class the latter nevertheless regarded the governor with respectful awe.

Gordon's first three years were peaceful enough and were unmarked by serious quarrels with his ministers. They allowed him some latitude in dealing with problems in which they had little interest or which they were unwilling to tackle because of possible political repercussions.

The first matter to claim Gordon's attention was the necessity of creating an efficient provincial defence force since he recognized the threatening aspect of affairs in the United States. New Brunswick had not been disturbed at the opening of the American Civil War and opinion in the province was at first in favour of the North. But the "Trent Affair" and the beginning of the Northern blockade of Southern ports which curtailed New Brunswick's trade combined to change provincial opinion first to neutrality and then to a bitter hostility toward the North. This was strengthened by the Anglophobic tone of the press in neighbouring Maine and other Union states. The year 1861 closed in the colony amid feelings of gloom and anxiety concerning its defencelessness, which was only partially relieved by the arrival at Saint John, in the dying hours of December, of some 6,000 British troops on their way to Canada.

No adequate facilities existed for the reception, in the middle of a

Honourable Arthur Gordon, 1856

Government House, Fredericton, New Brunswick, *circa* 1865

North American winter, of so many men, or for their transport over several hundred miles of snow-covered wilderness to the St. Lawrence. Furthermore, the provincial authorities had only a few days' notice of their imminent arrival. The local ministry did not know what to do. Gordon went outside the strict line of duty and assumed complete command. In the last four days of December, he commandeered schools, temperance halls, car sheds, and the customs house; he arranged for beds, bedding, and stoves, and directed the work in person. All was ready when the troops arrived. "So perfect were the arrangements and so good the provisions furnished that although it was the depth of winter not one death took place."[13] On the overland journey to Quebec the men suffered scarcely a frostbite. Only the thought that those (his father and Sir James Graham) who would have cared most about this, his first administrative achievement, were dead, and could give him no word of pleasure or approval, marred Gordon's satisfaction.[14]

Although the arrival of British troops for the defence of Canada raised morale in New Brunswick, because it demonstrated the mother country's concern for the safety of the colonies, it added little to the strength of the province. Virtually defenceless, it had only a small garrison of royal troops consisting of several officers and a few dozen men, and some fifty companies of volunteer, unpaid militia with a total strength of over 1,800. The latter, Manners Sutton had formed on his own initiative but they were untrained and in no condition to meet any serious attack from Maine. Furthermore, until 1862, despite urgings by the governors and pressure from the Imperial government, the provincial ministry showed little concern and had refused for more than ten years to spend any money on defence. In 1851, the legislature had suspended the operation of the militia act and in 1856 had renewed the suspending act for a further nine years. New Brunswick argued in justification of its stand that it had no wars of its own making. Its relations with its only potential enemy, the United States, had been good since the settlement of the boundary question in 1842, and even cordial after the signing of the reciprocity treaty in 1854. The province did not expect war and had therefore no need for defence. If it became involved in war simply because it was a British colony, then it was Britain's duty to protect it.

[13]Rev. J. W. Millidge, "Events of the Decade 1860–1870," *Collections of the New Brunswick Historical Society*, IV, 320–26. Millidge wrote from personal observation.

[14]Gordon's diary, 31 Dec. 1861, Stanmore Papers (N.B.). Sir James Graham, who had held the Admiralty under Aberdeen, had been a close friend to Gordon. He died about two weeks after Gordon's arrival in New Brunswick.

This state of affairs persisted until 1862 when increasing hostility between the Northern states and the British North American colonies persuaded New Brunswick politicians that they must provide for an efficient defensive force. Gordon was then able to obtain a vote of £2,000 annually, for three years, to carry out a reorganization of the militia. It appeared that a force strong enough to repel all but a full-scale invasion would soon be created; but a serious difficulty arose: if the assembly were to vote money for the militia, it desired to control that body. It therefore passed a bill making the lieutenant-governor ex-officio commander-in-chief of the militia.

Hitherto the lieutenant-governors had successfully argued that, although vested in the same man, the offices of lieutenant-governor[15] and commander-in-chief of the local militia were separate. They had consequently discharged the latter office without reference to politics. If the new act were to go into effect, the lieutenant-governor would be compelled to accept the advice of his council in matters relating to the militia. Gordon felt sure that it would soon become a political football and a source of party patronage. He admitted that a similar law had been enacted in Canada, but that colony was "a great and flourishing state" and among its politicians were to be found "some patriotism, moderation and statesmanlike superiority to mere personal antipathies or favouritism." New Brunswick was but "a petty province" where, though such qualities were to be found in many who took no share in politics, he sought "almost in vain for evidences of their existence among those . . . engaged in public life."[16] He refused to sanction the bill and himself proceeded with the gradual reorganization of the militia.

Gordon found his experience with the Aberdeenshire militia useful to him and his work progressed so well that by the time of the Fenian scare in 1866 he had over a thousand trained, paid militiamen under his command and a large body of volunteer, unpaid reserves. There can be little doubt that the existence of this force went far to prevent serious Fenian raids against the province.

The Lieutenant-Governor believed that his success with the militia merited some expression of approval by the Secretary of State, but Edward Cardwell, who succeeded the Duke of Newcastle in 1864, complained of unsatisfactory progress even though New Brunswick's paid

[15]Gordon and his predecessors, although technically only lieutenant-governors, were in fact governors and corresponded directly with the secretary of state for the colonies rather than through the governor-general of British North America who was technically governor of New Brunswick.

[16]Gordon to the Duke of Newcastle (confidential), 7 July 1862, Stanmore Papers (N.B.).

militia was proportionately larger than Canada's. Cardwell's lack of generosity derived from his impatient urge to reduce the Imperial government's expenditures for colonial defence and his belief that in over-stressing New Brunswick's military weakness he might induce her to join with the other British North American colonies for greater security.

The outstanding matter with which Arthur Gordon had to deal as lieutenant-governor of New Brunswick was the projected unification of the British North American colonies. For that reason, and because Gordon's part in this movement has hitherto been misunderstood, much of the remainder of this chapter must be devoted to it. Most historians of Canadian Confederation have regarded Gordon as an opponent of the union who used his official position to try to prevent its realization. This view has been based upon incomplete evidence. Now that Gordon's private papers have become available it is possible, indeed it is obligatory, to come to very different conclusions concerning his rôle in the agitation for Confederation.

The union question was not new when Gordon arrived in North America. Politicians had talked of it periodically for a number of years, and from time to time governors of the colonies had written dispatches in which they had discussed the merits of the various forms of union: a legislative union of all the British North American colonies; the dissolution of the 1841 union of the Canadas and a federal union of all the colonies with a continuation of the local legislatures; a regional legislative union of the maritime colonies perhaps to be followed by a federal union with the two Canadas.

Gordon formed his first opinions concerning union just after reaching Halifax, when he read two of Lieutenant-Governor Mulgrave's dispatches on the subject. The first of these (30 December 1858) pointed out "the folly of federation," and Gordon "fully concurred" in this view. The other (1 March 1860) argued the case for a maritime legislative union. Gordon did not agree so fully with it, believing that "the difficulty would be nearly as great as of effecting a real [i.e., legislative] union of the whole of Canada [i.e., all the British North American colonies]—the result far less brilliant and . . . far less useful."[17] After he had had some experience of the petty, personal, and corrupt nature of politics in New Brunswick, however, he began to adopt a more positive attitude to maritime union, and to believe that it might, by creating a larger political community, attract a better class

[17]Gordon to Newcastle, 23 Dec. 1861, Stanmore Papers (N.B.).

of politician and so lead to higher public morality and better government. Yet he was never exclusively a maritime unionist as Canadian historians have frequently charged. The larger legislative union was never far from his mind.

In January 1862, he commented that if he were secretary of state for the colonies he would refuse any further concessions to the maritime governments until the three lower colonies were united into one.[18] Nevertheless a week later he wrote that "every effort should be made to bring about a union of the three Lower Provinces, or of all with Canada."[19] In March, with his first session of the legislature behind him, he concluded that "the only chance for these provinces would be their union, either with Canada or with each other."[20] Two months later he assured Newcastle of his support of the projected Intercolonial Railway "because it is an essential step towards that union of the Provinces which I look upon as the only chance of securing anything like respectability in the conduct of their public affairs."[21]

Gordon proved his interest in the larger union by hard work on behalf of the Intercolonial. That railway, or a hard and fast commitment to build it, was a necessary preliminary to union. With the support of Leonard Tilley, the provincial secretary and leading minister, Gordon bullied his executive council into accepting on behalf of the province a fair share of financial responsibility. As a result, he made his first enemy, Albert J. Smith, who in 1862 resigned the office of attorney-general in which he had succeeded Charles Fisher in 1861. Gordon also attended the railway conference in Quebec in 1862 where he did what he could to bring about the preliminary agreement between the colonies for building the Intercolonial.

The conference at Quebec was followed by another in London. On the return of the New Brunswick and Nova Scotia delegations, the legislatures of those colonies passed the measures required to give effect to the agreements made at Quebec and London. When, however, Canada failed to follow suit, and thus repudiated the agreement, the public in New Brunswick and Nova Scotia was deeply angered. The suspicions then engendered concerning the good faith and trustworthiness of Canadians were to constitute a strong barrier to subsequent negotiations for the union of the colonies.

Gordon was extremely annoyed with the Canadians for bringing the

[18]Gordon to Lord Monck, 25 Jan. 1862, Stanmore Papers (N.B.). Lord Monck was governor-general of the British North American colonies.
[19]Gordon to DeGrey, 3 Feb. 1862, Stanmore Papers (N.B.).
[20]Gordon to Wilberforce, 16 March 1862, Stanmore Papers (N.B.).
[21]Gordon to Newcastle, 12 May 1862, Stanmore Papers (N.B.).

Intercolonial to a standstill. His ire is evidence of the frustration of his hopes for legislative union of British North America. It can scarcely be cited as evidence of his desire for maritime union.[22] On the contrary, had he favoured the smaller union over the larger he would have been pleased with the action of the Canadians in scuttling the Intercolonial. Now that the larger union appeared to be ruled out, however, Gordon turned to maritime legislative union as an alternative. Should it be accomplished, it would not prove a stumbling block to the legislative union of all the colonies, and should a later movement for the union of British North America take a federal rather than a legislative form, Gordon regarded the prior legislative union of the maritimes, or at least of New Brunswick and Nova Scotia, as absolutely essential. Otherwise, the local legislatures would continue to function. Gordon fervently desired their abolition because he had come to believe that the lower provinces were too small and parochial for the satisfactory working of responsible government.[23]

Gordon had no quarrel with responsible government as such; indeed, he believed it to be the only system under which the North American colonies could be retained within the Empire. But he had not been many weeks in New Brunswick before he became aware of the low standards of political morality which prevailed not only in the executive council and legislature but among the general public as well. The Liberal or Reform party, led by Tilley and Charles Fisher, had been in power, except for one brief interval, since 1854. It had lost its original reforming zeal and had grown smug and fat on patronage and graft. Tilley was undoubtedly the best and most highly principled member of the council, but he was "by no means without a strong share of the leaven"[24] which infected the others and he joined in "the thoroughly oriental view of truth"[25] then held in New Brunswick. Fisher, according to the Duke of Newcastle, was one of the worst politicians in North America.[26]

In 1859, Manners Sutton had written of the Tilley-Fisher régime that there was "not one member . . . or any single individual among their supporters, either in or out of the Legislature, whom I could recommend for the grant of any token of Her Majesty's personal grace or favor, without the risk (I might say the certainty) that their eleva-

[22]See W. M. Whitelaw, *The Maritimes and Canada before Confederation*, 189.
[23]Gordon to Palmer, 27 April 1863, Stanmore Papers, 49217.
[24]Gordon's diary, 29 Jan. 1862, Stanmore Papers (N.B.).
[25]Gordon to Cardwell, 17 July 1865, Cardwell Papers, PRO 30/48-6/39. Hereafter the PRO reference will not be cited for these papers.
[26]*Ibid.*, 20 Nov. 1865.

tion above their fellow Colonists would tend to depreciate the honor conferred."[27] Gordon observed that "as a rule, to be a member of the Assembly is a proof that a man is uneducated and is not a gentleman. . . ."[28] The members of the assembly were often grog-shop keepers, stage drivers, or lumberers, and could scarcely write a letter. They had little respect for the institution to which they belonged, as was clearly demonstrated when the Speaker of the assembly resigned in order to accept a position as sheriff's officer and keeper of a county gaol.

In 1858 the executive council, on Manners Sutton's insistence, had accepted responsibility for initiating legislation but the council's fear of offending any section of the colony prevented it from giving strong and vigorous leadership. Consequently "log-rolling" and parochialism continued in the assembly much as before. One of the members for Charlotte County made clear the restricted outlook and "native son" philosophy of the ordinary member when he said:

> Mr. Speaker, when a bill's before this house I always asks what's it going to do for Charlotte. I ain't got anything to do with the Province. I sits here for Charlotte and if they tells me it'll do good to the Province but do harm to Charlotte then says I "I go in for Charlotte." And if they tells me it'll harm the Province but do good to Charlotte then too says I "I go in for Charlotte."[29]

The general public evidently viewed parochialism, bribery, and corruption with equanimity. It had placed Charles Fisher at the head of the poll in York County in 1861, just a few months after he had been dismissed from office as attorney-general for using his official position for jobbing and speculating in Crown lands. The better-educated and wealthier class, secure in its independence and prestige, saw no reason to soil its hands with politics. Those of that class who did offer themselves for election were usually defeated by more unscrupulous men and by the prevalent democratic sentiment that good education and independent position were marks of aristocracy. The opposition Conservative party afforded no hope of salvation. It had never recovered from its defeat in 1854 and, by the sixties, differed from the Liberal party only in the fact that it was out of power and wanted to be in, and the Liberal party was in and wanted to remain.

Having examined all of these circumstances, Arthur Gordon concluded that New Brunswick had regressed since the introduction of responsible government and that the lower provinces were too meagre,

[27]Manners Sutton to Bulwer-Lytton, 2 March 1859, PRO CO 188/132.
[28]Gordon to Gladstone, [?] Jan. 1864, Gladstone Papers, 44320.
[29]*Ibid.*

poor, and thinly populated for responsible government ever to work satisfactorily. He feared that if these colonies were to unite with the Canadas on a federal basis they would simply wallow deeper and deeper in the morass of mediocrity and maladministration because the central government would attract the few capable politicians which they possessed. He attempted to forestall this evil and to create the conditions for an improvement in the government of the maritime colonies by promoting their legislative union. He reasoned that by creating a larger political community a better class of politician would be attracted and responsible government could be made to work without the corruption and pettiness which then characterized it in New Brunswick.

Throughout the summer and autumn of 1863 and the first half of 1864 Gordon worked for maritime union. His only means was persuasion of his advisers. His chief ally was the antipathy of the maritime politicians to the Canadians who had left the lower provinces in the lurch over the Intercolonial. The convention of maritime politicians which met at Charlottetown, Prince Edward Island, in the autumn of 1864 to discuss maritime union was in great measure the result of Arthur Gordon's activities.

As the Charlottetown Conference approached, Gordon was optimistic about the chances of its success. On his return from leave in England, late in the summer of 1864, he found all the members of the Nova Scotia government and all but one of his own council agreed that federal or legislative union with Canada was impracticable.[30] Since no counter-attraction now existed, maritime union might be expected to go forward. However, the Charlottetown Conference had barely assembled and dispensed with the preliminaries when a strong uninvited Canadian delegation appeared and asked to be allowed to discuss the union of all the British North American colonies. Like the camel in Aesop's fable, the Canadians, on gaining admission, took over. They argued so convincingly that the maritime delegates agreed to put maritime union aside and take part in a further conference, later in the year at Quebec, to agree upon resolutions on which a union between the lower provinces and Canada might be based. The sudden interest of the Canadians in union and their unexpected appearance at Charlottetown was stimulated largely by political circumstances in the united province of Canada. Lower and Upper Canada could no longer work in double harness. They desired immediate separation and the establishment of a federal union which would include at least some of the

[30]Gordon to Cardwell, 12 Sept. 1864, PRO CO 189/9.

maritimes. As George Brown, the leading opposition politician in Upper Canada, put it when Gordon asked him why Canada could not have allowed maritime union to take place first: " 'Because we can't wait. We are *not going to be tied to Lower Canada,* for twelve months more.' "[31]

Although Gordon was sorry to see maritime union brushed aside he was not unhappy with the proposal made at Charlottetown by several of the Canadian delegates, especially by Galt and Macdonald.[32] They favoured a union consisting of a strong central government with local legislatures occupying a subordinate position similar to municipal institutions.[33] Such a strongly centralized federal union amounted almost to legislative union, and Gordon prepared to accept it. He had no confidence, however, that the maritimes would do so because what Galt and Macdonald meant by "federal union" was not what the inhabitants of the maritimes meant by it. To the latter it entailed

. . . the retention of the machinery of the existing local governments, the expenditure within each Province of the Revenue raised from it except the quota to be paid towards federal expenses, and the preservation of the existing Legislatures in their integrity with the cumbrous addition of a central parliament to which the consideration of some few topics of general interest are to be confided under rigorous restraints prompted by a jealous care for the maintenance of provincial independence [and] facilities for local jobbing.[34]

Gordon correctly believed that the character and methods of the public men in Canada would soon ensure that their views on union would fall into line with popular concepts, partly from fear of unpopularity and partly because they wished to render some form of union more palatable. Gordon expressed these views to Edward Cardwell, the new secretary of state for the colonies.

Cardwell at first fully agreed with Gordon in desiring a strongly centralized union and felt sure that it would be created. Lord Monck, the governor-general, had assured him of this and, in October 1864, Cardwell informed Gordon that "there is no idea of that feeble Legislature which you so justly object to; . . . they [the Canadians] wish a strong central Legislature with subordinate municipal institutions. . . . We all agree in favouring a complete fusion not a federation."[35] A month later he repeated his assurances. "It signifies little," he wrote, "what name is employed. What we wish is a central and strong Government,

[31]Gordon to Cardwell (postscript), 30 Jan. 1865, Cardwell Papers.
[32]A. T. Galt was the finance minister and John A. Macdonald the prime minister of Canada.   [33]Gordon to Cardwell, 12 Sept. 1864, Cardwell Papers.
[34]*Ibid.*   [35]Cardwell to Gordon, 14 Oct. 1864, Cardwell Papers.

as distinguished from a number of small states united by a feeble bond."[36] Within the next few days Cardwell received a copy of the Quebec Resolutions, which he read and passed on to the cabinet. He believed the cabinet would approve the resolutions and he wrote to Gordon saying that he would soon have to instruct him to "promote the scheme of the Delegates to the utmost of your power."[37] The Quebec Resolutions, however, obviously did not provide for the "complete fusion" of the colonies or for the reduction of their legislatures to the status of "municipal institutions." Cardwell had therefore made an about-face in his attitude to the principle upon which a union was to be based.

The reason is not difficult to discover. As Whitelaw has pointed out,[38] little evidence exists that Cardwell had thought deeply about political constitutions or, indeed, that he was even much interested in them. Still, he must have been able to see the difference between a "complete fusion" and the kind of union offered by the Quebec Resolutions. Cardwell was primarily concerned with saving money for the Imperial Treasury. He believed that the Quebec Resolutions would provide the North American colonies with the means to undertake their own defence and thus relieve the mother country of an onerous financial burden. He was also a politician, one who "sometimes watched too closely the currents of public opinion, and was too critical of those who (as he used to say) 'never looked out of a window'."[39] Frederic Rogers, permanent under-secretary of state for the colonies, about this time (December 1864) wrote an illuminating passage concerning his chief: "Cardwell is happily absent. . . . The constant presence in his mind of the House of Commons and the leader of the Opposition is a terrible nuisance."[40] On this view of Cardwell's political outlook, it may be suggested that when the Quebec Resolutions appeared to be popular in British North America, but more importantly in British cabinet and political circles generally, Cardwell was prepared to adopt them and to drop his strongly expressed preference for a "complete fusion."

Before he received instructions to promote the Quebec Resolutions, Gordon had been urging on Cardwell the necessity and feasibility of making changes in the proposed union in the direction of greater central control. Even though he believed that these changes might not be accepted and that the proposed union would have mischievous results,

[36]Ibid., 12 Nov. 1864.
[37]Ibid., 26 Nov. 1864.
[38]Whitelaw, Maritimes and Canada, 276.
[39]Selborne, Memorials: Part II, Personal and Political 1865–1895, II, 244.
[40]G. E. Marindin, ed., Letters of Frederic, Lord Blachford . . . , 1860–1871, 252f.

he was prepared to acquiesce in a policy he did not approve and to promote it when advised to do so by his government.[41] He could not, however, say things he did not believe, or recommend as beneficial that which he considered injurious. Cardwell might therefore remove him if he saw fit. If the Secretary of State chose to allow him to remain, Gordon could do what, in the opinion of his advisers, was necessary to accomplish the union: "sanction the necessary amount of corruption; and approve the wholesale removal of officeholders of respectability."[42] Still the Lieutenant-Governor felt embarrassed and, on 2 January 1865, a few days after receiving Cardwell's instructions to promote federation, he sent in his resignation.[43]

Gordon had several reasons for wishing to resign. He found the powerlessness of his position as lieutenant-governor humiliating.[44] He disagreed with the principle upon which union was to be based. Most important, he thought that Cardwell might wish a governor more favourable to his own views. He would much rather resign than have the Secretary of State think him negligent in his duty. He believed it improbable, but not impossible, that federation would be defeated in New Brunswick but if it should he was sure Cardwell would hold him responsible.[45] Although he asked Cardwell to defer accepting his resignation until after the next mail because he had received information that a Fenian raid was planned (and a resignation in such circumstances would seem like running away),[46] his offer was a genuine one. The Secretary of State, however, saw no reason to accept it.

Meanwhile, discussions had taken place between Gordon and the Tilley council regarding the course of politics for the coming year. The life of the assembly was due to expire in June and elections had to be held by that month at the latest. The council at first (mid-December 1864) intended to hold another session before dissolving, but it did not wish to bring the Quebec Resolutions before the legislature at that session.[47] Gordon was so advised.[48] His instructions from Cardwell, which arrived late in December, compelled him however to urge his

---

[41]Gordon to Cardwell, 19 Dec. 1864, Cardwell Papers.

[42]Ibid.

[43]Ibid., 2 Jan. 1865.

[44]Ibid.; also Gordon to Wilberforce, [Jan. 1865], Stanmore Papers (N.B.).

[45]Gordon to Cardwell, 3 Feb. 1865; Cardwell Papers; Gordon to Palmer, 2 Jan. 1865, Stanmore Papers, 49217; and Gordon to Sir Edmund Head, 8 Feb. 1865, Stanmore Papers (N.B.).

[46]Gordon to Cardwell, 2 Jan. 1865.

[47]Tilley had indeed promised, in a speech at Carleton on or about 24 Nov. 1864, that no judgment on the Quebec Resolutions would be sought from the legislature until after elections.   [48]Gordon to Cardwell, 19 Dec. 1864.

council to take action on the resolutions. Union was intimately connected with the Intercolonial Railway; discussion of union in the legislature would lead inevitably to controversy over railways, because the proponents of a rival of the Intercolonial, the European and North American Railway, were active and vociferous especially in Saint John, the seat of Tilley's power. Some of the members of the council wished to hold another session before dissolution so they might receive pay for two sessions in 1865 instead of one,[49] but they were overridden by Gordon and Tilley. Tilley wished to postpone the elections as long as possible so he could prepare the electorate for federal union, but he was eager to avoid a pre-election session of the legislature. In fact, he did not dare call a session before the election. "Had we met the House," he later explained to Galt in reply to Canadian criticism that the union question should have been dealt with by the existing legislature, "we would have been compelled to have taken a course [concerning railway matters] that at the Elections in June would have defeated the Government Members [Tilley and Watters] and their supporters, five in all for the city and county of Saint John."[50]

Yet to postpone the elections until June without meeting the assembly would be difficult, not to say dangerous. It was customary for the legislature to meet early in the year, and the opposition would find it easy to discover the real reason for the omission and to make capital out of it. Moreover, many of Tilley's own supporters in the assembly would be incensed at the delay in collecting their stipends of £80, and some would feel that they ran the risk of losing their seats and thus their stipends. To delay the elections also meant going counter to the Canadians, Cardwell, and Gordon, all of whom for one reason or another desired an early decision. Although Tilley himself wished the delay in order to persuade the public to accept the Quebec Resolutions, his party had been in power almost continuously since 1854 and had to expect to lose seats no matter when the election came. If, then, he could not be sure of passing the union resolutions in the old assembly, how could he be sure of doing so in the new?

Tilley's dilemma was plain and painful. He could hold a session of the legislature thus ensuring his own defeat at the elections,[51] or he could choose between calling early elections or late elections. Whichever course he followed, he and his Liberal party ran the risk of defeat. Although he

[49]*Ibid.*, 30 Jan. 1865.
[50]Tilley to Galt, 6 March 1865, quoted by A. G. Bailey, "Railways and the Confederation Issue in New Brunswick, 1863–1865," *Canadian Historical Review*, XXI, 381.
[51]See Tilley's admission to Galt quoted above.

preferred to postpone the contest, he allowed Gordon to persuade him to choose early elections (March 1865), a course which led to temporary defeat. It does not follow, however, that the choice of the other road would have led to victory, or that Gordon was wrong in persuading Tilley to call immediate elections or Tilley for allowing himself to be persuaded. Delay might, conceivably, have led to an earlier victory, but it might also have led to a less temporary defeat than that which occurred.

The result of the elections surprised and shocked the Lieutenant-Governor. He had never anticipated the defeat of the leading members of the government.[52] He had noted in December that, although the union had little positive support, those desiring it were more earnest than those opposing it, and the former had the "means of influence at their command which here seldom fail of effect."[53] In his final forecast before the elections he had estimated that the new assembly would contain fifteen members in favour of Confederation, eighteen against, and eight purchasable members. The government could thus expect to find a majority.[54] Gordon had, however, over-estimated the strength of local issues in a contest which introduced a new concept antagonistic to the isolationism and parochialism of the cultural backwater that was New Brunswick.

Tilley and Fisher were deeply chagrined by their defeat in the elections. Cardwell and the Canadians were disappointed because without New Brunswick, the geographical keystone, federal union could not proceed. The Canadians asked for and obtained from Cardwell a decided expression of Imperial policy favouring union which, it was felt, would have a marked effect in persuading the loyal people of New Brunswick to reverse their decision. Fisher and Tilley (and Tupper of Nova Scotia) were parties to this plan and to an attempt to saddle Gordon and MacDonnell, the lieutenant-governor of Nova Scotia, with the blame for the defeat. They bluntly declared that their actions had "insured the defeat of the measure."[55] Fisher wrote to Macdonald: "I know everyone that he [Gordon] might be supposed to have the least influence with in any way, violently opposed Confederation, a state of things I cannot think could exist without his procurement in some way."[56] Gordon, then, was to be made the scapegoat, and what he had feared—that Cardwell would suspect him should New Brunswick reject the Quebec Resolutions

[52]Gordon to Cardwell, 18 March 1865, Cardwell Papers.
[53]Ibid., 19 Dec. 1864.
[54]Ibid., 27 Feb. 1865.
[55]A. G. Bailey, "The Basis and Persistence of Opposition to Confederation in New Brunswick," Canadian Historical Review, XXIII, 387.
[56]Fisher to Macdonald, 5 April 1865, quoted ibid.

—had come to pass. What is the truth? Did Gordon ensure, or seek to ensure, the defeat of the proposed union?

The answer to both parts of this question must be an unqualified "no." Sound and adequate causes for Tilley's defeat[57] existed aside from any interference by the Queen's representative. In addition, the governor of a colony possessing responsible government simply did not have the power or means to effect any marked change in public opinion. Moreover, the election was not close, and even if Gordon had worked against Tilley the result would have been nearly the same. Judging from the result of the election and from the year's delay needed, in not unfavourable circumstances, to reverse the decision, one may conclude that a difference of three months in the timing of the elections of 1865 would not have greatly affected the result. Gordon certainly did not defeat federation.

Neither did he seek to ensure the defeat of the proposed union. Gordon did not desire the defeat of the Tilley party and actually looked forward to its victory. He viewed with keen anticipation the prospect of the abolition of his office which the coming of the federation would ensure, and he awaited eagerly another appointment that would give more scope for his talents.[58] He wanted to leave New Brunswick because the amenities it offered were insufficient to atone for the disgust he felt at the powerlessness of his official position.[59] He had, it is true, by dint of

[57]The causes of the defeat of the unionists in the election of 1865 have been fully detailed by D. G. Creighton in *John A. Macdonald: The Young Politician*, and by A. G. Bailey in two articles in the *Canadian Historical Review*: "Railways and the Confederation Issue in New Brunswick, 1863–1865," XXI, and "The Basis and Persistence of Opposition to Confederation in New Brunswick," XXIII. The leading cause of Tilley's defeat was the opposition of the supporters of the European and North American Railway who feared that this railway, which they believed would ensure the continued prosperity of New Brunswick (which had been based upon the reciprocity treaty with the United States) by connecting the province with New England, would remain unbuilt should New Brunswick enter Confederation and thus be committed financially to the support of the Intercolonial Railway. Other people feared that once Confederation had been achieved the Canadians would refuse to assume their proper share of the cost of the Intercolonial. Roman Catholics feared interference with their land settlement policies in the area to be traversed by the Intercolonial. Some believed the Quebec Resolutions would result in the central government being too strong. Others, like Gordon, thought it would be too weak. Confederate speakers were able to tell the people only what New Brunswick would probably receive as a result of union, not the price she would have to pay. Finally, but by no means least among the causes of Tilley's defeat was the fact that his government had been long in power and had inevitably made enemies.

[58]Gordon to Wilberforce, 12 Sept. 1864 and 16 Nov. 1864, Stanmore Papers (N.B.); Gordon to Layard, 25 March 1865, Layard Papers, 39114.

[59]Gordon to Cardwell, 24 Oct. 1864, Cardwell Papers; Gordon to Gladstone, 26 Feb. 1865, Gladstone Papers, 44320.

much persuasion and management, been able to build up and to maintain over his council a degree of ascendancy which lasted until 1864 when he took his first leave of absence. But when he returned, he found that his influence had evaporated; the council had reasserted itself and its members met every hint of opposition from Gordon with threats of resignation, since they knew that he could not form a new government.[60] He was driven to declare that he was viewed by the council simply as its clerk.[61] For a man of Gordon's character, such a rôle was intolerable. He hoped fervently that the whole question of union would be settled by spring and that he would be enabled to return to England by the end of the summer of 1865 at the latest.[62] The defeat of the Tilley ministry in March blasted this hope. It is hardly likely that he worked or lent such influence as he possessed to bring this about. So much for the allegations of the corrupt Charles Fisher upon which much of the criticism of Gordon's activities in the 1865 elections has hitherto been based.

There were still other reasons why Gordon could not have sought to defeat federation. Such a defeat would ensure the victory of the American-sponsored European and North American Railway at the expense of the Intercolonial. Gordon had worked hard for the Intercolonial and he was decidedly anti-American. Furthermore a Liberal defeat would bring to power, as head of the new ministry, Albert Smith, the one man with whom he had never agreed and who had openly boasted of being his enemy.[63] He could scarcely wish this result; nor could he foresee that the new ministry would be so divided within itself that he would have more power than he had ever experienced under its predecessor. Finally, no lieutenant-governor would willingly have placed himself in the uncomfortable constitutional position in which Gordon now found himself. Until the March elections his duties as an officer of the Crown and as a governor responsible to his council had coincided. He had had simply to carry out Imperial orders which, although he disagreed with them, were approved by his advisers. Now he had to promote the same Imperial policy with advisers who opposed that policy but whose own policies concerning union he deplored. Was he to act as

[60]Gordon to Wilberforce, [Jan. 1865] and 16 Nov. 1865, and Gordon to Head, 18 Feb. 1865, Stanmore Papers (N.B.).
[61]Gordon to Head, 18 Feb. 1865.
[62]Gordon to Wilberforce, [Jan. 1865].
[63]There are many evidences in the Stanmore Papers (N.B.) of the mutual antipathy of Gordon and Smith (for example, Gordon's diary, 18 Nov. 1861, and Gordon to Waterfield, 27 Jan. 1863). Smith had gone into the opposition following his resignation as attorney-general in the Tilley government. In opposition he used his undisputed demagogic talents to decry the Intercolonial and to promote the European and North American Railway.

the governor of a colony possessing responsible government should act, and accept the advice of his constitutional advisers, or was he to carry out the orders of the Crown and thus be forced to deal with the official opposition and so act unconstitutionally?

To both Gordon and Cardwell that choice was obvious. Unless the new government could be persuaded to adopt the federation policy of its predecessor, Gordon must regard himself as being primarily an officer of the Crown and must carry out the policy of the Crown even if it meant that he had to consult and act with the leader of the opposition. Cardwell was, however, doubtful of Gordon. He feared that Gordon held opinions regarding the necessity of a strong union so firmly that he would not be able or willing to obey orders not wholly in conformity with those opinions. Gordon deeply resented Cardwell's suspicion. He had carried out his orders. He had even gone beyond them in endeavouring in January 1865 to prevent G. L. Hatheway's resignation from the council and in attempting before the elections to weaken the opposition by trying to induce J. C. Allen (who was to become Smith's attorney-general after the change of government) to join the Tilley council. He had also, he wrote to Cardwell, kept his criticisms of the Quebec Resolutions to himself. He had, of course, informed the Canadian government and the leading members of the Tilley council of his views before the Quebec Conference while the preliminary agreement reached at Charlottetown still admitted of modification; but after that he had kept quiet. He believed that not more than half a dozen people outside the Tilley government had known his opinion and even within the council some members supposed him to be a warm advocate of the Quebec scheme.[64]

So sure had Gordon been of a unionist victory that early in March he had accepted, what he had been assured was a promotion, the governorship of Hong Kong. After Tilley's defeat he changed his mind. He wanted to scotch the current rumours in New Brunswick and England that he was being recalled because of dissatisfaction with his administration. He had recently made a proposal of marriage and he preferred, if accepted, to bring his bride to New Brunswick because its climate was much healthier than that of Hong Kong. He wished also to demonstrate to Cardwell his willingness to carry out orders. Provided that the Secretary of State was prepared to give him his confidence he would remain in New Brunswick and work to reverse the electorate's

[64]Gordon to Cardwell, 22 May 1865, Cardwell Papers. Support for Gordon's contention is to be found in an editorial in the 16 Sept. 1865 issue of the pro-Tilley and self-admitted anti-Gordon *Morning Telegraph* which said: "The Governor had not given any person reason for thinking that he was unfavourably impressed with the Quebec Scheme."

decision.[65] Gordon expected that this would take some time and he and Tilley agreed that it was too soon (May 1865) to make the attempt. Opinion had not changed much, he informed Cardwell, and of this he was a better judge than the Canadians "who speak of this province without the same responsibility [and whose opinions] are accepted by you in preference."[66] He demonstrated to Cardwell his willingness to carry out orders when, in the late spring and early summer of 1865, a revival of the cause of maritime union originated in Nova Scotia. Although personally pleased and still believing that maritime union would be a useful preliminary to federation, he dutifully obeyed Cardwell's wish to prevent the movement gaining ground.[67] He simply failed to appoint delegates to a proposed conference.

In August Gordon sailed for England. Despite the rumours which were circulating both in the North American colonies and in England and which led him to write to Cardwell that he would be much disappointed "if the reasons which were not considered sufficient to justify my resignation are considered sufficient to require my recall,"[68] there is no foundation for the assertion that he was being recalled. Actually he was returning to England to be married. He had applied for leave in the regular manner but since Cardwell had heard of his plans and had sent congratulations Gordon did not await formal approval.

The wedding festivities and honeymoon kept Gordon away from the Colonial Office, but he had one interview with the Secretary of State. It was, according to Gordon, a most unpleasant one. Cardwell "never forgets that he is ones [sic] master which is right and never lets one forget it oneself which is more questionable. On the other hand he never remembers that the relative positions of master and man have not always been what they now are."[69] Cardwell continued to show that he distrusted Gordon and that he feared that he would not work zealously to promote union. To add insult to injury, he demanded of the Lieutenant-Governor written assurance that he would use his influence on behalf of union.[70] Gordon's pride was deeply wounded. He was an English gentleman whose word was his bond. He had given his promise. Why then should he be compelled to put it in writing? He was reassured by Bishop Wilberforce: "It is 'nasty' and like him; but I think that is all. He

[65]Gordon to Cardwell, 22 May 1865.   [66]Ibid., 5 June 1865.
[67]Ibid. See also Whitelaw, Maritimes and Canada, 279f.
[68]Gordon to Cardwell, 30 June 1865, Cardwell Papers.
[69]Gordon to Wilberforce, 14 Oct. 1865, Stanmore Papers (N.B.). Cardwell had been an ordinary M.P. when Gordon was both M.P. and private secretary to the Prime Minister.
[70]Cardwell to Gordon, 29 Sept. 1865, Cardwell Papers.

wishes I presume to be able to defend himself against attack."[71] Gordon than gave Cardwell the required assurance but in a stiff and formal manner. So long as he had the honour, he wrote, to hold any employment under the Crown, he would always endeavour to the best of his ability to carry out the orders he received through the secretary of state or any other authorized channel. Should he from any cause feel himself unable to carry out those orders, it would be his desire and duty at once to retire.[72] He refused a request, which he received from Cardwell an hour before he was to start back to New Brunswick, to delay his sailing and return to London to consult Monck and the Colonial Office regarding federation. He left England highly incensed with Cardwell, but by the time he and his wife reached Halifax he had calmed down sufficiently to repeat his assurances and ask the Secretary of State to be patient because, if federation were to be accomplished, it would be necessary to act slowly and cautiously.[73]

Before his journey to England, Gordon had formulated an approach to the problem. He had planned to take advantage of the strong differences of opinion within the Smith government in order to create a coalition between one of its factions and Tilley and a group of his more respectable supporters. The divisions in the government, however, had not come to the fore as early as he had expected and his plan was frustrated. Actually the Smith government appeared at first to be strongly united and it resisted resolutely the attempts made by Cardwell to use New Brunswick's military weakness as a lever to force it to accept union with Canada. On 1 April, less than a month after the formation of the new government, Cardwell instructed Gordon to point out to his ministers that, while England was very willing to exert herself in defence of her colonies, the colonies should also exert themselves. The government's reply to this was to vote three times as much money for the militia as its predecessor had done in 1864, and ten times as much as had been voted annually until 1862. In June Cardwell put on more pressure. He wrote to Gordon:

You will . . . express the strong and deliberate opinion of Her Majesty's Government that . . . all the British North American Colonies should agree to unite in one Government. . . . The Colonies must recognize a right and even acknowledge incumbent on the Home Government to urge with earnestness and just authority any measures which they consider to be most expedient on the part of the Colonies with a view to their own defence.[74]

[71]Wilberforce to Gordon, 1 Oct. 1865, Stanmore Papers (N.B.).
[72]Gordon to Cardwell, 5 Oct. 1865, Cardwell Papers.
[73]Ibid., 26 Oct. 1865.
[74]Cardwell to Gordon, 24 June 1865, PRO CO 188/192.

This dispatch was for publication throughout the colony, and it drew from the executive council a vigorous reply which concluded thus:

To confer on this Province a right of self-government would have been mockery if, in consequence of its claims to deference as a protector, the wish of the mother country was in all cases to be followed whenever expressed, whatever the opinion of those to whom the power of judging has been solemnly entrusted by the Sovereign and Legislature of Great Britain, and who, being on the spot, and fully conversant with the subject, consider themselves not unable to judge with respect to their own affairs. When a wish is expressed by Her Majesty's Government, it will be received with that deference which is due to suggestions emanating from so high a source, and will be considered with an anxious desire to meet the views of Her Majesty's advisers; but if such views should unfortunately not coincide with the views of those on whom alone the responsibility of action in the Province falls, the Committee [of the council] feel assured that Her Majesty's Government will expect and desire that the Government of this Province should act according to their own convictions of right, and in conformity with the sentiments of the people they represent.[75]

The original draft of this reply had included, at Gordon's insistence, an admission "that a Union may be formed on terms acceptable to us," but this was struck out and a declaration substituted that the people of New Brunswick were opposed to any closer political connection with Canada than that afforded by the tie of a common allegiance.[76] Truly the Smith government at this time felt its oats! Almost certainly, however, Cardwell's pressure contributed to the government's early strength.

As so often happens, the lapse of time accomplished what Cardwell and Gordon had failed to do. When the latter returned from England in the autumn of 1865, the rifts in the Smith Government had begun to be apparent, and Gordon again prepared to take advantage of them. Shortly after his return he received a visit from George Brown of Upper Canada and they "confidentially settled the whole course of operations to be pursued"[77] in effecting New Brunswick's adherence to federal union. There would be no resort to a dissolution of the House. Instead, satisfactory resolutions were to be adopted by making or buying a union majority in the existing legislature. There was a good chance of this plan succeeding because the government was rapidly weakening and Gordon's power was correspondingly enhanced.

Gordon found it a delightful government with which to work because,

[75]Reply of the executive council of New Brunswick in committee, 12 July 1865, to Cardwell's dispatch to Gordon, 24 June 1865, "Correspondence respecting the Proposed Union of the British North American Provinces," Parliamentary and Colonial Office Papers, July 1866 to March 1867, PRO 30/6-70.

[76]*Morning Freeman*, 23 April 1867.

[77]Gordon to Cardwell, 20 Nov. 1865, Cardwell Papers.

as he said, "its members do *nothing* and look to me to write their minutes and dictate their measures."[78] It was so rent by factions that it could not act. It contained three main schools of thought. There were those who favoured a stronger central government than that which the Quebec Resolutions would provide and who believed that the terms of union should contain written assurance of the construction of the Intercolonial. There were those who opposed any union with Canada and who demanded that the European and North American Railway be undertaken as a public work. Finally, there were those who thought the Quebec Resolutions took too much independence away from New Brunswick and who believed that the reciprocity treaty with the United States could be renewed and the European and North American Railway constructed privately. It was possible that the first or last of these groups, or perhaps both, might, under certain circumstances, be persuaded to support the proposed union. By the early spring of 1866 Gordon was ready to bring the union issue to a head.

Meanwhile the government had suffered severe blows. Charles Fisher had defeated an anti-union candidate in a by-election in York County in the previous November. Tilley while out of office was conducting a campaign on behalf of union and was making progress. R. D. Wilmot, next to Smith the most important man in the council, had been converted to the federation cause after a visit to Canada. The government had lost many of its most ardent supporters through its failure to undertake the construction of the New Brunswick section of the European and North American Railway as a public work. Smith and Attorney-General Allen had made an unsuccessful journey to England in an attempt to change Cardwell's mind. Smith had also made an abortive journey to Washington to obtain a renewal of reciprocity. His policy was now bankrupt. He had no real alternative but to accept the policy of the opposition.

On Smith's return from Washington, Gordon firmly tackled him. Smith admitted that he was not averse to union on principle and agreed to put a resolution favouring union through the legislature. When the legislature met in March 1866, the speech from the throne served notice on the opponents of union that a change in policy was imminent.[79] Had it not been for the jealousy of Fisher and the Liberals there is little doubt that Gordon's plan would have worked and that federation would have been carried without the delay of another election.

When the debate on the speech from the throne began, Fisher moved an amendment, not on the union issue but on the competence of the

[78]Gordon to Waterfield, 15 Jan. 1866, Stanmore Papers (N.B.).
[79]*Journal of the House of Assembly of New Brunswick*, 1866, 10–12.

government to protect the colony against the Fenian menace. The debate on this point dragged on for about three weeks and effectively prevented action on federation. If Smith was insincere in his promise to Gordon and wished for an excuse for delay, the opposition willingly provided it. It is clear that, as Macdonald suspected, "Fisher was playing Mr. Smith's game."[80] He was putting party before principle, and saying to Smith in effect: "You prevented us carrying Confederation; we shall prevent you." A coalition was thus plainly impossible. Cardwell and the Canadians were impatient, and Gordon, feeling that he could countenance no further delay, decided to force the issue.

The legislative council, which contained a good unionist majority, had meanwhile debated the throne speech briefly and decided upon a reply strongly favouring union on the basis of the Quebec Resolutions. Gordon determined to receive the address of the legislative council and to reply to it in terms warranted by his instructions. A committee of the legislative council waited upon him at twelve o'clock on 7 April to present the address. Gordon could not communicate officially with his ministers until he had received it. He sent immediately for Smith, but the latter did not appear at government house until nearly three o'clock, the hour at which Gordon had promised to reply to the legislative council. Smith advised Gordon against his proposed reply which "rejoiced to believe that the avowal of your desire that all British North America should unite in one community, under one strong and efficient government, cannot but tend to hasten the accomplishment of this great measure."[81] Smith refused to consult the other members of the executive council and to return in half an hour, and the committee of the legislative council refused to wait longer. Gordon therefore determined to deliver his proposed reply. On 13 April the ministry resigned and raised a storm over the Lieutenant-Governor's "unconstitutional" action.

Gordon formed a new council headed by R. D. Wilmot and Peter Mitchell,[82] a member of the legislative council. Nevertheless it was impossible that this caretaker government could command support in an assembly dominated by Smith's followers, who were clamouring for Gordon's head and who passed, by a good majority, a motion of censure upon him. New elections were inevitable. What would be the issue: federation, or the Lieutenant-Governor's "unconstitutional" behaviour?

[80]Macdonald to Tilley, 6 Oct. 1866, quoted by Creighton, *The Young Politician*, 439.
[81]Gordon's reply to the legislative council, 7 April 1866, quoted by James Hannay, *Life and Times of Sir Leonard Tilley*, 307.
[82]Later Canada's first minister of marine and fisheries.

Smith's position on the union question was weak. Because of his failure to obtain a renewal of reciprocity, to extract from Cardwell better terms for New Brunswick than the Quebec Resolutions offered, and to guarantee construction of the western extension of the European and North American Railway by undertaking it as a public enterprise, he could offer no alternative to some form of union. He had already agreed to support union, "provided one could be obtained upon fair and equitable terms."[83] Gordon, by making public his correspondence with him, forced him to admit this in the legislature. Smith had not fulfilled his promise, demonstrating to his anti-union supporters that he had been prepared to betray either them or Gordon. His best approach to the elections seemed to be to divert public opinion from the union question by raising a cry against the Lieutenant-Governor's interference with the sacred principle of responsible government.

Tilley was unnecessarily worried by the intrusion of this question. He had forgotten the lesson of 1856 when the "unconstitutional" procedure of Manners Sutton had failed Tilley as an election issue.[84] Now, as events were to show, the constitutional issue would fail Smith. Actually, as an issue, it was perhaps more advantageous than not for Tilley because there was still much disapproval of the Quebec Resolutions and, as Macdonald later told him, he was never in a position to fight an election on them alone.[85] It was easier to defend Gordon than it was union.

Moreover, Smith did not have much of a case against Gordon. The lieutenant-governors of New Brunswick had never admitted that they need accept advice as long as they could find new advisers who commanded a majority in the assembly either before or after a dissolution. Gordon, however, had clearly acted unconstitutionally in failing to consult his ministers before replying to the legislative council. Yet his failure was as much Smith's fault as his own. Smith could not take advantage of Gordon's error because it was generally known that he had hidden for several hours to delay receiving the Lieutenant-Governor's summons to appear at government house on the day the legislative council presented its address.

Cardwell, who had refrained from commenting adversely on Gordon's unconstitutional procedure, evidently thought that it might prove a

[83]*Journal of the House of Assembly of New Brunswick*, 1866, 217.

[84]See J. K. Chapman "The Mid-Nineteenth-Century Temperance Movement in New Brunswick and Maine," *Canadian Historical Review*, XXXV, 43–60. Manners Sutton had forced the Fisher-Tilley ministry to resign, and had found new advisers who were sustained by the voters in the ensuing elections.

[85]Macdonald to Tilley, 6 Oct. 1866, quoted in Creighton, *The Young Politician*, 439.

disadvantage to Tilley and the unionist cause. He suggested to Gordon that in order to avoid angry correspondence with his former advisers he might do well to accept the governorship of Trinidad which had recently fallen vacant. Gordon did not like criticism at any time. He found the imprecations being showered upon him by his discomfited ex-ministers particularly painful because, with the exception of Smith himself, he liked them and considered them more respectable than their predecessors. Nevertheless he rejected Cardwell's suggestion. His sudden departure from New Brunswick would give the impression that the Secretary of State disapproved of his conduct which in turn would give authority to the views of his attackers and perhaps prejudice the election. He wanted the satisfaction of reporting complete success and receiving credit for accomplishing a difficult task, and he wanted to stay until he had dealt with the threat of a Fenian invasion of New Brunswick. Cardwell acquiesced, and Gordon remained until October.

During the election campaign the Fenian menace became serious and, by alerting public opinion to the greater security to be found in union with the other colonies, contributed to the unionist victory in June. It also gave Gordon much to do. As commander-in-chief of the New Brunswick militia he had to see to its preparedness and, in co-operation with the regular troops, to its stationing. He travelled thousands of miles in a few weeks performing his task with efficiency, success, and considerable enjoyment. It is safe to say that had the Fenians carried out their threatened invasion of New Brunswick they would have met with ignominious defeat. As it was, their small-scale raids were repulsed on the borders and they eventually returned to the bar-rooms and tenements of New York and Boston with the grins on the other side of their Irish faces.

The unionists won the elections in 1866 as easily as their opponents had the previous year. They polled about 60 per cent of the vote, and only six of the twenty-two members who had signed the motion of censure against Gordon were re-elected. Gordon was gratified that he had been able to carry out Cardwell's orders to do what he could to ensure the success of the federal cause. Nevertheless he continued to believe that union on the basis of the Quebec Resolutions would prove illusory. He hoped that the Imperial government would make modifications which would greatly strengthen the central government at the expense of the provinces, and so render the union "a true and durable one."[86]

There was now some chance that this might be done as Lord

[86]Gordon to Monck, 24 Nov. 1866, Stanmore Papers (N.B.).

Carnarvon had replaced Cardwell at the Colonial Office in June 1866. Gordon and Lord Monck, who, somewhat to Gordon's surprise, were almost entirely agreed on the necessity of changes and on their nature, made suggestions to Carnarvon providing for a closer union. Carnarvon accepted almost all of them, but he could not persuade the colonial delegates to the London Conference to agree to them. He therefore allowed "those who were to lie in the bed to form it after their own fashion."[87]

The course of Arthur Gordon's first administration had not been smooth, affected as it was by external influences over which he could exercise little control. Although Gordon was a man of great energy and administrative skill and one who, as George Brown remarked, thought for himself, he had not found his victories in New Brunswick entirely satisfying. He had prepared for the reception of the troops in 1861, prevented a railway strike and riot in 1862, created an efficient militia, and provided for the defence of the colony against the Fenians. He had filled vacancies in the judiciary with men of acknowledged ability and impartiality rather than with men who had simply served their party well. He had helped to place the colony upon the path which the Imperial government, the Canadians, and the provincial Liberals wished her to take. These were important but not great accomplishments. He had failed to gain what he most wanted: to raise the level of political ability and morality by abolishing the legislatures of the smaller colonies through legislative union of all British North America or of the maritime provinces. That he failed was no fault of his. Had he been successful in helping to create a legislative union of all British North America, no doubt the level of politics would have been raised; but the maritime region would have suffered from much the same economic disabilities it has experienced in the last ninety years. Had he, however, brought about a legislative union of the maritimes before federal union took place, the results would have been more beneficial. Not only would better politicians have come to the fore, but the region probably would have been sufficiently united and strong to have fought more successfully than it has been able to do against the centralization of industrial development in Ontario and Quebec.

The year 1864 marks a dividing line in Gordon's administration of New Brunswick. Until he went on leave that summer his relationships with both the secretary of state and his own ministers were friendly. The Duke of Newcastle commended the work of the youngest governor in

[87]Monck to Gordon, 16 March 1867, Stanmore Papers (N.B.).

the colonial service, and Gordon's ministers deferred to his judgment to such an extent that he felt he really ruled as well as reigned.[88] During his absence his influence with his ministers vanished and, except briefly during the Smith régime, he was never able to win it back. In 1864 also, his relationship with the secretary of state deteriorated, when Edward Cardwell replaced the Duke of Newcastle in that office.

Gordon and Cardwell had known each other for more than ten years and were friends though not close friends. They should perhaps have worked well together. Nevertheless, each gave the other grounds for complaint. Cardwell had the businessman's virtues and some of his faults. He was single-minded and conscientious; but he came from a prosperous mill-owning family and tended to treat the governors under his command as factory superintendents. He was long on criticism and short on compliments. Gordon thought him officious, distrustful, and patronizing. But Cardwell too had cause to lament. The Lieutenant-Governor wrote him frequent letters insisting upon his own point of view respecting the union proposals. Gordon seemed to want too much praise and to require too much personal attention. "I know no other Governor," Cardwell finally wrote, "who has expressed himself more freely upon both . . . matters and men [than you]."[89] Cardwell correctly believed that Gordon was temperamentally unsuited to the task of governing a colony having responsible government. He assured him that he would be happier in a Crown colony where he would possess wider powers.[90] With both of these judgments Gordon was in complete agreement.

Gordon left New Brunswick with both regret and relief. It had been his home for five years and, on the whole, a happy one. He was sorry to leave "its glorious climate, its wild free forest life, and the splendid river"[91] he knew so well. He had grown attached to government house and had made a number of good friends. Nevertheless, he welcomed his escape from "the thraldom of such a set"[92] as his ministers. Their standards and philosophy had not been his. They had no more been able to tolerate a challenge to their authority by an outsider inclined to benevolent despotism than he had been able to stomach their corrupt practices, parochial outlook, and petty party quarrels. They were doubtless as glad to see the last of Gordon as he was to bid them farewell.

[88]Gordon to Palmer, 1 Jan. 1863, Stanmore Papers, 49217; and Gordon to Wilberforce, 15 Jan. 1863, Stanmore Papers (N.B.).

[89]Cardwell to Gordon, 1 July 1866, Cardwell Papers.   [90]Ibid.

[91]Gordon's diary, 1 Oct. 1866, Stanmore Papers (N.B.).   [92]Ibid.

III

TRINIDAD, 1866–1870

☙

I. BACKGROUND AND PROBLEMS

GORDON ASSUMED the governorship of Trinidad late in the autumn of 1866 after a leisurely journey from New Brunswick by way of Niagara Falls and New York. Despite Trinidad's smaller size and population, both Gordon and the Colonial Office considered his appointment a promotion. Trinidad's revenues, exports, and imports were nearly on a par with New Brunswick's; but, more important, Trinidad was a Crown colony in which the position of governor carried greater power and responsibility than in self-governing New Brunswick.[1]

Gordon found his new post most agreeable. "It is almost necessary," he wrote, "to have been Governor of such a Province as New Brunswick fully to relish the pleasure or indeed fully to feel the responsibility of such a government as this."[2] In New Brunswick he had considered himself " . . . not only a mere puppet, but a puppet in the hands of men . . . generally ignorant and almost always dishonest."[3] There he had been "dragged helplessly through the degrading dirt which a powerless 're- sponsible-government' Governor . . . [had] patiently [to] endure."[4] In Trinidad he had no parliament and no "blessed responsible ministers," and instead of "such men as Mr. Fisher of New Brunswick and the cobblers, tinkers, tailors, and thieves, who with a few exceptions were

[1]The governor's salary in Trinidad was £3,500 compared with £3,000 in New Brunswick.
[2]Gordon to Waterfield, 24 Nov. 1866, Stanmore Papers, 49249.
[3]Gordon to Cyril Graham (private secretary to Lord Carnarvon), 24 Nov. 1866, Stanmore Papers, 49244.
[4]Gordon to Carnarvon, 24 Dec. 1866, Stanmore Papers, 49244.

the politicians of that region,"[5] he had well-educated English gentlemen with whom to work. Here he had his first opportunity of making his mark, of ruling rather than reigning, of becoming master in the fullest sense, of demonstrating his ability to govern in the interests of all. The prospect filled him with energy and joy.

Gordon eagerly desired to begin the reformation of Trinidad. Aware, however, that every administrator on taking office inherits problems deriving from the successes and failures of his predecessors, he did not act precipitately. He painstakingly undertook first to learn the nature of his legacy. He travelled extensively about the island, read the dispatches of former governors, and sought information from colonial officials and private persons, and not until October 1867, at a public luncheon on one of the estates, did he make his first statement of general policy. He felt, he announced, that a governor should really govern and should be a living force to those over whom he ruled. He should be bound to them by ties of sympathy that would enable him to divine how far he could lead them in any course. This sympathy should make his acts the embodiment of national feeling and dispose the governed to acquiesce in his decisions as just and in his opinions as right, simply because they were the opinions and decisions of one they trusted and loved. He would, he said, attempt to realize this ideal. He made it clear that he intended to be his own prime minister.[6] Gordon asserted, in effect, that he would follow a policy of benevolent dictatorship. Such a policy appealed to him, especially after his New Brunswick experience. Certainly he could have followed no other with any chance of success in the conditions prevailing in Trinidad.

Froude once remarked that, in the absence of other uses for them, the West Indies "have been made to serve as places where governors try their 'prentice hand' and learn their business before promotion to more important situations."[7] Typically, this generalization is not altogether correct. It does serve, however, to indicate the calibre of the governors Trinidad had had from its conquest until the advent of Arthur Gordon. During that period only Sir Thomas Picton, the first British governor, Sir Ralph Woodford (1813–28), and perhaps Lord Harris (1846–54) had been capable and successful governors. The normal weakness and inefficiency of Trinidad's governors, the hands-off policy assumed by the Colonial Office, and the direct and indirect effects of the abolition of

[5]Gordon to Rogers, 24 Sept. 1867, and Gordon to A. J. Blackwood (senior clerk in the Colonial Office, 1840–67), 24 Oct. 1867, Stanmore Papers, 49244.

[6]*Trinidad Chronicle*, 22 Oct. 1867.

[7]J. A. Froude, *The English in the West Indies or the Bow of Ulysses*, 91.

slavery and the adoption of free trade accounted for the acute problems that Gordon found on his arrival. To understand how revolutionary Gordon's administration was, we must trace briefly the island's history during the previous quarter-century.

By the late forties Trinidad and the other British sugar islands had begun to suffer from the abolition of slavery and the withdrawal of the preference in the British market which colonial sugar had hitherto enjoyed. Despite rising world consumption the price of sugar fell. At the same time costs of production increased because of a labour shortage arising from the refusal of most of the former slaves to work on the plantations. They had instead become wanderers or squatters on the Crown lands. Consequently Trinidad had to import labour from India on short-term indentures. This practice drained the colony's financial resources because the Indians, when their terms of indenture expired and they were at the peak of their efficiency as estate labourers, either returned to India at the colony's expense or, like the negroes, squatted on the Crown lands. Hoping that the Indians would re-indenture themselves and that the negroes would return to work on the plantations, the planters exerted their influence to keep the cost of acquiring Crown lands high so that these groups would be unable to establish themselves as independent small-holders. As a consequence squatting became widespread. This resulted in destruction on the Crown lands and the creation of a serious social problem as large numbers of people removed themselves from the civilized portions of the colony.

The depression in the island's chief industry during the forties and fifties had other unhappy consequences. It led the government to curtail or postpone many desirable public works and, in the fifties, to reduce civil service salaries; the latter development tended to discourage the best men from entering the public service, thus contributing to a decline in its efficiency. A further weakening of the civil service leading to loose administration of public institutions resulted from inadequate supervision, by successive governors, of their officials and from the fact that "a family compact guarded the avenue to preferment"[8] and prevented investigations from running their proper courses. Thus by the 1860's, an overwhelming need existed for an expansion of public works and a reformation of the colony's public service and institutions.

The depression, however, was not responsible for all Trinidad's ills. Another source of great dissatisfaction arose from the attempt of the small Anglo-Protestant minority to make the island not simply a British possession but a British colony. This movement began during the

[8]T. Fitz-Evan Eversley, *The Trinidad Reviewer for the Year 1899*, 84.

governorship of Sir Henry McLeod (1840–46). Until then almost complete religious equality had prevailed. McLeod became the first governor to decline patronage of the Roman Catholic church—the church of the majority of the inhabitants. He also agreed to the passage of the ecclesiastical ordinance of 1844. This established the supremacy of the Church of England in Trinidad and perpetuated and magnified existing differences between Protestant and Roman Catholic. Lord Harris's establishment of a secular primary school system further alienated Roman Catholic opinion. Sir Charles Elliott, who succeeded Harris in 1854, allowed the Anglo-Protestant faction to bully him into refusing to recognize Roman Catholic Archbishop Spaccapietra and into withdrawing the latter's salary until the Colonial Office ordered it to be paid. Tension increased in 1863 when Governor Keate authorized an ordinance establishing civil marriage, making religious marriages in unauthorized places (such as death-bed marriages) null and void, and declaring any clergyman a felon if he solemnized a marriage in non-conformity with the ordinance.[9] Roman Catholics were dissatisfied also by the establishment, in the same year, of the Queen's Collegiate School, a secular secondary school. They wished, rather, government-assisted denominational schools.

The ultra-English Protestant party in Trinidad was led by Charles W. Warner, the attorney-general from 1844 to 1870. Throughout his tenure of office, he was next to the governor the most influential man in the colony. Indeed, between Harris's retirement and Gordon's assumption of the governorship, Warner probably had greater influence than the governors. He had "jockeyed" Elliott into premature retirement, had embittered several years of Keate's term by personally humiliating him,[10] had usurped the right to draft all legislation, and later became the chief opposition to Gordon's policies.

One of the colony's leading lawyers, Warner was well-connected by professional and blood ties with the most powerful elements in the community: the planter and commercial classes. Energetic, combative, and shrewd, and a highly competent law officer, he was also a skilled politician. Few in Trinidad were free from his power or influence. Few dared to defy him even when a governor opposed him. Most people reasoned that the governor would remain only a few years but that Warner would be with them always and might revenge himself upon

[9]This ordinance was modified by Governor Manners Sutton in 1865.

[10]H. J. Pantin (a Trinidadian planter) to Gordon, 26 Sept. 1867, Stanmore Papers, 49237; and Wenkstern (editor *Trinidad Chronicle*) to Gordon, 24 May 1868, Stanmore Papers, 49235.

those who had shown him opposition. It is fairly accurate to say that from 1845 to 1865 government policy was much what Warner decided it should be. He was the special advocate of the planters, and in so far as their welfare coincided with the colony's his influence was beneficial. In his opposition to the creole of non-British extraction and to the Roman Catholic Church, it was not so beneficial. He was responsible for the attempt to deprive Archbishop Spaccapietra of his salary; his was the hand behind the marriage ordinance; his was the loudest voice raised in behalf of a purely secular educational system. To him denominational schools would become "hot beds of Proselytism embittering religious differences already bitter enough."[11] He did not realize that he himself had created much of the religious bitterness. He desired harmony in the colony but did not understand a policy of mutual concessions; nor did he see that an aggressive Protestant policy could lead only to an aggressive Roman Catholicism.

Why was Warner so successful in having his policies implemented? Why did neither the governors nor the Colonial Office veto them? For the most part the governors were either too weak to resist him or too much in sympathy with his general aim of making the island British. The Colonial Office gave its (sometimes reluctant) sanction because it believed that those on the spot knew best what measures were needed and because it unconsciously applied to the Crown colonies that doctrine of non-interference in internal colonial arrangements which had succeeded in the self-governing colonies. It may also have felt disinclined to oppose the legislation of a colony whose depressed condition had resulted for the most part from Imperial policies. Regardless of the reasons why an anti-Catholic policy had been carried on in Trinidad,[12] that policy had, by the middle sixties, aroused bitter antagonism among Roman Catholics. They demanded greater religious equality and radical changes in the educational system. To these demands Protestants showed no disposition to surrender.

By the time Gordon arrived in Trinidad some of its problems had become soluble. The island had recovered from its long depression. Revenues had increased from £88,000 in 1850 to £185,000 in 1860 and £226,000 in 1866. Exports had risen from £319,000 in 1850 to £715,000 in 1860 and £1,022,000 in 1866.[13] It now became possible,

[11]Warner to Gordon, 11 Nov. 1869, Stanmore Papers, 49235.

[12]The British government had, in the 1830's, provided an opportunity for such a policy by its failure to sustain the terms of the capitulations which had guaranteed to maintain the French, Spanish, or Dutch character of the colonies of conquest.

[13]Trinidad "Blue Books," PRO CO 300/76,77,78.

with good management, to raise civil service salaries, improve the public institutions, and undertake needed public works. The improved financial and economic condition of the colony enabled the planters to accept the government's plans for bettering the conditions of the Indian labourers and to run the risk (which they fancied they took) of opening the Crown lands to legitimate settlement. They could now agree to a reduction in their purchase price, a reduction that, as Gordon saw, was the only way to curtail squatting and to civilize the back-country areas. Religious and educational problems also became soluble because the Colonial Office, shaken in its trust of "the men on the spot" (i.e., colonials) by the Jamaica rebellion of 1865, was prepared to give the governor full support in his legislative attempts to end social inequality. If the Colonial Office had ever seriously entertained a policy of anglicizing the non-British elements in the Crown colonies it now abandoned it. As Gordon put it in 1869: "Trinidad although a British possession is not a Colony of Englishmen and . . . the attempt to force uncongenial laws and habits upon races subject to her rule is one which England has definitely and forever renounced."[14]

Although the time for curing Trinidad's troubles was more opportune than for many years, ultimate success depended upon the governor's intelligence, energy, and strength of character. Would Gordon be astute enough to find adequate answers to the colony's problems? If so, would he be able to overcome the opposition which his proposals for reform would inevitably encounter? His was the power in theory. Could he exercise it? For more than twenty years governors of Trinidad had shared, or had been forced to share, their autocratic power with a local clique led by Charles Warner. Would Gordon reassert the lost supremacy of the governor? Could he lay the foundations for greater economic progress and prevent the social fabric of the colony being rent by further factional disputes? In short, was Arthur Gordon the man for the job?

Sir Frederic Rogers, permanent under-secretary of state for the colonies from 1860 to 1871, once wrote that the West Indian colonies "very commonly find out when they have got a Governor who is really anxious to make himself useful."[15] At the end of Gordon's first year in the island the Trinidad press was unanimous in his praise. All of the editors expressed themselves in vein similar to that of the editor of the *San Fernando Gazette* who wrote that Gordon had "grudged no exertion in furthering any object for the benefit of the Colony. . . . He is possessed

[14]Gordon to Frederick Warner (member of the legislative council), 22 Sept. 1869, Stanmore Papers, 49244.
[15]Rogers' minute on Rushworth's dispatch, 8 Nov. 1866, PRO CO 295/236.

of a head, a heart, and a will, all of which are interested in promoting the welfare of the Island. . . . By some inexplicable freak of the Colonial Office, Trinidad has at last got 'the right man in the right place'."[16]

II. TOWARDS SOCIAL HARMONY

Gordon viewed the antagonism between Briton and non-Briton, Protestant and Catholic, as the most immediate and pressing problem facing him upon his arrival in Trinidad. The Roman Catholic clergy early drew his attention to the inferior educational and religious positions occupied by the non-British Roman Catholic majority and stressed the desirability of a change. Gordon wished to help for several reasons. Although an aristocrat and a strong High-Church Anglican, he shared the growing English regard for religious liberty and equality. Perhaps his concern for Roman Catholic disabilities also derived from his early manhood when, influenced by the spirit of the Oxford Movement, he seriously considered joining the Roman church. The fact that Trinidadian Roman Catholics were mostly French and Spanish did not weaken his sympathy for them. While unmistakably and loyally British himself he had few jingoistic tendencies.[17] Doubtless the fact that he had travelled widely in Europe and the Middle East and spoke French enabled him better to understand and share the feelings of non-Britons. He could, therefore, look upon the educational and religious institutions of Trinidad with an almost complete absence of bias and with a desire to deal justly with the claims of competing groups. In the end he was able to effect a thorough reform of the educational system and to re-establish religious equality in the colony. The former was both more important and more difficult than the latter, and a detailed study of it reveals quite clearly Gordon's capacities as governor.

Until 1851 the only schools in Trinidad, besides a few private schools for the children of the well-to-do, were denominational schools. The government gave them some financial support but did not inspect them, and the standard of teaching was low. It became obvious to the Governor, Lord Harris, that a general system of primary education would have to be established, but he realized that the colony could not afford to establish and support both Anglican and Roman Catholic schools. Thus he passed the education ordinance of 1851 setting up free secular schools

[16]*San Fernando Gazette,* 9 Nov. 1867.
[17]Gordon shared Gladstone's hatred of Turks because he believed the Turks responsible for Britain's entry into the Crimean War which had brought his father's political downfall, a hatred reinforced by his own travels among them in 1861.

in each ward (district). A board of education, consisting of the governor and such other members as he chose to appoint, administered the new system and appointed an inspector who visited and reported upon each school each quarter. Local administration fell to the wardens or magistrates who raised the funds to erect and operate the schools. The colonial government provided funds to train a body of skilled teachers.

For several reasons the new system did not work well. The teachers were still not good enough. The wardens and magistrates had many other duties to perform and, moreover, found it very difficult to raise money for the schools. The board of education seldom met. To make matters worse, the Roman Catholics, who at first had acquiesced in the secular system, gradually veered to a most uncompromising opposition to it. Besides, the Protestant clergy, who with one or two exceptions had professed support for the new system, did much to subvert it by establishing denominational schools in competition with the ward schools. In some cases Anglican clergymen insisted on giving religious instruction in the ward schools and on teaching the Anglican catechism to Roman Catholic children. Hopes that the ward schools would supersede all others and assume a national character went unrealized. In 1868 about 2,900 pupils were attending the secular and about 2,800 the denominational schools.[18] The exclusion of religion from the curriculum of the secular schools had aroused the antagonism, rather than the interest, of the Roman Catholics who believed religious training of greater importance than education. One of the most liberal and well-educated Roman Catholic laymen in the colony, who had been a strong admirer of Lord Harris, characterized the latter's educational system as "altogether Godless" and charged that it taught the people that the state did not care about religion.[19] In short, by the middle sixties, the ward schools had become virtually derelict—a nobody's child.[20]

At first glance Gordon did not think the ward schools an entire failure. He believed the teaching fair and the attendance by children of both creeds good. He admitted that children grew up without religious training—an especially deplorable fact when they lived in such close contact with Chinese and Indian "heathens." Nevertheless, though himself a supporter of denominational education, he did not feel inclined

[18]Minutes of the legislative council of Trinidad, 19 Nov. 1869, enclosed in Gordon to Granville, 5 Feb. 1870, PRO CO 295/250.

[19]Dr. L. A. A. De Verteuil, *Trinidad: Its Geography, Natural Resources, Administration, Present Condition, and Prospects*, 2nd ed., 458.

[20]"The Report of Patrick Joseph Keenan," p. 9, Paper no. 1 of *Papers on the State of Education in Trinidad*, Parl. Pap., 1870, L (450), 650–808. Further references to Paper no. 1 will be cited as Keenan's report.

(taking into account the divided character of Trinidad's population and the increased expense entailed by duplicating schools) to recommend its readoption. To him secondary education offered greater opportunity for reform and to it he early turned his attention.

Two recently established schools comprised the secondary educational system of the colony in 1866. The first, the Queen's Collegiate School, founded in 1863, was a government-assisted day-school based upon the secular principle. It had been intended to serve the whole island, to provide students with a basis for higher education abroad, and to help Roman Catholic and Protestant understand and respect one another. Roman Catholics, already exasperated at the anglicizing policies of the Warner faction, rejected it and, in opposition, founded the College of the Immaculate Conception (commonly St. Mary's College). This school, wholly supported by private funds, offered a secular programme inferior to that of the Queen's Collegiate School. Since, however, it gave religious instruction, offered boarding facilities, enrolled students at a younger age (10), and did not reject illegitimate children, it proved more popular than the Queen's Collegiate School. By 1866 St. Mary's had an enrolment almost double that of its rival, and Roman Catholics demanded that the governor withdraw government aid from the Queen's Collegiate School.

Although Gordon did not think the Roman Catholic protest unreasonable, he wished neither to withdraw the grant to the collegiate school nor to divide it between the two schools. To withdraw it would mean the end of the collegiate school and hence of the attempt to fuse the races and creeds of the colony. To divide the grant would simply substitute two less efficient schools for the one good one. "What I should propose," he wrote in December 1866, "would be to retain the [Queen's] College as an institution occupying with regard to certain licenced schools the sort of position—*parve componere magis*—which an English University occupies with regard to the Colleges therein."[21]

During the next few weeks his proposal underwent some elaboration, and he was now recommending the establishment of a new collegiate institution to be governed by a council consisting of the governor and an equal number of Roman Catholic and Protestant members. The governor would appoint the principal, and, subject to the governor's approval, the college council would appoint the professors.[22] Students would become

[21]Gordon to Cyril Graham, 24 Dec. 1866, Stanmore Papers, 49244.
[22]The two professors of theology, one Roman Catholic and one Anglican, were to be nominated by the archbishop of Port-of-Spain and the bishop of Barbados respectively and subject to the approval of the government of Trinidad.

members of the college by entrance at any secondary school licensed by the college council. These schools, in the first instance, would be the collegiate school, which would have to make provision for boarders, and St. Mary's. Each licensed school would be governed by a superior chosen by the founders or trustees, and tutors appointed by the superior. Superiors and tutors would have to be approved by the college council, which might require tutors to pass examinations. Tutors might hold professorships in the college but professors, except for the professors of theology, need not be tutors in the schools. Students would be required to attend all college lectures and to pay fees, which would be divided between the college and their school with the larger proportion going to the latter. The state would pay the salaries of the principal and professors of the college including the professors of theology. It would also pay the salaries of the superiors of the schools and assist each school in proportion to the number of pupils it contained. In framing this plan Gordon sought to ensure to Trinidad the advantage of better professors than two or more private seminaries could obtain even with state aid. He wished to combine this benefit with the "undoubted advantages which a system of boarding schools offers for the more complete . . . training of the pupils; and above all, publicly to recognize, by the establishment of Professorships of Theology, the function of Religion in Education."[23]

This was a good proposal. It contained many educational advantages and met many Roman Catholic criticisms of the existing system. Gordon communicated it to Roman Catholic Archbishop Gonin of Port-of-Spain, hoping that the latter would welcome and accept it. For a time it appeared that he might. Gonin at first called it "fair," "pretty fair," and "very fair," and although it was not everything he desired he seemed prepared to accept it as the best available compromise. However, the bishops of his diocese pounced upon the plan, one of them objecting to "any intercourse whatever between Catholic boys and others whether at school or elsewhere."[24] Gonin therefore renewed his petition to the Governor asking either that the collegiate school be abolished and its funds turned to general educational purposes, or that its grant be divided between the two schools.

Gordon would neither accept this petition, nor give up his plan. He wrote to Archbishop Manning in England asking why, if neither bishops nor parents in New Brunswick had objected to Roman Catholic children mixing with Protestants for secular instruction, Trinidad should be

[23]Gordon to Archbishop Gonin (most private), 16 Jan. 1867, Stanmore Papers, 49244.
[24]Gordon to Archbishop Manning, 9 May 1867, Stanmore Papers, 49244.

different. He warned that because all five professors of Queen's Collegiate School were university graduates[25] the educational advantages offered by that purely secular school would attract more and more Catholics of the higher class. He thought his own plan the best and most expedient arrangement for securing daily religious influences without sacrificing the right of Protestants to share in the advantages of superior education and without sowing seeds of dissension for the future by rearing the young people in ignorance of and antipathy towards one another. Could Manning not use his undoubted influence to secure the approval of the Roman Catholic clergy of Trinidad?[26] Manning replied that, although Gordon's proposals seemed very considerately drawn and evinced a disposition to deal justly with the principles of the Roman Catholic church, he felt no mixed education to be possible. He strongly urged proportional help to Protestant and Roman Catholic denominational education.[27]

Before receiving this discouraging and uncompromising reply Gordon had written to the Colonial Office seeking the Secretary of State's approval of his proposal and of the concessions to Roman Catholic opinion he had made in it. He believed the approval of the Colonial Office would be difficult to obtain. Consequently he sent Archbishop Gonin's criticisms of the existing secondary school system to the Secretary of State and painted a gloomy picture of the Queen's Collegiate School himself.[28] By this act he badly over-played his hand.

Although acknowledging the high quality of secular education in the collegiate school, the Archbishop charged that the school neglected religion, cost more, contained fewer students, and sent fewer graduates to English universities than had been anticipated. Only about one-third of its students were Roman Catholics "so that the spirit of union and friendship . . . between Catholic and Protestant" had been confined to very few. Furthermore, since St. Mary's had sprung up by private enterprise, it was no longer necessary or desirable for the government to continue to assist a secondary school whose students came mostly from the middle and upper classes.[29] When the Colonial Office read this argument in conjunction with Gordon's unfortunate admission that "an institution founded and maintained at a great expense by the Government as an instrument of affording educational advantages to the whole island has practically become little more than a day-school for the

[25]All but the principal and second-master were Roman Catholics.
[26]Gordon to Manning, 9 May 1867, Stanmore Papers, 49244.
[27]Manning to Gordon, [June] 1867, Stanmore Papers, 49235.
[28]Gordon to Buckingham, no. 72, 24 May 1867, PRO CO 295/239.
[29]Gonin to Gordon, 2 April 1867, enclosure no. 2, *ibid.*

children of the wealthier protestant families in Port-of-Spain,"[30] it decided to abolish the collegiate school entirely.

It did not surprise Henry Taylor, senior clerk in the West Indies department of the Colonial Office, that private enterprise had been more than a match for the collegiate school.

I have always thought it questionable whether the taxpayer at large sh[oul]d be made to pay for the education of the rich. It is no doubt of great importance to the Poor that the rich sh[oul]d be educated & if rich Colonists w[oul]d not have their children educated without a School supported from public funds, it might be right that a school for the rich sh[oul]d be so supported. But it is a remark as old as Adam Smith that this sort of support is the anodyne of educational institutions & that they are only kept aware and alert when their support depends upon their exertions & the customers whom their reputation attracts.[31]

Sir Frederic Rogers considered Gordon's remark concerning the collegiate school "conclusive ag[ain]st its being maintained by taxation in a Colony wh[ich] is not Protestant. . . ."[32] Sir Charles Adderley, the parliamentary under-secretary, although a strong Protestant, also believed that any mode of terminating the tax for the education of the rich must be a good thing.[33] The original draft of the dispatch in reply to the Governor did not preclude consideration of a government college, but the final draft acknowledged the failure of the collegiate school, ordered its abolition, and stated the Secretary of State's disapproval of a government college in connection with private denominational schools. It suggested that the collegiate school grant would be most advantageously applied in raising the salaries of schoolmasters in country schools.[34]

This dispatch shocked Gordon. He had badly underestimated the strength of religious and economic liberalism in the Colonial Office. Yet convinced of the rightness of his own judgment of the colony's affairs, he was not prepared to accept this decision without a struggle. In

[30]Gordon to Buckingham, 24 May 1867.

[31]Taylor's minute, *ibid.*

[32]Rogers' minute, *ibid.*

[33]Adderley's minute, *ibid.* Adderley was uncomfortable concerning the whole question of changes in religion and education as a further minute (28 Sept.) demonstrated. "Is it wise [he asked] on the petition of a R.C. Abp, . . . to decide that Priests' Salaries should be increased, Presbyteries built [these were the subject of two further petitions in April 1867] . . . to pronounce the Collegiate S[chool] a failure, & [say] that its funds might be better disposed of? . . . Are we prepared to initiate such changes in approp[riation]s [with] a revenue already overcharged for eccles[iastica]l and Educ[ationa]l purposes and that just as we are withdrawing Imp[erial] aid & local Acts are about to expire which the Legisl[ature]s may refuse to renew, & the House of Commons may press Gov[ernmen]t to oppose?"

[34]Buckingham to Gordon, 12 Oct. 1867, PRO CO 295/239.

December 1868, in a private letter to Secretary of State Buckingham, he admitted that it had been "foreign to his object" to dwell upon the collegiate school's advantages. If, he said, he had supposed that any danger of its abolition existed he would have added a great deal to show how successful it had been despite grave obstacles. He warned that any attempt to destroy it would "raise a formidable opposition" among Protestants and thus "revive bitter party animosities." The Archbishop, with his clergy, had given him more cordial support than any other body in Trinidad, but "after all we must remember that he is a Dominican Monk and, as such, no very fair or unprejudiced judge of a system of mixed education."[35]

A month later Gordon, in a further attempt to save his plan, wrote a long dispatch in which he noted and corrected a number of the Archbishop's errors because, he told Buckingham, they "have no doubt obtained Your Grace's credence and may therefore influence Your Grace's judgment."[36] He went on to stress the two aims of the collegiate school: to bring up together boys of diverse race and religion, and to provide a sound system of education which would raise the tone of character and the standard of acquirements of the better classes of the island. It had been eminently successful in achieving the latter. Of late years every boy over sixteen had passed the Cambridge Local Examinations in which Trinidad and Liverpool stood together at the head of the list. Its graduates seemed "more manly and cultivated" than young men who had not been brought up at that school, and the school had been of "incalculable advantage to the Government and the Colony" as a source of honourable and efficient men for the junior departments of the civil service.[37] Admittedly the collegiate school appeared to have been less successful in achieving its other object. However, even if Roman Catholics were much more numerous than Protestants they were also much poorer[38] and it would be unreasonable to expect them to attend the more expensive collegiate school in comparable numbers.[39] To strengthen the case he now made, Gordon sent comments by Chief Justice Knox and Charles Warner. Knox wrote that "if we bear in mind the pressure used to prevent [Roman Catholic] boys . . . from attending . . . we may well be surprised, not that they should be comparatively few but that there should be so many." Warner alleged that the priests had

[35]Gordon to Buckingham (private), 9 Dec. 1867, Stanmore Papers, 49199.
[36]Gordon to Buckingham, 8 Jan. 1868, PRO CO 295/243.
[37]Ibid.
[38]The Solicitor-General reported in 1868 (Eversley, *Trinidad Reviewer*, 14) that six-elevenths of the wealth of Trinidad was owned by Roman Catholics.
[39]Gordon to Buckingham, 8 Jan. 1868.

used pressure to get Roman Catholic parents to withdraw their children from the collegiate school but, he added, "it is scarcely fair to put forward the success of such influence as an argument [against the school]."[40]

Gordon next proceeded to examine the consequences of abolishing the collegiate school. It could be effected only at the cost of removing the ablest officers of the government, "for the Attorney General, I am certain, and one at least of his colleagues, I believe, would never consent to . . . such a measure."[41] What would be gained? Unless abolition of the school were to be followed by transference of half its grant to St. Mary's, the Roman Catholics who opposed the collegiate establishment would remain unsatisfied. If half the grant were to be transferred, those Roman Catholics who supported the collegiate school would be irritated and the Protestants outraged. "The ablest of the servants of the Crown would have been expelled from their offices; and the Government would have to encounter at all points the unsparing hostility of former friends directed by men of no small capacity."[42] The Governor concluded his argument by asserting his impartiality concerning the collegiate school. He admitted being an advocate of the denominational system in education, but, he added, "I am not blinded by my own prepossessions or able to avoid recognizing the fact that the satisfactory adoption of such a system is here wholly impracticable whether as applied to the higher or the lower branches of study. . . ."[43]

Gordon refused to obey Buckingham's instructions to abolish the Queen's Collegiate School; nor would he give up his plans for the establishment of a new royal college. As a result, final decisions on both matters were to be delayed for two years. In the meantime the Governor turned his attention to the primary school system.

Archbishop Gonin had asked for a return to the denominational principle in primary education at the same time that he had petitioned for the abolition of the collegiate school. The "God-less" ward schools must go. The state should aid denominational schools and inspect them. Teaching should be in English. Quality would be ensured by the spirit of emulation which would exist between denominational schools. More children would be taught, and the colony would be saved through daily religious instruction from its "state of vice and immorality" as illus-

[40]Comments by Knox and Warner, enclosure no. 9, *ibid.*
[41]Gordon to Buckingham, 8 Jan. 1868.
[42]*Ibid.*
[43]*Ibid.*

trated by the high rate of illegitimacy.[44] So ran the Archbishop's argument.

Gordon continued to think better of the primary system than the Archbishop, though he agreed that lack of religious instruction in the ward schools constituted a serious evil. He proposed to cure it by insisting that every clergyman give religious instruction in each ward school in his district a stipulated number of times. Any clergyman failing to follow this regulation would lose some of his salary. Sir Frederic Rogers agreed to this. "It seems," he wrote, "a duty which ought to take precedence of almost any other."[45] Buckingham concurred and said he would not abolish the ward schools without further information about the deficiencies of their pupils in religious knowledge and the number of hours devoted by clergymen to religious instruction. He advised Gordon to appoint a commission to examine these matters.[46] Gordon agreed with the suggestion of a commission but told the Secretary of State that the inquiry would be more satisfactorily and efficiently conducted were it to be made by an inspector sent out from England whose examination should encompass the whole educational system, not simply questions of religious instruction. In the meantime he would appoint a local commission to inquire into the amount of religious instruction given in ward schools. Such a commission might disarm any clergy not disposed to accept the findings of an impartial layman. Buckingham accepted this suggestion and appointed Patrick J. Keenan, one of the Dublin school inspectors, as special commissioner.

Meanwhile Gordon appointed H. B. Darling, a Protestant, and J. M. Farfan, a Roman Catholic, as commissioners to examine religious instruction in the ward schools. Their report, or, to be more accurate, reports, became available in October 1868 and reflected the religious attitudes of their authors. Taken together, however, they presented "a lamentable picture"[47] of the lack of religious instruction in ward schools. Darling observed that, for the most part, religious training "did not

[44]Gonin to Gordon, 2 April 1867, enclosure no. 3 in Gordon to Buckingham, 24 May 1867. In the back-country ward of Mayaro the illegitimacy rate was 80 per cent between 1848 and 1868 and even in Port-of-Spain, where the predominantly Roman Catholic population was ministered to by the Dominicans, the rate was 54 per cent. (See Keenan's report, 34.)
[45]Rogers' minute on Gordon to Buckingham, 24 May 1867.
[46]Buckingham to Gordon, 12 Oct. 1867.
[47]Kortright to Buckingham, 6 Oct. 1868, enclosing Darling's and Farfan's reports, PRO CO 295/245. C. H. Kortright, lieutenant-governor of Tobago, administered the government of Trinidad during Gordon's two absences in England in 1868 and 1869.

extend beyond the teaching of the Lord's Prayer, the Apostles' Creed, the Ten Commandments, and the Church Catechism. . . ." He found no single instance of observance of the rule requiring a pupil to present to his schoolmaster a certificate signed by his clergyman stating the number of days in the preceding quarter upon which he had received religious instruction. Many of the clergy were ignorant of this rule, and the half holy-days had become half holidays. Darling recommended modifications of the system, but did not wish to depart from the secular principle.[48] Farfan was much less constructive than Darling. He wanted the ward schools replaced by denominational schools. Roman Catholics ought not to be required to pray with persons of other faiths. They should not attend the same schools. Furthermore boys and girls ought to have separate schools; "their continued contact can only lead to the most pernicious consequences!"[49]

Keenan had the somewhat dubious benefit of these preliminary studies when he arrived in Trinidad early in 1869. He stayed about two months, conducted a thorough inquiry into both primary and secondary education, and completed his report in July after his return home. Gordon received a copy just as he was taking ship for Trinidad on the expiration of his leave of absence. He found himself in almost complete agreement with Keenan's recommendations respecting primary education. He differed from him in only one major point. Keenan had advised vesting the management of each local school in the clergyman whose religion was that of the majority of the pupils in the locality. Gordon thought it more expedient in areas where religious groups were nearly evenly balanced and where circumstances did not warrant establishing separate schools to continue the ward schools and require the clergy to give religious instruction on stated days. Lord Granville, the new secretary of state, agreed, and requested Gordon, subject to this modification, to implement those aspects of Keenan's report which applied to primary education. On 21 December 1869, the legislative council carried, by a majority of ten to three,[50] a series of eleven resolutions establishing the new primary system.

The new system consisted of state-managed schools (in line with Gordon's modification of Keenan's report) and privately-established and -managed schools assisted by the state. The latter were not strictly denominational schools because they could not be exclusive. A compromise had been achieved between the secular and the denominational

[48]Darling's report.
[49]Farfan's report.
[50]Charles Warner and two unofficial members voted against the resolutions.

and in Gordon's words had "set at rest" the controversy over primary education "in a manner which affords a triumph to no party, and which is admitted to be fair and equitable."[51] The Colonial Office expressed its pleasure at the Governor's "judicious & energetic endeavours to place the education of the people in Trinidad on the best footing which local circ[umstance]s w[oul]d permit."[52]

The new primary school system did not gain acceptance without protest. A small but vigorous and noisy opposition sprang up during the interval between the council's approval of the resolutions in December 1869 and the passage of the education ordinance four months later. It was headed by A. B. Knox, the son of the Chief Justice, a cocoa planter named Billouin, and Dr. Mercer, whom Gordon had dismissed as resident physician of the Colonial Hospital for maladministration. Knox disliked Gordon and for two years had assailed him in the press in terms which Gordon had been assured were libellous. Mercer's opposition came from a desire for vengeance, and Billouin's from ignorance. The latter called Gordon "a puppet Governor" (presumably of the Archbishop), "a humbug of a Governor," and "a d—d short-sighted Governor."[53] The opposition was short-lived. It got as far as forming an education league to procure a fairer trial for Lord Harris's system, but made little impact. The small newspaper which supported it failed; the magistrates countered its propaganda; Knox became perturbed over Billouin's irresponsible speeches; the general public acquiesced in the new system; and the league died.

The dispute over primary education had been settled, but not that over secondary education. During his leave of absence in 1868 Gordon had explained his position (on secondary education) more fully than he had in his dispatches and private letters, and the Secretary of State agreed to suspend further consideration of the topic until he had received Keenan's report.

Keenan found both secondary schools well-managed and efficient. Both offered education of a high standard, though the pupils of the collegiate school were weak in religious knowledge and those of St. Mary's in mathematics. The collegiate school found favour with the public servants but the people flocked to St. Mary's "because the . . . introduction of the religious element . . . is more acceptable to them."[54]

[51]Gordon to Granville, 24 Dec. 1869, PRO CO 295/248.
[52]Taylor's minute, 14 Jan. 1870, *ibid.*
[53]L. M. Fraser (a magistrate) to Gordon, 1 Feb. 1870, copy enclosed in Gordon to Granville, 10 March 1870, PRO CO 295/250. Gordon's short-sightedness was physical not mental.
[54]Keenan's report, 62.

The collegiate school suffered by not being a boarding school, "but the principle of secularism . . . renders boarding impracticable; a fact which goes to show that . . . the secular idea is unsuitable to Trinidad . . . where the homes of the people are scattered. . . ."[55] The lack of boarding facilities and the high fees prevented coloured children from attending the collegiate school. The inability of St. Mary's to offer places at moderate terms because of lack of state aid prevented coloured children from attending that school. These were the major weaknesses that Keenan found. He recommended establishing a university of the West Indies. This, he felt, would supply a great need in the islands and enable the various colleges to conduct their own secular and religious training. Should this be found impracticable then the colony should give aid to privately-founded, independent, and self-regulating superior schools according to the results of examinations to be conducted under the direction of the board of education by examiners drawn from the teachers of those schools. The grant to the Queen's Collegiate School should be withdrawn and the proceeds of the education tax employed for the general purposes of education.[56]

Gordon considered a university of the West Indies impracticable for the time being and he strongly criticized Keenan's alternative plan of state-assisted denominational schools. It would prove impossible to obtain masters of the quality of those at the collegiate school. It was already difficult "to induce men of ability . . . to undertake the work of education in the West Indies; but that difficulty would be increased, if instead of being Public Officers in the receipt of a handsome fixed salary, and only liable to be removed by a formal process, the Masters . . . were dependent for their position and remuneration on the caprice of some irresponsible individual, or body of individuals, and were destitute of any official status or public character."[57] It would also prove more difficult to bring together students of different creeds in denominational schools than in a single college under government control.[58] The Governor expressed these views to Lord Granville and called attention to the plan which he had suggested in 1867 and which he still believed "would be acceptable to all parties as a compromise, though in itself perhaps wholly satisfactory to none."[59]

The Secretary of State agreed that the time was not yet ripe for a university of the West Indies. Otherwise, he inclined to Keenan's pro-

[55]Ibid., 63.
[56]Ibid., 70.
[57]Gordon's message to the legislative council, 7 March 1870, enclosed in Gordon to Granville, 10 March 1870.
[58]Ibid.   [59]Gordon to Granville, 8 Sept. 1869, PRO CO 295/248.

posals and requested the Governor to prepare a scheme founded on them.[60] Gordon acknowledged this instruction on 12 December 1869, and on 10 March 1870 he forwarded a plan, noting that he had submitted it to the legislative council three days earlier. In this plan Gordon had adhered to his original arrangement for an independent staff of professors, appointed by the governor and paid by salary entirely from public funds, who would form a new royal college.

Robert Herbert, the newly appointed assistant under-secretary, disapproved strongly of Gordon's proceedings though not of his plan. In promulgating his resolutions the Governor had, Herbert considered,

by no means complied with Lord Granville's request . . . that he should prepare and *submit to him* a scheme of secondary Education founded on certain suggestions then given to him. On the contrary, he has *published* a scheme differing from that suggested.

I do not think he should be encouraged to throw over instructions and exercise his own discretion in a delicate & much controverted question like this. . . . It should I think be pointed out to him that the course which he has followed is not that which he was desired to take.[61]

Rogers, however, counselled that any answer to Gordon's dispatch be delayed "till we see how the scheme is taken."[62] Granville acquiesced and, in the meantime, asked Keenan for his comments on Gordon's scheme. Surprisingly, Keenan found little fault with it. Instead, he commended the Governor for so nearly bringing the educational affairs of the colony, "the adjustment of which to many persons seemed hopeless," to a satisfactory and successful issue.[63]

H. L. Hall has remarked that the governor of a Crown colony should have discernment enough to know when to act illegally for the good of his colony.[64] To this we might add that the Colonial Office forgives him if successful and reprimands him if not. Although not illegal, Gordon's failure to follow Granville's suggestions was irregular as was his failure to await Granville's approval of his resolutions before incorporating them into the education ordinance of 1870. Undoubtedly had either the legislative council or any definite group in the colony actually objected to the changes in secondary education, Gordon would have received a reprimand from the Secretary of State. By two amendments, however, Gordon gained a smooth passage through the council for his resolutions. The first assured the secularists that there would be no direct religious

[60]Granville to Gordon, 12 Nov. 1869, Parl. Pap., 1870, L (450), 102.
[61]Herbert's minute on Gordon to Granville, 10 March 1870.
[62]Rogers' minute on Gordon to Granville, 10 March 1870.
[63]Keenan to Granville, 28 April 1870, Parl. Pap., 1870, L (450), 124–27.
[64]H. L. Hall, *The Colonial Office*, 111.

teaching in the royal college. The second set Roman Catholics' minds at rest by exempting students who so wished from any of the royal college lectures in those subjects in which they had already received efficient instruction.[65] Gordon allowed this second amendment on the understanding that Roman Catholics would sincerely support the royal college and would affiliate St. Mary's with it. He told the Roman Catholics point-blank that unless they were prepared to honour that understanding he would restore the original wording of the provision. No doubt many among both Roman Catholics and Protestants gave their support with reservations. The Archbishop merely acquiesced in the arrangement and was the only leading religious figure in the colony who did not attend the Governor's inauguration of the royal college on 3 June 1870. But no colonial voice ventured to oppose the scheme. Neither did the Colonial Office offer any criticism of the plan or of the Governor's irregularities in bringing it about. Instead, Gordon deservedly gained a reputation in the Colonial Office as a good educationist.[66]

Gordon had early seen the danger of Trinidad becoming a particularist society. He tried to avoid this through educational changes that would set at rest the antagonisms generated prior to his tenure of office, and ensure future understanding, toleration, and unity. He forced both secularists and denominationalists to compromise. Neither got all they wanted, but both recognized that Gordon desired to deal fairly with them and that the education ordinance of 1870 gave them everything they had any prospect of getting. The inauguration of the royal college, attended as it was by most of the leading Protestants and Roman Catholics and the staffs and pupils of both secondary schools, was a good omen for future social harmony.

Gordon's educational reforms contributed significantly to education itself aside from the impetus they gave to social harmony. The number of schools and scholars increased greatly. In 1868 there were 35 publicly-assisted schools containing 2,836 pupils. By 1890 there were 181 such schools and 19,855 pupils: a tremendous increase even allowing for the doubling of the population of the island during the interval. The quality of teachers also improved[67] and the royal college functioned satisfactorily. Gordon's education ordinance of 1870 as it applied to primary education continued in force with but minor modifications until 1890. Then a new ordinance was passed but it retained the main

[65]The college council was to be the judge of what constituted "efficient instruction."

[66]Robert Meade's minute, 30 Aug. 1871, on Gordon to Kimberley, 25 July 1871, PRO CO 167/534.

[67]Eversley, *Trinidad Reviewer*, 148.

principles underlying Gordon's primary system and scarcely altered the secondary system. These facts surely demonstrate the success of Gordon's educational measures.

Roman Catholic dissatisfaction during the late 1860's in Trinidad did not confine itself to education. It included a concern over the inferior position of their church to the Anglican church, an inequality which had prevailed since the ecclesiastical ordinance of 1844. Gordon proposed to repeal this ordinance, not to please the Roman Catholics but "to do them justice."[68] However, alive to the certainty of strong Anglican opposition, he awaited a suitable opportunity for an indirect approach to the question. It came in 1869 with the death of the Anglican archdeacon. Gordon thought it unnecessary to appoint a successor and decided to abolish the office and save the salary attached to it. The Attorney-General and Solicitor-General both considered it necessary to repeal part of the ordinance of 1844 before discontinuing the salary of an official of the Church of England so Gordon took advantage of their legal dictum to repeal the whole ordinance. He directed the preparation of a new ordinance which, although guaranteeing Anglican incumbents a life interest in their offices and salaries, looked both to the gradual disestablishment of the Anglican church in Trinidad and to the creation of a state ecclesiastical fund in which all Christian churches would share according to the number of their adherents.[69]

The Colonial Office thoroughly approved Gordon's ecclesiastical ordinance of 1870, because the latter conformed to the principle of religious equality that had been arrived at during the four years since the Jamaica rebellion. That event had convinced the Colonial Office of the mismanagement of the internal affairs of the West Indian colonies by the men on the spot and of the need for the Crown to take a more active interest in and exercise a more positive influence over them if injustices were to be avoided. As Henry Taylor put it: "The Crown alone could represent the interests of the inhabitants."[70] The Colonial Office did not find it easy to work out a satisfactory religious policy in a large number of colonies each containing several churches. The magnitude of the difficulty is obvious. Baptists in Jamaica rejected state aid on principle; Roman Catholics in Grenada preferred disendowment to

[68]Gordon to A. P. Marryat (an unofficial member of the legislative council), 7 March 1870, Stanmore Papers, 49244.

[69]The Anglicans, Roman Catholics, and Wesleyans in Trinidad accepted, but the Presbyterians and Baptists declined state aid. (De Verteuil, *Trinidad*, 172.)

[70]Henry Taylor to Granville, 15 Oct. 1869, filed with minute paper 12066/80, PRO CO 295/252.

endowment which did not include themselves; and Anglicans in St. Vincent preferred disendowment to endowment which extended beyond themselves.

The short way out of this complicated situation for the Colonial Office would have been to separate church from state entirely. It could hardly make this move when Granville held that "the moral & religious culture of the subject race [is] the paramount object to be considered,"[71] and when Henry Taylor, whose influence in the Colonial Office was still strong, protested that in the West Indies "to renounce state aid is simply to renounce Christianity."[72] The Colonial Office thus eventually decided on religious equality which would entail the disestablishment of the colonial churches. Letters patent would not in future be issued to colonial bishops and bishops' salaries would no longer be defrayed from Imperial funds. Questions concerning the creation of new Anglican bishoprics would be decided by Anglicans in the colony affected. Local church bodies would be established to govern the internal affairs of each church and to administer its funds. State aid would be granted to all churches in proportion to their membership and the work each did, but any church would have the option of refusing such aid. This financial readjustment was to be carried out gradually so that individual clergymen would not suffer hardship and Anglicans would not be too profoundly shocked by the necessary reduction in the amount of state aid given to their church.[73]

Although the dispatches give no indication that Gordon derived his religious policy for Trinidad from the one which the Colonial Office worked out for the West Indies as a whole, it does not seem likely that Gordon formulated his policy independently. He had begun to think about it as early as the Colonial Office did, but the similarity of the two policies is too much for coincidence. His visits to England in 1868 and 1869[74] provided opportunities for consultation and cross-fertilization of ideas on the subject.

[71]*Ibid.*

[72]Taylor's minute, 29 Nov. 1870, on Kimberley to Longden, 6 Jan. 1871, PRO CO 295/252.

[73]Important documents relating to the development of the new religious policy are: Minute paper 12066/70 appended to Longden to Kimberley, no. 172, 15 Oct. 1870, filed in PRO CO 295/252; and *Copy or Extracts of Despatch or Despatches from the Secretary of State for the Colonies to the Governor or Governors of any of the West Indian Colonies, setting forth Ecclesiastical Grants, and to the establishment of Religious Equality in such Colonies,* Parl. Pap., 1871, XLVIII (269), 565. A. Caldecott, *The Church in the West Indies,* chap. VI, gives a summary of religious changes in that area.

[74]The birth of a daughter took place in England in 1869 and Gordon obtained a short leave to be near his wife during this, her first, confinement.

Anglicans in Trinidad opposed the ecclesiastical ordinance less strongly than might have been expected. Charles Warner and two unofficial members of the council attacked it on second reading and defended the ordinance of 1844. The latter, they said, had not given the Anglican church any status or position superior to the Roman Catholic church. Obviously nonsense, their comment was contradicted by Warner's own previous dictum that the salary of an official of the Church of England could be abolished only by legislation. The salary of any Roman Catholic official could, however, be abolished by a simple resolution of the legislative council. With the Colonial Office, a strong governor, and the Bishop of Barbados (who considered the new ordinance "right and proper")[75] arrayed against it, the opposition yielded.

The repeal of the ordinance of 1844 and the passage of the ordinance of 1870 ended the hegemony of the Anglo-Protestant minority in Trinidad. Although it retained its influence, it never again attained the dominance it had held prior to Arthur Gordon's régime. Within a few months its chief spokesman, Charles Warner, lost the attorney-generalship[76] and so most of his authority and influence. The "British Party" never recovered from these blows.

III. LAND AND LABOUR

Had Arthur Gordon done no more than bring about a just settlement of Trinidad's educational and religious controversies his governorship could be judged successful. But he accomplished much more. He fostered the economic and social growth of the colony, and, in solving the problems of the Crown lands and squatting and in improving the indenture laws, he reduced lawlessness and suffering among a large number of its labouring population.

When Gordon went to Trinidad, only about 7 per cent of the island's 1,754 square miles was cultivated.[77] The remainder consisted chiefly of unalienated Crown lands containing large tracts of virgin forest and large areas suitable for cane, cacao, and similar crops. With a population expanding fairly rapidly[78] it might have been expected that significant acreages of Crown land would be sold, thus adding not only to the colony's revenue but to its economic growth. Instead, scarcely any public

[75]Gordon to Granville, 4 Feb. 1870, PRO CO 295/250.
[76]See below, pp. 95–96.
[77]Trinidad "Blue Book," 1866, PRO CO 300/77.
[78]Trinidad's population increased from 84,438 in 1861 to 109,638 in 1871.

land was sold,[79] and large areas were being ravaged by squatters whose numbers were rapidly augmented from year to year by immigrants from Venezuela and the other West Indian islands,[80] and by negroes and free Indian labourers from the settled portions of Trinidad itself.[81]

Although the island had known small-scale squatting from the beginning of European settlement, it did not become a problem until after the emancipation of slaves in 1838. By 1842 squatting had reached such proportions that the government promulgated an Imperial order-in-council (6 October 1838) which authorized magistrates to remove squatters from Crown lands. This action, however, proved ineffective, so Lord Harris, soon after his arrival as governor of Trinidad, attempted to regularize squatting by offering the squatters legal titles to their lands under certain conditions. Those who did not comply with the conditions would find themselves summarily evicted under strengthened laws.[82] The scheme began well and ended badly: 1,090 squatters filed petitions for their lands before the end of 1847, but only 295 completed their titles by 1866.

Several reasons lay behind the failure of the scheme. Delays in surveying, the costliness of the land and of the procedure for acquiring title, and the refusal of the wardens to evict squatters as long as they paid ward rates,[83] all encouraged squatters to continue in their illegal occupations. In addition, the planters lost interest in the whereabouts of the free labourers once Indian indentured labour became firmly established. No longer did they urge the government to suppress

[79]Between 1847 (when Lord Harris offered Crown lands for sale at an upset price of two pounds per acre) and 1866, only 3,423 acres were sold: Edward Rushworth's "memorandum relative to squatting and the management of the crown lands and also to the appointment of a surveyor general," enclosure no. 6 in Rushworth's dispatch of 19 June 1866, contained in enclosure no. 1 (papers relating to the occupation, sale, and management of the Crown lands) in Gordon to Buckingham, no. 80, 8 June 1867, PRO CO 295/239. Hereafter this is cited as Rushworth's memorandum. Rushworth administered the government of Trinidad from April to November 1866.

[80]These numbered about 2,000 a year. "Of their existence no trace [was] to be found in the more settled portions of the Colony." (Gordon to Buckingham, 8 June 1867.)

[81]Escaped slaves from the United States and slaves freed from slave ships were another source of squatters in the early sixties. Almost immediately they left the estates to which they had been allotted and took refuge in the more remote portions of the island. (Memorandum of Henry Mitchell, agent-general for immigrants, enclosure no. 3 in Gordon to Buckingham, 8 June 1867.)

[82]Ordinance 10 of 1848 and Ordinances 15 and 16 of 1852.

[83]Gordon could find no record of any case of the government proceeding against a squatter, although wardens occasionally had done so.

squatting. Indeed the problem generated so little interest that no dispatches between 1855 and 1865 even alluded to it.

By the latter year, however, some of the Indians whose indentures had been served had begun to squat upon the Crown lands. The planters then became alarmed lest newly-arrived Indians also take to the woods. These fears again focused attention upon the problem of squatting. At the same time others expressed a new interest in the Crown lands, hitherto regarded in the colony more as a liability than an asset. Economic conditions had improved, and capital became available for the expansion of agriculture. In 1865 a local group petitioned the government for permission to purchase Crown lands for cacao, cotton, nutmeg, and other plantations in lots of not less than eighty acres at ten shillings an acre. In the following year a company was formed which applied for a grant of eighty square miles of the public domain. The government refused these requests but through them became aware of the growing interest in the Crown lands and of the need for deciding soon on a policy for their sale and regular settlement. This could not be done without first dealing with the squatters.

Manners Sutton had begun to come to grips with these people before he left Trinidad early in 1866. He estimated the number of squatters to be about 800 (with their families, some 3,000 persons) occupying approximately 5,000 acres. He determined not to ignore them any longer and ordered the wardens to stop collecting rates from them. This action would warn the squatters that the government would no longer accord them inactive forbearance. It would prepare them, moreover, to accept the liberal terms he decided to offer them whereby they might convert their illegal occupancies into legal proprietorships.[84] He suggested to the Secretary of State that squatters be allowed to pay for their lands in four equal annual installments at the upset price of two pounds per acre with eviction to follow nonpayment of any installment. The same terms should be extended to those non-squatters who might in future purchase Crown lands at auction because it would be undesirable to give better terms to those who had knowingly violated the law than to those who had respected it. He thought the high upset price necessary because the employers regarded it as a protection against the dispersion of their labourers. He recommended that purchase by installment be allowed only in certain districts so that settlement could be carried out in an orderly fashion.

[84]Manners Sutton to the Secretary of State, 6 April 1866, enclosure no. 1 in Gordon to Buckingham, 8 June 1867.

Manners Sutton was not interested primarily in pushing back the frontiers of settlement in Trinidad or in expanding its agriculture. Indeed, he regarded "the withdrawal of large numbers of the inhabitants of the Island from established settlements, and from the vicinity of churches, schools, and other civilizing influences, as a very serious evil. . . ."[85] He concerned himself rather with alleviating the harmful results of squatting of which "the loss of Crown Land Revenue is the least, while the lawless habits, and the tendency to relapse into barbarism . . . are the greatest."[86] He saw that the only way to civilize the squatters was to introduce civilizing agencies among them; but he did not see that this could be done only by defying the planters and reducing the cost of land to a level which would not merely induce the squatters to become proprietors but would also attract many new setters to the Crown lands.

Manners Sutton's recommendations were open to objections, one of which was the probability that few squatters would pay the installments to complete their titles. Furthermore he made no provision for dealing with a second and totally different class of several thousand squatters[87] who had no intention of becoming purchasers of land on any terms. They lived in great misery in remote, heavily-forested, and only partially-explored regions. They planted only quickly-harvested crops of maize and rice and moved every two or three years. Because their dwellings were dirty, squalid huts their mortality rate was very high.[88] Despite their misery, they found their semi-savage life, "out of reach of such natural enemies as the Policeman and Schoolmaster," irresistible and in its pursuit they endured "any amount of privation unassociated with the payment of money."[89] They had become squatters to be free of the controls and obligations of civilized life. It was unlikely that they would voluntarily become landed proprietors.

Despite drawbacks, Manners Sutton's scheme was more liberal and practicable than any previous one, but no decision on it was reached

[85]Ibid.

[86]Ibid.

[87]This class consisted of ignorant creoles and half-savage Africans of various tribes: Mandingoes, Foulahs, Hausas, Yorubas, Ashantis, and Congos. It included some escaped slaves from the United States and many of the slaves freed from the slave ships. (First report of Robert Mitchell, commissioner for the ward of Montserrat, 28 Dec. 1867, enclosed in Gordon to Buckingham, 8 April 1868, PRO CO 295/243. Hereafter cited as Robert Mitchell's first report.)

[88]The Yorubas were an exception. They were good, industrious cultivators, built wooden houses, and subscribed to a general fund upon which they could draw in case of illness or accident. (Ibid.)

[89]Memorandum of Henry Mitchell in Gordon to Buckingham, 8 June 1867.

before he left the colony. As mere temporary administrator of the government, Edward Rushworth could scarcely be expected to undertake bold measures, although he did perform a worthwhile service for Gordon by making a report of the views and actions of previous governors concerning squatters and the Crown lands. He also stated his opinion that the nomadic class of squatters could be handled by combining stringent legislation against squatting with "a well devised and systematically pursued plan of opening up these [Crown] lands by the creation of new plantations, especially . . . of cacao . . . and also by the foundation of new settlements in the vicinity of those plantations with small holdings for the industrious and independent laborer."[90] Thus, almost immediately on arrival, Gordon was able to acquaint himself with the background of the problems of squatting and the Crown lands and with the views of his predecessors on these "most urgent" matters.[91] Furthermore he had at his command the opinions of the Colonial Office and the Imperial Land and Emigration Board,[92] both of which had already studied Manners Sutton's recommendations and Rushworth's memorandum.

T. W. C. Murdoch, of the Land and Emigration Board, was of two minds concerning Manners Sutton's plan. Were Trinidad to be regarded as a sugar colony only there would, he thought, be reason to hesitate in attracting labourers to settle on the Crown lands by offering them the right to buy land on installments. But Trinidad could not be so regarded and in any case settlement by labourers was to some extent inevitable.[93] Nevertheless he rejected the installment plan in favour of reducing the price of land from forty shillings per acre to twenty on lots of not less than forty acres and requiring the whole sum to be paid within a month. He believed this latter plan would serve the three purposes of putting a price on wild land: to prevent speculation, to provide a source of revenue, and "to prevent men without capital, . . . who ought to be labourers for wages, becoming landowners."[94]

Lord Carnarvon rejected Murdoch's philosophy. He believed that the attempt to regulate the price of land to prevent its purchase by labourers had actually promoted squatting. In his view the main object

[90]Rushworth's memorandum.

[91]Gordon to Cyril Graham, 24 Dec. 1866, Stanmore Papers, 49244.

[92]This board advised the Colonial Office on colonial Crown land policy and also on indentured labour.

[93]Murdoch to Rogers, 12 May 1866, enclosure no. 1 in Carnarvon to Governor of Trinidad, 20 Aug. 1866, copy included in enclosure no. 1, Gordon to Buckingham, 8 June 1867.

[94]Murdoch to Rogers, 2 Aug. 1866, enclosure no. 2 in Carnarvon to Governor of Trinidad, 20 Aug. 1866.

in the disposal of land should be "the favourable grouping of the population." Toward that end labourers should be given reasonable facilities for settling on freeholds near plantations, churches, and schools. He favoured the installment plan for both settled and nomadic squatters but thought that the latter should be offered better sites than those they then occupied. Future efforts to restrain squatting should "partake as little as possible of the character of a struggle with nature."[95]

In January 1867 Gordon submitted, confidentially, all of the correspondence relating to squatting and the Crown lands to the legislative council. He did not comment upon it and made only a few remarks of his own upon the subject in his covering memorandum. What he did write, however, showed by implication that he was concerned mainly with the development of Trinidad's economy. Squatting must be abolished before better use could be made of the colony's resources. Although not yet thoroughly acquainted with the affairs of the island he saw plainly that "one of its chief wants is . . . a denser population."[96] By June, he had travelled extensively throughout the colony and had first-hand information for the proposals which he now laid before the legislative council and the Secretary of State.

Gordon rejected Manners Sutton's installment plan as unworkable in practice and proposed to reduce the upset price to twenty shillings per acre[97] and to collect this sum together with fees and costs of survey from the purchaser on delivery of the grant. He suggested that funds from land sales be used to build roads, that new cacao plantations be exempted from ward rates for five years, and that efforts be made to resettle squatters in closer contiguity. He proposed finally that he should appoint a commissioner to carry his plan into effect.[98] He hoped, he told the council, that all would agree on the general principles of his plan if not on its details and that the members would be willing to leave him "a large measure of discretion" in applying its principles. After he assured the planters that where formerly people simply took the land they would in future be compelled to pay for it, the resolutions passed with negligible opposition.

Gordon did not intend legislating at this stage. He wished first to prove his scheme experimentally in the Montserrat district in which

[95]Carnarvon to Governor of Trinidad, 20 Aug. 1866.

[96]Gordon's memorandum to members of legislative council, Jan. 1867, enclosure no. 2 in Gordon to Buckingham, 8 June 1867.

[97]Except for village lots for which the upset price would be forty shillings per acre.

[98]Minutes of the proceedings of the legislative council of Trinidad, p. 52, 1 June 1867, PRO 298/34.

squatting was most prevalent. The resolutions (which committed the council to his scheme), when added to his power as judge of the Court of Intendant[99] and his executive power as governor, gave him the necessary authority. Feeling that any effective agreement with the squatters could be made only on the spot by an authorized agent of the government, he proceeded to create the Montserrat Ward Union and to appoint Robert Mitchell[100] as warden and commissioner for the settlement of Crown lands. Mitchell knew the dialects of French and Spanish spoken by the creoles and had a "remarkable power of influencing the colored population." An active and hardy man, with tact and judgment, Mitchell exactly suited the task facing him.[101]

Gordon gave Mitchell instructions not as literal and rigid rules but as an intimation of general principles and an indication of points requiring special attention. These instructions[102] illustrate the complexity of the whole problem, the liberal spirit with which Gordon was prepared to deal with the squatters, and the surprising breadth of knowledge he had acquired on the matter after a residence of but seven months.[103] He directed Mitchell to transform scattered illegal occupations into systematic, consolidated, legal holdings, a procedure which he felt to be less an end in itself than a means of improving the conditions of the squatters and a method of making land available to those who wished to begin new forms of agriculture on a larger scale. Gordon divided the squatters into seven classes. Those who had received Crown grants should not be interfered with against their wishes. Those who had paid the whole purchase price of their land but had not paid the fees or taken out a formal grant had "a virtual possessary right" which it would be wrong to abrogate. Squatters who had petitioned for their land and had paid some portion of the price had also acquired a right

[99]The Court of Intendant in Trinidad performed the duties of a Crown land department. It was Spanish in origin and consisted of the governor as judge, one of the puisne judges as assessor, and a clerk or escribano. The court could decide points of law and grant or reject applications for land but had no executive power. For the conduct of that branch of a Crown land department, the intervention of the governor in his executive capacity was necessary.

[100]The son of Henry Mitchell.

[101]Gordon to Buckingham, 8 June 1867.

[102]Draft enclosed *ibid.*

[103]A minute by Taylor on Gordon's comments concerning a land dispute illustrates Gordon's extensive local knowledge. Taylor wrote: "It is a singular exhibition of minute topographical knowledge and one can hardly tell how a Gov. of a large Colony comes to be possessed of it. But I believe Gov. Gordon goes about a great deal in the Island, sometimes *walking* 25 miles in a day." (Taylor's minute, 4 Oct. 1868, on Gordon to Rogers, 28 Sept. 1868, PRO CO 295/246.)

to remain. Nevertheless, because it might be desirable to move them they should be offered a third more land elsewhere, compensation for buildings and crops, and a price of twenty shillings an acre instead of the forty shillings which they would pay should they choose to remain where they were. To deal with the fourth and largest class, consisting of those who had had their land surveyed and had paid ward rates but had neither petitioned for a grant nor paid any part of the purchase price, would require "the utmost discretion" because that class included those who should receive equal treatment with the third as well as those who had "less claim on the forbearance of the Government than many of the following [or fifth] class." This latter group consisted of those who had not paid ward rates but had petitioned for a grant and had had their land surveyed, many sincerely believing that the completion of a survey constituted a licence of occupation. Gordon thought it "impossible not to regard with indulgence a not unnatural error." He left Mitchell free to deal with the fourth and fifth classes as he saw fit. Squatters of the sixth class, made up of those who had petitioned for their land but had neither had it surveyed nor paid ward rates, should be offered perhaps one-quarter more land elsewhere plus compensation. If they rejected this offer they should be treated with those of the last (seventh) class who had simply squatted. Mitchell might, if it was convenient, offer these groups an equivalent amount of land to be selected by the government. If they refused this offer he was to evict them under Ordinance 15 of 1852.[104]

Gordon realized the impossibility of creating a symmetrical division of the land owing to the broken nature of the country and the fact that grants were to be based upon the acreage actually occupied by the squatters. He instructed Mitchell to make the division as symmetrical as possible but to act "not so strictly according to a pre-arranged system as according to the exigencies of the particular case and the dictates of common sense." Mitchell should bear in mind that "however desirable it may be to consolidate the settlers . . . it would be dearly paid for were it attained at the price of exciting general discontent and a spirit of disaffection towards the Government. . . . So far as it is possible, what is done . . . should be accomplished through . . . tact and persuasion . . . , not under the influence of fear, or by the authority of force."[105]

Owing to Mitchell's knowledge, energy, and understanding, the Montserrat pilot-scheme made rapid progress. In December 1867, the

[104]Draft instructions to Mitchell, enclosed in Gordon to Buckingham, 8 June 1867.   [105]*Ibid.*

Commissioner reported that 408 squatters had applied for 5,533 acres and that new settlers had bought or petitioned for some 3,000 acres of unoccupied land. Large tracts had been cleared, a village had been established, and roads, bridges, and a police station were under construction. Montserrat was, he thought, fast losing its lawless and inaccessible character.[106] Encouraged by this report, Gordon asked permission to extend operations to another district and to appoint an assistant commissioner. The Colonial Office agreed. Buckingham was so impressed by Gordon's and Mitchell's success that, on Rogers' suggestion, he ordered copies of the dispatches and reports dealing with squatting in Trinidad to be sent to Jamaica where a similar problem existed.[107] Excellent progress continued throughout 1868. Visiting Montserrat early in 1869, Gordon remarked that Mitchell's second report (February 1869)[108] had "failed to do justice either to the magnitude of his operations, or the success which has attended them." He believed the suppression of squatting in Montserrat to be in sight.[109] "There is nothing," wrote Murdoch of the Land and Emigration Board, "that requires any interference on the part of the Home Government. On the contrary the operation cannot, it appears to me, be better left than in the hands of the governor and Mr. Mitchell."[110]

The Montserrat scheme had demonstrated that squatting could be suppressed. It did not prove that it could be prevented. Gordon felt sure squatting would reappear unless Crown lands could be settled in an orderly manner. This could be ensured only by reducing the cost and simplifying the procedure of acquiring those lands. During his leave of absence in the summer and autumn of 1868, Gordon formulated the alterations he proposed to make in the manner of disposing of Crown lands. The bases of his plan were prompt payment and local sales. He recommended, first, that an applicant for Crown land be required to pay one-half the upset price when filing his application and the remainder of the price on the day of sale, and, secondly, that sales be conducted by the wardens on fixed days after due notice. Murdoch thought the requirement respecting payment a little too stringent but the problem might "safely be left to Mr. Gordon to decide" and if the requirement proved a deterrent to purchasers the governor ought to have

[106]Robert Mitchell's first report.
[107]Buckingham to Sir John Grant, 23 June 1868, filed with Murdoch to Rogers, 19 May 1868, PRO CO 295/246.
[108]Robert Mitchell's second report enclosed in Gordon to Granville, 10 March 1869, PRO CO 295/247.
[109]Gordon to Granville, 24 March 1869, PRO CO 295/247.
[110]Murdoch to Rogers, 13 April 1869, PRO CO 295/249.

authority at his own discretion to relax it.[111] Without any hesitation the Colonial Office sanctioned Gordon's proposals which he intended to make the basis of legislation on his return to Trinidad. Meanwhile, however, other plans which threatened both to nullify the Governor's land settlement programme and to limit his executive authority had been formulated in Trinidad.

When Gordon left for England in June 1868, the legislative council, the borough council of Port-of-Spain, and the public had presented him with laudatory addresses commending him on his energy, integrity, enlarged and liberal views, his zeal for the advancement of the colony, and his enthusiasm for promoting the welfare of all of its inhabitants.[112] He might therefore legitimately have assumed that his policies and authority would be secure during his absence. On the contrary, however, he knew that the opposition would take advantage of his absence to attack him and his plans. Indeed, the opposition had already, at the beginning of the year, made one abortive sortie against him by attempting to ruin the *Trinidad Chronicle*, the newspaper that supported him. On that occasion a representative of the opposition, Thomas Finlayson, "the âme damné of the attorney general,"[113] told its editor, Otto Wenkstern[114] that his colleagues knew they could not take the necessary steps for the removal of the Governor as long as the leading newspaper fought his battles for him. That newspaper must therefore go. Wenkstern, he said, had chosen to ally himself with a governor whom they disliked and who was ruining the country. Should Wenkstern withdraw his support from the Governor all would be well with the *Chronicle*; but if he refused the English merchants would withdraw all their advertising and so ruin the paper. Wenkstern remained firm and in three days the paper lost virtually all its advertising and verged upon bankruptcy.[115] The editor appealed to Gordon, who saved him by awarding the *Chronicle* an extensive government printing contract and by making him a small personal loan. The opposition circulated a rumour

[111]Murdoch to Rogers, 27 Oct. 1868, PRO CO 295/246.

[112]Kortright to Buckingham (separate), 8 Sept. 1868, PRO CO 295/245. It is interesting to note that when Dr. De Verteuil moved in the council that an address be presented to the Governor, Charles Warner moved as an amendment "that it is inexpedient for this Board to address any Governor on any other occasion than those of his assuming and retiring from the Government of the Island." The amendment was lost, seven to four. (Minutes of the proceedings of the legislative council of Trinidad, p. 98, 23 June 1868, PRO CO 298/35).

[113]Wenkstern to Gordon, 18 Jan. 1868, Stanmore Papers, 49235.

[114]Wenkstern was a well-known London journalist until, for reasons of health, he emigrated to Trinidad about 1864. There, with the backing of one of the leading planters, he published and edited the *Trinidad Chronicle*.

[115]Wenkstern to Gordon, 18 Jan. 1868, two letters, Stanmore Papers, 49235.

that the loan amounted to $1,000, but this exaggeration encouraged those who were wavering in their support of the Governor to believe that he would not stand by and see his friends ruined.

Wenkstern, until he died in 1869, kept Gordon informed of the opposition's schemes and undercover propaganda. A few days after the events described above, he reported a plan to get rid of Gordon. The plotters did not intend to send a memorial to the Secretary of State but rather to "abuse and calumniate" the Governor, to make hostile demonstrations to him, "perhaps even to bribe people to hoot him in the streets until your Excellency when once out of the country, shall think with horror of returning to it." He went on to quote one of Gordon's opponents as saying that he would not mind paying the Governor as much as £5,000 a year if the English government were to send "a gentleman and not a thief and a blackguard."[116] After Gordon's departure in June 1868, the opposition lost no time in building up its organization and pressing its attack on the Governor. The Trinidad Reform Association, which had formerly existed to fight against Charles Warner, was now revived to fight for him. Warner, himself, with some success, attempted to dominate Kortright, the administrator in the Governor's absence.

Wenkstern regarded these activities with consternation and suggested to Gordon that the private individuals concerned be "crushed" and that "certain officials" (by which he meant Charles Warner) be removed to another colony. But Gordon wrote, reassuring Wenkstern:

I am not the least afraid of any opposition they or others may offer. . . .
The permanent officers of the Colonial Office, Sir Frederic Rogers, Mr. Elliot, and Mr. Taylor are warm allies of mine, and I am so fortunately situated that changes of Government make little difference to me in point of interest or influence. My [half] brother, the Duke of Abercorn, is a power amongst the Tories, and on the other side are my closest personal friends. I have lately been staying with the Duke of Argyll, who will probably be the new Colonial Minister, and am now just come from Hawarden, where I remained with the Gladstones till he commenced his "stumping" tour. I had much conversation about Trinidad with both, and know that I may be sure of their agreement in my views, as well as of their disposition to support me from old affection. . . .[117]

Nevertheless, news that Warner had drafted, and was pushing through the council, two ordinances (24 and 25 of 1868) dealing with squatting and Crown lands caused Gordon annoyance and deep concern.

[116]Ibid., 23 Jan. 1868.
[117]Gordon to Wenkstern, 15 Oct. 1868, Stanmore Papers, 49244.

Ordinance 24 provided for the abolition of the Court of Intendant[118] and transferred its records to the surveyor-general. It required that sales of Crown land take place in Port-of-Spain in the presence of the surveyor-general. It established an upset price of two pounds for village lots, of ten shillings for lagoon lands, and of one pound per acre for all other lands. It further provided that no lands (except village lots) be sold in lots of less than 16 or more than 400 acres, that all lands be sold and the Pitch Lake leased to the highest bidder; that planters be allowed to purchase lands adjacent to their estates upon which they had encroached; and that all grants under the ordinance *be signed by the attorney-general in proof of his allowance of the same.*[119] "This [ordinance] if carried," wrote Gordon, "will be a *death blow* to all my land settlement schemes. It is aimed at me, and I am astonished that this should not have been perceived."[120] The ordinance did pass the council and (together with Ordinance 25 making provision for the plantation and settlement of Crown lands) was forwarded by Kortright on 5 October 1868. Although under the impression that both ordinances represented the Governor's policy, Kortright had, however, not assented to them.

Danger lay not so much in the ordinances themselves (the Colonial Office could simply withhold its assent), but rather in the possibility of rousing the local legislators against the Governor should the Colonial Office refuse assent during his stay in England. The members of the council would naturally attribute the refusal to his influence. Their annoyance might prejudice his future usefulness, especially if on his return he forced them to pass legislation contrary to that already honoured by their votes. Gordon knew where responsibility lay for the introduction of the two ordinances. They had, he told Ebden, "been passed through the Council by the Attorney General in opposition to his [Gordon's] known views."[121]

Warner had three probable motives for his action. First, although he had called Gordon's plan for suppressing squatting "a large and states-manlike" measure,[122] he did not wish to allow the lower classes to settle on the Crown land and so become independent of planters and other

[118]See above, p. 73, fn. 99.

[119]Murdoch to Rogers, 27 Oct. 1868.

[120]Gordon to Wenkstern, 15 Oct. 1868.

[121]Ebden's minute, 29 Oct. 1868, on Kortright to Secretary of State, no. 160, 5 Oct. 1868, PRO CO 295/245. Richard Powney Ebden was a clerk in the Colonial Office.

[122]Newspaper clipping giving an account of the introduction of Gordon's resolutions to the legislative council, enclosure no. 5 in Gordon to Buckingham, 8 June 1867.

employers. The Montserrat scheme had allowed many scores of labourers to become small landed proprietors. Such a development, he felt, should not continue. Unless squatting could be prevented by simple repression, the colony would have to tolerate a certain amount of it. Secondly, Warner was not above using his official position to advance his personal interests.[123] The terms of Ordinance 24 were not closely drawn. This fact would result in much litigation from which, as a practising lawyer, he might expect to profit. Thirdly, Ordinances 24 and 25 both restricted the governor's authority and the former gave Warner, as attorney-general, a veto on all sales of Crown land. Warner's power and influence, threatened and waning under the impact of a strong-willed governor, might thus, at least in part, be restored.

Gordon did not intend to inquire into the circumstances surrounding the passage of the two ordinances. He would, he told Rogers, simply pretend that those concerned had made an honest error.[124] He contented himself with persuading the Land and Emigration Board and the Colonial Office to withhold assent from the ordinances and allow him to draft the legislation he desired. In this he had no great difficulty because they considered him an able man and believed that to allow him to "take his own course on his own responsibility . . . [afforded] the best chance . . . of securing the public interest."[125] Moreover, although both the Land and Emigration Board and the Colonial Office agreed with one feature or another of Ordinances 24 and 25 they disagreed among themselves,[126] and Gordon was able to take advantage of their differences to have his own way.

Gordon thus returned to Trinidad "backed by the authority of the Crown, and the confidence of the Colonial Office,"[127] and fully prepared to meet any opposition. He had always said, he wrote to Otto Wenkstern, that he should not return unless he saw the means of carrying out his policy.[128] He must have been greatly encouraged by the demonstration which greeted him at Port-of-Spain.[129] Yet his welcome was not unanimous. The Trinidad Reform Association continued to oppose him. It planned to fight him on every point and to prevent the passage of any measure good or bad, until he either resigned his governorship or placed

[123]See below, pp. 95–96.

[124]Gordon to Rogers, 9 Nov. 1868, PRO CO 295/246.

[125]Rogers' minute, 3 Dec. 1868, on Murdoch to Rogers, 30 Nov. 1868, PRO CO 295/246.

[126]Murdoch to Rogers, 30 Nov. 1868, and minutes.

[127]Gordon to Wenkstern, 15 Oct. 1868.

[128]*Ibid.*

[129]See the 8 December 1868 issues of the *Trinidad Chronicle* and *Port of Spain Gazette* for accounts of this popular demonstration.

himself under the protection of Charles Warner.[130] Since the Governor had power to push any measure whatever through the council he ignored these attacks and, for tactical reasons, continued to treat Warner as a friend.

A few weeks after his arrival Gordon received a dispatch from the Colonial Office instructing him not to assent to either Ordinance 24 or Ordinance 25, and agreeing to his proposals for dealing with the Crown lands. In one respect, however, the Colonial Office failed to meet his desires. It withheld the authority to dispose of land without settled rules as to price. As originally drafted the dispatch had conceded this power, but Rogers had come round to Murdoch's view that the executive would soon be accused of jobbing, and Granville had agreed to a change in the dispatch.[131]

In February 1869, Gordon told the council that Ordinances 24 and 25 had not been sanctioned because they differed from regulations already determined upon by Her Majesty's government. Legislation would be necessary, however, to ensure the success of the plan authorized by the Imperial government. Such legislation should not be too detailed. Any gaps could be filled later.[132]

The new ordinance (8 of 1869) for management and disposal of Crown lands passed a full meeting of the council with only one dissenting vote. It followed closely the "prompt payment and local sales" plan submitted by Gordon to Rogers the previous September and sanctioned by the Duke of Buckingham on 2 November.[133] There was but one change of any importance: the powers of the Court of Intendant with reference to the disposal of Crown lands were conferred on the governor exclusively as intendant of Crown lands.[134] Murdoch took it for granted that the ordinance did not authorize the governor to alter the regulations for the disposal of Crown land without the previous sanction of the secretary of state. The Colonial Office confirmed the ordinance.

To illustrate the correctness of Gordon's view of the necessity of centralizing authority and leaving the governor free, except for general rules, to dispose of Crown lands, the following instance is appropriate. In the spring of 1869 a group of twenty-five Indians eligible for return passage to India offered to remain in Trinidad if given free grants of

[130]Wenkstern to Gordon, 19 Feb. 1869, Stanmore Papers, 49235.

[131]Granville to Gordon, 19 Dec. 1868, and Rogers' minute, 15 Dec. 1868, on the draft, PRO CO 295/246.

[132]Minutes of the proceedings of the legislative council of Trinidad, pp. 7–9, Governor's message, 23 Feb. 1869, PRO CO 298/35.

[133]See above, pp. 75–76.

[134]The Court of Intendant was retained for the enforcement of ward rates and some other purposes.

land. Under the regulations Gordon could not dispose of Crown land except by public auction. Nor had he time to consult the Secretary of State because the Indians' ship was about to sail. Nevertheless he accepted their proposal. He agreed to grant each of them ten acres in lieu of their passages to India.[135] An additional forty-five Indians quickly followed the original applicants, and Gordon had land surveyed for them in the neighbourhood of the estates upon which they had served their indentures. Thus, even with the wide powers that Ordinance 8 had conferred upon him, Gordon had been forced to exceed them in the interests of a movement which he considered of "incalculable advantage" to the colony.[136]

The administration of Ordinance 8 fell upon Robert Mitchell, whom Gordon appointed sub-intendant. He first devised simple forms and books to enable the wardens to handle local sales with ease and efficiency. He next undertook to ascertain the extent of squatting throughout the colony and urged wardens to send in lists of all squatters in their districts. He himself supported them and in nine months travelled 3,000 miles in the back country. Describing his journeys he wrote:

I thus came personally into contact with the squatters in every form, from the comfortable occupant of a flourishing cocoa plantation, surrounded by paid assistants who did all the rough work for him, to the solitary squatter whose presence in the vast woods is only betrayed by the ring of the axe, and the thin column of smoke rising among the trees, and the chief part of whose property consists of the maize or rice planted on an acre or two of ground, and the palm-thatched rancho he has built. To each and every one of them whom I have encountered, (and their number is considerable) I have made it my duty when we met, to explain in their own language or jargon . . . the advantage to be derived from compliance with the laws and regulations now in force, and from the injury certain to result to themselves, from a longer persistence in an illegal course. I have ever found ready listeners among these people. Their astonishment at seeing a white man alone in the interior of the forest, without a guide, is extreme, and they realize probably for the first time, that they have not succeeded in placing themselves beyond the reach of authority, or the power of the law.

In those districts I have had time to visit, considerable sums have been paid in by the better class of squatters for the lands they hold; those who never intended to pay have absconded, and the rest, without exception, are straining every nerve, to make up the requisite amount to buy their little holdings. Many . . . who never dreamed of becoming landholders, attracted by the facilities . . . have come forward as purchasers.[137]

[135]The government of Trinidad was responsible for payment of the fare to India of any Indian who desired to return there on completion of his indenture. The cost ranged between twelve and thirteen pounds.

[136]Gordon to Granville, 22 May 1869, PRO CO 295/247.

[137]Mitchell's report as sub-intendant of Crown lands, 23 March 1870, printed copy enclosed in Gordon to Granville, 8 April 1870, PRO CO 295/250.

The investigations of Mitchell and the wardens revealed that squatting was more widespread than anyone had suspected. Even some of the main villages were situated, at least in part, upon unalienated land. With the application of the principles of the Montserrat scheme throughout the colony, Mitchell calculated, however, that by the end of 1870 the great bulk of the squatters would have purchased their lands or quietly resigned them to more industrious men.[138]

The new rules of procedure for purchasing Crown land[139] were so much simpler and cheaper than the old that they encouraged prospective settlers. Sales of public land between 1856 and 1865 had amounted only to 1,895 acres. After 1869 they steadily increased and, between 1878 and 1887, totalled 71,000 acres.[140]

The rapid increase in the number of landowners brought about by converting squatters into proprietors and by encouraging new settlers on the Crown lands made it more than ever desirable to simplify and cheapen the procedure for transferring and registering land titles. In 1863 the Duke of Newcastle had suggested these changes, but Governor Keate had not considered them desirable. Gordon had his attention called to them early in his administration but had been advised locally that such a reform would be too difficult to accomplish because it would adversely affect existing interests—presumably the lawyers whose practices would suffer. It was not a serious matter as long as it affected only a few hundred landowners of substance; but title to a small lot cost as much to register or transfer as to a large one, and the numerous new small-holders and peasant farmers could not afford to take the required legal steps. Gordon, therefore, passed an ordinance, based upon the Torrens Act in New South Wales, to facilitate registry and transfer of titles. The Colonial Office whole-heartedly approved it and agreed that it should take effect from 1 January 1871. Undoubtedly this legislation would have benefited the colony greatly but Gordon left Trinidad just after he transmitted it to the Colonial Office. His successor did not proclaim the ordinance and it was still not in force in 1884 although it

[138]*Ibid.*

[139]Under these regulations the warden furnished the intending buyer with the petition, helped him fill it in, and calculated the upset price of the lot at twenty shillings an acre. The buyer could either pay this sum, plus survey fees, at once and receive a 10 per cent discount, or pay half and the remainder within eight days of sale. The warden then forwarded the petition to the office of the intendant for decision. The intendant's office immediately informed the warden of the decision and at the same time ordered the Crown surveyor to complete a survey of the property within a month. After the survey the warden gave twenty-one days' notice and put the land up for auction on the last Thursday of the month. If no other applicant appeared the warden declared the petitioner the owner. The intendant then issued a grant.

[140]Eversley, *Trinidad Reviewer*, 115.

had never been repealed.[141] No doubt the legal profession in Trinidad profited.

Arthur Gordon's land reforms wrought a profound change in the character of the colony. They ensured rapid settlement and civilization of the uninhabited or irregularly-occupied areas of the island. They saved much of the natural resources from spoliation at the hands of squatters. They filled a void in the social structure by creating a new independent peasant class. This class introduced intensive, efficient, and diversified farming methods which enabled the colony to withstand more easily future breaks in the sugar market.

Although Gordon greatly improved the lot of the negro and coloured inhabitants of Trinidad by his land reforms he did not neglect that other, increasingly large, section of the labouring class—the Indians. Indians had begun to arrive in Trinidad in 1845 and twenty years later numbered some 10,000. Although better treated than their compatriots in neighbouring British Guiana, and very much better than those in Mauritius, their lives were grim. Mortality was high. Wages were low. Many, if not a majority, failed to earn enough during their first year on the island to feed themselves.[142] The planters displayed a callous attitude towards them. "One planter and one *only*," reported Gordon, "takes real thought for his coolies and he is laughed at by his neighbours."[143] Few thought it inhuman for Indian women to have to take their infant children to the fields with them and leave them lying in the sun and rain. Gordon accounted for this attitude by observing that "the most humane man cannot live long in an atmosphere of hardship and inhumanity without having his feelings blunted and his perceptions obscured by the tone of those around him, and by the sights to which he is habitually accustomed."[144]

When Indians first came to Trinidad, Lord Harris had attempted to safeguard their interests. "My desire is," he wrote to Gladstone, ". . . never to lose sight of the fact that the coolies are placed here under peculiar circumstances as utter strangers in a foreign land, and therefore requiring the zealous and unceasing care of the Government."[145] After his departure no one paid much attention to them until Manners Sutton and Rushworth made better provision for receiving

[141]De Verteuil, *Trinidad*, 465.
[142]Gordon to Marryat, 7 March 1870, and Gordon to W. F. Burnley (an absentee planter), 25 Jan. 1870, Stanmore Papers, 49244.
[143]Gordon to Bishop Wilberforce, 20 July 1867, Stanmore Papers, 49214.
[144]Gordon to Burnley, 24 March 1870, Stanmore Papers, 49244.
[145]Lord Harris to Gladstone, July 1846, quoted by De Verteuil, *Trinidad*, 456.

immigrants by giving them clothing and allowing them several days rest before agreeing to their allotment to estates. In 1865 Manners Sutton passed an ordinance permitting planters to establish estate hospitals for their coolies,[146] his intention being to relieve overcrowding in the colonial hospitals and to provide the Indians when ill with sufficient nourishment, medicine, and hospital accommodation free of charge. Since the planters seemed reluctant to build hospitals, Rushworth made the ordinance compulsory and further allotment of coolies contingent upon the planters' compliance with it.

By the beginning of 1867 hospitals had been built, or were under construction, on all but 13 of the 155 estates employing indentured labour.[147] By the autumn of that year Henry Mitchell, the agent-general of immigrants, reported "a marvellous relief to the Colonial Hospitals [and] a marked diminution of sickness on Estates."[148] Although the mortality rate was lowered by the provision of hospitals, it remained high particularly among new arrivals. Rushworth and Henry Mitchell had suggested that malnutrition might be the major reason because the Indians would starve themselves and their families in order to save money. They proposed that the planters provide the coolies with rations and deduct the cost from the wages instead of allowing them to feed themselves out of their wages. Gordon agreed and, in May 1867, forwarded a so-called "rationing ordinance" to the Secretary of State. It required the planters to supply rations to their labourers for the first year of the indenture. Buckingham thought the ordinance should be permissive, but Gordon insisted that the employers would then obey it only if they found it to their financial advantage. The Indians, if also given a choice, would reject the rations. Buckingham then agreed and Gordon proclaimed the ordinance. It amply fulfilled expectations. During the year ending 30 September 1869 (the first year the rationing ordinance was in force), 450 coolies died out of 9,563, or 4.7 per cent. Those who were in their first year and subject to the rationing ordinance lost 4 per cent of their number, compared with 7.3 per cent the previous year.[149] Second and third year coolies who had been weeded of their

---

[146]During the latter half of the nineteenth century the term "coolie" was used both officially and privately in place of the longer "Indian indentured plantation labourer." No disparagement of the Indians was intended and the author intends none in his frequent use of it in this book.

[147]Gordon to Carnarvon, 26 Jan. 1867, PRO CO 295/238. The thirteen estates which refused to build hospitals could no longer employ indentured labour.

[148]Report of Henry Mitchell, 18 Sept. 1867, enclosure no. 1 in Gordon to Buckingham, 20 Sept. 1867, PRO CO 295/240.

[149]The reduction in 1869 is the more remarkable because that year was the unhealthiest on record owing to a severe outbreak of yellow fever.

TABLE I*

Year	Mortality rate (percentage of first-year coolies)
1865 (no hospitals)	12
1866 (92 hospitals)	8.9
1867 (142 hospitals)	7.29
1868 (142 hospitals)	7.3
1869 (142 hospitals and rationing ordinance)	4

*Annual report of the Agent-general of Immigrants for the year ending 30 Sept. 1869, enclosed in Gordon to Granville, 8 April 1870, PRO CO 295/250.

weaklings lost 7 per cent and 4.2 per cent respectively.[150] Table I indicates the impact of the hospital and rationing ordinances upon first-year Indian immigrants. Gordon was so pleased with the success of the rationing ordinance that he decided to extend the period to two years. The planters agreed because Henry Mitchell convinced them that better health and increased strength enabled the coolies to do more work.

The Governor next proceeded to improve the lot of Indian women. They, like the men, were bound to work 280 days a year in the fields and were liable to the same penalties for failure. Child-bearing and illness often prevented them from completing their schedule. Consequently when a man completed his term his wife still had time to serve. The husband usually remained on the estate, but he did so unwillingly because he suspected that his wife's lost time was being exacted in order to retain him. Gordon found it revolting that a woman should be sent to gaol for the crime of attending her infant, and that pregnancy and illness were not recognized by law as causes for exemption from punishment for neglect of work. He therefore reduced the number of compulsory working days for women so they would be free at the same time as their husbands. He recognized pregnancy and illness as legal excuses for non-performance of field work. Finally, he substituted fines or additional labour for imprisonment for women convicted of breaking the labour laws. The planters did not at first favour these changes, but, helped by a reduction of 50 per cent in the indenture fee paid the government for female labourers, most planters eventually recognized their justness.

In June 1870, as a final piece of legislation, Gordon passed a new immigration ordinance consolidating all previous laws on that subject. At the same time he seized the opportunity of making several changes of importance to the Indian immigrants. He transformed the estate medical officers into civil servants thus enabling them to force the

[150]Gordon to Granville, 6 April 1870, PRO CO 295/250.

planters to comply with their directions. Moreover, no estate could have any more Indian labourers if the mortality among its coolies exceeded 7 per cent, or if 15 per cent failed to earn six pence a day during the preceding year. Immigration officers were given power to inquire on oath into the cause of any disturbance on the estates and to have the troublemakers arrested. Finally under Gordon's persuasion the planters agreed to drop claims to lost time except where a coolie had been convicted in a magistrate's court for breach of contract or absence without leave. To compensate the planters for this concession Gordon reduced the immigration fee for men as he had previously reduced it for women.[151]

Gordon brought about his improvements in the immigration laws with remarkably little opposition from the planters. There were several reasons for his success. First, the planters of Trinidad seem not to have been such a bad lot as those of British Guiana and Mauritius. No doubt they were callous, but they were not cruel, and many genuinely came to recognize and respect the humanity implicit in Gordon's proposals. Then, too, they respected the law and had not fallen into the habit of subverting it since they had been held in check by the magistrates, whose status was as high as their own. Again, although the improvements in the condition of the labourers cost the planters money, they were better able to afford the expense than formerly. Most important of all they realized that Gordon would be reluctant to deprive them of coolie labour and so ruin them, but that he would not hesitate to take such action if they adamantly refused to accept the reforms he felt to be necessary.[152]

Another governor, less prompted by humanitarian sentiments than Arthur Gordon, might have been content to allow the legislative council, on which the planters had strong representation, to legislate, as it saw fit, on behalf of the Indians. Gordon, however, saw the coolies not as expendable machines which might be replaced (although at some cost) by new ones from India, but rather as human beings requiring protection in their new and unfamiliar industrial surroundings against both their employers and their own cupidity. His immigration legislation was strongly paternalistic; but industrial serfdom unleavened by governmental

---

[151]Gordon to Granville, 25 June 1870, PRO CO 295/251.

[152]Nearly twenty years later, Gordon had the satisfaction of hearing that some of his strongest opponents were citing his coolie immigration laws and his Crown land administration "as the two great measures which have pulled the Colony through its great trials." (David Wilson [private secretary to Gordon in New Brunswick, later Sir David Wilson, K.C.M.G., governor British Honduras, 1897–1903] to Gordon, 10 May 1888, Stanmore Papers, 49264.)

intervention soon degenerated into slavery, as experience in British Guiana[153] and to a greater degree in Mauritius[154] was to show. The improvements which he made in Trinidad gave it probably the strongest legal system for the protection of indentured immigrant labour of any country in the Empire.

IV. PUBLIC INSTITUTIONS AND PUBLIC WORKS

For a complete picture of Gordon's reforms in Trinidad brief mention must be made of his improvement of the civil service and public institutions and his revival of public works including better facilities for transportation and communication. These measures were important to the well-being and development of the colony. Gordon had the foresight to envisage their utility. However, despite rising revenues, the colony was far from "easy-street" and, in face of the necessity (urged on him by the Colonial Office) of reducing the debt of £172,000, Gordon found difficulty in obtaining money for public works. Moreover, inflation, resulting from better times, aggravated the problem of low civil service salaries. From the outset of Gordon's administration various groups of civil servants petitioned him for higher salaries. Their need was obvious. Their salary cuts of the fifties remained unrestored and rising living costs[155] reduced their purchasing power still further. Almost all of them were financially embarrassed. Gordon observed that "a man over-whelmed with debt is far more under the control of his creditors than of his official superiors, or the Governor."[156] He saw two ways in which to increase salaries: either to take the money out of surplus revenue or to lower the cost of the establishment by a sweeping reduction of offices and a vigorous weeding out of inefficient officers. He rejected the first method since it would mean prolonged deferment of needed public works. The second would prove difficult because almost every public officer in the colony had ties of birth or marriage with almost every other public officer, and any reduction in their numbers

[153]*Report of the commissioners appointed to enquire into the treatment of immigrants in British Guiana*, Parl. Pap., 1871, XX [C-393], 483–689; Gordon to Granville, no. 46, 8 April 1870, PRO CO 295/246.

[154]See below, chap. IV, sec. III.

[155]The rise in living costs is indicated by the following comparison of prices in dollars and cents in 1855 (in parentheses) and 1867: beef (.06) .25; mutton and pork (.25) .30; butter (.18) .60; cheese (.10) .40; bread (.05) .07; eggs (.20) .60; potatoes (.80) 1.20; wool suit (22.00) 36.00. Rents and servants' wages also showed marked increases. (Enclosure no. 3 in Gordon to Buckingham, 23 Oct. 1867, PRO CO 295/240.)

[156]Gordon to Buckingham (letter), Sept. 1868, received 22 Sept., PRO CO 295/246.

would be resisted by the civil service as a whole. Unless he had the hearty co-operation and avowed support of the Secretary of State the Governor felt unwilling to incur the odium of making such a proposal.[157]

Although usually eager to reduce colonial establishments, the Colonial Office did not encourage Gordon in his proposal because it appeared that any reduction would be eaten up by the salary increases. Buckingham thought that salary increases in Trinidad would lead to demands elsewhere. Taylor did not believe that a rise in the cost of living could be a sufficient reason for an increase in salaries. Rogers disagreed. He felt that where a bargain had been made and the conditions changed the bargain should be adjusted.[158] Despite Rogers' view and the Governor's urgings, Buckingham did not agree to consider specific suggestions until late in 1868. Gordon then proposed amalgamation and abolition of offices totalling over £9,000 and salary increases of about £3,500 annually. The latter included annual increases for the lower ranks of the civil service and straight increases for a number of higher officials[159] and members upon whom extra work would fall because of amalgamation of offices. A net saving of some £5,500 resulted, which, by further amalgamations during the following year, Gordon increased to £8,000. He thought he could point to these savings without vanity because "they are due far less to any exertions of mine than to the vigilant and unremitting scrutiny of the auditor general, Mr. Eagles."[160] The Governor had, however, provided the initiative and given Eagles the opportunity to exercise his special talents. The Colonial Office gave credit to both.[161]

By taking advantage of deaths, resignations, and promotions Gordon carried out his consolidation of the civil service gradually. This action and the salary increases disarmed criticism. His improvement of several of the public institutions caused greater dissent. Of these the leper asylum came under his eye first. He found the wards filthy, the patients ragged and insubordinate. He dismissed the medical superintendent and accepted the resident inspector's resignation. The former, a man of mixed race, charged that he was a victim of the Governor's racial prejudice. Since Gordon had appointed a number of coloured men to office, the charge was so demonstrably unjust that the meeting called to protest the doctor's dismissal ended with cheers for the Governor.

[157]Ibid.
[158]Minutes on Gordon to Buckingham, 23 Oct. 1867.
[159]Gordon recommended that his successor should receive a salary of £4,000, an increase of £500.
[160]Gordon to Granville, 24 Nov. 1869, PRO CO 295/248.
[161]Minutes, Ibid.

Gordon's next move, however, ran into more serious opposition. Needing to increase the staff of the leper asylum and to keep the cost as low as possible, he accepted the offer of a group of Dominican nuns to come to Trinidad to care for the lepers. Munro Pasea, an unofficial member of the legislative council and supporter of Charles Warner, moved in council "that this Board had learned with regret that His Excellency the Governor has placed the charge of the Leper Asylum under Ladies of the Dominican Order, inasmuch as it gives the appearance of a religious denominational character to the Institution."[162] Although the motion was seconded by Frederick Warner and debated, Pasea withdrew it, surely a sign that it enjoyed little support. Despite this reverse, a group of Protestants led by the Anglican archdeacon petitioned the Secretary of State to ensure that "no Public Institutions supported out of the general funds of the Colony should be confided to the care of members of any Religious Order so that all who desire to avail themselves of the benefit of such institutions may do so without fear of any proselytising influence or interference with their religious beliefs."[163]

Had the Governor intended placing the leper asylum under the control of the nuns the petition would have been justified even though but five of the seventy-odd lepers were Protestant. But a Protestant layman was to manage the institution, a Protestant clergyman was to attend Protestant lepers, and the nuns were to form only part of the staff. Gordon felt no surprise at the petition. The Anglican clergy, he told Rogers, had "long been accustomed to consider Protestantism a necessary badge of all Government institutions in Trinidad."[164] The Secretary of State, who replied to the petition in terms suggested by Gordon, gave assurance that he contemplated no change in the character of public institutions, denied that any such change had been made in the leper asylum, and asserted his belief that objections to the sisters on the score of their religion were unreasonable.[165] This ended the controversy. The nuns did their work well, and the Protestants in Trinidad felt genuine sorrow when, in 1869, nine of the thirteen nuns died of yellow fever.

The colonial hospital in Port-of-Spain also came in for reform. A

[162]Minutes of the proceedings of the legislative council of Trinidad, p. 92, 1 May 1868, PRO CO 298/35.
[163]Protestant petition enclosed in Kortright to Buckingham, 24 July 1868, PRO CO 295/244.
[164]Gordon to Rogers, 15 Sept. 1868, PRO CO 295/246.
[165]Buckingham to Gordon, 16 Nov. 1868, PRO CO 295/246. Buckingham concurred in the petitioners' view that the nuns ought not to be allowed to lodge visitors in any part of the asylum buildings.

subcommittee of the hospital board uncovered evidence of both widespread administrative inefficiency and systematic looting of supplies. It implicated Dr. Mercer, who had supervised the hospital since 1854. Mercer had been in trouble on several previous occasions and had avoided dismissal in 1861 only because of his social connections. He now came under the scrutiny of the council. It found him negligent and inefficient in his administrative capacity, but did not recommend his dismissal. Kortright did, and Gordon and the Colonial Office concurred. Planning on reorganizing the staff of the hospital so as to include a surgeon general, a master of administration and supplies, and a resident surgeon, Gordon recommended Mercer for the last position. Mercer, he said, had not been intentionally dishonest. He had been a poor administrator but a good surgeon. The Colonial Office while concurring in Gordon's reorganization would not accept Mercer. Taylor expressed the office's attitude: "The frauds and embezzlements of public servants in Trinidad have been scandalously frequent & the offenders have almost always been allowed to escape to the Spanish Main or elsewhere. . . . If the Gov[ernmen]t does not do what it can to protect the public against its servants it will have no redress."[166]

Gordon continued his efforts to improve the health of the community by creating the Department of Public Health. He reduced the number of medical officers and increased the public duties and the salaries of those that remained. These changes resulted in a much more efficient health service at a moderate increase in cost which neither the Colonial Office nor the Treasury had any difficulty in sanctioning.

Expanding revenues and falling establishment costs gave the colony annual surpluses by which the debt was reduced. With this development Gordon began to see some prospect of undertaking a broad programme of necessary public works. His list was formidable: a water supply for the rapidly growing town of San Fernando; a combined police barracks and court house for both San Fernando and Port-of-Spain; new buildings for the leper asylum and house of refuge; a telegraph line between Port-of-Spain and San Fernando; dredging of the harbour at Port-of-Spain and the mouths of the rivers along the Gulf of Paria; and, above all, new roads and repairs to existing ones.

To carry out such a programme required an efficient department of public works, and the Colonial Office approved Gordon's request to re-create the office of surveyor-general and to find a man to fill it. In

[166]Taylor's minute on Gordon to Buckingham, 24 Dec. 1868, PRO CO 295/245.

February 1867, Gordon described to Carnarvon the kind of man he wanted. He should have energy, enthusiasm, originality, patience, judgment, and impartiality. He should be a man of method and system, with a taste for the details of organization and the power to enforce his decisions. He should be active and inured to life in the tropics. "It may be difficult," wrote Gordon in a masterly understatement, "to select a man combining all these various qualifications. . . ."[167] Taylor thought the Governor "might as well have described the attributes of a glorified spirit."[168] Still, the Colonial Office could surely have done better than to appoint L. H. Moorsom. Totally incompetent and lacking every desirable attribute, Moorsom obstructed rather than promoted public works. Gordon had again to abolish the office of surveyor-general to get rid of him.[169] Forced to rely on local talent, the Governor placed the department in the hands of its superintendent, J. Meagher, and took a much more active part in planning than he would have taken with a competent surveyor-general. Public works then progressed rapidly. All of the projects referred to above were either completed or under construction when Gordon left the island. Of these, the improvement and extension of roads were the most important and necessary.

Hitherto road construction and maintenance in Trinidad had been almost wholly the responsibility of the wards. The wards had neither the personnel nor the financial resources to maintain existing roads let alone to build new ones. Consequently many highways had fallen into such a state of disrepair that the shipment of sugar was hindered.[170] New roads had not followed expanding lines of settlement. Early in his tour of duty Gordon concluded that the colonial government would have to provide greater financial assistance to the local authorities for maintaining and constructing secondary roads, and itself would have to build either a system of primary or royal roads or a number of railways. He believed railways might be cheaper in the long run because Trinidad's soft subsoil made road maintenance expensive. The colony would, however, have to float a loan to cover the initial expense. The Colonial Office would not sanction a loan at this time, and railway construction did not begin until the administrations of Gordon's successors, J. R. Longden and H. T. Irving. Gordon therefore turned to the alternative.

He had two major problems in undertaking road construction: finding

---

[167]Gordon to Carnarvon, 25 Feb. 1867, PRO CO 295/238.

[168]Taylor's minute, *ibid.*

[169]Moorsom went to Hong Kong as surveyor-general at £1,000 a year, an increase of £200 over his Trinidad salary.

[170]Gordon to Graham, 24 Nov. 1866 and 24 Feb. 1867, Stanmore Papers, 49244.

a source of revenue and overcoming the prejudice of the Colonial Office in favour of the principle, long followed in Trinidad and other colonies, that roads were the concern of local rather than central authorities. He solved his first problem with funds from the rapidly expanding surplus revenue and by diverting part of the revenue derived from the so-called "wharfage tax,"[171] placed on all imports into Port-of-Spain. The ordinance which levied this tax expired during Gordon's absence in 1868. Since it produced such a good revenue, the council re-enacted the ordinance and decided to devote its proceeds to the filling of a swamp, generally considered a hazard to the health of Port-of-Spain. Gordon argued that since nearly all the colony's imports came through Port-of-Spain the tax was a general one. Its proceeds should, at least in part, be devoted to a general and not a local purpose such as the filling of the swamp. Both Buckingham and Granville felt the swamp to be a source of epidemics but Granville did reluctantly concede Gordon's argument. In 1869 Gordon was able to apply £4,000[172] from surplus revenues and £2,500 from the wharfage tax to road construction. This was three and a half times as much as the colonial government had contributed in 1867. On 1 April 1869, he extended the wharfage tax until 1878 thus ensuring funds for the government's contribution to road building for a further ten years. At the same time he provided by ordinance for the completion of three royal roads at government expense and under government supervision. Maintenance of the royal roads would be undertaken by the department of public works although local authorities would share the costs. The wards would continue to construct, repair, and provide the bulk of the funds for secondary roads. Although recognizing Gordon's departure from the principle of local responsibility for roads, the Colonial Office thought his case for governmental intervention conclusive. His programme, which greatly facilitated transportation and the settlement of the Crown lands, was successfully concluded by his successor, James Longden.

V. GORDON'S RELATIONSHIPS WITH COLONISTS AND COLONIAL OFFICE

Although hardly "a glorified spirit" Arthur Gordon might well have been describing himself when he specified the kind of man he wanted as surveyor-general.[173] As governor of Trinidad he exhibited great energy, enthusiasm, and originality, as well as patience, judgment, and impartiality. Displaying power to enforce his decisions he revived the long

---

[171]First levied in 1852 and continued in 1864.
[172]Increased to £10,000 the following year.   [173]See p. 91.

dormant authority of the gubernatorial office. He governed dictatorially but not arbitrarily, finding it "much easier to rule despotically with moderation"[174] than to "exercise a limited authority with tact and persuasiveness."[175] Gordon wrought profound and progressive changes in Trinidad's life and institutions. He freed it of the religious tensions that prevailed on his arrival. He gave it a settled population, an expanding economy, better labour laws, improved public services, a more efficient civil service, and a vastly better system of internal communication and transport.

It was scarcely to be expected that Gordon could carry through such a radical programme without resistance from some segments of the community or disagreements with the Colonial Office. He experienced powerful, but not widespread, local opposition to his régime and to many of his measures, but throughout his administration, he retained the sympathy of the bulk of the population. Moreover, no difference ever arose between him and his legislative council as a body. Colonial interests frustrated only one of his measures (simplification of land transfers) and delayed only one other (consolidation of the statutes) beyond his term of office. The Colonial Office aborted none of his policies.

Gordon's relationships were almost entirely satisfactory with the three secretaries of state—Carnarvon, Buckingham, and Granville—under whom he served all but the last few weeks of his administration. Buckingham aroused Gordon's ire once when he failed to confirm one of the Governor's provisional appointments. Gordon observed that "the judicious selection of proper candidates for local employment is among the most important duties of a Colonial Governor, and that if his administration be on the whole one entitling him to confidence, he may fairly anticipate that some weight will be attached to his opinion upon the relative merits of local candidates for employment. . . ."[176] Buckingham dropped the argument and confirmed the appointment. Granville, too, annoyed Gordon on one occasion. In 1868 Buckingham offered Gordon the governorship of British Guiana, a considerable promotion.[177] With much business in hand in Trinidad, Gordon decided to refuse the offer, to Henry Taylor's great relief.[178] Before he refused he extracted a

[174]Gordon to Wood, 12 Feb. 1868 to 25 May 1868, Stanmore Papers, 49235.
[175]Gordon to Rate, 8 June 1867, Stanmore Papers, 49235.
[176]Gordon to Buckingham, 16 April 1868, PRO CO 295/243.
[177]British Guiana paid its governor £5,000 plus £2,000 for contingencies compared with Trinidad which paid only £3,500.
[178]Taylor wrote: "The change which I have been apprehending for Trinidad is one which w[oul]d have given me great concern." (Taylor to Gordon (private), 7 Oct. 1868, Stanmore Papers, 49199.)

promise from Buckingham that, as compensation, Tobago should be attached to Trinidad—a suggestion which, with Rogers' support, Gordon had put forward a year earlier. Buckingham left office without keeping his promise, and Granville, who succeeded him, reversed his decision. Gordon complained to Gladstone of this breach of faith but to no avail.[179]

Apart from these slights to his prestige, Gordon, normally a frequent critic of his superiors, found few causes for complaint. Nor did the Colonial Office often find reason to complain of him. When one or other of its members did so he was overborne by the others. Gordon's reputation advanced rapidly. Granville in 1869 offered him another promotion —the governorship of Mauritius. "If," Granville wrote, "the offer should be an agreeable one to you, it will be pleasant to me to think that I have made the best choice out of the number of candidates who have presented themselves, and not presented themselves, and that it is coupled in my mind with the memory of one [Lord Aberdeen] for whom I had cause to feel the greatest admiration and attachment."[180] There is further evidence of his esteem for Gordon. Gordon asked to remain in Trinidad temporarily because he was afraid that the important reforms which he was in the process of making would not be completed if he left at this stage. Granville then asked Sir Henry Barkly, the governor of Mauritius to stay on for six months beyond the expiry of his term, telling Gordon that if still in office then, he would probably renew the offer. Had it not been for Charles Warner, Gordon would have completed his governorship of Trinidad with an unblemished reputation in the Colonial Office.

Throughout Gordon's term Charles Warner openly and covertly opposed every departure from the old British ascendancy line of colonial policy.[181] Realizing that Warner acted largely from conscience, and wishing to make as much use as possible of his undoubted abilities, Gordon exhibited great patience. He went so far as to obtain Granville's permission for Warner to oppose the educational reforms in the legislative council. By the autumn of 1869, however, he saw an opportunity of retaining Warner's services and, at the same time, of restricting the scope of his opposition. He proposed to make him chief justice to fill the vacancy left by the recent death of Chief Justice Knox. This position would allow Warner, who would become an unofficial rather than an official member of the council, to vote as he liked. It would allow the Governor to have a new attorney-general upon whose official vote

[179]Gordon to Gladstone, 24 April 1869, Gladstone Papers, 44320.
[180]Granville to Gordon, 6 July 1869, Stanmore Papers, 49199.
[181]Gordon to Granville (confidential), 23 Oct. 1869, PRO CO 295/248.

he could rely and upon whose co-operation in preparing legislation he could depend. It might also preclude Warner, as the highest judiciary figure in the colony, from leading an opposition outside the council. Granville objected to " 'kicking people upstairs' in consequence of their bad qualities"[182] and refused to accept the suggestion.

Lord Granville once asked Taylor why Warner had been retained so long as attorney-general in view of his opposition. Taylor answered that "he is a man of considerable abilities & of more influence than any other person in the Is[lan]d & that he w[oul]d probably do more mischief out of office than in office."[183] Warner's own realization of this fact probably prompted him to submit his resignation about the end of November 1869. He had another, more powerful reason. His extravagance and consequent perennial financial difficulties had led him into conduct unbecoming to a barrister or to his special position as attorney-general. The scandal was about to break, and he must have known that he ran great risk of dismissal from office without pension.

By taking advantage of his powerful position in the colony, Warner had brought pressure upon the executors of an estate—both of whom were public servants—to lend him the principal of that estate. He agreed to pay interest to the two legatees, the illegitimate children of the deceased to whom Warner had been legal adviser. He also agreed to pay the son's share of the principal on the latter's coming of age and the daughter's share at her coming of age or on her marriage, whichever occurred first. The son received interest and, looking on the loan as an investment, made no protest when Warner failed to pay the principal. The daughter received no interest and, when she married, no principal. Warner even had the temerity to act as her adviser in the case which she attempted to bring against him and to charge his fee against the amount he owed her.[184] The daughter (Senora Adelaida Mijores) then petitioned the Crown for redress of grievances. At this point Warner submitted his offer of resignation alleging as his reason the differences between himself and the Governor on matters of policy. Convinced that Warner's true reason was his awareness that Adelaida Mijores' petition was about to be forwarded to the Secretary of State, Gordon replied that because Warner's support of government policies was not absolutely essential he did not think his resignation necessary "on the grounds stated." When Warner rejoiced that the Governor saw "no reason" for his resignation

[182]Granville to Gordon (private), 31 Dec. 1869, Stanmore Papers, 49199.
[183]Taylor to Rogers, Jan. 1869, filed with Gordon to Buckingham, 16 Nov. 1868, PRO CO 295/245.
[184]Gordon to Secretary of State, 9 Dec. 1869, with enclosures, PRO CO 295/248. See also Taylor's minute, 9 Jan. 1870, on this dispatch.

Gordon drew his attention to his words "on the grounds stated."[185] There the matter rested until late February 1870, when the Governor received Lord Granville's reply to Senora Mijores' petition.

Granville directed an inquiry not only into Warner's conduct in the Mijores affair but into Warner's "pecuniary position." Having regard for Warner's long public service and large family, Gordon delayed taking immediate action on this instruction since it probably would result in Warner's losing his pension. He consulted the Colonial Secretary and then sent for Warner. Admitting that he was going beyond the bounds of offici; l duty he told the Attorney-General that he wished to be in possession of his resignation before acquainting him with communications he had received from the Secretary of State. Warner inquired whether Gordon intended recommending him for a pension and, receiving an affirmative reply, wrote his resignation. Gordon then informed him of Granville's order and gave him an opportunity to withdraw his resignation. Warner refused and left with warm expressions of thanks for the consideration the Governor had shown him.[186] He repeated his thanks a few days later in a letter enclosing an "official" resignation.[187] In this letter Warner stated that since he could not admit it to be his duty to submit to the inquiry into his pecuniary position he had no alternative but to resign.[188] He was willing, however, to submit to an inquiry into the Mijores affair itself.[189]

Since Warner had shown himself willing to undergo this inquiry, had resigned before learning of Granville's order (though he must have guessed its nature), and had now paid Adelaida Mijores what he owed her, Gordon did not feel "compelled to carry further . . . the proceedings [respecting Warner's pecuniary position] which he had been directed to institute."[190] He recommended the former Attorney-General for the most liberal pension possible[191] and certified that he had discharged his duties with "diligence and fidelity"![192]

The Colonial Office took a dim view of Warner's misdeed and of the

[185]Gordon to Charles Warner, 8 Dec. 1869, Stanmore Papers, 49244, and Gordon to [Ebden], 17 Nov. 1870, PRO CO 295/254. Warner later denied that his offer of resignation was prompted by a desire to escape an inquiry. (Warner to Kimberley, 8 Oct. 1870, PRO CO 295/252.)

[186]Gordon to [Ebden], 17 Nov. 1870.

[187]Warner to Gordon, 17 March 1870, Stanmore Papers, 49235.

[188]Ibid.

[189]Gordon to Granville, 24 March 1870, enclosing Warner's resignation, PRO CO 295/250.

[190]Ibid.

[191]Ibid.

[192]Warner's application for pension, enclosed in Gordon to Granville, 24 March 1870.

Governor's action in recommending him for a pension. Its reply to Gordon's dispatch followed Taylor's minute which said that if Warner wished to avoid an inquiry he must tender an unconditional resignation in which case he would receive no pension. If he wished a pension he must submit to the inquiry.[193] The executive council then held the inquiry. It found Warner guilty of conduct unbecoming his professional character as a barrister and his special position as attorney-general. His conduct, it said, had tended to bring the administration of justice into contempt and to prejudice the reputation of the public service. It recommended that he be censured but not dismissed from office.[194] Taylor considered the executive council's recommendation far too lenient. He questioned whether Warner's conduct had been consistent with holding office under the Crown or retiring with a pension. He thought Gordon, who had conducted the inquiry until its final day and had meanwhile returned to England, ought to be asked for his written opinion.[195] Herbert agreed except for the last suggestion: "I hardly think [he wrote] that Gov[ernor] Gordon's judgment of character & conduct is generally correct enough to be of very great value in a case of this kind, and in this particular matter he has much astonished me by recommending Mr. Warner for a pension, 'on the most liberal scale possible' . . . at the very time when he was calling upon him to answer this disgraceful charge."[196] Herbert recommended Warner's final dismissal without pension. Kimberley, who replaced Granville as secretary of state in June 1870, was less severe. He found Warner's conduct "reprehensible" but granted him a pension of two-thirds that to which he would normally have been entitled.[197]

Had Warner now accepted his dismissal from office on a reduced pension with good grace, Gordon would have escaped much of the Colonial Office's distrust of his judgment which was to bedevil his administration of Mauritius. But Warner, who had real reason to show gratitude to Gordon, chose rather to blame him for his predicament. He wrote to Kimberley charging that Gordon had indirectly forced him to resign by telling him that Sir Henry Taylor disliked him and that the Colonial Office would lay hold of any handle to get rid of him. He could not accept a reduced pension without making himself party to what "is

[193]Taylor's minute on Gordon to Granville, 24 March 1870. Such unusual harshness by the Colonial Office reflected its tendency, after the Jamaica rebellion, to interfere in the internal affairs of Crown colonies.
[194]Longden to Kimberley, 8 July 1870, PRO CO 295/251.
[195]Taylor's minute, 2 Aug. 1870, ibid.
[196]Herbert's minute, 5 Aug. 1870, ibid.
[197]Kimberley's minute, 5 Aug. 1870, ibid.

intended as a stigma upon me." He did not accept the Secretary of State's view of his conduct, nor, he cautioned, "will it be accepted by the community."[198]

This letter drew some interesting minutes from the Colonial Office staff. Ebden wrote: "Mr. Gordon is not very guarded in his communication and his unguarded communications are unfortunate in coming to light."[199] Taylor defended Gordon: "Before coming to the conclusion that Mr. Gordon has been indiscreet, it may be well to enquire whether Mr. Warner's statement of what he said is correct. The result of the enquiry before the Council and otherwise was not such as to inspire confidence in the accuracy of his statements."[200] Herbert was disposed to believe Warner. "Previous experience of Mr. Gordon,"[201] he wrote, "renders it but too probable that what Mr. Warner says he said to him is (more or less) correctly quoted. I should be disposed to call upon him for an explanation without using any unnecessary terms of compliment."[202] Rogers and Kimberley agreed that Gordon should be asked for his remarks. Gordon admitted that he could not remember the "exact phraseology of long and familiar conversation" but, he continued, "Mr. Warner's memory gravely misleads him if he now thinks that his resignation was prompted by arguments or language on my part such as those to which he refers."[203]

Ebden considered Gordon's explanation "rather lame" and his memory not very distinct. "We know that he is rather incautious and it w[oul]d be singular that Mr. Warner should recollect it if Mr. Gordon did not say something like it."[204] The wise and experienced Taylor again rose to Gordon's defence:

> I can easily imagine Mr. Gordon to have said *something like* what Mr. Warner imputes. A word or two makes all the difference in such cases, & the context of a conversation may give a totally different complexion to one or two detailed sentences. Nor is it often possible for a scrupulous man to state positively what passed or did not pass in a conversation which took place many months ago. . . . As to the apparent inconsistencies in the course taken by Mr. Gordon I do not find it difficult to understand them on my

[198]Warner to Kimberley, 8 Oct. 1870, enclosed in Longden to Kimberley, 8 Oct. 1870, PRO CO 295/252.

[199]Ebden's minute, 4 Nov. 1870, *ibid.*

[200]Taylor's minute, 5 Nov. 1870, *ibid.*

[201]Herbert had been Gladstone's private secretary from 1855 to 1858. He had known Gordon then; but they had been out of contact from 1859 to 1868, the years Herbert spent in Australia. Herbert entered the Colonial Office only in 1870.

[202]Herbert's minute, 6 Nov. 1870, on Warner to Kimberley, 8 Oct. 1870.

[203]Gordon to [Ebden], 17 Nov. 1870.

[204]Ebden's minute, 22 Nov. 1870, *ibid.*

theory of Mr. Gordon's nature and character. He had lived in a friendly intimacy with Mr. Warner & at the same time Mr. Warner had done what he could to oppose some of his favorite measures. The conduct of Mr. Warner towards Adelaida Mijores might very well excite his indignation. The spectacle of a man of brilliant talents who had ruled supreme over the Colonial society for a long course of years falling into utter ruin & disgrace in the last stage of life, might very well excite his pity. The person so disgraced had been his opponent. Impulses of indignation, generosity & pity in a man of ardent temperament explain to me the inconsistencies in question [that is, how Gordon could condemn Warner's actions and at the same time recommend him for the most liberal pension possible].

Mr. Gordon has ability, industry, energy & public spirit in abundance. What he wants is dryness.[205]

Acting on Herbert's suggestion[206] Kimberley drew Gordon's attention to his own admission that he had gone "beyond the strict bounds of official duty" and to the fact that "Mr. Warner has no doubt availed himself in an unexpected and very unsatisfactory manner of the advantage which you, . . . too kindly, afforded him."[207] This, the Secretary of State felt, might be a lesson to Gordon to be careful in his private and personal relations with colonists, official or not. The tone of the letter was gentle. Kimberley had, he said, no thought of conveying censure but rather of making suggestions for the future guidance of "a gentleman whose services have been so distinguished and valuable."[208] Gordon, in reply, admitted that his course had been irregular, although he suggested that there had been extenuating circumstances and regretted that he had incurred Lord Kimberley's disapprobation. He agreed too, that a governor should exercise great caution in his relationship with those he governed.[209]

Prior to the unpleasantness arising out of the Mijores affair, Granville had renewed his offer to Gordon of the governorship of Mauritius. Gordon accepted with some reluctance. He feared that "the mortar is hardly dry, and that the house which I have built will fall if its props and scaffolding are suddenly removed."[210] He knew that he had done much in Trinidad but that much remained to be done. He knew also that in few other colonies might he expect to "reign again with the same absolute & unchecked power."[211] He had, however, twice refused promotion and thought he might not soon be offered another if he again refused.

[205]Taylor's minute, [22 or 23] Nov. 1870, ibid.
[206]Herbert's minute, 23 Nov. 1870, ibid.
[207]Kimberley to Gordon (confidential), 12 Dec. 1870, PRO CO 295/254.
[208]Ibid.
[209]Gordon to Kimberley (confidential), 14 Dec. 1870, PRO CO 295/254.
[210]Gordon to Palmer, 10 March 1870, Stanmore Papers, 49217.
[211]Gordon to Waterfield, 24 March 1870, Stanmore Papers, 49249.

Gordon left Trinidad reluctantly and most Trinidadians looked upon his departure regretfully. The new editor of the *Chronicle* observed that the retiring Governor

has made himself more felt than perhaps any single Governor we ever had since Picton and Woodford. . . . He has made his mark and left his stamp amongst us if ever a Governor did. By a large body,—larger we think in the progress of time, he will be remembered as one who did things of great and permanent good for the Colony;—by others and also a numerous body he will be looked back on as one who came hither only to subvert existing institutions. . . .[212]

In presenting its customary address on the departure of a governor, the legislative council expressed the desire of its members

to bear testimony to the ability and energy which you have displayed. . . . Your administration has been shorter than we had reason to expect, but will long be remembered for its fairness and impartiality, irrespective of creed and race, and the recognition of native claims to public employment. . . . Future generations will look back with gratitude to Your Excellency's administration, and your name will long be remembered by those who will owe to Your Excellency their prosperity and security.[213]

It went on to praise in fulsome terms each of the measures carried out under Gordon's direction.

Concerning this address, Sir Henry Taylor, who had been head of the West Indian department of the Colonial Office since 1825, wrote that it differed from most of its kind "in being true from beginning to end." He continued:

I think that Mr. Gordon has done more for Trinidad in the 4 years of his adm[inistratio]n than any of his Predecessors since 1824. He has been laborious & public spirited & singleminded, & having to encounter a good deal of opposition to some of his most important measures he has nevertheless succeeded in carrying along with him, at last, the great body of the Colonists including some of his more intelligent opponents, & I imagine that the unofficial members of Council in giving their support to this address may be taken to represent the sentiments of the educated Colonists generally.[214]

Robert Herbert agreed with Taylor's praise of Gordon's good qualities and felt that the Colonial Office should express to Gordon its satis-

[212]Editorial in *Trinidad Chronicle*, 24 June 1870. Wenkstern was no longer editor having died the previous year.

[213]Minutes of the proceedings of the legislative council of Trinidad, pp. 79–80, 21 June 1870, PRO CO 298/35.

[214]Taylor's minute, 15 July 1870, on farewell address presented to Gordon by the legislative council of Trinidad, transmitted in Gordon to Kimberley, 24 June 1870, PRO CO 295/250.

faction with the just and well-merited testimony to his services contained in the address. Nevertheless, he did not consider Gordon deserving of unmixed approval and added that he wished that Gordon's "judgment and discretion were at all times equal to his energy and ability."[215] Rogers agreed "in admiring Mr. Gordon's energy, ability & public spirit & also in admitting that he is sometimes over eager & excited about his work."[216]

With a successful, productive, and satisfying administration behind him, Arthur Gordon left Trinidad early in July 1870. He did not take up his new post immediately. His wife was expecting her second child and he remained in England until after her confinement. On 10 January 1871, a few days after the birth of his son,[217] he sailed for Mauritius with no presentiment that the next four years would be the unhappiest of his career.

[215]Herbert's minute, 15 July 1870, *ibid.*
[216]Rogers' minute, 15 July 1870, *ibid.*
[217]George Arthur Maurice; "Maurice" in honour of Gordon's appointment to Mauritius.

IV

MAURITIUS, 1870–1874

I. "MAUDITE MAURICE"

ARTHUR GORDON's new jurisdiction embraced the island of Mauritius and several other small dependencies of which the Seychelles archipelago was the largest. With an area of just under half a million acres, Mauritius, in 1871, had a population of 317,069. Sugar and its by-products accounted for the bulk of the exports. When Gordon arrived on 17 February 1871, neither he nor the Colonial Office knew much of the colony's importance or conditions.

In Britain the status of Mauritius as a colony of importance derived partly from Napoleonic days when, in French hands, it had been a thorn in the flesh of the Royal Navy, and partly from the years after its conquest when, as a diminutive British naval station, it occupied a strategic position on the route to India. Few appreciated the extent to which the Suez Canal had already reduced its naval and military value. Concerning the internal conditions of the colony, the Colonial Office knew that, as in Trinidad, the French Roman Catholics had suffered from discrimination. It knew that the island had recently experienced heavy losses from hurricanes and that it had become increasingly unhealthy because of an inadequate sanitary system and the presence of malaria. It was, however, unaware that malaria had become endemic and that the rapid cutting of the forests had reduced and polluted the supply of fresh water. It knew nothing of the wretchedness of the Indian population, free and indentured alike, nor the extent to which the governor's power had been curtailed during the previous twenty years.

There were several reasons for this surprising ignorance. The Colonial

Office had insufficient time and staff for its responsibilities. (It dealt with matters called to its attention but did not, at least until Robert Herbert became permanent under-secretary, seek information.) In Mauritius, as in the West Indies, it had followed a hands-off policy since the early forties, leaving matters to the men on the spot. The latter, namely, the governors and administrators, too frequently refused to make themselves unpopular with the colonists by intervening to correct abuses, and allowed events to take their natural course.[1] The Mauritians, however, shared responsibility for the grim conditions in the colony and the scarcity of information concerning them. One reliable observer[2] in 1872 remarked upon the "extraordinary" character of the Mauritian people and "their wonderful loyalty" to the island. "They resent as treason anything that disparages the Island or the Planting interest, and how double-dyed a traitor not only he is thought who exposes, but who would not conceal at every cost, all that might be reprehensible in any planter, until he has been fully exposed."[3]

Once Gordon had revealed to the Colonial Office the truly miserable conditions prevailing in the colony, Herbert, who had been made permanent under-secretary, concluded that "Mauritius has been allowed to drift during the last 20 years or so upon every rock & shoal which common prudence must have avoided; and having the most costly Government (perhaps) in the world, it has been the worst governed country, or not far from it."[4] Much of this misgovernment had resulted from a gradual weakening of the power of the Crown within the legislative council. Before 1849 the legislative council of Mauritius had contained seven officials bound to vote as the governor directed, and seven unofficials. The governor had two votes—a deliberative vote and, for emergencies, a casting vote. The first departure from this classical concept of Crown colony government came in 1849. Earl Grey, the father of responsible government in British North America, perhaps

[1]On more than one occasion in the course of his career Gordon charged the Colonial Office with preferring as governors men who did not draw attention to abuses. The Colonial Office, he felt, did not like to be reminded that all was not for the best in the best of all possible worlds.

[2]William Edward Frere (Sir Bartle Frere's brother), who, with Victor Williamson, composed the Royal Commission which inquired into the condition of Indian immigrants in Mauritius in 1872–73.

[3]Frere to Gordon, 6 Sept. 1872, printed in Stanmore (Arthur Hamilton Gordon), *Mauritius: Records of Private and of Public Life, 1871–1874*, I, 678. Future references to this collection of Gordon's Mauritius papers will be in abbreviated form, *Maur.*

[4]Herbert's minute, 7 Oct. 1872, on Gordon to Kimberley, 21 Aug. 1872, PRO CO 167/545.

wishing to effect a similar evolution in the Crown colonies, confided to Sir George Anderson, whom he had just appointed to Mauritius, that "a favorable influence" might be exercised over the conduct of affairs by adding to the council "two or more members unconnected with the extreme party in the Colony. . . ." He instructed Anderson to appoint to the council as many persons as he saw fit "during pleasure," and "to select them either from persons not holding office or from persons holding office."[5] In future, therefore, the legislative council could, and did, contain the seven officials, and an indeterminate number of two kinds of unofficials: office-holders, who might or might not vote for government measures, and private citizens. As succeeding governors received instructions similar to Anderson's, and as they were given no power to declare vacant the seats of members absent for prolonged periods, the number of unofficials in the council gradually increased until it reached thirteen.

Sir Henry Barkly had difficulty with his council on several occasions and, though "an able tactician,"[6] did not always succeed in having his measures passed. There are "many evidences" that instead of forcing a collision with the opposition, and thus a reform, he temporized with it.[7] Despite his difficulties he showed no interest in Buckingham's cautious proposal in 1868 for a revision of the constitution and advised "very strongly against leaving . . . any of the unofficial members" out of the list contained in Gordon's instructions.[8] His advice was accepted and although Gordon's instructions allowed him to declare a seat vacant if the member were absent for six months, they also contained a power "almost amounting to an order" to fill the places of absent unofficials with acting appointments.[9] Thus he occupied a position in relationship to his council little if any stronger than his predecessor.

If much of the evil condition of Mauritius could be attributed to the governor's lack of power, much could be laid to Barkly's contentment with it, his inactivity,[10] his penchant for seeing eye to eye with the

[5]Lord Grey to Anderson, 17 May 1849, quoted by Charles Cox, senior clerk of the Eastern Department, in his long and interesting minute paper (3 Feb. 1872), summarizing the history of the legislative council of Mauritius. (PRO CO 167/537, 223–470.) Herbert, in a marginal note on this minute paper, called Grey's instructions to Anderson "very unfortunate."

[6]Herbert's minute, 5 Feb. 1872, on Gordon to Kimberley, 14 Dec. 1871, PRO CO 167/537.

[7]Cox's minute paper, 3 Feb. 1872, ibid., and a marginal note by Herbert.

[8]Henry Holland's minute, 5 Feb. 1872, ibid.

[9]Herbert's minute, 16 Jan. 1872, ibid.

[10]Herbert wrote that "it would be an endless matter to follow up all his sins of omission in Mauritius." (Herbert's minute, 12 Feb. 1874, on Gordon to Kimberley, 9 Jan. 1874, PRO CO 167/559.)

planters,[11] his desire to make life easy for himself,[12] and his unwillingness to prejudice the popularity he and Lady Barkly enjoyed in Mauritian society.[13] It is true that Sir Henry governed Mauritius during a period of natural disaster—hurricanes, droughts, and crop failures—but surely this was the time for vigorous leadership, not weakness and complacency.

In contrast to Barkly, Gordon immediately began to chafe at the curbs on his power imposed by the unofficial majority in the council, but he spent a year convincing the Colonial Office that change was imperative. As late as January 1872, Kimberley was still writing that "It does not follow . . . that because in petty W[est] Indian communities, where there are hardly whites except a few Estate Agents, it is expedient to place the whole power in the hands of the Govt., such a system would work well in Mauritius where there are I believe a considerable number of white Creoles holding a respectable position, & jealous of Government interference."[14] He did not think Mauritians easy people to deal with but suggested that much caution be employed in making constitutional changes whereby the executive would have greater authority.[15] He would do nothing until after he had read a history of the Mauritian constitution prepared by Charles Cox early in February 1872. Even then, though one of the assistant under-secretaries, Robert Meade, held that "we should endeavour eventually to make Mauritius completely a Crown Colony,"[16] and Herbert believed that Mauritian remonstrances ought to be "boldly faced" when "the power weakly given them is taken back,"[17] Kimberley failed to take drastic steps. Instead, he informed Gordon that he should simply fail to fill vacancies in the council until the number of unofficials equalled the number of officials—a slow process. To carry important

[11]Barkly had been a West Indian plantation owner himself and, perhaps not unnaturally, got into the habit of "hob-nobbing" with the planters in Mauritius and of doing "much to acquire . . . popularity of which they . . . were the dispensers. . . . " (Petition of the Old Immigrants of Mauritius presented on the 6th of June 1871, with observations by Adolphe de Plevitz, 25.)

[12]Gordon's diary, 2 May 1871, Maur., I, 72.

[13]Lady Gordon to her sister Jane Ryan, 28 Oct. to 16 Nov. 1871, Maur., I, 297.

[14]Kimberley's minute, 18 Jan. 1872, on Gordon's dispatch, 14 Dec. 1871. Although Kimberley, in the course of two tenures of office as secretary of state for the colonies, eventually came to understand that coloured populations in the colonies suffered through being left to the less than tender mercies of white settlers he could not bring himself to interfere drastically with what he considered the God-given right of whites to be masters wherever they numbered an appreciable minority of the population. Occasionally he "talked big" but his actions fell far short of what was necessary.

[15]Ibid.   [16]Meade's minute, 16 Jan. 1872, ibid.

[17]Herbert's minute, 5 Feb. 1872, on Cox's minute paper, 3 Feb. 1872.

measures in the meantime, the Governor might appoint office-holders as unofficial members of the council in order to "swamp" the regular unofficials. This "unusual power" should, however, be used only "under a strong sense of its necessity."[18] Gordon might have been more successful in persuading the Colonial Office of the true condition of Mauritius and the desirability of giving the governor greater power had some of the staff not suspected his judgment as a result of the Warner-Mijores controversy and also because of the pressure which he exerted during his first months in Mauritius to be relieved of his post.

In contrast to his initial impression of New Brunswick and Trinidad, Mauritius struck Gordon unfavourably. Its "bourgeois—et très bourgeois" society[19] repelled him. Some twenty years later Sir Arthur wrote this unflattering commentary on the Mauritian society of his day:

There is nothing so offensive as a French bagman, and most of the existing planters were more or less of the Bagman class. The French families settled in the island were for the most part of later importation and of a lower class than those in Trinidad, but such as they were they had in great measure disappeared and been replaced by their own overseers and managers. The moral condition of the Colony was worse than that of Trinidad, which is saying a good deal. Excepting those who had been brought up in the convents, or at home, under the strictest old-fashioned French surveillance, most of the young ladies had encountered adventures more or less scandalous; while of the married women we will only hope that the gossip which left few reputations untouched was even more malicious and contained an even smaller substratum of truth than that of other places. The tone of the men was . . . even lower. . . . Too generally the planters had mistresses, usually half-castes, while the overseers and managers almost invariably lived with Indian women; and I was assured that the provision of pretty coolie girls was almost a recognised form of hospitality on a plantation when the visitors were young men. The traditions of the time of slavery . . . were retained all the more vividly owing to the fact that comparatively few of the Creoles had left the island, and had consequently a most exaggerated idea of its importance and their own. . . .[20]

Nor was Gordon greatly impressed by the calibre of his officers.

[18]Kimberley to Gordon (confidential), 14 Feb. 1872, PRO CO 167/537. The disadvantage of appointing office-holders as unofficial members of the council was that, while they would feel compelled to vote with the government on the occasion of their appointment, there was no way of ensuring their continued loyalty. Most were closely connected with the planters—indeed many owned or held shares in plantations—and were thus insufficiently disinterested to be able to take a broad view of questions. Others feared unpopularity if they voted contrary to the interests of the plantocracy. It was true that office-holders were appointed "during pleasure," but it would have been invidious to appoint a man simply to give the government an extra vote on a single occasion.

[19]Maur., I, 124.

[20]Ibid.

Edward Newton (the colonial secretary) though "a gentleman, cultivated and agreeable," firmly believed that planters were perfect. For several years he had exercised an authority nearly as great as that of Charles Warner in Trinidad[21] and had promoted similar policies. B. G. Colin, the procureur-general (attorney-general), needed to be held by a "tight rein," but he was a clever, essentially honest man "out of whom one may get good work—more than any of his colleagues."[22] Ward, the auditor-general, possessed "the instincts of a gentleman, and once had some ability, but drink and debauchery [had] addled his brains and destroyed his body."[23] Kerr, the treasurer, was an "honest, thoroughly well-meaning man . . . in no way distinguished as to capacity or knowledge."[24] General Smyth, the officer commanding the troops, who had administered the government after Barkly's departure, Gordon found "a sensible though not specially clever English gentleman; thoroughly honourable and loyal, with some sense of humour, and quite safe, reticent, and reliable."[25] Chief Justice Shand was "very inferior" to Chief Justice Knox of Trinidad. The senior puisne judge, "an old Creole idiot," had been on the supreme court since 1832. John Gorrie, the third judge, was clever but "rough and vulgar in manner . . . and not a man to inspire confidence."[26] The magistrates, with one or two exceptions, had come under the control of the planters. The minor civil servants were characterized by their "extreme feebleness," and "jobbery and nepotism were all but universal."[27] These might be considered as opinions too hastily conceived by a disillusioned man, but they were borne out in all essential respects by subsequent events and the findings of the Royal Commission which sat in Mauritius in 1872–73.

Governors usually expected uncongenial societies and weak civil services. Gordon was no exception. For relief from the cares and difficulties of office he looked to the company of his wife and children who planned to follow him within a few weeks. Possessed of a sense of family over-developed even for the nineteenth century, his disappointment knew no bounds when he realized that he ought to forbid their

[21]Gordon's diary, 23 Feb. 1871, *Maur.*, I, 30; and Gordon to Lord Richard Cavendish, 11 Nov. 1872, *Maur.*, II, 34.

[22]Gordon's diary, 23 Feb. 1871, *Maur.*, I, 30f.

[23]*Ibid.*   [24]*Ibid.*   [25]*Ibid.*

[26] Extract from letter to Lord Richard Cavendish, June 1871, *Maur.*, I, 124f. Gordon eventually revised his opinion of Gorrie and had him transferred to Fiji as chief justice.

[27]*Maur.*, I, 124–25. This judgment is confirmed by Sir George Bowen (governor of Mauritius 1879–82) who wrote that "paltry patronage is in Mauritius the most mischievous form of corruption." Quoted by P. J. Barnwell, *Visits and Despatches (Mauritius 1598–1948)*, 269.

coming. Both the chief medical officer and General Smyth, who had forbidden his own family to come to the island, advised him that he would endanger his wife's health and probably lose one if not both of his children if he allowed them to come. A month after his arrival Sir Arthur wrote privately to Kimberley with "some embarrassment and much vexation" to ask for another post because he could not undertake to separate himself from his wife and young children. Although willing that his family should face "*uncertain* risks" he could not expose them to "definite danger."[28] He telegraphed[29] to his wife ordering her to stay in England and wrote explaining the situation. He asked that she work "to bring interest to bear" to have him appointed to the under-secretaryship about to fall vacant at the Colonial Office or, failing that, to have him re-appointed to Trinidad. He could hardly bear to think of the children, he concluded. "Nevil will utterly forget me. George, (I shall never call him Maurice now), will be a great child before I know him."[30] Gordon himself attempted to bring interest to bear by enlisting the support of Gladstone[31] and Bishop Wilberforce.[32] To both he expressed his desire for the assistant secretaryship at the Colonial Office in which he considered he could be useful "for no one there has much knowledge of Crown Colonies."[33]

In mid-April Gordon received two pieces of news: first that he had been made a K.C.M.G.—an honour he had refused in 1868—and secondly that his family were on their way, by the troopship *Tamar*, via the Cape. He had known for a week or two that his telegram had not been in time to prevent their sailing. True, they would arrive at the end of the unhealthy season, but he still had great misgivings. "If I could stop them I would, but as I cannot I must . . . make Rachel think I think she has done right in coming . . . [but] their coming . . . will not remove or diminish the absolute necessity for soon giving up the post."[34] His friends at home did not seem to understand the danger. They assumed that with his family joining him he would be content to stay. Herbert, Sir John Shaw-Lefevre, and Sir Henry Taylor, all wrote in this vein. Taylor, with unconscious irony, concluded his letter by wishing Sir Arthur and Lady Gordon as much happiness in Mauritius as Paul and

[28]Gordon to Kimberley (private), 8 March 1871, *Maur.*, I, 42f.

[29]Telegrams from Mauritius had to be mailed as far as Aden.

[30]Gordon to his wife, 8 March 1871, *Maur.*, I, 41. Gordon later decided to nickname his son "Jack."

[31]Gordon to Gladstone, 8 March 1871, Gladstone Papers, 44320.

[32] Gordon to Wilberforce, 9 March 1871, Stanmore Papers, 49214.

[33]*Ibid.*

[34]Gordon's diary, 15 May 1871, *Maur.*, I, 81.

Virginia.[35] Gordon again pressed Kimberley and Gladstone that he might be sent back to Trinidad. "If I go back there & finish all I began I shall be able to do some good in my generation, & shall not have lived wholly in vain."[36] So convinced was he of the decline of Mauritius that he suggested to the Secretary of State and to the Prime Minister that Mauritius be exchanged with the French for Chandernagore.[37]

Gordon's importunities understandably annoyed Kimberley. The intercession on the Governor's behalf of Taylor and Herbert, and intervention by Gladstone, Sir Roundell Palmer, and probably one or two other members of the cabinet doubtless did little to improve his frame of mind. To Gladstone he wrote: "I have no prejudice against Sir A. Gordon but I am bound to say he is not going the way to raise my opinion of him. He writes to me very discontented, *wailing* letters, & seems to forget that there is always good work for a man to do who will perform his duty whatever & wherever it may be."[38] Kimberley told Palmer that private convenience had to give way to the interests of the public service,[39] and he informed Gordon that "credit is to be obtained where there are difficulties to overcome, not where all is smooth sailing. . . ."[40] Palmer supported Kimberley's stand and although sympathizing with Gordon nevertheless suggested to him that he stiffen his spine.[41]

Acting on the advice of his father-in-law, who had talked with Gladstone, Gordon decided to apply for leave on grounds of health— he had suffered badly from hay fever[42] ever since his arrival—and return to England to plead his case in person. Should he not be given leave he would resign. Much to his surprise, the Colonial Office, believing that there was little point in keeping him there if he was not up to his work, granted his application.[43] Meanwhile Gordon spent a few weeks in the Seychelles where his health improved so dramatically that he asked that

[35]Taylor to Gordon, 15 May 1871, *Maur.*, I, 154.

[36]Gordon to Gladstone, 2 June 1871, Gladstone Papers, 44320.

[37]*Ibid.* At first he suggested Pondicherry but on second thought felt the French would consider it too valuable to be exchanged for so miserable a possession as Mauritius.

[38]Kimberley to Gladstone (private), 6 June 1871, Gladstone Papers, 44224.

[39]Kimberley to Palmer (private), 3 July 1871, copy enclosed in Palmer to Gordon, 18 Aug. 1871, *Maur.*, I, 276.

[40]Kimberley to Gordon (private), 6 July 1871, Stanmore Papers, 49199.

[41]Palmer to Gordon, 11 Aug. 1871, *Maur.*, I, 275–77.

[42]Gordon's hay fever was at times so bad that it amounted almost to a serious illness, depriving him of his "strength and spirits," and making his eyes so weak he could scarcely see. (Lady Gordon to her mother, 15 Feb. 1872, *Maur.*, I, 435.)

[43]Minutes on Gordon to Kimberley (separate), 22 Sept. 1871, PRO CO 167/535.

his leave be deferred for a year. Kimberley gladly received the news that he had made up his mind to stay and apply himself energetically to making the best of the situation in Mauritius.

Throughout this exchange the Secretary of State treated Gordon with tact and forbearance. It is difficult not to sympathize with his annoyance at Gordon's importunities and the intervention of the latter's friends. Moreover, colonies did not profit by frequent changes of their governors, as Gordon himself more than once asserted, and it would be difficult to find another post in keeping with Sir Arthur's talents. Yet, if Kimberley's belief that Gordon deliberately darkened his picture of Mauritius is understandable, so, too, are the Governor's fears for his family's health and his conviction that the Colonial Office rather than promoting had inadvertently demoted him.

TABLE II*

Year	Births	Deaths
1861	7,857	6,814
1862	10,837	13,719
1863	11,169	11,666
1864	11,499	11,649
1865	12,118	12,042
1866	12,134	11,702
1867	10,568	40,114
1868	9,436	18,403
1869	9,977	11,295
1870	11,157	7,426
1871	11,803	8,171

*Gordon to Kimberley, 21 Aug. 1872, PRO CO 167/545.

The danger of living in Mauritius was real as the vital statistics in Table II indicate. When he received these figures Kimberley minuted: "It is curious after Sir. A. Gordon's jeremiads about the insalubrity of Mauritius to observe that the death rate in 1870 & 1871 was lower than in any years since 1861."[44] The statistics, however, took no account of a vast number of non-fatal illnesses. Furthermore the lower death rate in 1870 and 1871 resulted largely from the great malaria epidemic which had already carried off the weaklings in 1867 and 1868,[45] but, in part too, from the now general use of quinine by the creole and European

[44]Kimberley's minute, 1 Oct. 1872, on Gordon to Kimberley, 21 Aug. 1872, PRO CO 167/545.
[45]During the first six months of 1867 nearly 26,000 deaths occurred in Mauritius, some 14,000 out of a population of 80,000 in Port Louis. The high death rate resulted from a shortage of quinine. Government institutions had none to spare and private stocks sold for £27 per ounce at public auction.

population. Indians of course could not afford quinine and, despite a general increase of 100 per cent in its consumption in 1872 over 1871, deaths from malaria again increased. In 1873, more than 11,000 people died,[46] and in Port Louis the percentage of deaths from malaria rose from 50 in 1871 to 64.[47] Significantly also, life insurance rates, which had increased by 21 per cent between 1867 and 1869, did not fall with the falling mortality rate of 1870 and 1871.

Most of the chief officials lived in the hills near Réduit—one of the healthiest regions of the colony—but even they suffered badly. By June 1871, of those who had held high office eighteen months earlier, the general (Smyth's predecessor), the procureur-general, the Anglican bishop and his successor, the Roman Catholic bishop, were dead. The treasurer, "paralysed and helpless" from malaria, was about to be sent home to England. The auditor-general, "with a constitution utterly shattered," was to go in October. The collector of internal revenues and the officer of the civil status had resigned "with health wholly ruined." The collector of customs, wretchedly ill, subsisted "on blue pill and quinine." The colonial secretary had frequent attacks of fever and had lost both his wife and only child within a year.[48] In all, between 1867 and 1871, 310 civil servants died and 53 had been compelled to retire through ill-health.[49]

Gordon's opinion that Mauritius had become a less important colony than Trinidad was equally justifiable. Largely undeveloped, the latter offered possibilities for a flourishing economy based upon a variety of industries. By contrast, almost all of Mauritius was devoted to sugar cane; the soil was showing serious signs of depletion; and what little forest remained was being rapidly cleared for new sugar plantations to replace worn-out ones. Furthermore the colony was losing its importance as a naval base and port-of-call, and was a million pounds in debt— *per capita* about three and a half times as much as Trinidad. General Smyth, after more than a year in the island, agreed with Gordon that it was unlikely to become prosperous or healthful again.[50]

Whatever the justification of Gordon's case or Kimberley's suspicion, the mutual respect and confidence between Colonial Office and governor,

[46]Gordon to Kimberley, 9 Jan. 1874, *Maur.*, I, 383f.

[47]Newton to Kimberley, 4 April 1873, PRO CO 167/552; and Newton to Kimberley, 29 May 1873, enclosing reports of chief medical officer, PRO CO 167/553.

[48]Gordon to Palmer, 29 June 1871, *Maur.*, I, 143.

[49]Memorial of the members of the civil service of Mauritius, enclosed in Newton to Kimberley, 16 Oct. 1873, PRO CO 167/555.

[50]Smyth to Kimberley, 18 Sept. 1871, PRO CO 167/535.

necessary for satisfactory colonial government, disintegrated. For a time the Colonial Office was unconvinced that some reforms suggested by Gordon were urgent. On his part, Gordon came to believe that Kimberley disliked him and deliberately passed him over for promotion in favour of men less capable and deserving than himself.[51] Despite his lack of confidence in the Secretary of State, his ill-health, his hatred of the island, and his hopes of soon leaving it, Gordon nevertheless energetically began to set Mauritius to rights. Within three months he saw his task clearly and planned his action. "There is an Augean stable to cleanse," he wrote, "and reforms wanted which it will be difficult to touch without raising a storm. . . . However, some things should be done which will not be unpopular, and if I begin with them, they may help me to success in more difficult work."[52]

Gordon felt that he might safely grant to the Seychelles a degree of independence from Mauritius, give greater recognition to the French language, customs, and people in Mauritius, divide government aid more fairly between the Roman Catholic church and the Church of England, and pass legislation to protect the water supply and to conserve and add to forest lands. His more difficult and unpopular tasks would be to improve sanitary arrangements, reduce establishment costs, and revise the laws governing Indians.[53] Sir Henry Barkly had ignored almost all of these increasingly urgent reforms. He had been content to reign as a constitutional monarch and to allow the Colonial Office to believe that harmony and justice prevailed. In Barkly's place there was now a man eager to rule and to force his superiors to recognize the injustices and cleavages in colonial society, a man who astonished the inhabitants by the determined way in which he set to work.

II. THE SEYCHELLES DEPENDENCY

Although almost all of Gordon's problems in Mauritius had greater importance than that of reforming the Seychelles dependency, most

[51]There are many evidences of Gordon's belief that Kimberley disliked him and discriminated against him, and some evidence that his belief was correct. On one occasion Kimberley offered Gordon South Australia which it is difficult to consider a promotion. He refused him Jamaica when Sir John Grant retired in 1873. Lady Gordon, who spent most of this period in England in close contact with Liberal politicians, firmly belived that "anything will be better for us than Lord Kimberley." (Lady Gordon to Gordon, 2 Feb. 1874, *Maur.*, II, 474f.) I do not think, however, that Kimberley was ever deliberately or consciously unkind to Gordon.

[52]Gordon's diary, 23 May 1871, *Maur.*, I, 84f.

[53]*Ibid.*

required much investigation before he could tackle them. Moreover, they would severely tax both his energies and his power, so that he needed good health and some assurance of Colonial Office support before undertaking them. As yet he had neither. Attracted to the Seychelles because its problems would be relatively simple to solve and because its healthfulness would offer relief from the enervating atmosphere of Mauritius, Sir Arthur sailed for Port Victoria in August 1871.

The Seychelles, which one observer likened to "Loch Lomond, the Bay of Naples, and Tahiti all thrown into one,"[54] consisted of nine islands and a number of islets, some 50,000 acres in all, with a hot but pleasant climate. "All is so quiet and so luxuriant," Gordon exclaimed. "Everything grows as if it felt pleasure in growing."[55] The more he saw of the islands, the more they captivated him. Tropical fruits, spices, and vegetables grew in abundance, but, except for the coco-nut, sugar cane, coffee, cacao, and vanilla, little attempt was made to cultivate the land. Coco-nut oil was the major export, but coffee and cacao were becoming more important.

The population (11,037 in 1871) comprised a handful of European planters (mostly French), a hundred or more planters of mixed blood, and some nine to ten thousand labourers, nearly all negroes, either Africans captured from the Arab slave dhows or descendants of the slaves of the French. The Africans served five-year indentures to the planters and then customarily squatted on Crown land. This practice had the usual results: a shortage of labour and spoliation of the natural resources. Concerned only with labour, the planters demanded that they again be free to import Africans captured from Arab slavers.[56] Should this be done, roads, hospitals, and schools already required for a rapidly growing population[57] would become even more essential. The growing importance of the Seychelles as a port-of-call after the opening of Suez necessitated building a mile-long pier across the lagoon at Port Victoria.

These projects required money and energy. Captain W. H. Franklyn,[58] the civil commissioner or administrator, had made some progress on them by using prison labour, but lack of legislative authority and money sadly frustrated local efforts. A thousand miles of ocean precluded Mauritius taking much interest in its dependency and such as it did take

[54]A. E. Havelock to Gordon, 14 Feb. 1874, *Maur.*, II, 485.
[55]Gordon's diary, 5 Sept. 1871, *Maur.*, I, 216.
[56]Importation of Africans had been suspended in the late sixties.
[57]An increase of 50 per cent had taken place during the previous decade.
[58]Formerly captain of a merchantman and a magistrate at Vancouver Island. So enormously fat that he had to be carried, he was, nevertheless, an energetic and conscientious administrator.

seemed to be directed to spending in Mauritius the revenues collected on behalf of the Seychelles. Gordon, passing through Port Victoria on his way to Mauritius, perceived that the dependency would make little progress unless, in some degree, severed from the Mauritian government. His first official visit confirmed this impression, and he consequently proposed to create a small council to which he would give power to impose taxation and make by-laws, subject to confirmation by the governor of Mauritius. He would give it authority also to vote annual estimates and accounts of revenues and expenditures, subject to audit in Mauritius. In brief, he decided to give the Seychelles what Earl Grey had suggested over twenty years earlier: a municipal government.[59] General control of legislation and policy would rest with the governor and legislature of Mauritius.

The Secretary of State sanctioned the proposal. It could be implemented in three ways: by order-in-council, by issuing a new commission and set of instructions to the governor, or by ordinance of the legislature of Mauritius. The Colonial Office chose the last, and from its point of view, the simplest. Gordon concluded from his experience of the council in Mauritius that, however carefully he might frame the ordinance, the council would suggest foolish and objectionable modifications which he would be powerless to resist. Hence he asked that his plan be implemented by order-in-council, and the Colonial Office, although it thought Sir Arthur unnecessarily afraid of his council, honoured his request. On his birthday in 1872 Gordon inaugurated the new constitution and appointed a council or "board of civil commissioners." The latter consisted of Franklyn (as chief civil commissioner, the sole executive authority), A. Esnouf, the district judge, and J. H. Brooks, the government medical officer, as the official members, and three planters as the unofficials. Esnouf and Brooks held their seats as individuals not by virtue of their offices.

The first sessions of the board, at which Gordon himself presided late in 1872, produced several useful ordinances. These provided for a public hospital, assistance to education, forest conservation, a loan to improve the water supply of the capital, division of the islands into wards to facilitate collecting rates and taxes, arbitration of disputes arising from the expropriation of land for public roads, and, finally, medical treatment for indentured Africans and government inspection of the estates upon which the Africans worked.[60] Gordon believed the experience that the board thus gained would enable it to function satisfactorily without him,

[59]Gordon to Kimberley, 16 Oct. 1871, PRO CO 167/536.
[60]Gordon to Kimberley, 17 Dec. 1872, 15 Jan. 1873, *Maur.*, II, 63, 98.

but he underestimated the part played by his own personality and position. Within two months after his second official visit the board had reached a deadlock. Brooks and Esnouf misunderstood their functions as civil commissioners. At least, they professed to regard themselves co-equal with Franklyn in his executive capacity and considered that they should personally approve legislation before being asked to vote for it. They combined with the unofficials to prevent measures which they believed inimical to their personal interests.

Brooks was particularly unco-operative. The most energetic man in the islands, he thought that a public hospital would curtail his private practice, and that Gordon's and Franklyn's policy of encouraging traders to settle in the islands would encroach upon the trading monopoly he had built up.[61] Esnouf, a gentleman "as gentlemen go in Mauritius,"[62] had no love for the Seychelles. Prompted by a desire to leave the Seychelles as quickly as possible, and perhaps also by a wish to fulfil the Mauritian prophecy that the dependency would founder if the guiding hand of the parent colony were removed, he struck a blow at the revenue by reducing to nominal sums the fines that he imposed. Sir Arthur realized that Esnouf and Brooks were not suitable official members, but they were the best-educated men in the islands and he could find no one better qualified. Franklyn lacked the personality to control them, but his death in April 1874 gave Gordon the chance to appoint Captain A. E. Havelock,[63] a very able administrator, as chief civil commissioner. Thereafter progress resumed and the board passed two important postponed measures: one to establish a bank, the other to suppress squatting. The former took effect in 1874 during Gordon's last visit, but the latter was only beginning to take effect at that time.

Having established the legislature in 1872, Gordon went on with his other plans for the Seychelles. He improved the administration of justice and reduced its cost by making it possible to try at Port Victoria, instead of Mauritius, all criminal cases except capital offences, and all civil cases to a value of £50. He obtained the sanction of the Colonial Office for a number of increases in the establishment, most significantly the appointment of George Barrow[64] as collector of revenues and secretary to

[61]Brooks wanted to make enough money to retire as soon as possible. He had, however, a "charming Greek wife for whose sake much [was] forgiven him." (Gordon's diary, Sept. 1873, *Maur.*, II, 324.)

[62]*Ibid.*

[63]Later Sir Arthur Havelock, eventually a governor and Gordon's successor in Ceylon.

[64]Barrow was one of the few journalists in Mauritius who had supported Gordon's policies.

the chief civil commissioner, and of Dr. William MacGregor[65] as second government medical officer, justice of the peace, inspector of schools, officer of the civil status, and inspector of Africans. He granted, and won Colonial Office approval for, the petition of the planters to resume importing Africans captured from Arab slave traders. He accompanied this by regulations to ensure better treatment of African plantation labourers and better care for those who were too old or ill to work.

In 1872, H. M. Stanley charged in England that Africans were being taken to Mauritius and the Seychelles to be sold as slaves. However, no Africans had arrived in Mauritius for five years, and those who had come earlier had served their indentures and by 1872 enjoyed unrestricted freedom. Gordon indignantly rejected the accusation as it applied to the Seychelles. The planters, he noted, paid a fee for each indentured African to defray the government's expense in caring for them on landing. True, the fee, by exceeding this expense, produced a slight government profit, but this was unintentional. The planters paid wages, and the Africans had recourse to the law. He thought planters on the whole faithfully observed the regulations, but he would be better able to tell after Dr. MacGregor carried out his first inspections.[66]

MacGregor's visits to the plantations proved that Stanley's charges contained more than a little truth. "The stories of short payment in some cases, and of deficiency in food in others," wrote George Barrow, "are enough to make one blush for civilised humanity. . . ."[67] Later he added "the only difference between slavery at Seychelles and slavery at Zanzibar . . . is that at Seychelles the price of the commodity is lower, and the time it lasts of shorter duration."[68] Much as Gordon liked the Seychelles, he sadly conceded that "the feelings and traditions of slavery still subsist among the colonists. . . ."[69] In describing the condition of the Africans to his wife, he wrote:

Of course . . . [it] is better than it would have been had their voyage been continued, and they had been sold at Zanzibar or in the Persian Gulf or Arabia. But I think the benefit they derive from our intervention is only such as to call for very moderate thankfulness on their part. They are as much separated from their homes and families as if they had continued their voyage. . . . They are hired out to planters, to work for five years, which, no doubt, they regard as slavery, though as they receive wages, and are at the

[65]MacGregor (later Sir William) became one of Gordon's most valuable assistants in Fiji and afterwards was governor of New Guinea, Lagos, Newfoundland, and Queensland.

[66]Gordon to Kimberley, 16 Jan. 1872, *Maur.*, II, 106–8.

[67]Barrow to Gordon, 20 Aug. 1873, *Maur.*, II, 261.

[68]Barrow to Gordon, 2 May 1874, *Maur.*, II, 593.

[69]Gordon's diary, [Nov. 1873], *Maur.*, II, 323.

end of five years free men, it is not so really. . . . [But] they must live the rest of their lives among a people whose ways, thoughts, and habits are wholly strange to them. On the other hand, they escape murder and violent ill usage. . . . Their condition, I should say, was better than that of the average slave—decidedly so—but not equal to that of domestic slaves of a superior class under a kind master.[70]

After MacGregor began his rigorous inspections the government prosecuted planters for failure to observe the regulations, and it refused further allotments to those found guilty of mistreating their labourers. Even membership in the board of civil commissioners did not exempt planters from punishment, as one of the unofficial members (leMarchant) learned. Thereafter, the condition of the Africans improved. Nevertheless, a sharp watch had to be maintained because experience was accumulating to show that, where a colony employed indentured labour, planters evaded or subverted the regulatory laws unless checked by an efficient system of government inspection. The traditions of slavery died hard in Seychelles as they did in Mauritius.

The introduction of six or seven hundred Africans a year led Gordon to consider the education of their children. They should not, he felt, be allowed to grow up in ignorance. He approached the Roman Catholic nuns, whom he found willing to educate the girls at small cost to the government. He instructed the Chief Civil Commissioner to work out a plan for educating the boys, but Franklyn died before he had done much work on the plan. Havelock had not had time to do much when Gordon paid his last visit to the dependency. In his final public appearance Sir Arthur warned the Seychellois that unless they soon made better provision for the education of African children they could scarcely expect to receive more immigrants.

The educational problem in the Seychelles was not confined to Africans. The dependency had no government schools, and such denominational schools as it did have were starved for money and consequently were bad. Gordon offered government aid to any denominational school adopting a conscience clause. The Roman Catholics accepted his offer. The Anglican Bishop of Mauritius rejected it because he believed the Roman Catholic population to be a legitimate field for Anglican missionary activity. He also asserted that Church of England schools in the Seychelles were mission schools (though they received but £32 a year from the Society for the Propagation of the Gospel) and thus eligible for government aid without adhering to a conscience clause. He clung to this position despite his shock at discovering, during a visit, how really

[70]Gordon to Lady Gordon [July or Aug. 1874], *Maur.*, II, 678.

bad the Anglican schools were. Consequently in 1874 (the year when government aid to education began) the Roman Catholic schools, but not the Anglican, received grants.

Sir Arthur left the Seychelles for the last time late in August 1874, with the satisfaction of having at least conferred "positive benefits . . . on . . . a small community."[71] He had placed the islands on the constitutional path to colonial status which fostered in their inhabitants a feeling of self-reliance and control over their own destinies. He had protected the weak, provided better social services, and improved the administration of justice. Finally, he had taken steps to conserve the natural resources of the islands and to encourage the growth of trade and agriculture. The Seychellois had good reason to regret the departure of the first governor who took any interest in them. Gordon unquestionably devoted more time to the dependency than its size, population, or importance warranted; but all but one of his visits took place during the course of journeys to and from England. Moreover, the improvement in his physical and mental well-being resulting from his sojourns there induced him to defer his resignation as governor of Mauritius. He was thus able to initiate important reforms which otherwise might have been long delayed.

III. INDIAN IMMIGRANTS

One of Sir Arthur Gordon's major contributions to Mauritius lay in his vast improvement of the condition of its Indian population. This reform occupied so much of his time and made him so unpopular among the planters and the merchants that several other important projects remained uncompleted when he resigned. So dreadful and disgraceful were the conditions of the Indians, free and indentured alike, that had Sir Arthur done nothing more in Mauritius than draw the attention of the Colonial Office to them, his governorship would have been worthwhile.

Very early in his administration Gordon realized that the colony's labour system had many defects. Because, however, to his amazement, the protector of immigrants no longer inspected the estates, Gordon could not obtain reliable information. Indeed, he found it extremely difficult to obtain any information whatever, because public opinion exerted "a moral [and] to some extent even a physical terrorism" over the local officials which made them reluctant to provide it.[72] In April

[71]Gordon to Selborne, 15 Jan. 1873, *Maur.*, II, 109.
[72]Murdoch to Herbert, 10 Jan. 1872, PRO CO 167/548.

Government House, Port-of-Spain, Trinidad, 1866

Sir Arthur and Lady Gordon, 1875

Le Réduit, the Governor's Residence, Mauritius

1871, Sir Arthur began to make some inquiries of his own into conditions on the estates and discovered that the magistrates had not uncovered even the planters' grosser abuses of their indentured labourers. Early in June he received a petition from the "old immigrants" (those Indians who had completed their indentures) asking that he remove their grievances. He decided to refer this petition to the "police inquiry commission," which he had determined to establish in consequence of Judge Gorrie's allegation that the police habitually arrested Indians on suspicion and tampered with their evidence "contrary to the maxims and usages of English law."[73] He did not appoint the commission before leaving on his first official visit to the Seychelles because he hoped that the Acting Police Commissioner, who would probably obstruct the inquiry, would soon leave the colony.

During the Governor's absence, Adolphe de Plevitz, a German manager of a small estate, who had helped the old immigrants prepare their petition, grew tired of waiting for action and published a pamphlet containing the petition and his own observations upon it. The publication completely shattered the conspiracy of silence over the true conditions of the Indians which the Mauritian community (perhaps as much unconsciously as consciously) had established and maintained over the years. It caused a tremendous furore throughout the colony—a storm which Gordon had hoped to avoid through quiet investigation and gradual reform.

De Plevitz in his observations attacked the whole immigration system denouncing recruiters in India (". . . the more they lie, the greater the profits"); the protector in Mauritius (". . . his office was instituted to facilitate . . . oppression"); planter ("[he] pays . . . very nearly what he chooses"); police (". . . it is an absurdity to speak of justice . . . at the discretion of the Police"); magistrates ("[they] are nearly all . . . more or less directly interested in the sugar plantations"); and the legislative council ("[it has] wholly deprived the poor Indian . . . of the rights of citizenship . . . [and] almost put him without the pale of humanity").[74] He also criticized Gordon's predecessor. Barkly, de Plevitz correctly stated, had acted contrary to the will of Her Majesty, as expressed in his commission, by assenting to laws placing restrictions and disabilities on persons not of European birth or descent which did not apply to persons of European birth or descent.[75]

[73]Gorrie to Gordon, 26 April 1871, *Report of the Royal Commissioners appointed to enquire into the treatment of immigrants in Mauritius*, Parl. Pap., 1875,XXXIV [C-1115], 1, 22. Hereafter this report will be cited as *Report, 1875*.
[74]*Petition of the Old Immigrants of Mauritius with observations by Adolphe de Plevitz*, 19–24, hereafter cited as De Plevitz. [75]*Ibid*.

The unrestrained nature of the colonists' reaction to these charges indicated either a guilty conscience or an absurd belief in their own purity. It also demonstrated how thin a veneer of liberalism and tolerance overlay the Mauritian character. The prevailing temper is illustrated in the following editorial:

Il n'y avait qu'un sot, capable de porter une accusation semblable, méconnaissant en tout point la fierté et l'orgueil des Mauriciens. Il n'est que trop vrai, pourtant, que cette fierté et cet orgueil, qui enfantaient des prodiges, se sont bien effacés, puisque vingt milles Créoles restent froids et impassibles, en écoutant l'accusation qu'un misérable étranger porte contre eux dans un écrit public, où ils sont considérés comme des hommes se parjurant devant les tribunaux, et sous serment, pour six pence! Si vous avez horreur du sang (nos mœurs sont devenues si douces), mettez-vous donc, Créoles, cinq ou six pour payer les frais d'un procès, et poursuivez donc ce calomniateur qui n'a pas craint de vous jeter l'injure à la face, en vous appelant menteurs, et en disant à haute et intelligible voix que vous vous parjurez pour six pence.

Allez-vous nous forcer à entrer dans l'arène, nous qui sommes partisans de la peine de fouet et de la peine de mort! Est-ce qu'il se rencontrerait plus l'énergie, plus de véritable courage, plus de juste fierté dans le cœur de ceux qui disent et qui comprennent que le sang est nécessaire pour lever tous les affronts du genre de celui que toute la Colonie a reçu d'un malheureux pamphlétaire! Faites donc punir par les lois l'ingratitude de cet homme, à qui l'on accorde "le vivre, le couvert," et l'hospitalité. Il lui faut une leçon; accordez lui donc ce que son bon génie réclame de vous pour sauver son âme.[76]

Journals more restrained in their language called de Plevitz a libeller of the colony and demanded that the Governor deport or at least prosecute him. Gordon refused to act. The first would be tyrannous; the second, improper. Besides, he considered de Plevitz's charges mainly true. He tried nevertheless to quell the creoles' anger. He reminded them that similar charges in the past had neither harmed the colony nor put a stop to Indian immigration, and that if the charges proved untrue they had nothing to fear. Despite the Governor's conciliation de Plevitz became the victim of a prearranged assault encouraged by the newspapers. Lots were drawn for the privilege of striking de Plevitz with a stick. The honour fell to Jules Lavoquer, who set upon the "libeller" in the street. After the attack both were arrested. Lavoquer was released on bail immediately; de Plevitz, not until the next day. Gordon now intervened but, knowing that no jury in Mauritius would convict Lavoquer, tried him before a magistrate. A public subscription paid Lavoquer's fine and presented him with the stick—adorned by a silver plate carrying a suitable inscription—with which he had struck the blow for the honour

[76]Extract from *Progrès Colonial*, 1 Oct. 1871, quoted in *Maur.*, I, 280–81.

of Mauritius. The *Commercial Gazette* told Gordon that "by his undisguised bias" against Lavoquer he had driven the people "to doubt his justice," and it correctly warned him that his "future career as Governor of Mauritius [would] be beset with difficulties."[77]

Nor was this the end of the affair. Gordon received a petition bearing 900 signatures expressing full approval of Lavoquer's conduct and disapproval of his persecution, and asking again that he expel de Plevitz from the colony. One of the unofficial members of the council demanded that the Governor do something to refute de Plevitz's charges. The chamber of agriculture asked him either to rebut "the malicious assertions contained in this libel . . ." or to name a competent commission to report on the condition of Indians employed in the sugar industry.[78] To all of these demands for action against de Plevitz Sir Arthur returned a polite but firm rebuff. A government, he thought, should deal with acts, not with criticisms and opinions.[79] He congratulated the chamber of agriculture on its willingness to have a commission of inquiry.

Knowing that any commission which he himself might appoint would be subject to intimidation,[80] Gordon refused to appoint one. This led the chamber of agriculture to demand a royal commission. One member told him confidentially that the planters believed a show of willingness on their part would induce the Secretary of State to conclude that such a commission was unnecessary.[81] When Sir Arthur pointed out the expense and the delay in reforming the immigration system that would result from the appointment of a royal commission, the chamber thought he was confessing weakness and insisted on it. At least, he reflected, the planters would not be able to say that he had forced a royal commission upon them.[82]

Gordon himself had mixed feelings about the appointment of a royal commission. On the whole he favoured it because he doubted "the length to which the Colonial Office would go" in supporting his own reform of the system.[83] He wished, however, to have credit for accomplishing it without outside assistance. He had also to consider the effect that a delay in correcting abuses might have not only in prolonging the suffering of the Indians but in increasing the colony's difficulties in acquiring fresh levies. The Indian government, unilaterally, could halt

[77]*Commercial Gazette*, 26 Oct. 1871.

[78]Resolutions of the chamber of agriculture, 13 Nov. 1871, *Maur.*, I. 307.

[79]Gordon's speech in the legislative council, 14 Nov. 1871, *Maur.*, I, 301.

[80]It had been almost impossible to obtain a lawyer to conduct the prosecution of Lavoquer. One who did agree to do so was intimidated and withdrew.

[81]Postscript to Gordon to Kimberley (confidential), 10 Nov. 1871, PRO CO 167/536.   [82]*Maur.*, I, 467.   [83]*Ibid.*, 466.

emigration. Indeed, in July 1872, it threatened such action.[84] Apart from this danger, however, Mauritius had found it difficult to compete for Indian labour with the West Indies, which paid higher wages and provided return passages. As the answer to this problem, the immigration committee of the Mauritius legislature suggested that the Secretary of State be asked to prohibit other colonies from offering coolies better contracts than Mauritius. Further, it recommended an increase in the pay, not of the Indians, but of the recruiters, by giving them a higher bounty on each recruit.[85] Obviously then, the Mauritians, if left to themselves, would take no reform measures. Sir Arthur therefore decided to recommend the appointment of a royal commission and, at the same time, to persuade the council to pass resolutions favouring reform of the chief abuses in the immigration system. If the royal commission came, the resolutions, if passed, would form an important admission of the necessity for change. If it did not, they would make a good foundation for an ordinance which those who had voted for them would find difficult to resist.[86]

These resolutions, six in number,[87] were based upon Lord Kimberley's dispatch of 16 December 1871,[88] which in turn was based upon suggestions made by Gordon in September.[89] They ran as follows: (1) Indians were to be guaranteed a return passage to their homeland after a stipulated period of years; (2) they were to have an earlier claim (than under existing law) to cancellation of contract for its non-fulfillment by the employer; (3) no immigrant would be allowed to re-indenture himself until after the expiry of his previous indenture; (4) medical attendants on the estates were to be appointed by the governor and be paid as the governor, with the advice and consent of the legislature, should direct; (5) the protector of immigrants was to be empowered to refuse further immigrants to any estate on which the mortality (non-accidental or non-epidemic) had been excessive or of which the owner had been convicted of habitual ill-usage; and (6) the governor was to have authority to remove immigrants from unhealthy estates or estates where he was satisfied they had been ill-used.[90]

Gordon had quite markedly impressed C. Antelme, a leading member

[84]A. D. Hume to the Colonial Secretary of Mauritius, 13 July 1872, enclosed in Gordon to Kimberley, 20 Sept. 1872, PRO CO 167/541.
[85]Gordon to Kimberley, 9 Feb. 1872, PRO CO 167/541.
[86]*Maur.*, I, 467.
[87]Actually seven, but the third was the corollary of the second and was considered with it.
[88]Kimberley to Gordon, 16 Dec. 1871, PRO CO 167/537.
[89]Gordon to Kimberley, 21 Sept. 1871, PRO CO 167/535.
[90]For the full text of these resolutions see *Maur.*, I, 507–8.

of the chamber of agriculture and an unofficial member of the council. Consequently Antelme undertook to persuade the other unofficials to support the resolutions provided he was allowed to cover himself by proposing verbal amendments. Gordon accepted this arrangement and late in March 1872, in a rather elaborate tongue-in-cheek speech,[91] introduced them in the legislature. Except for the first he did not intend to press any to a vote unless it appeared to enjoy near unanimous support. He could not risk defeat and thus prejudice the operation of the commission.[92] He carried the second, third, and fourth resolutions unanimously. He postponed a vote on the first resolution and did not even call for one on the last two. On 21 May he reintroduced the first resolution and carried it by his own deliberative vote. He might perhaps have been more successful, but Antelme had given the gist of the resolutions to the chamber of agriculture.[93] As a result the newspapers put pressure on the unofficials to reject them. The *Commercial Gazette* howled that Gordon had the colony at his mercy and that all hope of his listening to reason had vanished. It demanded that the council refuse even to discuss the resolutions.[94] When the council passed the three, the *Gazette* charged Gordon with having " 'deceived, duped, and over-reached' every member."[95]

If the colony disliked the Governor's resolutions, the Colonial Office disliked his handling of them. Herbert, who called himself Gordon's "friend and well-wisher"[96] and who usually supported him, wrote:

Sir A. Gordon is delighted at the manner in which he has carried his resolutions, one of which he postponed, two he withdrew, & the remaining three were modified & re-written by the opposition—almost as brilliant a performance . . . as the passing of the great Conservative Reform Act in this country. He creates all sorts of trouble & discredit for himself by his mental

[91]See *Maur.*, I, 496–506. Kimberley did not find himself inspired by Gordon's "prolix speeches and messages." He disapproved of "sober Britons playing the rôle of excitable Celts." Herbert thought the speech "undoubtedly able & not too florid for the French-Colonial taste." (Kimberley's minute, 20 May 1872, on Gordon to Kimberley, 4 April 1872, PRO CO 167/542; and Herbert's and Kimberley's minutes, 5 and 6 June 1872, on Gordon to Kimberley, 2 May 1872, PRO CO 167/543.)

[92]Kimberley determined on the royal commission on 10 Feb. 1872, and Gordon received word of this on 17 March, eleven days before he introduced his resolutions although he had given notice on 12 March of his intention to introduce them.

[93]This is another example of Gordon placing too much confidence in the integrity and judgment of colonials.

[94]Extract from *Commercial Gazette* quoted by Gordon in his diary, 27 March 1872, *Maur.*, I, 493.

[95]Gordon's diary, 2 April 1872, *Maur.*, I, 510.

[96]Herbert to Gordon, 19 Dec. 1873, *Maur.*, II, 404.

& moral obliquity & tortuousness; and seems quite unable to learn that the man who straightforwardly & steadily maintains his opinions is more popular and more successful than he who attempts to make things pleasant by concealing some parts of his views & modifying others after he has once committed himself to them.[97]

Kimberley also questioned Gordon's proceedings although respecting his courage for attempting contentious reforms.[98] When later Sir Arthur got the resolution favouring return passages through the council, Herbert thought it better than nothing but of little value because it was not to be followed at once by legislation.[99] Although Kimberley had told Gordon in December that return passages for Indians "should be at once re-established,"[100] he now believed that Gordon had "acted with great want of judgment in pressing the question pending the inquiry" by the royal commission.[101] Not wanting to increase the Governor's difficulties he remained silent on the subject except for a private letter saying there was now nothing to do but wait for the report of the commission.[102] The Colonial Office could afford a more patient attitude than Gordon, who felt much pain at the continued abuse of over 200,000 people by the planters and police.

Nothing more clearly illustrates the antipathy of Mauritius to reform, or the slight chance which Gordon by himself had of quickly revolutionizing its immigration system, than the time it took him to reinstitute government inspections of the sugar estates and public reaction to those inspections. He began this process in September 1871. The ordinance did not pass until mid-December and a thorough probe did not begin until late February 1872. The planters had no objections to inspections provided they were forewarned of the inspector's arrival and of the questions he would ask. But when, on the Governor's orders, the protector of immigrants descended upon them unannounced and asked all sorts of embarrassing questions, it was an entirely different matter. It was nothing but a "spy-system," a reflection upon their "honor and integrity" in which "the Home and Indian Governments, and previous Governors of Mauritius, were always justified in entertaining [a trust]."[103] The *Commercial Gazette* believed it substituted "the manoeu-

[97]Herbert's minute, 17 May 1872, on Gordon to Kimberley, 4 April 1872.

[98]Kimberley's minute, 20 May 1872, *ibid.*

[99]Herbert's minute, 3 July 1872, on Gordon to Kimberley, 27 May 1872, PRO CO 167/543.

[100]Kimberley to Gordon, 16 Dec. 1871.

[101]Kimberley's minute, 3 July 1872, on Gordon to Kimberley, 27 May 1872.

[102]Kimberley to Gordon (private), 4 July 1872, *Maur.*, I, 651.

[103]Gordon to Kimberley, 6 March 1872, and enclosure no. 2; PRO CO 167/542.

vres of Scotland Yard, . . . [for] statesmanlike measures." The colony, it said, would never be content to "rest under the burden of undeserved suspicion, and will seek every legitimate means to be relieved of it."[104] The French papers, with the exception of the *Sentinelle* which supported the Governor, adopted a similar tone.[105]

So unpopular had Gordon become, as a result of his failure to take action against de Plevitz, his reinstitution of inspections, and his resolutions, that public opinion welcomed the news that a royal commission had been appointed and would arrive in Mauritius shortly. Although fears had been expressed in the previous November that the commissioners might be men "imbued with prejudices, of peculiar and perhaps little education, or acquaintance with the world, . . . perhaps chiefly anxious to justify their appointment . . . ,"[106] Mauritians now believed the commission would restore the colony's reputation so wilfully damaged by Gordon. The editor of the *Commercial Gazette*, confident that the facts would vindicate the planters, feared that the Governor might attempt to keep information from the commissioners. He even suggested that the appointment of the royal commission indicated the Secretary of State's distrust of Gordon and presaged his recall.[107]

The royal commissioners, William Edward Frere and Victor Williamson, arrived in mid-April 1872. Their hearings and the report of the Police Inquiry Commission[108] published at their request early established the inadequacy of the laws ostensibly enacted to protest the Indians and confirmed Gorrie's allegations[109] and the validity of de Plevitz's charges. In August, H. N. D. Beyts, the protector of immigrants, reported to Gordon that "there is *decidedly* a turn in the tide of public opinion towards a recognition of the justice and soundness of your policy. . . ."[110] A month later one of the inspectors wrote that "feeling seems to be getting daily stronger in favour of inspection, and most of the planters do not hesitate to express their opinion that it is a misfortune that some one was not put to keep them in the right road years

[104]Extract from *Commercial Gazette*, n.d. enclosure no 2 in Gordon to Kimberley, 6 March 1872.

[105]See the files of *Le Cernéen, Progrès Colonial*, and *Sentinelle de Maurice* for February and March 1872.

[106]James Currie (president of the chamber of agriculture) to Gordon, 25 Nov. 1871, *Maur.*, I, 334.

[107]*Commercial Gazette*, 16 and 20 April 1872. That Gordon felt impelled to ask Kimberley to deny these rumours indicates both the weakness of his position in Mauritius and his lack of confidence in Kimberley's support.

[108]Gordon established the Police Inquiry Commission in December 1871. It reported in April 1872.

[109]See above, p. 119.

[110]Beyts to Gordon, 16 Aug. 1872, *Maur.*, I, 662.

ago."[111] No sudden or dramatic change of heart yet occurred. The papers continued to express their resentment of this meddling by Gordon and the royal commissioners in the internal affairs of Mauritius. However, as the commissioners continued their probe and it became clear that they were even more critical of the colony than the Governor, colonial indignation tended to focus less on Gordon and more on the commissioners.

By November the royal commission had nearly completed taking evidence, and Sir Arthur, feeling his assistance no longer essential, decided to take his deferred leave. Early in the month he sent his family home[112] via the Cape, and two weeks later sailed for the Seychelles, where he remained until mid-January 1873. He then paid a visit to India[113] and did not arrive in England until April. This leisurely homecoming was designed to give the commissioners time to complete their findings and to arrive home before him. Aware that Frere and Williamson respected him and agreed with him as to the difficulties of governing Mauritius, he believed that if they arrived at the Colonial Office first, he might be given a more cordial reception. This plan miscarried. Frere suffered a heart attack which prevented him and Williamson from leaving Mauritius until October 1873.

Gordon hoped never to return to Mauritius, but if he had to, he wished to take the report of the royal commission with him. As delay followed delay in the departure of the commissioners from Mauritius, and as his leave became more and more protracted, he felt it his duty to offer to return. Much to his disgust Kimberley accepted. Promising Lady Gordon to return within a year he left London about the end of September, arriving at Port Victoria on 20 October, and Port Louis on 23 November.

[111]George Jenner to Gordon, 4 Sept. 1872, *Maur.*, I, 675f.

[112]Lady Gordon and the two children spent nearly a year and a half in Mauritius, fortunately with no ill effects upon their health.

[113]Gordon's visit to India may have been prompted by a desire to see the "lay of the land" in case he should some day be offered an Indian presidency. If he did not have that ambition when he went there he soon formed it. In any case he travelled widely and formed some highly critical impressions of the administration and civil service of India. He wrote to his father-in-law as follows: ". . . the most disappointing impression I received was from a nearer contact with the Indian Civil Service. . . . Few seemed to *know* & fewer still to *care* anything about the natives & their habits of life or of thought: in fact there was often rather a pride in saying 'thank God I know nothing about the brutes'." (Gordon to Sir John Shaw-Lefevre, 16 April 1873, Stanmore Papers, 49224.) After his arrival in England he got up a memorial to the Duke of Argyll, the secretary of state for India, asking that the government of India take steps to preserve some of the historic buildings of India which he had observed falling to ruin. For the text and signatories, see *Maur.*, II, appendix C.

Although the *Overland Commercial Gazette* mourned the news of the Governor's return as a "general disappointment"[114] and a group of diehards continued to abuse him, Gordon now found himself much more popular in the colony. A motley crowd of some four or five thousand hailed his landing with cries of "Long live the liberator of the oppressed classes."[115] The *Sentinelle* called this demonstration "unprecedented" and a greater welcome than any governor had hitherto received,[116] but *Le Cernéen* deplored it as a "manifestation ridicule."[117] In reproving those journals which continued to stir the public against the Governor's policies, the *Vert-Vert* noted that Sir Arthur was "un homme à idées libérales et à principes séverès" and that "la partie réfléchie et sensée des habitants, s'est montrée réfractaire à un systême d'intolérance et de partipris qui compromet tous les jours l'interêt bien entendu de la Colonie, et qui ne tend à rien moins qu'à établir, entre gouvernant et gouvernées, une défiance et une suspicion nuisibles à tous."[118]

In part Gordon's new popularity arose from his policy of dealing justly with the French Roman Catholics[119] in matters concerning education, religion, and employment in the civil service—a policy which he had begun to implement before his leave and which the Roman Catholics had not forgotten. In part it stemmed from dislike and fear of the royal commissioners, whom one editor had compared to Minos and Rhadamanthus "of mythologique et infernale memoire."[120] Knowing that Frere and Williamson had judged them harshly, most of the colonists showed a disposition "to make up the quarrel" with the Governor and to enlist him on their side "to deprecate the wrath of the Colonial Office, when the day of trial comes."[121]

Although Gordon used his increased popularity to push other reforms, he could not force the "day of trial" on the coolie problem. Frere experienced another heart attack in England, and the commission's report did not appear until 1875. By that time Gordon had resigned. The report, however, belongs to Gordon's administration, and its findings have a place in any study of his work as governor of Mauritius.

[114]*Overland Commercial Gazette*, 14 Nov. 1873.
[115]Extract from the *Sentinelle* enclosed in Gordon to Kimberley, 12 Dec. 1873, PRO CO 167/556.
[116]*Ibid.*
[117]Gordon to Lady Gordon, 25 Dec. 1873, *Maur.*, II, 360.
[118]Extract from *Vert-Vert* enclosed in Gordon to Kimberley, 12 Dec. 1873.
[119]See below, pp. 135–40.
[120]*Le Pays*, 30 April 1873, quoted in Frere to Gordon, 27 April–2 May 1873, *Maur.*, II, 201.
[121]Gordon to Lady Gordon, 25 Dec. 1873.

The royal commissioners discovered that between 1843[122] and 1858 a shortage of labour had ensured that planters treated their coolies humanely. Deterioration began as the supply of labour greatly increased with resumption of private importations of Indians in 1855 and with the influx that followed the Indian Mutiny. Ordinance 30 of 1858 practically abolished the labourer's right to contract with the highest bidder. Magistrates' inspections of estates became ineffective in 1864. The annual inspection by the protector of immigrants, begun on the Duke of Newcastle's instructions in 1864, ceased in 1868. The latter inspection had never been effective in any case because Barkly had refused to allow the protector's clerk to run the office during the protector's absence. Barkly had been frightened because the protector's inspection had caused "some perturbation among the planters" and had been commented upon unfavourably in the press.[123] At the same time Barkly had told the magistrates that they must avoid "all semblance of official demand"[124] in obtaining statistics from the planters. The magistrates could scarcely fail to conclude that they would not receive official support should their inspections be other than perfunctory.

The commissioners noted that dilatory inspections and wretchedness among the estate labourers went hand in hand. Planters made no pretence of obeying existing laws for the protection of their labourers. Instead they effectively evaded or subverted them. They habitually neglected to pay wages on time, hoping by this means to force the Indians to re-engage themselves. They illegally docked $300,000 in wages annually,[125] forced their labourers to work when ill, and failed to provide housing and hospital accommodation. With a few exceptions the doctors, paid by the planters, made no attempt to treat the Indians. The magistrates almost invariably sided with the planters in any disputes with labour. In short, estate owners treated the Indians as they liked.

Unfortunately for the planters, disease and harsh treatment produced a high mortality[126] among the estate workers and discouraged old immigrants from re-indenturing. Consequently a shortage of labourers

[122]The year the Mauritian government took Indian immigration out of private hands.

[123]Barkly to Cardwell, dispatch no. 263, 1864, quoted in *Report*, 1875, 195.

[124]*Ibid.*

[125]Robert Mitchell to Gordon, 1 Sept. 1872, *Maur.*, I, 673. Gordon brought Mitchell from Trinidad, temporarily, to help in uncovering abuses in the Mauritian immigration system.

[126]Vital statistics for the Indian population of Mauritius at this period are scarce and unreliable because they were inefficiently collected by the magistrates and inefficiently compiled in the government offices; but such as they are they indicate a high mortality rate.

developed. Fresh contingents from India became harder to obtain because the West Indies offered better contracts. It was this situation, reported the commissioners, that produced the New Labour Law (Ordinance 31) of 1867, which aimed at making life so miserable for the old immigrants (of whom there were now many thousands) that they would have to seek refuge on the estates.[127] Perhaps this new law and the regulations passed under it in November 1868 and August 1869 might have been less harsh had it not been that, at the time, Mauritians felt extremely hostile to "old immigrants." Unable to account otherwise for the epidemic of malaria currently besetting the island, the Europeans placed the blame squarely upon the free Indians[128] who, in squalor and misery, crowded among them. Forgetting where responsibility lay for the continued presence in the colony of so many old immigrants and the lack of adequate sanitary facilities, European Mauritians by 1869 regarded the old immigrant as a "vagrant disguised." They distrusted "the genuineness of any employment which an Indian [might] adopt on his own account."[129] The *Commercial Gazette*, though deprecating any "coercive legislative measures as would in the least degree interfere with the personal liberty of an Old immigrant . . . ," still thought the law ought to insist that every Indian unable to give proof of employment or ownership of property be treated as a vagabond.[130] There would, it believed, be no "large demand for fresh labour if the Government were to adopt stringent legislative measures to force thousands of idle Old immigrants . . . to earn their livelihood. . . ."[131] The government ought to insist that no dwelling be inhabited by more than such number of "Indians" as it could accommodate in a sanitary condition. (Apparently it did not matter how many Europeans lived in one house.) No house ought to be let to any old immigrant who could not prove employment or a self-supporting income. "The law properly carried out in these respects, an additional supply of effective, productive labour would be brought on the market; and while the condition of the Indian would be bettered, while the sanitary condition of the colony would not fail to be improved, the planter would be enabled to obtain, for yet some years to come, the full amount of labour he may require, without the loss of time, the risk and the expense which attend its introduction from India."[132]

The *Commercial Gazette* spoke with the authentic voice of the planters. That "the measures eventually passed by the Legislature were

[127]*Report*, 1875, 106.
[128]*Ibid.*, 141–44.
[129]*Report of the Police Inquiry Commission*, appendix F 2, para. 27.
[130]*Commercial Gazette*, 13 June 1867.
[131]*Ibid.*, 18 June 1867.   [132]*Ibid.*, 14 June 1867.

in strict accordance with the opinions and recommendations put forward by these writers . . ."[133] indicated the planters' power. It is fair to add that the general public largely shared those opinions and recommendations.

Sholto Douglas, the acting procureur-general, submitted the draft of the new law to the council at the end of August 1867. In his introductory remarks he dwelt upon the idleness and filthiness of the old immigrants and the incidence of gang robbery among them. He considered stringent legislation necessary to protect the colony and the Indians themselves against such menaces.[134] The royal commissioners, however, could find nothing so peculiarly restricted to old immigrants as to warrant such distinctively class legislation as this ordinance proved to be. Many creoles were also idle and filthy, and estate labourers as well as old immigrants had committed gang robberies.[135]

The only opposition to the New Labour Law came on second reading from W. W. R. Kerr, the treasurer. He charged that, as matters stood, nearly everybody including public officials, unjustly condemned the old immigrants and refused to listen to their complaints. The new law, he said, would be purely the result of a general feeling of hostility against them. Sir Henry Barkly ridiculed him by comparing him to the odd juryman who, constantly in the box, always differed from the other eleven and complained that they were obstinate and wrong. The press and the chamber of agriculture joined in the attack. The latter stated its willingness to have an official investigation of Kerr's charges if the Governor were not convinced of their inaccuracy. Barkly, however, thought such an inquiry would be as useless as it would be mischievous and induced Kerr to withdraw his charges so that he (Barkly) would not be compelled to send them to the Colonial Office.[136]

The New Labour Law passed the council late in November, 1867. In the following year, after Barkly reported satisfaction with their operation, the Duke of Buckingham confirmed both the ordinance (31) and the regulations for the proper functioning of the ordinance. Stringent as these measures were, even more stringent regulations were adopted in 1869. Barkly, however, made no mention of these to the Colonial Office.[137] It is plain that the Colonial Office only partly understood the

---

[133]*Report*, 1875, 107.   [134]*Ibid.*, 109.   [135]*Ibid.*, 124.   [136]*Ibid.*, 124–25.

[137]Barkly sent home only the proceedings of the executive council which the Colonial Office did not customarily send to the Imperial Land and Emigration commissioners whose duty it was to report to the secretary of state on all laws affecting labour. Consequently the commissioners never saw these amending regulations although they did comment in their 29th annual report on the stringency of the ordinance itself which, they noted, subjected the old immigrants to a control applied in England only to men under tickets-of-leave. (*Ibid.*, 126.)

motives behind the new ordinance and knew little or nothing about the character of the regulations of 1869. These dealt with the unsanitary living conditions of the old immigrants. Barkly to his credit hesitated in passing the regulations, but unfortunately, at the crucial moment, he received a dispatch from Buckingham telling him that the government ought to prevent individuals being public nuisances and that it should destroy unsanitary buildings.[138] This seemed to provide him with the requisite authority and he passed the regulations. Buckingham had only the health of the colony in mind when he gave the Governor this advice. This was doubtless one of Barkly's motives also. Yet a strong suspicion must remain that, in increasing the severity of the regulations, he acted both to gain popularity and on the advice of the stipendiary magistrates. They had declared that the pass system, inaugurated by the New Labour Law, had not been working well, and that "the object to be kept in view should be to send more labourers onto the estates at reduced wages. . . ."[139]

Ordinance 31 of 1867 and the subsequent regulations degraded the old immigrant and took from him virtually every vestige of his former freedom. They reduced him to the "condition of a helot, or more accurately, to that . . . of 'the most absolute serf'."[140] He could live neither how nor as he pleased, nor could he give shelter to his relatives and friends. If he did not work he went to gaol as a vagabond. He had always to carry an identifying photograph and a police pass. If he lost them he had to pay twenty-two shillings (or two months' average wages) to replace them. To procure them he often had to walk as far as 150 miles. If found without them he was arrested and kept in custody, often for several days, until his papers could be brought and presented to the magistrate. He could be sent to prison if this papers contained errors or if the police made mistakes concerning the boundaries of the district for which his papers were actually in order. Some old immigrants served prison terms at hard labour (stone-breaking) because the estate upon which they worked changed hands thus causing a discrepancy in their papers. If an old immigrant lost his papers the law gave him eight days to raise the money for new ones. He could not, however, work as a day labourer without a licence, the fee for which had originally been four shillings, but by order-in-council had been raised to twenty shillings. Barkly did not report the increase to the Colonial Office. Unless the old immigrants could borrow the money he had to "hire out" to an estate or remain in the vagrant depot until

[138]Buckingham to Barkly, 6 June 1868, quoted *ibid.*, 140.
[139]*Ibid.*, 137.   [140]*Ibid.*, 138.

an engagement could be found for him. If he changed employers he had to go to the central police station of his district to have his papers put in order. Failure to follow this regulation made him liable to arrest as a vagrant and to a sentence of hard labour. The police enforced the new law with enthusiasm. They stopped Indian market gardeners carrying their produce to market and often delayed them on technicalities until their produce had spoiled. They conducted organized vagrancy hunts, arrested old immigrants in groups and charged them not individually, but collectively. The magistrates then sentenced them in batches numbering up to fifty. The Indians had no redress for false arrest.[141] Frere and Williamson found that all these atrocities actually did take place because, as they said, "in its administration, the [new] law was in too many cases carried out in its strictest and harshest letter, and, . . . in too many more cases, the administration went even beyond this. . . ."[142]

The labour system as it had operated under Barkly shocked the royal commissioners. They disapproved of everything about it. They found the laws for the protection of the estate workers too lenient and, if enforced at all, enforced only to the detriment of the Indians. They considered the New Labour Law and its regulations outrageous and the complaints enumerated in the old immigrants' petition fully justified. They considered the magistrates ignorant, the police reckless, the doctors inefficient, and the planters cruel.[143] Frere and Williamson followed Gordon in publicly rejecting the unworthy motives imputed by de Plevitz to Barkly[144] and to the council in passing Ordinance 31 and its regulations. Yet they noted that these measures had been based upon the reports of the magistrates and police inspectors who had urged them as a means of forcing old immigrants back to the plantations and that the colonial press and many of the general public had advocated them for the same reason. It is impossible to read their report without concluding that they believed the miserable condition of Indians, both on and off the estates, was attributable to the weakness of Barkly and the council in the face of public opinion.

The commission's recommendations concerning the immigration system closely paralleled the changes sought by Gordon in his 1872 resolutions. Lord Carnarvon, the new secretary of state, accepted them and, in slightly stronger form, forwarded them to Gordon's successor,

[141]De Plevitz; and *Report*, 1875, 16, 137–140.
[142]*Report*, 1875, 138.
[143]*Ibid.*, 557–84.
[144]Gordon in his diary, however, insisted that Barkly "must have sinned . . . with his eyes open." (*Maur.*, I, 85.)

Sir Arthur Phayre, in March 1875. The most important of these included strengthening inspections; ensuring prompt payment of wages; making the medical attendants civil servants; granting a right of return passage at the colony's expense; giving the protector of immigrants powers consistent with his title; prohibiting re-indenturing for periods of more than a year at a time; providing for an independent magistracy having no financial interests in sugar estates; and giving the governor power both to withdraw labourers from estates where they were abused and to refuse such estates fresh contingents.[145]

As to the old immigrants whose complaints had led to the appointment of the commission, Frere and Williamson contented themselves mainly with a full exposure of the abuses, making only a few specific suggestions for reform. Carnarvon went further and gave vehement instructions to Phayre. He must change the vagrancy laws at once, absolutely prohibit vagrancy hunts, punish the police for false and vexatious arrests, and deprive them of their right to receive a portion of the fines imposed on old immigrants for offences. Although Gordon had ended these practices, the law which had supported them remained. Carnarvon considered it ought to be revised at once. He also found objectionable the fee which the law required of an old immigrant before he could work as a day labourer. "It is not easy to understand," he wrote, "why a free man (which the old immigrant is supposed to be), should be required to pay a fee for exercising what is the common liberty of all men."[146]

Phayre acted on a number of these recommendations during his first year in office and, in 1878, by Ordinance 12, altered the whole immigration system to conform with the principles laid down by the royal commissioners and Lord Carnarvon. This ordinance remained in operation until 1922. The real improvement in the Indians' condition began, however, with Sir Arthur Gordon's resumption of efficient inspections in 1872[147] and with his curtailment by executive order of the harsh activities of the police against old immigrants. After those radical changes the Indians' progress and development followed a continuous course.[148]

---

[145]Carnarvon to Phayre, 11 March 1875. *Correspondence relating to the Royal Commission of Inquiry . . . in Mauritius*, Parl. Pap., 1875, LIII [C-1188], 15–21.
[146]*Ibid.*
[147]One of the magistrates exclaimed: "What *totally* changed practice now goes on in all departments compared to what prevailed fourteen months ago! Planters, Clerks, Police, Magistrates, etc., *have* to keep within the law." (J. G. Daly to Gordon, 14 Sept. 1872, *Maur.*, I, 687.)
[148]K. Hazareesingh, *A History of Indians in Mauritius*, 101.

IV. MEASURES FOR THE RELIEF OF ROMAN CATHOLICS

When Lord Granville offered Gordon the governorship of Mauritius he intimated that the colony had been governed in a true John Bull spirit.[149] His parliamentary under-secretary, William Monsell, told Gordon that the colonial authorities had favoured the "least religious elements" among the French, and that his "true mission . . . [would be] to draw the sympathies of the people towards us. . . ."[150] On arrival Gordon found he had not been misinformed, at least on this aspect of colonial life. It was Trinidad all over again. Having reformed the situation in that colony, Gordon looked forward to repeating his success in Mauritius. The comparative incompleteness of his victory was to result less from the forces arrayed against him in the colony than from his relative lack of executive authority and Lord Kimberley's failure to uphold the cause of religious equality for the sake of a few hundred pounds.

By the time Gordon arrived total state aid to the Roman Catholic church amounted to less than three shillings per member whereas to the Anglican it amounted to over fourteen shillings per member. Roman Catholics received only one-tenth of the amount voted to aid denominational schools; yet they maintained nineteen such schools compared with the Anglicans' fourteen. Although nineteen out of twenty pupils in the government-operated schools were Roman Catholics,[151] only Protestant prayers were said, the inspector was a bigoted Protestant, teachers were trained by a Protestant, most headmasters and most of the council of education were Protestant. Protestants under the leadership of Edward Newton, the colonial secretary, dominated the legislative council, where English was the only official language. Englishmen or Protestant members of Roman Catholic creole families filled most offices in the civil service. Gordon observed that although their change of religion might not have gained Protestant creoles their offices "they would not have obtained them had they retained their original faith."[152] During Sir Henry Barkly's administration Newton had been, for all practical purposes, prime minister. He took care that his nominees were Protestant.[153] He believed that if, in Mauritius, England had adopted

[149]Gordon's diary, 23 May 1871, *Maur.*, I, 84.
[150]Monsell to Gordon, [July or August 1869], Stanmore Papers, 49199.
[151]Except a few Indian schools whose pupils were Hindu or Muslim.
[152]Gordon to Carnarvon, 4 April 1874, *Maur.*, II, 522.
[153]He revived this policy when he administered the government during Gordon's long absence in 1872–73. Occasionally he made a mistake. He reported to Gordon in 1873 that the Roman Catholic Bishop had been anxious to appoint a Mr. Marie

"the same system that the Prussians are now [1873] doing in the con-
quered provinces of France, however 'brutal' such system may be, . . .
the effect would have been that this place would have been thoroughly
English. . . ."[154]

Gordon did not disagree with the ultimate aim of the English faction.
"Gentle pressure" might have done much to promote use of the English
language, and constant association with those of another faith might
have "insensibly loosened the bonds of Roman Catholic exclusive-
ness. . . ." The harsh and intolerant methods in use had been wrong.
They had simply aroused antagonism to England and resistance to
change. All he might now hope to do in the interests of justice would
be to create as much religious and linguistic equality as possible. He
announced this policy at a public dinner within a fortnight of his arrival.
It no longer mattered which party held power in Britain, he stated. She
no longer sought to introduce her own manners, laws, language, and
religion in her overseas territories. She accepted the fact that Mauritius,
though a British possession, was not an English colony. He himself
fully agreed with the mother country's new policy of governing her
dependencies "in accordance with their own interests and their own
wishes." He pointed to its success in Canada where, instead of a small
British party "maintained by artificial support," and a "sullen dis-
affected" population, there now existed a British party which com-
prehended the whole Canadian people. He concluded his speech with
the hope that everyone would co-operate in applying this policy in
Mauritius.[155]

Gordon did not for a moment mean to imply that Mauritius should
have self-government. There had been too much drift in that direction
already—a drift which he believed it necessary to reverse. He meant
only that Lord Durham's policy of assimilating the French Canadians
had been rejected for British North America with beneficial results and
that the same could be expected by abandoning the anglicizing policies
long practised in Mauritius. His speech earned him a popularity among
French Roman Catholics which never entirely disappeared even at the
height of the de Plevitz affair. It also won him the hatred of many
English officials and planters which never entirely disappeared either,

---

to one position but, said Newton, "I objected to him, as he is a Frenchman [viz.
Roman Catholic], and accepted Mr. Coutanceux instead, who I did not know
was also a Frenchman until it was too late!!" (Newton to Gordon, 9 Jan. 1873,
Maur., II, 93.)

[154]Newton to Gordon, 29 May 1873, *Maur.*, II, 220.

[155]Gordon's speech to the municipal corporation of Port Louis, 28 Feb. 1871,
Maur., I, 36–37.

even at the height of his popularity on his return from England late in 1873.

In implementing his policy, Gordon's first practical step was to reduce Newton to the status of a department head and to assume the "prime ministership" himself. He also allowed the use of French in the legislative council and took control over appointments to the civil service. Throughout his administration he saw to it that individuals were not excluded from preferment by reason of their origins, language, or religion.

Late in 1872 Sir Arthur began his reform of the educational system. It can be briefly summarized because education in Mauritius, although more efficient than Gordon had found it in Trinidad, suffered similar ills and he applied similar remedies.[156] He determined to maintain the secular character of the government schools, to give government aid to private primary schools which opened their doors to all and adopted a conscience clause and to private secondary schools which affiliated themselves to the royal college. In making these proposals to Kimberley he noted his "parental partiality" for the scheme he had established in Trinidad.[157] Kimberley in reply considered the Trinidadian system "one which may properly be followed in Mauritius, *mutatis mutandis* as closely as possible."[158] Sir Arthur won the consent of the council of education for his proposals just before he left the colony. Although legislation to give them effect had to await the arrival of his successor, credit for it belongs to Gordon and to Charles Bruce,[159] rector of the royal college, who assisted him industriously in drafting the ordinance.

The death in June 1871 of Anglican Bishop Huxtable opened the way for reform of religious establishments and endowments in Mauritius. Huxtable had accompanied Gordon to the colony in February, and his early death so soon after that of his predecessor led the Colonial Office to wonder whether it would be worthwhile to appoint another bishop. It asked Gordon for his opinion and for a report on religious affairs in Mauritius. Early in 1872 he complied with the request. He believed an Anglican bishop not only unnecessary but harmful to both the Church of England and the colony. In such a small island with such a tiny Anglican minority a bishop found insufficient scope for his talents and

---

[156]See chap. III.

[157]Gordon to Kimberley, 18 Dec. 1872, PRO CO 167/547.

[158]Kimberley to Gordon, 25 Oct. 1873, PRO CO 167/547.

[159]Later Sir Charles Bruce, governor of Windward Islands 1893–97, Mauritius 1897–1903.

spent his time quarrelling with the Roman Catholics or leading a clique among his own flock. Gordon suggested that Bishop Tozer of Zanzibar through occasional visits could perform all requisite services in Mauritius. Although Herbert agreed with this suggestion,[160] Kimberley decided to allow the Anglicans in Mauritius to decide the issue for themselves. They voted in the affirmative and Bishop Royston arrived in 1873.

Until his appointment to Mauritius Royston had served in India. Untouched by the spirit of toleration which for some time had characterized relationships between religious organizations in England, he believed the recent adoption by the Roman Catholic church of the dogma of papal infallibility portended an anti-Protestant crusade. Any efforts by the Roman church in the colonies to achieve parity of treatment with Anglicans he considered "ultramontane conspiracy . . . against the true liberties of man."[161] He looked to the Governor for support in the counter-crusade he prepared to launch against Roman Catholics. One of the first steps needed was to secure a reversal of the Secretary of State's decision denying him letters patent (viz. territorial jurisdiction).[162] The Colonial Office had long refused letters patent to bishops in responsible government colonies, had withdrawn them in two Crown colonies (Hong Kong and Gibraltar), and had decided not to issue them to future bishops of Jamaica and Barbados. It believed they ought to be dispensed with altogether. Royston and some of the Anglicans in Mauritius considered this a blow at the dignity of their church. On several occasions they petitioned[163] for the issue of letters patent but both Gordon and the Colonial Office were adamant.

This bigoted Low-Churchman, who refused to accept a lower status than former Anglican bishops, was a thorn in Gordon's flesh. Royston's attempts to use the schools to convert Roman Catholic children to

[160]Herbert minuted: "If we had less than half the present number of Anglican Colonial Bishops, I believe the Anglican church in the colonies would be in a very much better position than at present." (Herbert's minute, 20 Feb. 1872, on Gordon to Kimberley, 12 Jan. 1872, PRO CO 167/540.)

[161]Royston to Gordon, 17 Jan. 1874, enclosed in Gordon to Kimberley (confidential), 5 Feb. 1874, PRO CO 167/559.

[162]The abolition of letters patent meant that a colonial bishop could exercise his full jurisdiction only over those clergymen who voluntarily recognized his authority. It also meant that colonial clergy ordained by colonial bishops were disqualified from preferment in England or Ireland. Lord Blachford's Colonial Church Act of 1874 overcame this latter disability. (Marindin, *Letters of Lord Blachford*, 305.)

[163]On the last occasion, in 1874, the Bishop, quite irregularly, used the police to circulate the petition. They acquired several thousand names but, according to one Anglican chaplain, only about forty were worthwhile.

Protestantism and his refusal to countenance any decrease in the establishment or endowment of the Church of England or any increase in state aid to the Roman Catholic church or schools served to delay educational reform, to aggravate religious hostilities, and to keep alive resistance to Gordon's plans for religious equality. Major responsibility for preventing the establishment of religious equality in Mauritius does not, however, rest with Royston because the plans for its accomplishment had suffered a bad set-back before his arrival.

Early in 1872 the Colonial Office, struck by the disparity (in *per capita* terms) between the amount of state aid given to the Anglican and Roman Catholic churches, concluded that "in Mauritius, as in many other Colonies," both churches should gradually be disestablished.[164] Clergymen of both churches in receipt of salaries would continue to receive them until their deaths or resignations. Their offices would not be filled. At the same time the state would establish a concurrent endowment fund to aid both major churches on a basis of greater equality. In deciding how large that fund would be and how it would be divided Lord Kimberley had several choices. First, he might provide the Anglican church with a grant equal to the amount it already received as part of the establishment and raise the Roman Catholic grant to a proportionate amount. The Anglicans would then receive £4,099 and the Roman Catholics approximately £34,500.[165] He rejected this plan as too expensive. Secondly, in accordance with the principle worked out for the West Indies by Rogers and Granville between 1868 and 1870, he might gradually reduce the Anglican grant and increase the Roman Catholic until the amount each church received was proportionate to its membership.[166] This plan would have been ideal, and neither church could easily have resisted on any reasonable grounds. Kimberley rejected it because, in the interests of economy, he wanted to reduce the amount of state aid to the churches.

He chose a third course by which he would maintain the amount (£6,800) paid to the Roman Catholics as part of the establishment and at the same time reduce that paid to the Anglicans, not to an

[164]Kimberley to Gordon, 9 May 1872, *Maur.*, I, 606–8.

[165]Figures for religious adherents in Mauritius are not very accurate but at most the Church of England had 10,000 adherents and the Roman Catholic church 85,000. In 1872 the government paid £4,099 to the Church of England and £6,800 to the Roman Catholic church as part of the establishment. It made additional special grants which brought the sums received by the two churches to £7,333 and £11,549 respectively. Kimberley did not intend to continue these special grants for more than a short time.

[166]Under this plan Anglicans would have received about £1,150 and Roman Catholics £9,750.

amount (say £1,000) proportionate to their membership, but by half (£2,050). In other words he sacrificed the principle of religious equality in an attempt to ensure the Anglicans £1,000 a year more than they were entitled to, and to save the colonial treasury some £2,050 annually at a time when revenues were running well over £600,000 and showing a fair surplus.[167]

Not very surprisingly both communions rejected Kimberley's plan. The Anglicans would have rejected any scheme which reduced either the absolute sum or the relative amount they received from the colonial treasury. The Roman Catholics, who had petitioned for increased state aid, did not derive enough satisfaction from the prospect of seeing the Anglican grant reduced to ensure their support of the scheme. They now petitioned for abandonment of the proposed separation of church and state, for equalization of state aid through an increase in their own grant, and for help in constructing and maintaining their church buildings.[168] The Anglicans sent a memorial to the Secretary of State asking him to restore the former rights, privileges, and allowances of their bishop, to fill existing vacancies in their establishment, and to continue the grants to which they had been accustomed.[169] In the council Roman Catholic and Anglican members combined to oppose Kimberley's plan. Gordon who might have persuaded them to accept it, was on leave, and Newton, the administrator, either could not or would not do so.

Faced with all this opposition in the colony, as well as questions in Parliament, the Secretary of State decided (except for letters patent) to restore the former conditions. He instructed Newton to fill existing vacancies in the Church of England's establishment. In this happy issue Anglicans saw "the working of the good hand of Almighty God. . . ."[170] Roman Catholics had little reason to rejoice although their bishop now enjoyed the same status as his rival, and the Colonial Office showed a willingness to approve state aid for their church building programme. Gordon made the latter possible by reviving an old ordinance (54 of 1844) under which the state could provide a matching grant once the church itself had raised a stipulated proportion of the sum required.

After the Gladstone ministry fell in 1874 Gordon tried again to reduce the difference in state aid to the two churches. He proposed to

[167]For revenues at this period see below, pp. 140 and 146, fn. 202.

[168]Petition of the Roman Catholic bishop, clergy, and laity, enclosed in Newton to Kimberley, 29 May 1873, PRO CO 167/553.

[169]Memorial of the members of the Church of England enclosed in Newton to Kimberley, 2 May 1873, PRO CO 167/553.

[170]Royston to Newton, 13 Sept. 1873, enclosed in Newton to Kimberley, 18 Sept. 1873, PRO CO 167/555.

lower the Anglican establishment from thirteen to six clergymen and to leave that of the Roman Catholic at thirty-one. The Colonial Office thought his plan not substantially different from Kimberley's and believed it inexpedient to reopen the question until public indignation had subsided.[171] Contenting himself with warning Carnarvon that religious affairs would soon require serious consideration, Sir Arthur allowed the matter to drop.

If Gordon had had more time and fewer distractions, he might have shown greater willingness to press for reforms favourable to Roman Catholics. Still, he had achieved much on their behalf in government employment and education, and a little in church matters. It would be scarcely fair to reproach him for not having done more.

V. THE ESTABLISHMENT

A close relationship always exists between revenues and the cost of carrying on a government on the one hand, and the funds available for public works on the other. Obviously, if the cost of the establishment, of running the public institutions, and of servicing the debt bears a high ratio to the revenue, little money will be left for necessary or desirable public works. Nowhere, perhaps, is this better illustrated than in Mauritius in the early seventies.

Railway building and the calamities of the late sixties had saddled the colony with a large debt which took about one-tenth of the annual total revenue to service. The establishment, both in 1871 and 1872, cost £233,000, or 35 per cent of the average total revenue of £660,000. The public institutions took all but a small fraction of the remainder. The colony paid its way, but it could not find a sufficient surplus both to reduce its debt and to provide for the urgently required expenditures on sanitary works and conservation measures which might re-establish its health. Keenly alive to the life-and-death nature of this latter problem, Gordon gave financial matters his early attention. There were but two ways in which extra funds might be acquired: increasing the revenues and curtailing the fixed costs of government. The former implied raising taxation and the latter meant reducing the cost of the establishment. Nothing could be done about reducing the cost of servicing the debt without reducing the debt itself, and the public institutions offered little scope for savings.

Increased taxation offered some possibility but small probability of enlarged revenues. Gordon doubtless would have had co-operation of

[171]Gordon to Carnarvon, 4 April 1874, and minutes, PRO CO 167/559.

the council, especially of its unofficial members, in increasing the taxes of the lower classes. Those classes already bore an unfair share of the tax load because the planters, in their Barklyan hey-day, had so managed matters that the poorest classes paid about 12 per cent of their incomes in taxes, the professional and middle classes about 6 per cent, and the planters themselves about one per cent.[172] From some taxes planters were specially exempted.

The planters could certainly afford to pay more. The question was, would they? The record indicated that they would not. For example, early in 1870 before Gordon's arrival, General Smyth had managed to get the council to approve a new sanitary law. The Colonial Office had rejected it because the operating funds were to be drawn from the coolies in the form of an income tax to be deducted by their employers. The council had then substituted a house tax, but it, too, bore very heavily on the poorest classes, especially the Indians. Again the Colonial Office refused to sanction the law. Kimberley then suggested that funds be raised by combining an equitable graduated income tax with a uniform capitation or house tax. Gordon agreed that this might be a fair arrangement but realized that the upper classes would oppose the income tax for themselves and without it he did not feel justified in collecting the house or capitation tax. He could find no alternative direct tax the incidence of which would not be too uncertain or which would not be too expensive to collect. He turned, therefore, to the indirect field. He proposed an additional import duty on luxury items such as tobacco and spirits to yield £25,000 a year, and an additional export tax on sugar to yield a further £25,000. To prevent wealthier people who were not engaged in exporting sugar from escaping increased taxation, he proposed a levy on all salaries over a certain amount. Before forwarding these proposals to the Secretary of State,[173] he referred them to the finance committee of the council.[174]

The finance committee, perhaps forgetting in its wrath that on more than one occasion it had recommended taxing the old immigrants as a class, protested vigorously that a tax on sugar would be class taxation. Lord Kimberley rejected this argument because "the health of the Colony is of primary importance to those who make a profit from carrying on its chief enterprise, and whose business, by introducing a very large foreign population, has been directly the cause of the increased expenditure on sanitary objects which is now thrown upon the

[172]Gordon to Palmer, 29 June 1871, *Maur.*, I, 144.
[173]Gordon to Kimberley, 3 May 1872, PRO CO 167/543.
[174]Message to the legislative council, 19 March 1872, *Maur.*, I, 488–90.

Colony."[175] Nevertheless he thought the amount to be raised by the additional sugar tax ought to be reduced to £13,000 and that the other £12,000 should come from an import tax on rice and other grain.[176] He had no objection to the luxury tax, and it was imposed in mid-1872.

Despite Kimberley's concession to the planters, their representatives in the council showed the greatest reluctance even to discuss taxation for sanitary purposes. In September 1872, Gordon carried a motion to go into committee only by his double vote although, once in committee, the council passed, by twelve votes to seven, a motion that additional sums would be required in 1873. He got no further before going on leave in November. In his absence the council passed an ordinance (6 of 1873) imposing a sanitary tax to which Gordon certainly would not have consented. This ordinance, instead of imposing an export tax on sugar and an import tax on grain, imposed only the latter.[177] Furthermore, the council recommended that additional sums if necessary be raised by increasing licence fees and direct taxes. Robert Herbert disapproved:

> I do not think it likely that the Sec[retary] of State would be prepared to sanction an ordinance imposing . . . a tax on the poor man's grain & not at the same time taxing the rich man's export of sugar—the two taxes were suggested by Lord Kimberley as part of one scheme, but the [Finance] Committee [of Mauritius] do not consider it worth while to notice the recommendation from which they dissent, although they quote the despatch in favour of that which suits their views. . . . It will inevitably be said of them . . . that they . . . govern in the interests of a class.[178]

Kimberley prepared to sanction the ordinance despite Herbert's expectations and his own earlier remarks about the justice of a sugar tax. Whereas he had formerly considered an additional sugar tax not only admissible but possessing the advantages of graduating itself according to the producer's means and not being easily evaded,[179] he now found the imposition of an export tax "not easy to defend."[180] Facing the prospect of a clash with the planters over the immigration system, he wished to avoid offending them over taxation.[181] He therefore confirmed the ordinance and expressed his satisfaction with it.[182]

The most charitable view of Kimberley's action is that his anxiety for the health of the community prompted it. However, he had not been

[175]Kimberley to Gordon, 5 July 1872, *Maur.*, I, 650–51.
[176]*Ibid.*
[177]This was additional to the luxury tax on tobacco and spirits.
[178]Herbert's minute, April 1873, minute paper 5572/73, PRO CO 167/552.
[179]Kimberley to Gordon, 5 July 1872, *Maur.*, I, 651.
[180]Kimberley's minute, 6 April 1873, minute paper 5572/73, PRO CO 167/552.
[181]*Ibid.*   [182]Kimberley to Newton, 16 June 1873, PRO CO 167/552.

easy to convince of the colony's unhealthiness. "Smyth and Gordon," Kimberley had complained in 1871, "wish to make out that the island is uninhabitable."[183] He remained sceptical throughout 1872,[184] but a few days before approving the ordinance he had observed plaintively that "the colonists are deaf to all remonstrances against their apathy in sanitary matters."[185] Perhaps, then, his relief that the council had at last done something, even though not what he had recommended, led him to approve the ordinance. His attempt to cloak his retreat from insistence on an additional tax on sugar with an orthodox economic philosophy, must, however, be regarded as specious, because Gordon's recommendation had not been for the imposition of a new export tax but for an increase in an existing one. Kimberley's expression of satisfaction at such obvious class legislation as Ordinance 6 and his change of front in the face of colonial resistance were inexcusable. They served only to increase the obstructionism of the Mauritian planters and council and to dishearten any governor committed to fight for the interests of the poorer classes against a long-dominant exploiting cabal.

At the time of these unsuccessful attempts to force the planters to assume a fairer share of the tax burden, Gordon and the Colonial Office tried to discover a way to reduce the cost of the establishment. Since they could not reduce civil service salaries because of the high cost of living and the hazards to health, they had to look to reductions in the number of civil servants. Barkly had not thought the establishments admitted of any material reduction, but the Colonial Office wondered how such an immense civil service could be required in so small an island.[186] Kimberley instructed Gordon to reduce the heavy cost of government "in every way consistent with good government and the proper protection of the mass of the population."[187] This reservation was inserted at the request of Rogers, who believed that "the Council would be only too glad to retrench offices & duties valuable for the protection of the labourer."[188] Gordon agreed that the burden of the establishment ought to be reduced, but he drew attention to the colony's reluctance

[183]Kimberley's minute, 7 Aug. 1871, on Gordon to Kimberley, 30 June 1871, PRO CO 167/533.
[184]See Kimberley's minute, 1 Oct. 1872, on Gordon to Kimberley, 21 Aug. 1871, PRO CO 167/545.
[185]Kimberley's minute, 8 June 1873, on Newton to Kimberley, 2 May 1873, PRO CO 167/553.
[186]Holland's minute, 28 Feb. 1871, on Smyth to Kimberley, 11 Jan. 1871, enclosing the estimates for 1871. (PRO CO 167/532.) Henry Holland was legal adviser to the Colonial Office at this time.
[187]Kimberley to Gordon, 17 March 1871, PRO CO 167/532.
[188]Rogers' note on draft dispatch to Gordon, 17 March 1871. This note is the only indication I have found that the Colonial Office had its suspicions of the way Mauritius treated its labouring population.

to believe that its system could be improved. He also professed a lack of sufficient financial knowledge to deal with the situation.[189] Kimberley, however, told him that he desired "nothing more than that you should proceed deliberately and cautiously."[190]

In the estimates for 1872, Sir Arthur managed to make cuts in the existing establishment amounting to about £6,000, although the actual saving to the colony came to only £500 because of higher education costs, the opening of a new immigration office at Madras, and some unavoidable new appointments.[191] He did not believe he could make a thorough revision of the establishments without outside help. He could not do it himself without devoting so much time and thought to the details and machinery of each department that it would be fatal to his other equally important duties. He could not count on the Auditor-General who was either ill or drunk. He hoped to get Eagles from Trinidad on an acting appointment as auditor-general. The Colonial Office, although agreeable to this suggestion, "quite despaired" of getting the Mauritian establishments thoroughly revised. Herbert felt that "the Governor, whoever he may be, can never do it, as he cannot without great danger [endure] the unpopularity & undertake the labour involved."[192]

The Colonial Office therefore decided to appoint a commission to inquire into civil and general expenditures in Mauritius. To it Kimberley appointed Penrose Julyan, one of the Crown agents, with F. R. Round, a Colonial Office clerk, as secretary. He required Julyan to report upon the nature, amount, and manner of the work performed in each department,[193] the number of officers employed, the number required, the practicability of consolidation of offices and reduction in salary rates. He also asked him to examine the cost of operating the railways. Temporarily overwhelmed with work, Julyan did not go to Mauritius until the middle of 1873, at which time the Governor was out of the colony.

Although Gordon was usually jealous of his authority, there is no

[189]Gordon to Kimberley, 4 May 1871, PRO CO 167/533. This was nothing more nor less than another argument for being relieved of Mauritius. He had a thoroughly adequate knowledge of financial matters and his financial reports from all his governorships left little to be desired. Meade called them "most creditable" and thought nothing could be clearer. (Meade's minute, 9 March 1872, on Gordon to Kimberley, 11 Jan. 1872, PRO CO 167/540.)

[190]Kimberley to Gordon, 27 June 1871, PRO CO 167/533.

[191]Gordon to Kimberley, 11 Jan. 1872.

[192]Herbert's minute, 16 Jan. 1872, on Gordon to Kimberley (confidential), 14 Dec. 1871, PRO CO 167/537.

[193]Not to be included in the investigation were the supreme court, educational and ecclesiastical establishments.

evidence that he objected either to the appointment of the commission or to its personnel. In any case he hoped not to return to Mauritius. When that hope evaporated, and when, on his return journey, he met and talked with Julyan, his indifference disappeared and he became concerned with the commissioner's behaviour in Mauritius and with his recommendations.

The Governor had formed a poor opinion of Julyan even before this personal encounter. J. G. Daly,[194] the best of the Mauritian magistrates, had written that he considered him a gossip, a snob, and a cockney, no doubt clever in commercial affairs but lacking knowledge and experience of Crown colony administration.[195] If to this observation we add that Julyan was a doctrinaire proponent of colonial self-government, we have a reasonably accurate profile of him. His only direct experience of colonial government had been some commissarial and financial employment in Lower Canada and Australia prior to his appointment as a Crown agent in 1858. After Sir Arthur met him, he fully concurred in Daly's opinion. He called Julyan a "dirty little snob"[196] and "that unholy imperial apostate,"[197] who had fallen "completely into the hands of the enemy."[198] He charged the commissioner with having upset what little discipline the civil service had by the disparaging and familiar way in which he spoke of the Governor in the presence of public servants. Gordon also accused him of meddling in affairs outside the scope of his commission, and listening to, and believing, lies concerning men and affairs in the colony—lies which he repeated in the Colonial Office.[199] Doubtless, Gordon wrote disgustedly to his wife, the Colonial Office would prefer to believe Julyan rather than Frere and Williamson, the royal commissioners.[200]

Although Gordon was on the point of resigning his governorship by the time Julyan's report[201] appeared, neither this fact nor Herbert's assurance that the report contained little of an objectionable nature prevented Gordon from displaying a lively interest in it. Indeed, he pounced upon it and belaboured it. Not that all the recommendations were bad. On the contrary, many were sound and useful, especially where they concerned departmental efficiency. Their implementation by

[194]The son of Sir Dominick Daly, a contemporary colonial governor.
[195]Daly to Gordon, 25 June 1873, *Maur.*, II, 244–45.
[196]Gordon to Lady Gordon, 23 Oct. 1873, *Maur.*, II, 292.
[197]Gordon to Victor Williamson, 31 Jan. 1874, *Maur.*, II, 409–10.
[198]Gordon to Lady Gordon, 23 Oct. 1873.
[199]Gordon to Williamson, 31 Jan. 1874, and Gordon to Frere, 4 Feb. 1874, *Maur.*, II, 409–11.
[200]Gordon to Lady Gordon, 23 Oct. 1873.
[201]Julyan's report constitutes vol. 101, PRO CO 172.

Sir Arthur Phayre reduced the cost of establishments by about £6,000 or 2.5 per cent.[202] Otherwise, however, Julyan's recommendations were unsound in the light of Mauritian conditions, and it is difficult not to believe that he fell under the influence of the Governor's enemies.

Gordon deplored Julyan's proposed reduction of the governor's establishment as tending to weaken the governor's authority, which he had so painstakingly attempted to re-establish.[203] Such a reduction would entail a decrease in the governor's salary or a decrease in his staff or both. Sir Arthur did not object to a reduction in the governor's salary provided it took place at the proper time, that is, upon a change of governors. He had concluded that Mauritius now lacked the importance to warrant a £6,000 a year man as governor. Indeed, he himself had already made a recommendation to this effect and he stood by it.[204] Yet he could hardly accept a cut during his tenure without its reducing his prestige and giving the colonists grounds for believing that the Secretary of State did not appreciate his work.

On only a few occasions during the course of his career did Gordon concern himself with his salary. Rarely did he try to save. On the contrary, he usually made a point of spending his salary in the colony from which he drew it. Probably, as Cox implied, he had threatened to refuse the Mauritius appointment when the Secretary of State reduced the salary from £7,000 to £6,000 on Barkly's retirement.[205] Pride would account for this. He had recommended an increase in the governor's salary in Trinidad, though for his successor, not himself. He had fought with his ministers in New Brunswick over his salary, but on principle, because they were cheating him by paying him in currency rather than sterling. In short, from a mercenary point of view, a high salary did not often interest Gordon.[206] As a prestige symbol, however, it was quite another matter. Conceiving the governor to be partially in fact, and wholly in theory, the Queen's representative in the colony, Gordon considered that he should have a salary large enough to patronize charities liberally and to dispense a certain amount of "royal largesse."

[202]The average annual cost of the establishments was £227,000 between 1878 and 1880 as compared with £233,000 between 1869 and 1873. The percentage of the total revenue taken up by establishments also fell from 39 in 1869 to 33 in 1873 to 29 in 1879, but, for the most part, this was due to increasing revenues. PRO CO 172, vols. 97, 99, 106, and 107.

[203]Gordon's observations on Julyan's report filed with minute paper G/14736/74, PRO CO 167/562.

[204]Ibid.

[205]Marginal note by Cox on minute paper G/14736/74.

[206]On several occasions he had refused appointments carrying higher salaries than he was drawing.

This would increase the respect that colonists ought to have for their governor, which, in turn should enable him to lead them more easily. Gordon's awareness that neither the Colonial Office nor many contemporary governors shared his somewhat peculiar view of the governor's position in the colony probably accounts in part for his willingness that his successor should have a lower salary than his own.

Sir Arthur's reasons for opposing a reduction in the governor's staff were of a more practical kind. In order to be his own prime minister and to keep in close touch with the high officers of the government who lived scattered about in the hills near Réduit, he had been forced to establish a courier service of his own.[207] Consequently his establishment greatly exceeded Barkly's. The latter had managed with a small staff partly because he had allowed the colonial secretary to function as prime minister and partly because he had used civil servants attached to the colonial secretary's office. These practices, however, placed Sir Henry in the colonists' hands—a position Gordon refused to take. He insisted that he could not effectively administer the government without a large staff of his own. The Colonial Office agreed with him and rejected Julyan's proposal, Cox minuting that Mauritius required "a considerable amount of paternal Gov[ernmen]t."[208]

Julyan also recommended opening all public offices in Mauritius to competition among creoles, granting exceptional authority to the colonial secretary, reducing the salaries of the magistrates, making all future appointments from the colonial bar, and, finally, resuming the practice—discontinued in 1871—of allowing the police to share in fines imposed for minor offences. Although expenditures would have decreased had these proposals been adopted, their net effect would have been pernicious. Gordon had already gone as far as desirable in opening the civil service to creoles. He had introduced a modified form of competition which restricted entry to those of good character. Julyan's suggestion would have given employment in the civil service to the cleverest men without regard to their honesty and integrity. The large number of civil servants whom Gordon had to dismiss for dishonesty demonstrated the necessity for an insistence on good character in new appointments. Furthermore, most civil service posts were already held by creoles, and the Governor argued that a leaven of Britons ensured a broader and more disinterested attitude within the service than would be the case were it to be composed entirely of creoles.[209]

---

[207]Messengers had to be employed because postal services in Mauritius were too slow.   [208]Cox's minute on minute paper G/14736/74.

[209]Gordon's observations on Julyan's report, minute paper G/14736/74.

To grant the colonial secretary exceptional authority would simply be to revert to Barkly's system with painful consequences to the Indians and a new decline in the governor's power. To reduce the salaries of the magistrates would discourage the best men from occupying the bench, and ensure that the magistracy would fall even more under planter influence. To refuse to appoint any but creoles to the bench would virtually guarantee a complete absence of even-handed justice. Most magistrates were already products of the colonial bar. The only Englishman appointed between 1870 and 1874 was Daly. He, almost alone among the magistrates, had the desire, courage, independence, and the abstract concept of justice to enforce the law against all offenders regardless of class or race.[210] Lastly, Gordon argued, to allow the police to retain a portion of fines was again to revert to the state of affairs which he found when he first came to the colony. This recommendation also contradicted the findings of the Police Inquiry Commission and of the Royal Commission. Against Julyan's recommendations Gordon's arguments prevailed, and the Colonial Office did not adopt them. Had it acted on them, the trend which Sir Arthur had imparted to the administration in Mauritius would have been reversed and the paths of future governors would have been filled with obstacles.

The reform of the establishments was not one of Gordon's greater successes in Mauritius. He did see to it that reductions offset necessary increases. He did impose a better sense of discipline upon the civil service. "I found it bureaucratic," he wrote, "and have made it autocratic."[211] But he failed to reduce the cost appreciably. The major reasons were his prolonged absences from the colony, the postponements in the appearance of the Julyan mission which discouraged piece-meal reform, and the impossibility, to which Herbert had drawn attention, of the governor's managing a thoroughgoing reform.

VI. PUBLIC WORKS

Although Gordon was not able either to levy much new taxation or to obtain funds through a large reduction in the establishments, he did prevent governmental costs from rising. This fact, coupled with a gradually expanding revenue as prosperity slowly returned to the island,

[210]The need for magistrates of Daly's calibre was demonstrated in 1874 when he imposed a prison sentence on an engineer named Piddington for kicking an Indian—a not uncommon occurrence. If one can judge from the outraged feelings of the European community and the astonishment of the editor of Le Cernéen, such a sentence had never before been imposed. (Le Cernéen, 25 May, 1874.)

[211]Gordon to Lord Richard Cavendish, 11 Nov. 1872, Maur., II, 34.

allowed him during his last months in office to pass or prepare ordinances important to the health and natural resources of the colony. One of these was a new sanitation ordinance (8 of 1874).

Hitherto sanitary arrangements had been looked after by a weak general board of health and a large number of local boards. It had proved impossible in the past to implement useful measures because of local jealousies, lack of central direction, and disputes between boards over methods. Ordinance 8 did not establish a department of health because Sir Arthur did not think a reform of that scope would be accepted. It did, however, strengthen the general board of health and gave it emergency powers for use during epidemics. It also abolished the local boards and substituted for them sanitary guardians, appointed by the governor, assisted by inspectors appointed by the general board. Ordinance 13 supplemented Ordinance 8 and repealed the law under which money for sanitary purposes had been raised by special taxes. It provided that revenues from these taxes would in future go into general revenues and that money for sanitary purposes would be voted as part of the estimates. These two ordinances provided a much needed centralization of authority in sanitary matters. They received a warm welcome in the Colonial Office. Herbert and Carnarvon believed that, despite any protest which might come from Mauritius, the ordinances should be confirmed with strong approval.[212]

Sir Arthur regarded Ordinances 8 and 13 as only part of a general plan for improving the health of the colony. In his message to the council on 17 March 1874, he alluded to the need to prevent pollution of rivers, to conserve existing forests and water-courses, to ensure proper building standards throughout the island, and to provide for the observance of sanitary rules in the villages.[213] He had already appointed commissions to study and make recommendations concerning the first two. He had ordered preparation of a new building ordinance and had nominated a committee of the council to study the fourth. On 8 April, the council, without a division, passed resolutions favouring legislation to solve these problems.[214]

The new building ordinance received second reading just after Gordon left Mauritius (although being in the Seychelles he was still within the colony) and obtained Colonial Office sanction early in 1875. It took into account the report of the council committee on village sanitation and

[212]See minutes on Gordon to Carnarvon, no. 167, 22 June 1874, PRO CO 167/560.
[213]Message to council, *Maur.*, II, 492–98.
[214]Gordon's diary, 7 April 1874, *Maur.*, II, 530.

replaced the law of 1869 which, having passed at the height of bitterness against the old immigrants, had proved too strict for regular enforcement. The new ordinance contented itself with establishing general rules respecting buildings and their sanitary facilities, leaving much to be done by by-laws in Port-of-Spain and much to the discretion of the surveyor-general in the country districts.

In June 1874 Gordon forwarded to the Colonial Office the reports of the commissions on water pollution and forests and water-courses. These provided bases for further legislation related to the health of Mauritius. Of this legislation the most important was the ordinance (18 of 1874) for the protection and disposal of Crown lands, passed shortly after Sir Arthur Phayre's arrival. From the beginning of his administration Gordon had been struck by the rapid denudation of the forests and the resultant destruction of the land and pollution of the streams. In 1872 he tried to halt this trend which was having such an unfortunate effect upon the community's health. As a temporary measure pending a more comprehensive ordinance, he passed Ordinance 9 (1872) to check the rapid destruction of trees and undergrowth on the banks of streams. He himself did not prepare the later ordinance (12 of 1872) and, because it left the way open for large-scale "jobbing" by members of the council, the Secretary of State refused to sanction it. Even without this fault Kimberley would have rejected it because it contemplated compulsory purchase by the Crown of private lands for reforestation. He believed that private owners should not be compelled to sell land to the government, although he did not prohibit the Crown from cautiously purchasing lands adjacent to Crown lands or plots particularly suitable for planting forests. He authorized Gordon to spend up to £5,000 on replanting suitable Crown land.[215] In 1873 the council voted £1,200 for this purpose—a sum which would replant 300 acres of the 11,500 acres which required reforestation.[216] In July 1874 Gordon asked the Colonial Office to approve a vote of £3,000 for the purchase of certain forest lands required for the protection of the water supply. Herbert and Carnarvon reluctantly agreed, at the same time warning Sir Arthur Phayre to be very cautious in making future purchases. Although the sums spent were small Gordon made a start upon the physical rehabilitation of the island. Ordinance 18, which finally replaced Ordinance 9 of 1872, ensured that the new trend would not be reversed. It provided that

[215]Kimberley to Gordon, 30 July 1872, *Maur.*, I, 668–70.
[216]The total area of Crown land in Mauritius in 1873 was 54.79 square miles (about 8 per cent of the island's area) of which half was forested. Of the remaining half, 18.25 square miles required replanting. (Newton to Kimberley, 28 May 1873, PRO CO 167/553.)

Government House, Nasova, Fiji, 1876

Government House, Wellington, New Zealand, *circa* 1880

Queen's House, Colombo, *circa* 1885

A Scene near Queen's Cottage, Nuwara Eliya, *circa* 1885

the governor in executive council might dispose of Crown lands except those in the mountain reserves, the river reserves, or the Pas Géometrique.[217] (Lands in the last might be leased provided that the lessee planted trees.) It required the surveyor-general to plant trees on unleased Crown lands, allowed squatters to purchase Crown lands provided they were not required for public purposes, prohibited free grants of Crown lands except for religious, charitable, or educational purposes, and gave the surveyor-general authority to enter upon and survey private lands, and to appoint forest rangers.[218]

Although much of this new legislation failed to carry Gordon's name it may, nevertheless, be placed to his credit. He provided the initiative and appointed the commissions and committees upon whose findings it was based. Impressed by the number of reports and projected ordinances coming from Mauritius during the last months of Gordon's administration, one of the Colonial Office clerks noted that Sir Arthur Phayre would have plenty to do.[219] The latter, like Gordon, a "strong" governor, proved a suitable successor, carrying on the policies and implementing the measures which Gordon by resigning in mid-1874 had been unable to accomplish.

VII. RESIGNATION

Gordon had found his task in Mauritius far more exacting than that in Trinidad. It had been one thing in Trinidad to revive a power which had simply not been exercised for twenty years and to do it with the advantage of a slight beginning made by his predecessors and the encouragement of both Buckingham and Granville. It was quite another in Mauritius, where he had uncovered "a state of things . . . which," in Herbert's words, "we had not been led to expect,"[220] to attempt to re-create an authority which had suffered from anemia since 1849 and which Barkly had done nothing to resuscitate and much to kill. Moreover, in Mauritius, Gordon had, in Lord Kimberley, to deal with a secretary of state reluctant to believe in the appalling nature of Mauritian conditions, reluctant to admit that the colonists would not willingly make the necessary changes, reluctant to give the governor greater authority, and

[217]A belt round the island of not less than 250 French feet measured inland from the high-water mark.
[218]Phayre to Carnarvon, 10 Dec. 1874, PRO CO 167/561. One of the first forest rangers was Adolphe de Plevitz.
[219]R. J. S. Macdonald's minute, 14 Aug. 1874, on Gordon to Carnarvon, 24 June 1874, PRO CO 167/560.
[220]Herbert's minute, 13 March 1872, on Gordon to Kimberley, 9 Feb. 1872, PRO CO 167/541.

reluctant to face questions in Parliament by spokesmen for the Mauritian planters who rose to query the decisions of the governor even on minor points of discipline in the civil service. Unable, in the face of these difficulties, to make the governor supreme, Gordon managed, nevertheless, to make his will count for something, and to rescue the governor's office from being as much a dead-letter in Mauritius as it had become in the responsible government colonies. This was his most important achievement. Without it neither he nor his successors could have overcome the inertia of that isolated and ingrown society which had abandoned only those aspects of slavery which were disadvantageous to the ruling planter class. Without it he could not have accomplished or set in motion the reforms already discussed.

Although the revolution which he effected in Mauritius was less thoroughgoing and complete than the one he had made in Trinidad, it was nevertheless substantial. From it dates the rapid improvements which the colony experienced during the late years of the century: the betterment of the lot of the Indian immigrants, fairer treatment of Roman Catholics especially in respect to education and the government service, improvement in the island's health, and progress in the Seychelles dependency. That he accomplished so much with so little encouragement from anyone in the Colonial Office except Herbert and under the insults and abuse heaped upon him by a colonial society and press which hated him, his policies, and his philosophy of government says much for his determination and his devotion to duty.

As the time approached for him to comply with his promise to his wife to return to England within a year (by September 1874), Gordon decided to resign his governorship. From his first weeks in the colony he had made up his mind to remain in Mauritius for as short a time as possible. Indeed, his resignation had long been in Herbert's hands although he had not insisted on the Colonial Office's accepting it as long as such action might harm the public interest. By mid-1874 he had initiated all the major reforms he contemplated, and it seemed from Frere's repeated heart attacks that the report of the royal commission might be indefinitely delayed. There seemed little point in his remaining longer, and he asked Herbert to place his resignation in the hands of the Secretary of State. Now that Lord Carnarvon had replaced Lord Kimberley in the Colonial Office, Gordon expected a firm offer of new and more interesting employment.

As long as Lord Kimberley remained secretary of state, Gordon felt he would never be given an acceptable appointment. In the autumn of

1873 he concluded that his colonial career had come to an end and he considered a return to the House of Commons.[221] The dissolution of 1874 came too soon, however, and he gloomily contemplated a writer's life on Clapham Common.[222] His dejectedness grew with the appointment, to Jamaica, Ceylon, and the Straits, of men who had not held previous governorships. He could not really condemn these appointments because he himself objected so strongly to the office of governor being considered "*a profession*" that he was "always glad to see outsiders appointed."[223] Yet, he thought three in a row a bit much. What he found even more disheartening were Sir Henry Barkly's G.C.M.G. and Sir John Scott's[224] K.C.M.G. "Good Heavens!" he exclaimed to Victor Williamson, "what temptations the Colonial Office throws before one to shut one's eyes to all things unpleasant—to take life as it comes, and to smooth away all ugly roughnesses from the glossy surfaces of the picture of universal all-rightness which it is so comfortable to oneself to paint, and which the C. O. so earnestly desires to have painted."[225] To Lady Gordon, he added, "they ought to give me the Grand Cross or make me a Privy Councillor to balance this."[226]

Gordon was so certain of Kimberley's dislike of him that, despite his hatred of Disraeli and his love and respect for Gladstone, he almost welcomed the defeat of the government in 1874. He infinitely preferred the new Secretary of State to the old. Lord Carnarvon he considered "a perfect gentleman," not clever but devoted to his work, while Kimberley, he believed, "never cared to give his full attention to Colonial matters . . ." because he was "so bitterly disappointed at not being made Foreign Secretary on Lord Clarendon's death. . . ."[227] Whether or not Sir Arthur correctly assessed Lord Kimberley's attitude, his relationship with the Colonial Office improved after the change of ministers. When

[221]Lord Selborne told Gordon that he had been the subject of a cabinet conversation in 1873. (Gordon to Selborne, 26 Sept. 1873, *Maur.*, II, 269.) It may have concerned his return to Parliament or an under-secretaryship.

[222]He wished, when the opportunity offered, to prepare his father's correspondence for publication.

[223]Gordon to Selborne, 13 Oct. 1873, *Maur.*, II, 282.

[224]Sir John Scott, lieutenant-governor Labuan 1850–56, governor Natal 1856–65, British Guiana 1868–73, retired 1873.

[225]Gordon to Williamson, 27 May 1874, *Maur.*, II, 606–7.

[226]Gordon to Lady Gordon, 15 April–1 May 1874, *Maur.*, II, 565.

[227]Gordon to Selborne, 28 July 1874, *Maur.*, II, 668–69. There is no evidence to support this conjecture but it may account for the lack of friendship between Gladstone and Kimberley. Kimberley, while a member of all four of Gladstone's ministries, never once visited Hawarden. My authority for this statement is a remark made by Henry Gladstone to Professor Paul Knaplund in 1923 which the latter quoted to me in a letter dated 31 Jan. 1961.

Herbert informed him that Carnarvon would probably offer him the new colony of Fiji,[228] he happily returned to England in time both to keep his promise to his wife and to give his successor the benefit of his advice. He left Mauritius with a deep sense of relief although he confessed "to some qualms of conscience" because he foresaw that some of his friends would "have a rough time of it" and that Gorrie and Daly especially would encounter great difficulties.[229]

[228]Herbert to Gordon, 5 June 1874, *Maur.*, II, 660–61.
[229]Gordon to Williamson, 30 June 1874, *Maur.*, II, 641.

V

FIJI, 1875–1882

✤

I. FIJIAN PROSPECT

NO COUNTRY can have acquired a colony from more altruistic motives than those which prompted Britain to annex Fiji. Although Australians and New Zealanders, uneasy over French, German, and American activities in Oceania, had been urging the mother country to adopt a British "Monroe Doctrine" for the Pacific,[1] most British statesmen continued firm in their (by now traditional) anti-expansionism. Convinced that the Empire was already too large, the Imperial government abhorred the thought of adding to its overseas responsibilities. Only strong humanitarian pressures persuaded the authorities in 1874 to accept the proffered unconditional cession of the Fiji Islands.

For several years British humanitarians had been urging that it was Britain's duty to correct the abuses of the infamous Western Pacific labour traffic because the majority of those implicated in the traffic were British subjects, mostly Australians. Fiji would be an ideal base from which to exercise control. When it became obvious that the Pacific Islanders Protection Act of 1872—Britain's first attempt to control the activities of her subjects in the labour trade—had failed, the humanitarians increased their demands for action.[2] These coincided with growing

[1]Paul Knaplund, "Sir Arthur Gordon and Fiji: Some Gordon-Gladstone Letters," *Historical Studies Australia and New Zealand*, VIII, 1958, 282.

[2]The *Sydney Morning Herald* on 11 July 1878 noted that Britain annexed Fiji unwillingly and probably would not have annexed it except for the philanthropic aim of controlling the labour traffic. It noted, too, that the "economical party" in Britain had predicted "heavy and incessant raids on that most long-suffering mortal, the British taxpayer." (Enclosure in Des Voeux to Secretary of State, 19 Aug. 1878, PRO CO 83/17.)

political difficulties in Fiji itself. There, the interests of the predominantly British (Australian and New Zealand) white population conflicted with those of the Wesleyan-converted Fijians, and again humanitarian voices in England requested that the islands be annexed in order that the natives might be protected from settler exploitation. The Gladstone government refused to intervene in 1872 on the ground that "King Cakobau's[3] Government," the new local administration which represented both whites and natives, ought to have a chance to show its worth.[4] By the following year it had become obvious that the experiment had failed and that bankruptcy had overtaken the government. Appeals then came from Fiji for annexation, and Gladstone reluctantly sent a commission, comprising Captain Goodenough, commodore of the Australian station, and E. L. Layard, consul for Fiji and Tonga, to report on the Fijian situation.

Although the British government still hoped to avoid annexing the islands, the commission strongly recommended it. The Gladstone administration had fallen by the time the commission reported, but the new government proved almost as reluctant as the former to accept sovereignty over Fiji. Lord Carnarvon, to whom Disraeli left the decision, finally concluded, however, that he had no alternative and empowered Sir Hercules Robinson, governor of New South Wales, to negotiate with King Cakobau and the leading chiefs of Fiji an unconditional cession of their country to the Queen. On 10 October 1874 Robinson proclaimed Fiji a British colony.[5]

Gordon's connection with Fiji began in June 1873 when he offered either to go to Fiji as a commissioner to report on the expediency of admitting it to the colonial empire, or, if the British government decided to accept sovereignty over it, to undertake organization of the new colony's government.[6] Kimberley rejected this offer. Gordon therefore drew considerable pleasure from Herbert's letter which said that Lord

---

[3]Cakobau is the Fijian spelling. The word is pronounced and, in English, spelled, as "Thakombau." The major differences in spelling are that the Fijian "g" is rendered as "ng" in English, "b" as "mb," and "c" as "th." I have, however, employed Fijian spelling throughout because it is the form used in the documents of the period.

[4]Knaplund, "Sir Arthur Gordon and Fiji," 282.

[5]For detailed treatments of the annexation of Fiji see J. D. Legge, *Britain in Fiji, 1858–1880*; E. Drus, "The Colonial Office and the Annexation of Fiji," *Transactions Royal History Society*, 1950; W. P. Morrell, *Britain in the Pacific Islands*; R. A. Derrick, *A History of Fiji*; J. M. Ward, *British Policy in the South Pacific*.

[6]Gordon to Kimberley (private), 8 June 1873, Stanmore Papers, 49199.

Carnarvon agreed with him that Gordon was "in many ways qualified to make the best of that very queer bargain which appears almost certain to be forced upon us. . . ." Herbert doubted whether Fiji could raise sufficient revenue to pay for even the simplest Crown colony government, but, he added, "nothing but a despotism is thought of [and] if John Bull chooses to incur the cost, much good can be done in Fiji; and you are the man to do it."[7]

Gordon appreciated the "prospect of *founding* a colony." He would, he judged, make a serious error if he shirked "the greatest chance of *individual* action I have ever yet had—[It is] probably *the* point of my career. . . ."[8] Still, he hesitated. Lady Gordon had told him she would go anywhere that conditions were at all suitable for the children, but he feared the long exile would be a "terrible banishment" for his family.[9] Moreover, Gladstone and the Liberals had opposed the annexation of Fiji and, if he accepted, he did not wish to be considered a party renegade. Should he go to Fiji he hoped Gladstone would not attack the governor however much he might attack the annexation.[10] Gladstone, however, assured him that anyone who undertook the task of setting the new colony to rights would have the "greatest claim to forbearance if he cannot have support."[11]

Shortly after Sir Arthur's return to England Carnarvon privately and confidentially outlined to him the conditions under which the governor of Fiji would be required to work. "There are very few," wrote Carnarvon, "to whom I should think it desirable to speak thus unreservedly, especially in the great uncertainty in which I find myself & in which I must remain until I can receive Sir H. Robinson's written & detailed opinions as to the course to be pursued."[12] As things stood, however, it appeared that the governor must accept a low salary at first, stay for a full term or longer if he were successful "which in this case is an essential condition," and manage with but few assistants, although those who would accompany him would be as strong men as could be secured. Carnarvon made it plain that he wanted Gordon for the new post. Nevertheless, he gave him the option of refusing the appointment by adding that "Fiji is not the only place in which a

[7]Gordon to Lady Gordon, 15 July 1874, *Maur.*, II, 646–49.
[8]*Ibid.*
[9]Gordon to Gladstone (private and confidential), 4 Dec. 1874, Gladstone Papers, 44320.
[10]*Ibid.*
[11]Gladstone to Gordon, 6 Dec. 1874, Gladstone Papers, 44320.
[12]When Robinson had been sent to Fiji to accept sovereignty, he was asked to report on possible future policies.

colonial minister may hope to have the advantage of experience & ability such as yours."[13]

Gordon put off his decision for some weeks, but there can be little doubt that he would have accepted Fiji without the pressure which Carnarvon finally put on him by first obtaining the Queen's approval of the appointment and then asking him to accept it "as authorized by Her Majesty." The Secretary of State also arranged for him to be invited to Windsor where, as Gordon told Gladstone, conversation took place which made refusal difficult.[14] After a final reassurance by Carnarvon that his acceptance of Fiji would not mean a loss of status (as Gladstone and Cardwell had suggested), Sir Arthur agreed to take the post.[15] He felt certain that there lay the great chance to gratify his life-long ambition of making a name for himself. The Secretary of State felt he had done well for Fiji in securing Gordon as governor because he believed him to be "the fittest man within my knowledge to undertake a very difficult and equally delicate task."[16] In announcing the appointment to Sir Hercules Robinson he wrote: "Sir Arthur Gordon's ability, and his administrative experience in Colonies in which the coloured inhabitants form a large majority of the population, will, I doubt not, qualify him in a special degree for the work of organizing the new Government. . . . I am satisfied that there could be no greater mistake than to commit to weak or inexperienced hands the solution of such difficult questions as those which will have to be met at the outset in taking over the new dependency of Fiji."[17]

Late in March 1875, Sir Arthur, with his family, personal staff, and several of his administrative officers, sailed for Fiji. They reached Sydney in mid-May and remained there for nearly three weeks enabling Sir Hercules Robinson to brief Sir Arthur on Fijian affairs. Leaving his wife and children to follow in September, Gordon embarked for Fiji on 14 June and landed at Nasova, the temporary capital, on 25 June.

[13]Carnarvon to Gordon (private and confidential), 23 Oct. 1874, Stanmore Papers, 49199. This letter appears also in the Carnarvon Papers, PRO GD 6/39.

[14]Gordon to Gladstone (private and confidential), 4 Dec. 1874. It may be doubted that Carnarvon would have gone this far without a fairly definite understanding with Gordon. It may well be that Sir Arthur over-emphasized the pressure in his letters to Gladstone in order to neutralize any criticism which the latter might have had of his acceptance of the governorship of a colony whose acquisition Gladstone had opposed.

[15]Gordon to Carnarvon (private), 29 Dec. 1874, and Carnarvon to Gordon, 30 Dec. 1874, Carnarvon Papers, PRO GD 6/39.

[16]Carnarvon to Gordon, 27 Aug. 1878, in Stanmore, *Fiji: Records of Private and of Public Life, 1875–1880*, III, 165. References to these papers will be cited hereafter in abbreviated form as *Fiji*.

[17]Carnarvon to Robinson, 16 Jan. 1875, PRO CO 83/5.

After months of rain, "Queen's weather" welcomed the "Queen's chosen representative" to the islands. This led the editor of the *Fiji Times* to hope that "the beams of sunshine" augured a "glorious summer of prosperity and contentment."[18] Yet immediate prospects for the colony's future and Sir Arthur's success were gloomy. When he had undertaken "to reduce the Fijian chaos to order" many thought he had accepted a most unpromising job.[19] Within a fortnight of reaching Nasova Gordon thought so too. "I see my task here will be an uphill one," he told Carnarvon, "but with God's help & your support I believe much may be done. . . ."[20] Fiji's situation had greatly worsened in the interval between his acceptance of the governorship and his arrival. A prolonged spell of bad weather had ruined crops, reduced exports and imports, curtailed customs revenues, and brought the planters, already badly hit by falling cotton prices, to the verge of ruin. A much worse calamity had befallen the natives. In the first half of 1875 an epidemic of measles killed about 40,000 of the estimated population of 150,000 Fijians. Coming so soon after the beginning of British rule the disaster made the natives suspicious of British intentions. Certain irresponsible people among the European population encouraged native suspicions. The *Fiji Times*, for instance, insinuated that the administration (in particular John Bates Thurston, the acting colonial secretary) had deliberately introduced the measles in order to destroy the native race.[21] The insinuation of the *Times* was arrant nonsense, prompted partly by wishful thinking but mostly by hatred of Thurston, who had done his best to protect natives from white exploitation. Native suspicions were unfounded, but they presented a formidable obstacle to Gordon's successful administration of the colony.

The epidemic had two noteworthy ill-effects on Fiji's finances. The Imperial government reduced its proposed grant to the colony from £150,000 to £100,000,[22] evidently on the dubious reasoning that, because the native population had been decreased by a quarter, Fiji

[18]*Fiji Times*, 25 June 1875, extract printed in Parl. Pap., 1876, LIV [C-1404].

[19]*Sydney Morning Herald*, 11 July 1878, editorial enclosed in Des Voeux to Secretary of State, 19 Aug. 1878.

[20]Gordon to Carnarvon, 12 July 1875, Carnarvon Papers, PRO GD 6/39.

[21]Minutes on Robinson to Secretary of State, 17 March 1875, PRO CO 83/6. The epidemic occurred after Cakobau and his two sons, who had contracted mild cases of measles during their return voyage from a visit to Sydney, were allowed to land in Fiji before they had completely recovered. Responsibility for the disaster rested with the captain and medical officer of H.M.S. *Dido*. They failed to impress upon Layard the serious consequences that might result from failure to place the patients in quarantine.

[22]Gordon to Carnarvon, 9 May 1877, PRO CO 83/13.

would require a third less financial assistance. Secondly, the colony's revenues from customs and native taxes dropped, resulting in a large deficit in 1875 instead of the modest surplus which Robinson had expected.

Sir Arthur, therefore, faced a most complex task at the outset of his administration of Fiji. He had to establish his administration and create the essential services. He had also to provide a supply of labour for the planters and attract capital for the development of the colony. At the same time he had to undertake the procedure, outlined in his instructions from the Secretary of State, for settling the many hundred land claims. Moreover, without delay, he had to evolve a native policy that would allay the distrust caused by the epidemic and earn the future co-operation of Fijians, chiefs and commoners alike. To shoulder this burden was a formidable undertaking at best, but to shoulder it with only two-thirds of the Imperial assistance he had expected and with the colony's obviously heavy deficit would have been to attempt the impossible without dictatorial powers and a competent staff. Fortunately Sir Arthur possessed both. After a week in Fiji he wrote:

> You will think me very pertinaceous, very tiresome—possibly very importunist, but I, at whatever risk, feel compelled to repeat, *usque ad nauseam*, what I have several times said before. For God's sake, don't try to govern Fiji in detail from Downing Street. I will do my best to carry out honestly & loyally your views, and attain your objects, but unless you allow me almost entire liberty as to my *mode* of action, you will make it impossible for me successfully to carry on the government, and you have told me that success is essential to my stay.
>
> ... I am very happy and perfectly in my element. I am confident that, if let alone, I *can* & *shall* succeed, but you cannot conceive how differently many questions look when one is able to judge them on the spot from what they did in London. For one thing, I withdraw my opinion as to the constant presence of a man of war, and am of opinion that *no* military force, except a strong but cheap native police force, is needed. . . .
>
> My dear Lord Carnarvon; you told me I might rely on your support. Without that assurance, I would not have taken the post. Shew it by *trusting* me, & [by] supposing that I *can* deal with the circumstances which present themselves to me. I am not a bit afraid of *you* in this respect, but I am very much afraid of some of the old regular habitués of office, who won't or can't, see the difference between a long settled colony, and a new field. If I am to work *cheaply* I shall have in many ways to run counter to routine.[23]

The Secretary of State's reply to this impertinent letter could scarcely have been more satisfactory to Gordon. It not only assured him of Lord Carnarvon's "full confidence" and "full support," but promised him

[23]Gordon to Carnarvon (private), 2 July 1875, Carnarvon Papers, PRO GD 6/39.

"very free action" in dealing with the questions that would arise. It also flattered the pronounced streak of vanity and catered to the constant need for reassurance which ran intertwined in Gordon's character. Carnarvon wrote:

When I proposed to you to undertake the serious task of starting the Colony in its new life, it was amongst other reasons because I knew that you w[oul]d not need or look for the constant guidance from Downing St. which some Gov[erno]rs expect and which in some circumstances is necessary. Beyond this I know you will not expect me to go. You will, I am satisfied, appreciate my meaning and neither on the one hand doubt my sincere anxiety to give you every support and discretion, nor on the other hand understand my words to mean such an abdication of my own control as would—even when I can trust as fully as I can to you—be unusual & undesirable and such as I am sure you would not wish to ask.[24]

Sir Arthur, referring to the one reservation that the letter contained, replied that "any such 'abdication' of your powers . . . would be absurd, as well as wrong. All I require is to know that, as the Speaker says—'you will ever put the most favourable construction on my words & actions.' "[25]

Although Gordon, throughout his administration of Fiji, successfully attempted in his dispatches and vivid private letters to Carnarvon and Herbert to inform the Colonial Office of the condition of the country and its inhabitants, he kept his most important plans and policies to himself. Looking to the Governor to initiate plans and policies, Carnarvon nevertheless expected to be given a chance to refuse or modify them before they were implemented. Sir Arthur, however, informed the Colonial Office of them only after he had put them into operation. This procedure hardly endeared him to Herbert and Carnarvon, least of all to the "old regular habitués" of the office. Both the Secretary and Under-Secretary bore their ignorance with fortitude and although they disagreed with certain of Gordon's proceedings seldom reproved him.

Gordon not only asked for a free hand in formulating policies but insisted on nominating most of the officers who would be responsible for carrying out those policies. This earned him a mild rebuke from Herbert:

No man can be more considerate than Lord Carnarvon, and . . . I believe you are satisfied that what you ask is not only reasonable but necessary. Still . . . you are putting a very unusual amount of pressure upon the Secretary of State, who I honestly think cannot go very far in appointing persons entirely unknown to himself on the recommendation of the first Governor.

[24]Carnarvon to Gordon, 28 Sept. 1875, Stanmore Papers, 49199.
[25]Gordon to Carnarvon (private), 24 Dec. 1875, Carnarvon Papers, PRO GD 6/39.

I am sure you will remember that although there is the greatest value in your being strongly armed at first with men you can trust, the Government you establish must not be too *personal* in its nature, as you will not stay in Fiji forever.

Lord Carnarvon is not accustomed to stipulations from Governors as to their subordinate employees, and at all events you may as well let me know in the first instance what you feel you must demand.[26]

Nevertheless, Gordon succeeded, and all but one or two of the officers who formed his government and filled the major posts in the colony's civil service were his selections.

Surely no other colony of the day could boast a higher proportion of able administrators than Fiji. Outstanding among them were Dr. William MacGregor and Captain Arthur Havelock, both of whom had worked under Gordon in Mauritius, Charles Mitchell of Trinidad, and George Ruthven Le Hunte, a young graduate of Cambridge. All except Mitchell were destined to become successful colonial governors. So was John Thurston, whom Gordon found acting as colonial secretary in the temporary administration established by Robinson. Gordon rescued Thurston from the almost certain obscurity to which his unpopularity among the European population seemed to doom him. He at once recognized Thurston's ability and made him his chief adviser. As a result Thurston was able to devote the remainder of his life to Fiji, the last ten years as governor. He deserves to share with Gordon the paternity of modern Fiji.

Gordon had several other valuable assistants. David Wilkinson, a Fiji planter and a master of native dialects, became Sir Arthur's commissioner for native affairs. John Gorrie, whom he persuaded the Colonial Office to send from Mauritius, early replaced the ailing Sir William Hackett as chief justice. Alfred P. Maudslay, an intelligent young archaeologist, whom he had met at Brisbane and invited to visit Fiji hoping that he might find the means to employ him, became his general handy-man filling various offices (among them the colonial secretaryship) with distinction. Captain Louis F. Knollys, the Governor's aide-de-camp, and A. J. L. Gordon, Sir Arthur's private secretary, often found themselves employed on other than their nominal duties. Finally, there was Walter S. Carew, a long-time settler, who did useful work as Gordon's commissioner in the large island of Viti Levu on whose interior tribes he was an acknowledged expert.

Under Sir Arthur's guidance, this group of less than a dozen men brilliantly and successfully created and managed the colony through its first difficult years. That the Governor welded together this heterogeneous

[26]Herbert to Gordon, 19 Dec. 1874, Stanmore Papers, 49199.

collection of men, some of whom were markedly egoistic, bound them to himself by ties of affection and deep respect, and overcame their mutual jealousies and suspicions, especially those arising between the old "Fiji hands" and the men fresh from home, speaks much for his ability as a manager of men and a statesman.

Gordon did not assume the governorship immediately on landing in Fiji. E. L. Layard, the acting administrator, had received no orders from the Foreign Office to proceed to his consulate at Tonga and refused to leave Fiji and await orders in Sydney. Gordon decided consequently to allow the acting administration to continue temporarily. Although Herbert thought the arrangement "foolish & inconvenient," and Carnarvon believed it could not "conduce to good gov[ernmen]t,"[27] Gordon found it satisfactory. It relieved him of office work and gave him time to observe men and affairs so that when he took complete command on 1 September 1875 he was able to act decisively.

No special problem attached to the establishment of the government. The Colonial Office had decided that Fiji would be a Crown colony of a "very severe type." Power would rest with the governor, assisted by an executive council and a small legislative council consisting of four official and three unofficial members. Gordon decided to give the officials only acting appointments at first and to appoint the unofficials from among the men whose names had been suggested to him at a meeting of the European community. Such was the arrangement for the government of the European population and for the colony in general. As for the native community tentative arrangements had already been made. Sir Hercules Robinson, who believed that "for many years to come, Fiji can only be governed . . . through the instrumentality of the native chiefs,"[28] had appointed a native governor or *roko* over each of Fiji's twelve provinces and a sub-chief or *buli* over each of the country's eighty-two districts. Robinson had visualized the government issuing its orders to the *rokos* and *bulis*, who would then carry them out. Gordon was prepared to accept this organization but not the method. He proposed instead to accord the Fijians a large measure of "home rule," with what success will be seen in a later section.

II. FINANCE

The most urgent problem confronting Sir Arthur when he assumed the governorship of Fiji was that of finance. Unless he could solve it his

---

[27]Minutes on Gordon to Carnarvon (confidential), 27 June 1875, PRO CO 83/6.
[28]Robinson to Carnarvon, 20 Oct. 1874, PRO CO 83/5.

plans for Fiji would be jeopardized and his administration would be considered a failure. Moreover, because it was unthinkable that the British taxpayer could for long be asked to pay the cost of governing a colony, the Imperial government would be forced either to depend solely upon its warships to maintain order in Fiji or to turn it over to its white settlers to do with as they might. Although Gordon had once denied having special financial ability[29] he was to demonstrate in Fiji a capacity for fiscal innovation and management that marked him as an expert, and when he left the colony it was able to support itself.

Sir Hercules Robinson had estimated that in 1875 revenues would be just under £25,000 and expenditures nearly £18,000. Actually the government took in only about £16,000 and spent more than double that amount. At this rate bankruptcy would soon have overtaken the new administration, as it had the old, despite the Imperial grant.[30] The Colonial Office expected the colony to pay its way by the time the grant had been spent. It dared not ask Parliament for more. Hence Gordon had to find new sources of revenue, more especially since, unlike the Colonial Office, he was not content merely to establish an administration capable of maintaining order and protecting the natives from further exploitation. He believed that the government should play a positive rôle in colonial society, that it should help the natives and develop the economy. Consequently he contemplated a more elaborate and costly establishment than the Colonial Office did.

Gordon observed that neither the tax levied on the natives by Cakobau's government nor that instituted by Sir Hercules Robinson had produced much revenue. Since Britain had annexed Fiji for the natives' benefit and since most of the local government's revenues would be spent on their behalf, Sir Arthur reasoned that the natives ought to make a substantial contribution to those revenues. Robinson had abolished the poll-tax because many natives who had been unable to pay it had practically been sold to European planters. Gordon believed that the object of the poll-tax had not been primarily to raise a revenue but to force natives to work on white men's plantations. Had Robinson not abolished it Gordon would have. He also rejected Robinson's substitute, which had allowed the natives either to give twenty days' labour on public works or to pay an equivalent amount in cash. Most Fijians preferred work to cash payment and Fiji could not employ the number of labourers wishing to do public work. Gordon had to rule out this method of taxing. Since

[29]See p. 144.
[30]In theory this was not a grant but an interest-free loan to be repaid when the colony could afford it.

the natives used large quantities of imported cloth and cutlery, they made some contribution to customs revenues, but they bought few other articles on which duties were levied. Since, moreover, they did not consume large quantities of spirits, take out licences, or use stamps,[31] Sir Arthur concluded that only through some special tax could they be made to contribute much to the revenues.

On his voyage out to Fiji he had roughly outlined a plan founded on the Dutch system in Java as E. B. Money had described it in *How to Govern a Colony*, and it was this system, with major modifications, that he adopted. Under it Fijians would be required to pay their taxes in kind. Briefly, the method of imposing the tax was this: the government first decided what sum it required from the natives. It then called upon the traders to submit tenders for certain specified articles of native produce. In the light of the contracted prices the legislative council decided the quantity of produce required from the natives and assessed each province in accordance with its productivity. The native provincial council then assessed each district in the province; the district council assessed each village in the district; and the village authorities organized plantations and the labour of the villagers. The principle underlying assessments at each level was very close to the socialist principle of "from each according to his ability." One great difference between the native tax systems in Fiji and Java was that in the latter any surplus produce became the property of the government whereas, in Fiji, it remained the property of the natives to dispose of as they saw fit.

Gordon's native taxation scheme had advantages for both the government and the natives. From it the government derived a sizeable revenue at little cost[32] or inconvenience. Through it the government could encourage the Fijians to slough off their indolence, adopt better forms and methods of agriculture, and learn the value of their produce. Only by such gentle and persistent pressure, Gordon calculated, could Fijians be led to a higher stage of civilization without being debauched or having their will to live destroyed. Moreover, the taxation scheme was an important part of Gordon's whole policy of encouraging the natives to govern and do things for themselves.[33]

The natives found the new tax the least oppressive and disturbing of any they had yet encountered. No longer, in order to earn tax money, were they to be forced to labour half a year for the white planter or to

[31]Most Fijians could read and write their own language and were great letter writers, but Fiji had no internal mail service and letters had to be sent by courier.

[32]In 1878, for example, the cost of collecting £18,178 worth of produce was only £1,407.

[33]See below sec. III, especially the long quotations on p. 193.

sell their produce to a trader for a fraction of its value. Instead, they were to be confirmed in their traditional occupations of tillers of the soil and gatherers of its fruit. Working in village plantations to raise produce for taxation purposes did not seem strange to Fijians because they were accustomed to contribute to their chiefs' support by produce or labour. Finally, the Fijians were not far removed from communal life. They did not see themselves as individuals but only as part of a group. A communal tax they could understand and on a communal project they would willingly work. As John Thurston, who probably knew and understood Fijian society better than any other man, put it:

The individual, as regards rights and obligations, is not known to Fijian law. . . . They do and suffer as communities. . . . They are under the authority of one patriarchal head or Chief; hence they act well in communities, but as individuals they fail, for as a rule they have no individuality.[34]

Later, in recalling the remark made by Cakobau and other chiefs at Draiba in 1875 (" 'Whoever' said they, 'heard of a man building a house, or making a canoe, or forming a garden for himself?' "), Thurston commented:

No [Fijian] man dreams of making a garden, or building a house, for the simple reason that he does not feel himself to have any individual existence. He is only one of a brotherhood or family and can only think and act with its other members. His wants must be made known to his chief, who discusses the matter with the . . . old men of the village, and they decide what shall be done. If a garden is to be made, or a house is to be built the whole village assembles and the work is done. But for a man to attempt doing anything of the sort for himself is from a Fijian point of view either ridiculous or insolent.[35]

With these remarks in mind it is not difficult to understand why the two previous attempts to tax the natives failed and why Gordon's attempt succeeded.

In February 1876, Sir Arthur described his tax proposal in a long dispatch which he forwarded with an even longer memorandum on the same subject by Thurston. Together Gordon and Thurston made out a strong case for the scheme, Thurston explaining its consistency with native character and customs, Sir Arthur noting the failure and oppres-

[34]Thurston's "Memorandum upon the Establishment of District Plantations in the Colony of Fiji for the purpose of enabling the Native Population to Provide their Taxes in a manner accordant with Native Customs," enclosed in Gordon to Carnarvon, no. 22, 16 Feb. 1876, PRO CO 83/9.

[35]Thurston's "Memorandum on Native Taxation," enclosed in Gordon to Secretary of State, no. 47, 29 April 1878, PRO CO 83/16. This reference will be cited hereafter as Thurston's "Memorandum on Native Taxation."

siveness of previous tax policies and arguing the soundness of his own and the likelihood of its productivity. He cited the support of those (Thurston, Wilkinson,[36] and W. S. Carew) who knew the Fijians best, claimed that at Draiba the chiefs had "warmly advocated and strongly recommended" the plan, and quoted Early Grey to the effect that "the most convenient form of imposing a Land tax in a rude state of society, I believe to be that of requiring from all who cultivate the soil, a tithe or some fixed proportion of the produce."[37]

Intensely worried concerning Fijian finance, the Colonial Office took Gordon's scheme well in its stride. Fuller, one of the junior clerks, minuted: "Sir A. Gordon has hit upon a bold (& I suppose novel) plan. . . . Whatever may be decided upon when the Ordinance is received in an authenticated shape, there can be no doubt that Sir A. Gordon has reasoned out his scheme with pains & deliberation."[38] Malcolm, one of the assistant under-secretaries, spoke of it as "a measure wh[ich] . . . has [been] thought out with much care."

> It commends itself as being in accordance with native usage & therefore reasonable & likely to work well. . . . It can be worked by natives & will not shock them too much. . . . It is probable . . . that the Gov[ernmen]t will lay itself open to some misrepresentation and that we shall hear of charges against it of exacting forced labour from the natives. In reality however the system . . . is no more forced labour than the exaction of the income tax at home is robbery. . . .
>
> He [Gordon] ought . . . to be told that he should have communicated his ideas more freely to L[or]d Carnarvon. . . . We only hear of [his scheme] when it is too late to criticize. If however the Gov[erno]r raises £21,000 a year by it much may be forgiven.[39]

Herbert and Carnarvon agreed with Malcolm's remarks and sanctioned the ordinance.

Although the Colonial Office showed willingness to give Gordon's tax scheme a trial before condemning it, voices were soon raised against it in Fiji and Britain. The traders and planters in Fiji hated it, the former because it prevented them from making much profit out of the native produce earmarked for taxes, the latter because it allowed most natives to work for themselves. "The fact is," wrote Thurston, "that the trader looks upon the native as an ignorant being born to sell at the cheapest and buy at the dearest, to, or from him the trader. The Planter regards the native as a being specially adapted if not specially intended by

[36]At the time, the government's chief interpreter.
[37]Gordon to Carnarvon, 16 Feb. 1876, and enclosure, PRO CO 83/9.
[38]Fuller's minute, 1 April 1876, *ibid.*
[39]Malcolm's minute, 3 April 1876, *ibid.*

Providence to work for him the Planter."[40] Of course neither group revealed its motive for opposing the plan. Instead, they charged the Governor with exacting forced labour from the Fijians and with restricting their freedom as British subjects. The *Fiji Times*, with its normal irresponsibility, joined in the attack, even affirming that "this system is in Java, a Government Monopoly and *equally with the plan adopted in Fiji*, the produce is paid for by the Government according to its own notions of value and weight. This is fixed every year and is so fixed as to leave a large profit to the Government when the stuff is sold."[41] However well this described the system in Java it completely libelled that of Fiji as the editor must have known. Despite the fact that this too obvious concern of the planters, traders, and *Fiji Times* for the Fijians invited open disbelief, their cries of protest against Gordon's native tax were taken up and carried back to England by Attorney-General de Ricci when he returned home in 1876.

De Ricci's opposition was prompted perhaps by his inability to get the better of the Governor,[42] perhaps by a genuine if misguided belief that Fijians were being deprived of their rights. Unknown and uninfluential, he could not have stirred up much trouble by himself. However, Sir Charles Dilke, a strong opponent of the annexation of Fiji, now joined the attack. Speaking at Chelsea on 4 September 1877, Dilke criticized annexation as offering insufficient gain for the large expense England had incurred. Basing his remarks on de Ricci's observations, he affirmed that England's expenses in Fiji would have been appreciably greater but for the adoption by the Governor of the native produce tax which, he alleged, conflicted with the principles of English liberty. He likened the Fijian "culture system" to that of the Dutch in Java.[43] When Dilke repeated his charges in the House of Commons, Gordon felt obliged to refute them. He did so in March 1878, in an able dispatch[44] followed a month later by an exhaustive memorandum prepared by Thurston.[45] The latter showed that de Ricci had completely misapprehended the taxation scheme because he had never studied the ordinance which imposed it. Hence Dilke's charges lacked proper foundation.

After the Colonial Office received Gordon's March dispatch, which Herbert thought "very good" and worthy of printing, it did not worry

[40]Thurston's "Memorandum on Native Taxation."
[41]*Fiji Times*, 10 April 1878, quoted *ibid*. Thurston's italics.
[42]De Ricci had openly boasted that he would earn promotion by opposing the Governor as the Attorney-General at the Straits had done. (*Fiji*, I, 200.)
[43]*The Times* (London), 5 Sept. 1877.
[44]No. 37, 24 March 1878, PRO CO 83/16.
[45]Thurston's "Memorandum on Native Taxation."

much about the impact of Dilke's allegations upon public opinion. In any case Gordon's native produce tax had by now (1878) given such promise of becoming an excellent revenue producer that the Colonial Office was almost enthusiastic over it and disinclined to attach much weight to any criticism of it.

Sir Arthur, however, continued to worry about adverse public reaction to his scheme. He considered the native produce tax an integral and vital part of his whole native policy and rightly believed that without its revenue he would be unable to maintain a satisfactory government in Fiji. He further considered the Colonial Office to be unduly responsive to public opinion and believed it his duty to set the public right. Taking advantage of his year-long leave of absence in 1878–79 he prepared a paper, explaining and defending his tax policy, which he read before the Royal Colonial Institute in March 1879.[46]

Although English criticisms of the native tax practically ceased at this point, attacks continued in Fiji. In March 1879 George William Des Voeux, who acted as governor during Gordon's leave, forwarded a petition from the Fiji Chamber of Commerce which stated that legislators, colonists, and natives united in condemning the tax and alleged that the effects of the tax had been to prevent natives from working for Europeans and to ensure continuance of primitive native methods of agriculture.[47] The petitioners asked for an inquiry to demonstrate the truth of their allegations and to discover the real feelings of the Fijians. They hoped in this way, they said, to relieve the natives of the "injustice, oppression, and cruelty to which the ordinance under which they are taxed so exposes them, and which can but be regarded as a disgrace to a British Colony."[48] Gordon, to whom the Colonial Office sent the petition for his comments, replied that his dispatches and the paper he had given to the Royal Colonial Institute contained his answer to the petitioners.

The Secretary of State politely but entirely rejected the petition saying that it had been "the object of Her Majesty's Government in permitting what has been a novel experiment in the History of British Colonization to avoid too rude a shock to native customs and prejudices and to disturb as little as possible pre-existing forms of authority under which the natives were governed through their chiefs."[49] The tax proved too productive to forego on the ground that it was either antiquated or

[46]"Native Taxation in Fiji," *Proceedings of the Royal Colonial Institute*, X (1878–79). See also *Fiji*, III, appendix.
[47]Petition of the Fiji Chamber of Commerce, enclosed in Des Voeux to Secretary of State, 31 March 1879, PRO CO 83/19.
[48]*Ibid.*
[49]Secretary of State to Gordon, 13 Aug. 1879, PRO CO 83/19.

TABLE III*

	1873 (King Cakobau's gov't)	1875 (Robinson's plan)	1876	1877	1878	1879	1880
		(*pounds sterling*)					
Native taxes	6,000	3,499	9,843	15,103	18,178	19,885	15,485
Customs revenue			13,456	16,351	19,827	20,415	23,995

*MacGregor's memorandum enclosed in Des Voeux to Secretary of State, no. 126, 22 Aug. 1882, PRO CO 83/30. Gordon's estimate of £21,000 from the native tax would have been realized in 1880 but for the drastic decline in prices of primary products brought on by the general depression. Gordon preferred a drop in revenue to a forced increase in native production.

opposed by interested pressure groups. Table III shows the sums realized by Gordon's scheme during the first five years of its operation and demonstrates its value in relation to customs duties, the other major source of government revenue, and to the sums raised by King Cakobau's government and by Sir Hercules Robinson's plan. Des Voeux considered it "a remarkable and probably unprecedented fact [that] we are able to raise such a sum from a race like the Fijians without the presence either of soldiers or of armed vessels."[50] No other tax "could have brought an equal amount to the Treasury without danger to the peace of the colony and without complete disregard of what was due to those who had voluntarily ceded their country in return for a promise of protection."[51]

The native produce tax also fared well in promoting and gradually attaining the objectives of better agricultural methods, increased production, greater self-dependence, and greater knowledge among Fijians about the true value of their products. In 1878, despite the large amount collected for the tax, the natives produced and sold more for their private use than ever before.[52] When Gordon made a tour through the large island of Vanua Levu in 1877, he found everywhere signs of increasing prosperity and concluded that "socially as well as financially the new system of native taxation is working in the manner which was anticipated and desired."[53] Others with less desire than Gordon and Thurston to impress the home authorities also testified to the beneficial effects of the tax upon the natives. James Mason, an unofficial member

[50]Des Voeux's message to the legislative council, enclosed in Des Voeux to Secretary of State, 30 Dec. 1881, PRO CO 83/27.

[51]Sir George William Des Voeux, *My Colonial Service*, I, 357.

[52]Thurston's "Memorandum on Native Taxation." Copra exports, almost entirely the result of native production, increased from 1,530 tons (worth £25,300) in 1876, to 4,371 tons (£54,640) in 1877, to 5,311 tons (£79,700) in 1878. (Gordon's speech at Nasova, 16 Oct. 1879, *Fiji*, IV, 80.)

[53]Gordon to Carnarvon, 12 July 1877, PRO CO 83/14.

of the council, as a planter certainly did not approve of the natives' increased prosperity, but, after a recruiting expedition in Viti Levu where only 23 men out of 2,000 interviewed had engaged as labourers, he stated that the people of that district were better off and had better houses and larger plantations than before annexation. He noted that wages had increased by two pounds a year over the fifty-two shillings a year that planters formerly paid their Fijian labourers. Finally, Mason contradicted a missionary who charged that the Fijian population was declining.[54] "My own experience among the natives,—which is of some duration,—leads me to a different conclusion."[55]

Some early opponents of the tax eventually became strong supporters. R. B. Leefe (whom Gordon once called the most stubborn man he knew) constantly and conscientiously opposed the tax throughout Gordon's administration. In 1889, however, he wrote to say how mistaken his opposition had been. Having been British consul at Tonga he had seen what a "spurious and altogether hateful civilization" had been evolved "from the theory of individual as opposed to tribal responsibility."[56] Fijians after fifteen years of Gordon's taxation policy were, said Leefe, "essentially the same happy joyous contented people. . . . Their ideas have of course somewhat advanced and they have more money at command to buy the doubtful wants of civilization."[57] Tongans, who had once been as happy and contented as the Fijians, now after thirty years of "so-called freedom of individuals" had become "a nation the reverse of happy . . . without elasticity of spirits, . . . without joy in life, . . . worshippers of money for if they cannot get it to pay taxes they are ruthlessly sold up."[58]

[54]The charge was made by Rev. J. Rooney in a letter to the *Sydney Morning Herald*, 14 Aug. 1880. Gordon denied Rooney's allegations both as to the decline in Fijian numbers and the reasons given for it. Kimberley did not think Gordon borne out in his contentions, but Fuller believed that "any unprejudiced observer" would admit that Gordon's policies had not been prejudicial to the natives and that if their numbers had decreased it had been in spite of his efforts. "That it should be even a debatable question whether the population is decreasing now or not is in itself a proof that Mr. Rooney's allegations are unsound." (Gordon to Secretary of State, 8 Nov. 1880, enclosing clipping containing Rooney's letter; and Kimberley's and Fuller's minutes, PRO CO 83/23.)

[55]James E. Mason to Gordon, 18 Sept. 1880, enclosure no. 3 in Gordon to Secretary of State, 8 Nov. 1880, PRO CO 83/23. On his last point Mason may have been correct as far as the district he visited was concerned but Fiji as a whole was probably experiencing a slight decline in population.

[56]R. B. Leefe to Gordon, 1 Nov. 1889, Stanmore Papers, 49242. In Tonga individuals had a choice of paying their taxes in kind or money. There, as Thurston remarked, "eighty per cent of the population is in gaol or supposed to be." (Thurston's "Memorandum on Native Taxation.")

[57]Leefe to Gordon, 1 Nov. 1889.   [58]*Ibid.*

Francis Arthur Jackson, a Fiji planter, who must have resented Gordon's failure to acknowledge his letters protesting the tax, also changed his mind as he observed the results of the tax. In 1895 he wrote that, having seen it in operation under Gordon and his three successors, Des Voeux, Sir Charles Mitchell, and Sir John Thurston, he had come to believe it the right policy. He hoped that the English people would learn the facts about the produce tax instead of "the untruths circulated by Mr. Hogan M.P. and W. Fillingham Parr."[59]

Parr and men like him continued long after Gordon's departure to oppose the taxation scheme calling it "slavery," "forced labour," and an "infringement of the rights of British subjects." Nevertheless, the weight of evidence and the conversion of Leefe and Jackson into staunch supporters indicate that the produce tax conferred positive and even dramatic social and economic benefits upon the Fijians. Admittedly, it did not at once result in changes in their agricultural methods; but this is hardly surprising because, of all man's practices agriculture has been the most resistant to change.

The Colonial Office's view of the native tax was determined mostly by the revenue raised from it. As long as the sum increased every year all was well. When, however, the amount decreased in 1880 and again in 1881, several of the officials took a gloomy view of the tax's future. Edward Wingfield, one of the assistant under-secretaries, noted with a sigh in 1882 that "it was an experiment from the first & though it has answered fairly well hitherto some other arrangement may no doubt be accepted. . . ."[60] John Bramston suggested, what was easier said than done, that "the natives . . . [should] take to producing some articles of greater value & less liable to fluctuation in price than copra,"[61] which fell from £15/10/- per ton in 1879 to £8/10/- in 1881. The senior officials, considering the facts that no other system could produce as much revenue and protect the natives from exploitation, showed no disposition to alter it. Fijians thus continued to pay their taxes in produce until the turn of the century, and not until 1913 did cash payments become the accepted method of meeting them.

Although the colony's revenues increased steadily during Gordon's administration so did its expenditures. The Colonial Office kept pressure

[59]Jackson to Stanmore, 1 Dec. 1895, Stanmore Papers, 49242. Fillingham Parr was Gordon's worst enemy in Fiji. For some of his attacks see below, pp. 195–97.

[60]Wingfield's marginal note on minutes on Des Voeux to Secretary of State, 22 Aug. 1882.

[61]Bramston's minute, *ibid.* Bramston was also one of the assistant under-secretaries.

upon Sir Arthur to balance his budget. Gordon made great efforts to comply especially during his first two years in the colony before the revenues increased to a significant amount. Yet the task was hard. His domain was exceedingly large. Rapid communication between the islands proved difficult especially after the loss, in 1876, of the government steamer *Fitzroy*. Since the white settlers were scattered throughout the islands more magistrates were needed than if the people had been grouped in one or two areas. All of these circumstances led to a more costly establishment than the Secretary of State had first contemplated.

At the end of October 1875, Gordon forwarded his schedule of establishments. He estimated the cost at nearly £4,000 more than the amount authorized by the Secretary of State. Herbert saw no alternative but to sanction *"provisionally"* all of the Governor's arrangements "which he has carefully & laboriously considered, and, I am sure, believes to be as economical as possible."[62] He hoped, however, that Gordon would watch carefully for every opportunity to dispense with any appointments "which though necessary to bring the new administration into working order may not be required after it has been once organized." To show "that a moderate staff of competent persons can administer public affairs" in the colony would be, he believed, a "great credit" to Gordon and those under him.[63]

Although the Governor had promised to keep expenses down,[64] and had agreed that the cost of the establishment was out of all proportion to Fiji's revenues, he could not sacrifice what he deemed essential "to the true interests of the Colony."[65] Announcing regretfully that he could not reduce the cost below £20,000,[66] he nevertheless pointed out that in most new colonies establishment costs bore an undue ratio to revenues.[67] In an effort to reduce costs he had pledged himself to draw during his first year only £3,000 of his nominal £5,000 salary and did not ask outright for his full salary until 1877 when he believed that he would soon be able to balance the budget. From his reduced salary he even paid the expenses and, in some cases, the honoraria of men whom he

[62]Herbert's minute, 5 Feb. 1876, on Gordon to Carnarvon, no. 82, 30 Oct. 1875, PRO CO 83/6.

[63]Herbert's minute, 5 Feb. 1876, on Gordon to Secretary of State, no. 80, 30 Oct. 1875, PRO CO 83/6.

[64]Gordon to Carnarvon (private), 24 Dec. 1875, Carnarvon Papers, PRO GD 6/39.

[65]Gordon to Carnarvon, 6 May 1876, PRO CO 83/10.

[66]The cost of the establishment gradually ranged upward from this figure as the government undertook new essential duties but remained under £30,000 throughout Gordon's administration.

[67]Gordon to Carnarvon, 6 May 1876.

needed in government work but for whom he could find no place in the establishment. Despite the high cost of living in Fiji he kept his officers' salaries at a level which barely provided for the essentials. He amalgamated offices so that nearly every man on the establishment performed more than one job. The European magistrates, for example, were also issuers of licences, coroners, prison visitors, peace officers, inspectors of labour contracts, members of the provincial courts, and sometimes land commissioners. In several areas the magistrate was the only government official in a radius of perhaps a hundred miles. "What we are trying to do here," Gordon wrote at the end of 1877, "is similar to an attempt to make six magistrates suffice for the whole of the West Indian Windward Islands excepting Barbados."[68]

The Colonial Office recognized these efforts. In July 1876 Robert Meade, an assistant under-secretary, noted that "both the L[egislature] and C[ouncil] & Sir A. Gordon are thoroughly in earnest in keeping the expenditure down to the lowest point consistent with safety. . . ."[69] Malcolm, too, observed that the Governor was "struggling hard with his deficits & he is entitled to all the support we can give him."[70] Malcolm thought Gordon deserving of great sympathy in the difficult task of extending the government, hitherto confined to Levuka, over all the Fiji islands while trying to keep ordinary expenditures within ordinary revenues. "As far as one can judge he is setting about this task with zeal, energy & (as it appears to me) with judgment."[71] Meade correctly summed up the situation:

> If this country annexes Fiji in order to bring to an end the misgovernment & confusion which formerly reigned . . . there can be no doubt that it will have to supply the deficient revenue. It is impossible to govern in a cheaper fashion if we are to have all the machinery of a Colonial Gov[ernmen]t. Of course one Resident Magistrate with two or three subordinates aided by the naval captains could govern after a certain manner, but could not do that which England annexed the place in order to carry out.[72]

Until 1878 it appeared to the Colonial Office that the £100,000 grant set aside to pay the deficits would rapidly evaporate. Gordon estimated his deficit for 1876 at nearly £31,000. He proposed in his rough estimate for 1877 to reduce the cost of the establishment to £20,000. Annoyed at his failure to include the promised reductions in his final

---

[68]Gordon to Carnarvon, 31 Dec. 1877, PRO CO 83/14.

[69]Meade's minute on Treasury to Under-Secretary of State, 7 July 1876, PRO CO 83/12.

[70]Malcolm's minute of Gordon to Carnarvon, 7 June 1876, PRO CO 83/10.

[71]Malcolm's minute on Gordon to Carnarvon, 26 Jan. 1876, PRO CO 83/9.

[72]Meade's minute, *ibid.*

estimates, the Colonial Office refused to sanction them. Sir Arthur contended that insistence on cuts which he had judged possible *in extremis* would injure the efficiency of the government. Moreover, conditions in Fiji had improved since he had submitted his rough estimates. The revenue in 1876 had been £37,237 compared with £16,433 in 1875. He estimated it would be £49,050 in 1877 and that in 1878 ordinary revenues would balance ordinary expenditures.[73] Did this not justify his failure to make reductions harmful to the colony, and did it not also justify his retaining the whole of his nominal salary?[74] Although almost every one of Herbert's and Carnarvon's private letters during the latter part of 1876 and the first half of 1877, as well as many of the Secretary of State's dispatches, spoke of the continued "anxiety" of the Colonial Office over Fiji's finances, the "pressure at the Treasury," and the extreme importance of reducing "all expenses within the narrowest possible limits,"[75] Carnarvon nevertheless eventually approved the estimates.[76] Even then, consent came only after Sir Arthur, at his own personal expense, had sent Alfred Maudslay home to answer the Colonial Office's questions on Fijian financial matters.

As a result of Maudslay's visit and the continued improvement in Fiji's revenues, the Colonial Office began to regain confidence in the colony's future and to show less reluctance to sanction expenditures. Not that it had altogether refused desirable expenditures even when everything looked black, but it had agreed to them with reservations. It had accepted the necessity of appointing more medical officers but thought that they ought to be used as magistrates and registrars. It had agreed that the Fijian government had to have a boat to replace the lost *Fitzroy*, but hoped that the new vessel would enable Gordon to reduce the number of magistrates thus partly off-setting its cost.[77] The one increase that Carnarvon accepted unconditionally was the payment of Gordon's

[73]Gordon to Carnarvon, 17 Jan. 1877, Carnarvon Papers, PRO GD 6/39; Gordon to Selborne [Jan.] 1877, Stanmore Papers, 49217.

[74]Gordon to Carnarvon, 22 May 1877, PRO CO 83/13; Gordon to Carnarvon, 17 Jan. 1877.

[75]Carnarvon to Gordon, 9 June 1877, PRO CO 83/13; Carnarvon to Gordon, 3 April 1877, Carnarvon Papers, PRO GD 6/39; and Herbert to Gordon, 9 June 1876 and 10 Feb. [1877], Stanmore Papers, 49199.

[76]Carnarvon to Gordon, 11 Oct. 1877, PRO CO 83/14.

[77]In an October 1877 minute Carnarvon wrote: "Great as may be the need of economy—we must not allow undue reduction in the number of magistrates or the supervisory machinery of the gov[ernmen]t. I am disposed to believe that a considerable work is going on . . . and it w[oul]d be a great misfortune, for whatever cause, to interrupt the progress now being made. (Carnarvon's minute on Wilkinson to Gordon, 11 July 1877, enclosed in Gordon to Carnarvon, 10 Aug. 1877, PRO CO 83/14.)

full salary. By the latter part of 1876 this had become an important matter to the Governor. His decision whether to leave Fiji or remain rested largely upon it.

When Lord Carnarvon first offered Gordon the governorship of Fiji, Sir Arthur had been prepared "to devote to it the whole remainder of [his] official life,"[78] and he had not worried about the amount of his salary. "To obtain the services of any fit man," he had told Carnarvon, "you must give him enough to live on, and that is all that is necessary; for I have always considered that it is to the securing of his private fortune, and not his salary that a Governor should look for pecuniary benefits."[79] Yet he had not been in Fiji six months before he began to hint at his early retirement from the colony. In January 1876, he wrote to Lord Carnarvon that he would find it impossible to remain in Fiji without "a most damaging loss of respect" should Lord Carnarvon disapprove the native policy to which he had so committed himself. He would welcome removal on two grounds: Lady Gordon's dislike of life in Fiji, and the high cost of living. Besides, the governorship of Ceylon— a post to which he might in other circumstances expect to be appointed —was about to fall vacant.[80] In June, August, and September, he again drew attention to his wife's discomfort in "living in a birdcage"[81] and her loneliness during his long enforced absences from Nasova. He noted that he was spending £2,000 more than his salary on the public service and that, in justice to his children, he could not ruin himself for the convenience of Fiji. Nor could he send his family back to England, or to Australia for the Fijian rainy season, because he could not afford to keep up two homes. For these reasons, he thought he would soon be forced "with extreme reluctance" to hand over his unfinished work to other and, he hoped, abler hands.[82] Nevertheless, he "solemnly & sincerely" assured Carnarvon that "could I afford to do so, I had really much rather stay here than go to Ceylon. My heart is thoroughly in my work, and that work is of intense interest to me, difficult, and at times dispiriting, as it is."[83]

No one who has read Gordon's letters and dispatches from Fiji can possibly question the genuineness of his interest in the work there or his

[78]Gordon to Carnarvon (private), 25 Oct. 1874, Carnarvon Papers, PRO GD 6/39.   [79]Ibid.   [80]Ibid., 19 Jan. 1876.

[81]Government House, Nasova, was built in the native style. Lady Gordon's unhappiness in Fiji was not wholly the result of physical discomfort. It arose also from the fact that A. J. L. Gordon and Captain Knollys left her no voice in running the household. She later spoke of herself as a "cypher" when they "managed the house & everybody in it." (Lady Gordon to Gordon, 6–8 Sept. 1885, Stanmore Papers, 49226.)

[82]Gordon to Carnarvon, 19 June, 28 Aug., 27 Sept. 1876, Carnarvon Papers, PRO GD 6/39.   [83]Ibid., 27 Sept. 1876.

love for the islands and their people. How sincere, then, were his desires to resign his governorship? Were his hints simply part of a campaign to obtain the whole of his salary? Had he, perhaps, other motives in making them? He constantly feared that the Colonial Office might reject his policies. He knew that Carnarvon did not wish to appoint a new governor until the colony had become well-established. Was Gordon playing politics and threatening resignation in order to ensure approval of his policies? Fiji was experiencing difficult days in 1876. Did the Governor doubt his ability to balance the budget at any time and to place the colony on a firm financial footing? He had been told often enough that he had to do so or the wrath of the House of Commons would be visited upon both the Colonial Office and himself. Was he laying a line of retreat which, in the event of failure, he might use rather than face the disgrace of being recalled? No categorical answer to any of these questions is possible. It is highly probable, however, that if Carnarvon had not agreed to his drawing his full salary he would soon have resigned. By relieving Fiji of part of the cost of her establishment he had come to the end of his personal financial tether and could no longer care for his family in the manner he deemed proper. Much as he loved Fiji, had it come to a choice between the colony and his family he would have chosen his family.[84]

Carnarvon and Herbert received Gordon's plaintive letters with patience and fortitude. Their replies suggested that they appreciated his difficulties and would understand if he felt he had to resign. Interspersed with admonitions to be careful of expenditures they also sent him words of sympathy and encouragement.[85] Although, in the privacy of the Colonial Office, Carnarvon spoke of Sir Arthur's "defects of temper,"[86] only on one occasion did he lose his own. Early in 1877 Gordon proposed a scheme whereby he should become governor of New South Wales and retain Fiji at the same time.[87] Lord Carnarvon usually did not

[84]Against this judgment must be set Gordon's remark to his wife in 1880 that "If I was, of my own set purpose, to give up my work which I believe God meant me to do here, *for the sake* of my children, or to *seek* other employment, I should always fear Nemesis. . . ." (Gordon to Lady Gordon, 10 June 1880, *Fiji*, IV, 319.)

[85]See, for example, Carnarvon to Gordon, 18 Oct. 1876, Carnarvon Papers, PRO GD 6/39.

[86]Carnarvon's minute, 12 Oct. 1877, on Gordon to Carnarvon, 10 Aug. 1877.

[87]Gordon to Carnarvon, 27 Jan. 1877, Carnarvon Papers, PRO GD 6/39. Gordon's reasoning probably went rather like this: "If I can become governor of New South Wales, a self-governing colony, I shall have little to do there and can devote much of my time to Fiji. This arrangement will enable me to complete work in Fiji for which I shall not have time during the remainder of my term. Furthermore, my family will be able to live in Sydney, and I shall have a large enough salary to maintain them there and to visit them as my New South Wales duties dictate and my Fiji duties permit."

write minutes on Gordon's private letters but on this occasion he stated angrily, "Gordon's letters always provoke me & this not less than others. But the matter is settled. He must stay in Fiji & do his work there or he must come home."[88] Carnarvon's wrath soon evaporated. He got Herbert to suggest to Gordon that "the New Southwelshmen are very jealous of any temporary appropriation of their Governor to other uses. . . ."[89] He himself replied to Sir Arthur's outright request for his full salary,[90] saying "you have had severe work, you are I hope turning the corner of your financial difficulties, the addition is not a large one; and if it enables you . . . to carry out & complete your task I shall think it money well laid out in the interest of the colony."[91] When Lord Carnarvon resigned as secretary of state early in the new year, he felt he could not leave the department without writing Sir Arthur "a few lines of friendly farewell. . . . I have a great deal of pleasant retrospect and not the least pleasant part of that consists in believing that through your energy courage & administrative skill the annexation of the Fiji islands has been already to a great extent justified by its success. I am very much obliged to you for all the zealous cooperation which you have given me and for the good work that you have done."[92] Carnarvon's last official act was to ask the Queen to bestow upon Gordon the Grand Cross of the Order of St. Michael and St. George.[93]

Gordon deeply regretted the departure of Lord Carnarvon, who had always been a kindly and considerate chief and had approved and upheld his policies. He believed that Carnarvon, and Herbert to a lesser degree, had supported his views on native affairs against those of the rest of the Colonial Office staff.[94] Fearing that a new secretary of state might withdraw that support, Gordon looked forward with eagerness and anxiety to the leave of absence that Carnarvon had granted him.[95] He

[88]Carnarvon's minute, *ibid.* Gordon's letters did not "always provoke" Lord Carnarvon. He found Sir Arthur's fine descriptions of Fiji and its customs intensely interesting. It was Gordon's letters of complaint that he found provoking.

[89]Herbert to Gordon, 31 May 1877, Stanmore Papers, 49199.

[90]It was not until January 1877 that, considering the state of Fiji's revenues, Gordon felt justified in recommending it.

[91]Carnarvon to Gordon, 3 April 1877, Carnarvon Papers, PRO GD 6/39.

[92]*Ibid.*, 3 Feb. 1878.

[93]Gordon had been given a half-promise of a G.C.M.G. a few months earlier by Herbert, who had written to say that Sir Arthur Phayre had been given this honour and that Herbert feared Gordon might think he had been passed over. "Probably you will after all be before long the youngest G.C.M.G. . . ." (Herbert to Gordon, 21 [Dec.] 1877, Stanmore Papers, 49199.)

[94]Gordon to Selborne, 16 May 1878, Stanmore Papers, 49217.

[95]Herbert encouraged Gordon to come home for discussions. (Herbert to Gordon, 23 Nov. 1877, Stanmore Papers, 49199.)

would have an opportunity to explain his policies to Carnarvon's successor, Sir Michael Hicks Beach. If he approved them, Gordon would return to Fiji to complete his term of office. If not, he too would resign. When he appeared at the Colonial Office he found, rather to his surprise, "entire and most thorough approval of *all* that I had done—and a very handsome recognition of the success of my policy. . . ."[96]

Gordon should not have been surprised at his cordial reception. His policies were succeeding; there were strong indications of prosperity in Fiji, and, best of all, he had left the colony almost self-sufficient financially. To the Colonial Office, ever fearful of the Treasury and the House of Commons, the last was the most important. As long as Sir Arthur balanced his budget and kept the natives at peace he might continue to follow closely his own designs. Sir Michael Hicks Beach felt no urge to negate his predecessor's policies—why tempt fortune? Gordon even found the Colonial Office willing to support his plan for a loan to retire the liabilities of the pre-annexation government and to provide the funds for necessary public works connected with transferring the seat of government from Nasova to Suva.

In March 1875, Carnarvon had informed Sir Arthur that the British and Fijian governments "absolutely and entirely" declined to admit any obligation for the debts of King Cakobau's government and that no claim preferred by demand or as of right could be entertained. Nevertheless, the Fijian government might pay, "voluntarily, and as an act of grace," such of those debts as it considered just. "But with regard to the time and manner in which such payments are to be made the Government of Fiji must reserve to itself the fullest discretion."[97] After due inquiry Gordon's government decided that the just claims amounted to £80,000, but because the Colonial Office at first refused point-blank to consider Gordon's suggestions for further Imperial aid or for an Imperial guarantee of a Fijian loan,[98] claims would have to wait until Fiji could float a loan on her own credit.

Had the debts of the old government been the only extraordinary call upon the revenues it might have been possible, by the middle of 1877, for the Fijian government to have issued a loan large enough to pay them. Fiji, however, had other extraordinary expenditures facing her. Gordon estimated that the colony required a further £50,000, half for public works at Suva—which, after much time and trouble, he had

[96]Gordon to Selborne, 10 Sept. 1878, Stanmore Papers, 49217.
[97]Carnarvon to Gordon, 4 March 1875, PRO CO 83/5.
[98]Minutes on Gordon to Carnarvon, 9 May 1877, PRO CO 83/13.

chosen as the permanent capital—and half for various other projects such as building lighthouses, assisting the immigration of indentured labour, and speeding the work of the Lands Commission.[99] In all, therefore, Fiji required £130,000.

Despite Maudslay's preparatory work and Gordon's direct negotiation with the Colonial Office, various delays took place before the loan was issued. As a result, interest amounting to £15,000 accumulated on the debts owed on behalf of the old government; and the loan, when finally issued in 1881, ran to £150,000 instead of the contemplated £130,000.

Meanwhile the revenues continued to increase leading the Treasury to observe "with pleasure" that the finances of the colony appeared to be "rapidly attaining a satisfactory position," and to recognize "the exertions which Sir A. Gordon has made to attain this result. . . ."[100] On the last day of December 1879 Gordon, with pardonable pride, reported that Fiji had balanced its budget and expressed his belief that there was "no other instance on record of a dependency burdened as Fiji was before annexation, and receiving so inconsiderable an amount of pecuniary support from the Imperial Government, attaining in so short a time, an independent financial position."[101] Even though the budget had at last been balanced and some £14,000 remained unexpended of the grant-in-aid, Fiji's finances still required careful handling. Some branches of the civil service were badly undermanned[102] and almost all government officers were underpaid. Unless salaries could be raised the colony ran great risk of losing some of its most experienced servants. Moreover, as shown in 1880, almost any unexpected decline in revenues or increase in expenditures would throw the budget badly out of kilter. In that year revenue from native taxes fell and immigration cost unforeseeably increased leaving the colony with a deficit of £7,720.[103]

The deficit frightened the Colonial Office. Lord Kimberley, who had again become secretary of state, unfairly blamed Gordon[104] because

[99]For the work of this commission see below, pp. 204, 209.

[100]Treasury to Colonial Office, 2 July 1879, PRO CO 83/20 (Treasury 10610/70).

[101]Gordon to Secretary of State, 31 Dec. 1879, PRO CO 83/20.

[102]The colony was terrifyingly short of doctors.

[103]Des Voeux to Secretary of State, 12 April 1881, PRO CO 83/25.

[104]Meade to Treasury, 12 Sept. 1881, PRO CO 83/28. Lord Kimberley, who was generally partial to white supremacy, was not at first very favourable to Gordon's native policy which was so closely connected with the colony's finances. As time went by he viewed it more kindly, perhaps because, as Gordon in his dispatches from New Zealand took pains to point out, the peace which characterized native affairs in Fiji contrasted favourably with their threatening aspect in New Zealand where white supremacy prevailed.

before leaving Fiji, Sir Arthur had tried to ensure the retention of a competent civil service for his successor by approving modest increases in salaries. Forced by Kimberley to retrench, Des Voeux, who succeeded Gordon as governor of Fiji, curtailed some public works and cut many salaries. As a consequence of the latter action and his own defects of character, he lost within a year or two most of his senior administrators. By late 1882 only MacGregor and Le Hunte remained of the officers who had come to Fiji in 1875 and 1876. Had it not been for MacGregor, Le Hunte, and Thurston, and the small group of young men whom Gordon, almost entirely on his own responsibility, had brought with him on his return to Fiji in 1879, Des Voeux would have found it extremely difficult to carry on an effective administration.

When one considers the resources with which Sir Arthur Gordon began his governorship of Fiji, the colony was in remarkably good financial shape when he left it. It is true it carried a debt of £250,000, made up of the Imperial grant-in-aid or long-term non-interest-bearing loan of £100,000 and the 4.5 per cent loan of £150,000. However, the colony had been forced to assume debts of the former government that, with accumulated interest, amounted to £95,000. Of the remaining £155,000 of debt for which Gordon had responsibility, some £6,500 of the Imperial grant remained in the hands of the Crown agents after the deficit of 1880 had been met, £50,000 had been spent or earmarked for capital expenditures, and about £98,500 had gone to meet deficits on current account including that of 1875 for which Sir Arthur was only partly answerable. In brief he had managed to create and operate an effective administration for slightly less than the amount set aside by the Imperial government.[105] Furthermore, Gordon had increased the revenues fivefold in five years and, during the last three of those years, he had succeeded in balancing the budget once and in very nearly doing so twice. These were notable achievements.

III. NATIVE AFFAIRS

When Sir Arthur Gordon was appointed the first governor of Fiji no one in England had an inkling of the kind of native policy he would

[105]Some might argue that the debts of the old government were supposed to be paid out of the Imperial grant, and that the assessment made above is thus inaccurate. This argument is unsound because, in the beginning, the Imperial government admitted no responsibility for the debts of King Cakobau's government; the Imperial government had no accurate idea of their amount; and, finally, not even the Treasury suggested that those debts should be covered by the Imperial grant.

establish in the new colony. Beyond desiring that colonies should not add to British taxation, the public remained unconcerned with colonial affairs and most members of Parliament absented themselves during debates on colonial matters. The Aborigines Protection Society and the Anti-Slavery Society, the groups which took the most interest in native peoples, had successfully pressed for the annexation of Fiji. But neither they nor the Colonial Office considered that native policy should go beyond ending the abuses perpetrated upon natives by white planters and traders. Under the impact of Christianity and "abuse-free" commercial development native peoples should and would adopt civilized standards and practices. So ran humanitarian thought. Gordon's observations led him to conclude that such a policy resulted in hardship, injustice, and, eventually, decimation and destruction of the native race. If the British colonial system as hitherto practised was "incompatible with the preservation of a native population"[106] then, Sir Arthur judged, the system ought to be changed. In Fiji he perceived an opportunity to conduct an experiment through which, by preserving and strengthening Fijian society, he might enable the native people to attain a civilization of their own. When they had succeeded they would be able to stand by themselves and to accept such parts of Western culture as they wished. "If," he wrote, "the Fijian population is ever permitted to sink from its present condition into that of a collection of migratory bands of hired labourers, all hope, not only of the improvement, but the preservation of the race, need inevitably be abandoned. This result would be one, in my opinion, disgraceful to our rule. . . ."[107] Should his policy be successful, or even partly so, it would gain much for the Fijians and "for the credit of England."[108]

Gordon arrived in Fiji with no preconceived solution to the native problem; he waited to see and study the situation before making up his mind. He drew his ideas from various sources, from Thurston and Wilkinson, his own observations, and his historical knowledge of English and Scottish societies when they were at approximately the same stage of civilization as the Fijian. The native policy which Gordon created and slowly elaborated was dictated partly by experience and partly by his desire to prevent the destruction of the Fijian race. As he later put it, "policy and necessity pointed in the same direction as right and justice."[109]

[106]Gordon to Selborne, [?] Jan. 1877, Stanmore Papers, 49217.
[107]Gordon to Carnarvon, 9 Aug. 1877, Stanmore Papers, 49199.
[108]Gordon to Selborne, 13 Aug. 1877, Stanmore Papers, 49217.
[109]Sir Arthur Gordon, "Native Councils in Fiji," *Contemporary Review*, XLIII (1883), 711–31.

Gordon originally viewed the native produce tax as simply the most appropriate means of raising a revenue from the natives, but he quickly saw it as an instrument for improving them materially and socially. If Fijians were to be encouraged to become better farmers and to increase their agricultural production, they must be guaranteed sufficient land. Sir Arthur's land policy, therefore, first aimed at curtailing the exorbitant claims of white settlers. Once that object was achieved Gordon would find it desirable to restrict the Crown's own claims to land. If natives were to manage their lands and pay their taxes, and if, as Goodenough, Robinson, and Gordon all saw, Fijians could be ruled only through their chiefs, then Fijian political organization had to be strengthened and Fijian custom modified and codified. Such, in outline, was Gordon's native policy. In addition, he accepted, as a matter of course, the necessity for protective legislation to ensure that Europeans treated natives justly, and did not enslave them. Sir Arthur's successful insistence that "the natives . . . are the people—whose interests we have to consider . . ."[110] gives him a major claim to be judged the father of twentieth-century British policy in colonies with large indigenous populations.

Faced on arrival in Fiji with native unrest caused by the epidemic and the rumours as to the new government's intentions spread by the settlers, Gordon had as his first task to gain the confidence of the native population.[111] He continued the study of the language which he and his officers had begun during the voyage from England, and although he always found Fijian difficult to speak he soon learned to read and understand it. As always, he travelled in order to know the colony and its people. He made a point of showing respect and friendliness to Cakobau and other leading chiefs. Cakobau, for his part, demonstrated his loyalty to the new régime in every way, especially by insisting that the *rokos* whom he assembled at Bau in September 1875 publicly accept the Governor as their superior.

Sir Arthur took advantage of the Bau meeting and every other opportunity to persuade the chiefs, and through them the people of Fiji, that the British government had no wish to deprive them of their property, rights, or their customs, except those such as cannibalism, infanticide, and the sale of wives, which by now were almost universally condemned in Fiji. He assured them also of the Queen's personal

[110]Gordon to Carnarvon (private), 24 Dec. 1875, Carnarvon Papers, PRO GD 6/39.
[111]On the day Gordon landed in Fiji he sent Dr. MacGregor and Dr. Mayo, with medicines, off to the islands where measles still prevailed.

interest[112] in Fiji and of his own private and public desire to protect the people and help them to improve themselves. Ample proof that Gordon early won the confidence and obedience of the chiefs came in 1876 during the course of an uprising among the pagan cannibal tribes in the mountains of Viti Levu. Had it not been for the loyalty and co-operation of the *rokos*, the rebellion probably would have spread, and Gordon could not have suppressed it by the unorthodox, inexpensive, and highly effective method that he employed. In that case Sir Arthur would have been forced to call in a large body of regular troops to fight a long and costly war, and the sad history of the New Zealand Maoris would have been re-enacted in Fiji.

The rising of the highland clans was caused by the fact that many of the primitive mountaineers had never accepted either Cakobau's government or the cession of Fiji to Britain. Layard in January 1875 had persuaded some of them to renounce cannibalism and accept Christianity, but the introduction of measles at this meeting and the resultant great mortality led the highlanders to blame the government and to resume their former heathen practices. On the eastern side of the highlands alarm soon subsided but on the western side the tribes remained in a state of incipient revolt. In July 1875 Sir Arthur sent W. S. Carew and A. J. L. Gordon to assure them of the government's good intentions, but both that mission and a subsequent one by Sir Arthur himself only partly succeeded. In April 1876 the remaining dissident chiefs, having been told by white settlers that the government intended taking their land and introducing English law, threatened by the newly converted Christian tribes with forced conversion, and self-deluded concerning the invincibility of their rocky fortress,[113] decided to make one last attempt to save their waning influence. They began burning neighbouring Christian villages. The latter retaliated and the hill war was on.

Gordon believed that he could not allow the highland chiefs to go unpunished because they would interpret this as a sign of government

[112]The Colonial Office sent some of Gordon's most interesting descriptions of Fiji and its people to the Queen. The chiefs, at the close of their annual meeting, always sent her a letter, through Gordon and the secretary of state, to which she always replied.

[113]One night during the campaign against the mountaineers, as the moon shone on the white river mists and threw the black shadow of the rocky stronghold of Bukatia far over the plain, a cannibal priest appeared on the pinnacle and shouted the challenge: "Fire is unknown to my house in Bukatia." From below, in slow and measured tones, the beleaguring Christian army with one accord replied: "Wait till to-morrow." The next day Bukatia fell and its temple was burned. (Gordon to George Shaw-Lefevre, 6 July 1876, *Fiji*, II, 69–71.)

weakness. Knowing he could not arrest them without a fight, he ordered reinforcement of Carew's police force at Nasaucoko. He visited the area and called for a *levée en masse* from the districts most nearly affected. He directed each of the *rokos* of the other provinces to send thirty volunteers to the disturbed region, and sent post-haste to New Zealand for a hundred rifles. Gordon planned the campaign himself, and appointed Captain Knollys, with A. J. L. Gordon as his subordinate, to carry it out. Briefly the plan was to send a native force under Le Hunte to garrison Nasaucoko. Knollys would then, at the head of the native police and provincial levies, sweep down the Sigatoka. Simultaneously a native force led by A. J. L. Gordon, would clear the lower Sigatoka. Except for the fact that A. J. L. Gordon's advance preceded Knollys' this plan was followed and proved completely successful. The tribes on the lower Sigatoka submitted during the latter part of June and those on the upper part of the river in late July and early August after Knollys and his force captured the caves into which they had retreated. With all resistance at an end Sir Arthur disbanded his native army, which at its peak numbered about 2,000.[114]

In suppressing earlier rebellions it had been customary to burn villages, to exile the offenders, men, women, and children, to other islands as slave labour for the settlers, and to sell the vacant lands to planters. Sir Arthur took a different course. He impressed upon Knollys and A. J. L. Gordon that they were to prevent their native troops from committing the usual atrocities of raping the women and slaughtering the old men and children. They might burn villages only for purely military reasons. "I will not have the country devastated," he told them. "I give you fair warning you will have to give me a very strict account of every village burned."[115] Furthermore, Sir Arthur opposed wholesale deportations following defeat of the tribes. He felt it would be "more truly lenient and considerate" to imprison those who had taken a prominent part in the rebellion, to deport permanently a few of the more dangerous characters, and to inflict the death penalty on "the worst of those who had committed actual murder. . . ."[116] No one would be put to death unless, after having accepted the new government, he had become one of the plotters and originators of the rising; or had

---

[114]Memorandum by Gordon, Jan. 1877, for transmission to the Secretary of State, quoted in [Sir Arthur Gordon] *Letters and Notes written during the Disturbances in the Highlands (known as the "Devil Country") of Viti Levu, Fiji, 1876,* I, vi–xx. This work, in two volumes, bears the title "Story of a Little War" on the spine and this title will be cited in further references.

[115]Gordon to Knollys, 22 May 1876, *Story of a Little War,* I, 226.

[116]Memorandum, January 1877, *ibid.,* xvii.

been a traitor to the Crown, that is, had borne arms against the government while holding office in and drawing salary from the government; or had committed unprovoked murder of women and children. "I do not say," he wrote to MacGregor, who urged leniency, "that all belonging to these three classes *will* be executed, but that none will be so who do *not* belong to them."[117]

Sir Arthur took no pleasure in punishing the rebels. "My natural tendencies (which are not, I think, brutal), my strong sympathy with the native race, the natural shrinking one feels from the performance of a painful duty, all combine to make me desire, in each separate case, to pardon the offender; and it is only the exercise of reason and deliberate judgment which enables me to adhere to the course I marked out for myself on the first commencement of the outbreak. . . ."[118] He confirmed only 26 of the 70 capital sentences passed by the commissioner's court,[119] commuting the remainder to varying terms of imprisonment, mostly for five years at hard labour. Prison sentences were inflicted on some 120 rebels and permanent deportation was imposed on a few others. Gordon allowed the great majority of the highlanders to retain their lands but bound them to keep the peace, hand in their guns, and accept the authority of his government. To ensure their obedience he established Fort Carnarvon, with a garrison of over a hundred men, a few miles up the Sigatoka beyond Nasaucoko.

Gordon did take pride and pleasure in certain aspects of the war. The alacrity with which the provincial chiefs had provided volunteer troops proved to him that he had won the confidence of most of the Fijians.[120] The ability shown by Knollys and A. J. L. Gordon[121] in leading the campaign and controlling the native levies demonstrated, he

[117]Gordon to MacGregor, 22 July 1876, *Fiji*, II, 90. Gordon thought there might be one or two professional murderers on whom capital sentences would have to be imposed. MacGregor as administrator of New Guinea later faced a similar problem and applied the same solution as Gordon had done following the "Little War."   [118]*Ibid.*, 89–90.

[119]At various times between June and October 1876, Carew as commissioner, and Knollys, A. J. L. Gordon, and Le Hunte as deputy commissioners presided over trials. The highland area had been placed outside the jurisdiction of the supreme court when the colony was organized.

[120]Some provinces sent two or three times the requested thirty men. It may be suggested, however, that the young men enjoyed the prospect of a good fight.

[121]Sir Arthur sent Lord Carnarvon copies of many of the private letters he exchanged with Knollys, Gordon, and others during the conflict because, "vainly & selfishly perhaps," he wished him "to see how those . . . I have trained work for and with me. . . . Without that strong band of personal sympathy, without the power of selecting just the instrument which . . . one deems the fittest for the purpose—it would be almost impossible to get the work done which one has to do here." (Gordon to Carnarvon, 5 July 1876, Carnarvon Papers, PRO GD 6/39.)

believed, his judgment of men and vindicated his decision not to use Colonel Pratt and the detachment of Royal Engineers in suppressing the rebellion. He thought the completeness of the victory ensured peace for the future and its cheapness justified his refusal to accept Pratt's unofficial advice to call for 500 Indian sepoys or a West Indian regiment before tackling the hill tribes.

Although some white settlers doubtless felt that Gordon should have followed precedent and cleared the disturbed area of its entire population, the public, native and European alike, approved his measures. Even the *Fiji Times* applauded. It assured the Governor "that there is not a white man in the group, who, growl as he will, does not approve of the vigorous policy which has culminated so successfully for the best interests of the country, and thank in his heart, the authority which devised and carried it out." The editor made it plain, however, that the Governor must not expect any diminution in the grumbling of the white population.[122]

The only opposition Sir Arthur experienced came from Captain Havelock, the acting colonial secretary. Havelock, although a competent administrator, was an army officer who inclined to orthodox methods. So critical was he of the Governor's failure to employ Pratt and the Royal Engineers in the campaign that he quarrelled with Gordon, gave up his post, and returned to England.[123] Pratt's own feeling about being superseded by amateurs[124] is unknown. As a Colonial Office staff member wrote, "It would be interesting to know Col. Pratt's account of the transaction."[125] According to Gordon, Pratt opposed the use of the Royal Engineers on active service in the mountains. Neither did he wish native Fijian forces to be used. He believed that nothing ought to be done against the rebels until the arrival of reinforcements.

[122]*Fiji Times*, 26 Aug. 1876, extract enclosed in Gordon to Carnarvon, 30 Aug. 1876, PRO CO 83/10. The *Fiji Times* probably would have approved any policy, the more vigorous the better, against any segment of the native population.

[123]The quarrel did not destroy the friendship between Gordon and Havelock. There was coolness for a time, rather like that between Gladstone and Gordon after their return from the Ionian Islands in 1859. Gordon, however, recommended Havelock to the Colonial Office for further employment. Years later, Havelock wrote, "I sinned against you in thought word and deed, and I now express my sorrow. . . ." (Havelock to Gordon [Jan. 1889?], copy in Gordon's diary, 20 Feb. 1889, Stanmore Papers, 49265, f. 36.) When Gordon printed his Fiji records he omitted any reference to their dispute because Havelock had been "conscientiously and honestly" mistaken. (Stanmore to Havelock, 18 July 1897, Stanmore Papers, 49207.)

[124]Knollys was the only professional soldier taking part in the conflict.

[125]Fuller's minute on Gordon to Carnarvon (confidential), 18 Nov. 1876, PRO CO 83/11.

The Governor agreed with Pratt's first point but for different reasons. The use of white regulars, he believed, would have given a racial complexion (which he wished to avoid) to the struggle. Moreover the Engineers by themselves would not have been strong enough to defeat the rebels and any attempt to combine them with Fijian irregulars probably would have proved a fiasco. Each would have hindered the other. To have awaited reinforcements would have allowed heathens and Christians in Viti Levu to go on slaughtering each other thus continuing the decimation of the population begun by the measles. To have brought reinforcements would have incurred an expense which the colony simply could not have borne. As Des Voeux later suggested, the campaign "would have cost England probably a quarter of a million [pounds] or more for the carriage of troops from India."[126] Apart from gratuities to Knollys, A. J. L. Gordon, and MacGregor[127] and some tax remission to the provinces that had supplied forces, the suppression of the rebellion cost Fiji £1,991[128] and Britain nothing at all.

The Colonial Office was neither surprised nor disturbed when it first received news of the rebellion. Malcolm minuted at the end of June: "Outbreaks of this sort were only to [be] expected. This seems to be only a partial & isolated one."[129] Three weeks later, however, Malcolm thought it looked "very like a little war," and Herbert feared it was "a rather serious affair. . . ."[130] As Gordon's dispatches continued and the character of his punitive expedition became clear, the Colonial Office began to criticize the Governor. Its disapproval centred on two features of his conduct: his apparent failure to seek Pratt's advice, and his employment of A. J. L. Gordon both in fighting the rebels and in judging them after they had been apprehended. Fuller thought it "natural to expect some evidence in Sir A. Gordon's despatches that he had placed

[126]Des Voeux to Secretary of State, 15 Feb. 1881, PRO CO 83/25. One of the Colonial Office clerks noted in the margin of this dispatch "this [figure] is probably correct."

[127]These gratuities amounted to £650 in all. When the Colonial Office considered sanctioning them, Captain Ommanney (private secretary to Carnarvon), perhaps a shade enviously, exclaimed, "By an inscrutable but beneficent dispensation of Providence private secretaries become soldiers in Fiji, and soldiers become private secretaries in Downing St.!!" (Marginal note on Gordon to Carnarvon, 27 Sept. 1876, PRO CO 83/10.)

[128]This sum does not take into account the loss of the *Fitzroy* which went aground on a reef during the operations. She was valued at £6,000 and insured for £3,000. This loss, however, should not be charged to the costs of suppressing the rebellion because the vessel might have grounded any where at any time.

[129]Malcolm's minute, 28 June 1876, on Gordon to Carnarvon, 6 May 1876, PRO CO 83/10.

[130]Minutes on Gordon to Carnarvon, 7 June 1876, PRO CO 83/10.

himself in communication with Col[one]l Pratt, as the best military authority on the spot & the one . . . on whom the conduct of a 'war' [normally] would have devolved."[131] Meade considered that "however successful he [Sir Arthur] may have been on this occasion, he should be positively forbidden to go on the war path without the advice & sanction of the officer in command of the troops."[132] Meade also believed it "open to remark that the person who tried the prisoners was Mr. [A. J. L.] Gordon who had conducted the operations against them."[133] Both Herbert and Carnarvon added highly critical comments. The former noted that "it was expressly on account of the possibility of troubles with the Cannibal tribes that we sent the Royal Engineers to Fiji[134]—and now that the occasion for their employment, or at any rate for consulting the able officer in command of them, has arisen we find the whole duty of a Governor in regard to military matters entirely ignored and a very dangerous amateur war undertaken without a word as to the Officer Commanding."[135] Carnarvon minuted:

We must point out to Sir A. G[ordon] that he cannot pass over the off[ice]r in command; & that even with success the principle is a dangerous & objectionable one. . . .

Failure w[oul]d have involved more than the defeat of a few Fijian chiefs; it w[oul]d have compromised the whole of the Gov[ernmen]t & have made absolutely necessary the employment of the troops under very unfavourable cir[cumstan]ces. . . . There was a risk of failure. This makes the omission to communicate with Major Pratt a serious matter.[136]

Despite the brusque tones of Carnarvon's minute, the terms in which, two weeks later, he couched his private letter to the Governor revealed the care with which he handled Sir Arthur. He had, he said, read all of Gordon's private letters "with the greatest interest. . . ." Their "graphic description of the scenes & events & persons" had added a "picturesqueness to what was strange & wild enough of itself." They had made him appreciate the extent of "the primitive & simple civilization" of the Fijians. Carnarvon then congratulated Gordon on the success of his "well planned & conducted" expeditionary force. Some things he did

[131]Fuller's minute, 19 Aug. 1876, on a number of Gordon's dispatches dealing with the uprising. This and other minutes are contained in minute paper 10040, PRO CO 83/10.

[132]Meade's marginal note, minute paper 10040.

[133]Meade's minute, 22 Aug. 1876, ibid. The trial referred to took place on 29 June at Na Sigatoka.

[134]This was not the only reason the Royal Engineers were sent to Fiji. They were also to help with surveys and the construction of public buildings, and so forth.

[135]Herbert's minute, 27 Aug. 1876, minute paper 10040, PRO CO 83/10.

[136]Carnarvon's minute, 1 Sept. 1876, ibid.

not quite understand, as for example, why no reference had been made to Pratt and his soldiers. "I think you would have stood on firmer ground had you obtained Major Pratt's opinion and a general concurrence in the proceedings."[137]

This gently reproving letter crossed one from the Governor, who had finally got around to explaining his failure to consult Pratt officially or to accept his advice. Gordon's explanation contained the arguments noted above.[138] After he received Carnarvon's letter and the Colonial Office's official inquiry, he reiterated these arguments in a dispatch but, as Lord Carnarvon had foreseen,[139] he added that he had considered the suppression of the rebellion a police rather than a military action. There had been no need, therefore, to consult Pratt.

The Colonial Office rightly did not expect Sir Arthur's failure to use the Royal Engineers to arouse adverse public comment or to lead to awkward questions in Parliament. In any case success and economy were sufficient excuses for unorthodox methods. It took a less phlegmatic view of A. J. L. Gordon acting as both "general and judge"[140] and of the severe sentences imposed upon the rebels. Like Sir Arthur it feared public criticism. Herbert postponed bestowing the "marks of approval" that the Governor recommended for Knollys, A. J. L. Gordon, and a number of Fijians,[141] because he thought it probable that "we shall have some complaints of the trial & execution of the prisoners such as have already appeared in the New Zealand press[142] and it will be safer to wait."[143] Nevertheless little further criticism appeared,[144] and no complaints came from Exeter Hall.[145] Early in the new year the

---

[137]Carnarvon to Gordon, 14 Sept. 1876, Carnarvon Papers, PRO GD 6/39.
[138]See p. 188.   [139]Carnarvon's minute, 1 Sept. 1876.
[140]Herbert to Gordon, 19 Oct. 1876, Stanmore Papers, 49199.
[141]Sir Arthur recommended that the Roko Tui Nadroga and the Roko Tui Namose be given gold rings for their help and loyalty. Their tribes had been the most recently Christianized, the most threatened by the rebels, and the most likely to join the rebels. He recommended that the Roko Tui Ba and Yasewas' "conspicuous act of gallantry" in removing kegs of powder from a burning house be handsomely acknowledged. This was done eventually because, as Captain Ommanney noted, the act of gallantry "far surpasses many for which a V.C. has been given." (Minute on Gordon to Carnarvon, 30 Aug. 1876.) Knollys and A. J. L. Gordon were recommended for the C.M.G. which they later did receive.
[142]Critical articles appeared in the *Daily Southern Cross* which were answered by the *Sydney Morning Herald* and the *Fiji Times*.
[143]Herbert's minute on Gordon to Carnarvon, 30 Aug. 1876.
[144]A debate on Fiji took place in the Commons in the spring of 1877 in which Parnell attacked Gordon most vehemently. The House, however, would not listen to him. (George Shaw-Lefevre [Lady Gordon's brother] to Gordon, 28 May 1877, *Fiji*, II, 549.
[145]Headquarters of the English missionary and philanthropic societies.

Secretary of State carried out Sir Arthur's recommendations. Typically, Gordon felt a little let down when he learned that his own work had not been publicly recognized. Typically, he had no hesitation in telling the Secretary of State of his disappointment.

Although Gordon undoubtedly desired praise too frequently, he had nevertheless some grounds for his disappointment in this instance. He had acted quickly, decisively, and, by discarding professional advice, courageously, in dealing with the hill war. He had planned the strategy and wisely allowed the Fijian chiefs to determine tactics. The cost had been negligible and victory complete. As time was to demonstrate, Fiji had witnessed its last large-scale rebellion, as well as the last blow in behalf of regional independence against central authority. The vigorous and industrious highlanders of Viti Levu rapidly adjusted themselves to settled life. In 1880 Sir Arthur could report a striking change in the mountain areas. "There is now no district in which matters are more satisfactory or in which the native policy of the government has been more completely successful. . . ."[146] His measures and methods had again borne good fruit.

The little war in Viti Levu not only enhanced Gordon's own status and authority and confirmed that of his government throughout the group, but it impressed upon Fijians the possibility and desirability of working together for common purposes. Before the outbreak Sir Arthur, through the produce tax, had begun the task of improving native local and regional organizations and turning them to constructive purposes. By establishing the council of chiefs as a kind of federated Fijian parliament answering to himself as governor-general, he had begun to transform the loosely confederated imperium of Cakobau into a Fijian nation.

To Gordon, it was not enough for his government to recognize "the interests of all classes of the population as equal objects of solicitude."[147] Racial incompatibility too often frustrated the benevolent intentions of the rulers. Even where no conscious repulsion existed, want of imagination and lack of understanding of the native point of view produced similar results. He thought it probable that as much wrong had been inflicted "by the conscientious but narrowminded desire to act in accordance with maxims in themselves generally sound, but not of universal application," as by violence and tyranny.[148]

[146]Gordon to Secretary of State, 10 Nov. 1880, PRO CO 83/23.
[147]*Fiji*, I, 197.
[148]*Ibid.*

Under the influence of a desire to effect improvement, a pressure is put upon the native to adopt European habits, perhaps unsuitable, and almost certainly distasteful. He is subjected to laws which are strange to him, and which in some respects conflict with his own idea of justice, whilst he is aware that . . . the advantage in any contest under such laws is all on the side of those who have long been familiar with their operation. He is urged to simulate ideas which are unintelligible to him. Impatience at the ignorance and levity too frequently displayed by natives in authority, to say nothing of acts of real misconduct, leads to their services being set aside, and all native agency is replaced by that of white officials and magistrates. Something—perhaps much, perhaps little—is done for the native; nothing is left to be done by him, or in his own way.[149]

Sir Arthur considered such a policy rash, dangerous, and harmful.

At best the natives, bewildered and depressed, deprived of all interest and object in life, sink into indolence, apathy, and vice, and, exposed almost without any safeguard to snares and temptations innumerable, they lose position, property, self-respect, and health, and perish from off the face of the earth.

It is manifest that the more the native policy is retained, native agency employed, and changes avoided until naturally and spontaneously called for the less likely are these results to follow. But it is not enough to abstain from seeking hastily to replace native institutions by unreal imitations of European models.

The moral sense of a semicivilised race is often very unlike our own, but is not on that account the less real; and it would be a great mistake to suppose that it does not exercise a most powerful influence upon thought and action. . . . It is therefore of the utmost importance to seize, if possible the spirit in which native institutions have been framed, and endeavour so to work them as to develop to the utmost possible extent the latent capacities of the people for the management of their own affairs, without exciting their suspicion or destroying their self-respect.[150]

Gordon concluded that his wisest course was to preserve the existing native organization of village communities, to uphold the authority of the chiefs and local councils, and to maintain existing native laws and customs, modifying them where necessary but allowing native agencies to enforce them. He abolished the old department of native affairs, and as governor assumed direct control himself with the assistance of a native affairs board composed partly of Europeans and partly of natives. He defined by law the composition and functions of the existing district and provincial native councils—those "essential mainsprings" of Fijian social and political life—which, for many years, had "regulated every local transaction."[151] In future, district councils were to meet

149*Ibid.*   150*Ibid.*, 197–98.
151Gordon to Carnarvon, 16 June 1877, PRO CO 83/13.

monthly and provincial councils quarterly. To complete the edifice of native self-government Gordon eagerly seized the opportunity to create a permanent council of chiefs.

This "Great Council" or "Bose vaka Turaga" was an innovation. The chiefs had held meetings sometimes, but infrequently or irregularly; in future, the council would meet annually. It would consist of the *rokos*, the native stipendiary magistrates, and two *bulis* from each of the provinces. To the Great Council Sir Arthur gave responsibility for discussing matters affecting natives and for passing resolutions which, if approved by the governor, were forwarded to the Native Affairs Board for consideration. The Native Affairs Board had power to transform the resolutions into regulations that, subject to the approval of the legislative council, had the force of law. Gordon thought the method of transacting business, in what he called the "native parliament," much resembled that followed in its beginnings by the English Parliament. "The way in which all resolutions are presented to me together and receive answers is just that in which the representations of Parliament were made to the Angevin Kings."[152]

Although the Bose vaka Turaga had no direct legislative powers it wielded much more influence over legislation affecting Fijians than would a few natives sitting as members of an otherwise wholly European legislative council as in New Zealand. Among the measures for which, during or just after Gordon's administration, the Great Council was largely responsible were the native lands ordinance, the industrial schools ordinance, and legislation respecting native indentured labour. More than legislative advantages stemmed from the Great Council. Its regular meetings provided opportunities for airing grievances, settling disputes, and breaking down the insularity of the chiefs. The council gave the government moral support in disciplining delinquent chiefs. Perhaps most important, it provided the only link between all Fijians and aided the growth of a sense of national identity.

The Fijians welcomed Gordon's policy and plainly showed their desire to make it work. Said the great chief Ma'afu to his colleagues in 1875:

Let us be helpers truly. . . . It is a great work. Think of past years, of our desire to be united for purposes of Government. Think of the many attempts that have been made. Remember how hard it was to make any progress. Were we not near to ruin several times? Now the foundation of the house is fixed and firm. Let us build. What the Governor requires of us is to be

[152]Gordon to Mary Gladstone, 24 April 1880, L. M. Phillipps and B. Christian, *Some Hawarden Letters, 1878–1913*, 70f.

careful to recommend those things that we truly think are for the best. Let us manfully obey his every word, and further his desires. . . . We may yet live to see Fiji's peace firmly established, Christianity and civilization advancing, and all of us happy in our own homes. This is the day I have sought and desired to see.[153]

The Roko Tui Bua added:

It is as clear as the noonday that there is but one object in the Governor's mind. He is seeking for our true and real good, and we must be true and real helpers in his great and heavy task. . . . Our natural habits of indifference and our ready excuses for not having done our work will not do in this age. What is decided upon to be done we must do. The Governor is our true leader and helper, let our obedience be thorough.[154]

Wilkinson, the chief government interpreter, spoke of the earnestness of the chiefs' deliberations and their unity of feeling in discussing the subjects brought forward for consideration. "The absence of this unity has hitherto been one of the most serious drawbacks to the formation of a Government and to progress."[155] Near the end of Sir Arthur's administration, Wilkinson, who attended all the deliberations of the Great Council, marked the improvement in the council both in the spirit in which discussions were conducted and in the greater frankness amongst the superior chiefs.

The feeling is gaining ground that the Bose is not simply a great gathering together of chiefs and people but that it has important and real results extending to every part of the Colony. . . .
It is at the Bose alone, or more than anywhere else, the chiefs feel that while they are individually chiefs in their own Provinces they are nevertheless inseparably a part of the whole body. . . .
There is a manifest feeling of pride, that if their work be not perfection it shall be the best they are capable of.[156]

As the years of Gordon's governorship passed, the chiefs gradually realized that the council was to be a permanent and essential part of the new régime. As the council's sittings grew longer a fixed order of procedure had to be imposed. The successful working of the council and the sight of legislation growing out of its deliberations gave the

[153]Translation of Ma'afu's address to the council of chiefs at Draiba, Sept. 1875, by D. Wilkinson, printed in minutes of the council of chiefs enclosed in Gordon to Carnarvon, 16 Feb. 1876, PRO CO 83/9.
[154]Translation of Roko Tui Bua's address, Sept. 1875, printed in minutes of the council of chiefs, *ibid.* It should be noted that the Governor was not present at the Draiba meeting. The speeches are thus free of any imputation of flattery.
[155]Report of D. Wilkinson, the native commissioner, March 1880, enclosed in Gordon to Secretary of State, 11 April 1881, PRO CO 83/25.
[156]*Ibid.*

chiefs a self-confidence that enabled them to stand up for themselves and their people against the unwarrantable demands of settlers and missionaries.

Because Sir Arthur from the first had decided that direct control of native affairs should rest with the governor rather than the legislative council, the successful implementation of his native policy placed a tremendous burden upon him and his establishment. He himself presided at the opening of the Bose vaka Turaga and studied the resolutions passed during the session. He wrote constantly to the *rokos* urging them to their duties, chiding them when they failed, but always encouraging them. His letters had to be carefully phrased, for a Fijian who received too much praise was ruined and one who got too little gave up trying to do his job. The Governor also corresponded frequently with his native commissioners and the stipendiary magistrates and paid them visits when he could. He knew when and why the natives were depressed, discouraged, or dissatisfied, and he could take remedial measures quickly. He worked unsparingly[157] and he required a similar devotion to duty by his staff. For the most part he got it. Time-consuming and often exhausting, his conduct of native affairs was, nevertheless, a labour of love. Moreover, he believed, it was the work that God had called him to perform. Still, he sometimes found it dispiriting to realize how few understood his policy and of those who understood it, how few sympathized with it. Most of the settlers looked upon Fijians as encumbrances to be cleared away as rapidly, although as decently, as possible. Most of them deplored his attempt to make the natives self-supporting and self-governing. Many worked actively to frustrate the Governor's plans and to destroy native confidence in the government. This was especially true of that planter-cum-journalist, W. F. Parr, and of G. L. Griffiths, the proprietor of the *Fiji Times*, and his editor Solomons.

Parr, whom the Colonial Office considered "entirely untrustworthy"[158] if not slightly insane, posed as the friend of the natives and wrote

[157]Lady Gordon complained that "Arthur is so taken up with Fiji affairs that he can't realize what it is to me to be cut off from everything as I am. He has to work very hard—beginning to write at six o'clock in the morning for two hours before he dresses for breakfast, and then at work the whole day till half-past five o'clock, when he comes up to the drawing-room and reads to Nevil and plays with the children till their bed-time. . . ." (Lady Gordon to her sister Mrs. Ryan, [?] Sept. 1877, *Fiji*, II, 605.) But even when at play with the children he "was working [his dispatches] out in his mind. . . ." (A. P. Maudslay, *Life in the Pacific Fifty Years Ago*, 91.)

[158]Fuller's minute on Gordon to Secretary of State, 27 March 1880, PRO CO 83/22.

countless letters to the Colonial Office, newspaper editors, and public men in England defaming Gordon's administration. He charged that Gordon's native policy subjected Fijians to the same misrule as they had endured before annexation and "the same serfdom as in the olden days, with the exception of 'club law.' " He claimed that if natives were allowed to work for planters, the latter would protect them from "the tyrannical actions of the chiefs."[159] Parr asserted that "Ichabod is written o'er the land,"[160] and asked Herbert why Fiji was "cursed with a governor like Sir Arthur Gordon. . . . It seems to be his determination to ruin the country. . . . Everything he has done and is doing is contrary to the wishes of every planter."[161] Parr tried unsuccessfully to get William Forster, the London agent for New South Wales, to act as the agent for the Fiji planters and persuade the Colonial Office not to allow Gordon's return to Fiji when his leave expired in 1879. He alleged to Forester that Gordon was "hated by every native as well as by every white man."[162] Parr was almost certainly responsible for the totally false story that appeared in the *Fiji Times*, the *Sydney Daily Telegraph*, and *The Times* (London), that Fijians, in protest against taxation and slavery, had murdered and eaten a government agent.[163]

The fulminations of Parr did not worry Gordon unduly. He knew that no one in the Colonial Office, with the exception of James Lowther, Carnarvon's incompetent[164] parliamentary under-secretary, believed them. He knew that the Fijians happily accepted his policy. Moreover, after returning from leave he learned that "a number of the settlers . . . desire[d] to afford his policy a more cheerful support than . . . hitherto. . . ."[165] Yet he was not insensible "to the injury which may be done to me,—and to what I care much more for, the maintenance of the present system of native administration in Fiji—by the circulation of such stories [as Parr's]."[166] During a speech in October 1879, he gave

---

[159][W. F. Parr], *Fiji in 1877: The First Three Years since Annexation under Governor Sir Arthur H. Gordon, K.C.M.G., or A Crown Colony of a Very Severe Type*, pamphlet filed with PRO CO 83/18; copy also in British Museum.

[160]*Ibid.*   [161]Parr to Herbert, 28 March 1878, PRO CO 83/18.

[162]Parr to Forster, 17 June 1878, PRO CO 83/17 (Agents 12723).

[163]Gordon to Secretary of State, 8 Aug. 1881, and Fuller's minute, 23 Sept. 1881, PRO CO 83/27. No murder or act of cannibalism had taken place and the district in which it was alleged to have occurred was so remote that it had never been taxed.

[164]See George Shaw-Lefevre to Gordon, 28 May 1877, *Fiji*, II, 549.

[165]*Melbourne Argus*, 10 Jan. 1880, clipping enclosed in Gordon to Secretary of State, 27 March 1880. He observed to his wife that "I really believe I am getting a hold upon those who have hitherto been most hostile to me." (Gordon to Lady Gordon, 7 Jan. 1880, *Fiji*, IV, 162.)

[166]Gordon to Secretary of State, 8 Aug. 1881.

much notice (Kimberley thought "a great deal too much") to Parr's charges.[167] A few days earlier he had demonstrated to the colonists that, despite their antipathy, he and his policies had won respect at home, by disembarking (on his return from England) in full uniform and the scarlet silk gown of a Doctor of Civil Laws which degree Oxford had just conferred on him.[168]

The planting community and its spokesmen did not provide all of the opposition to Sir Arthur's native policies. The missionaries, especially the Wesleyan,[169] resented the gradual replacement of their influence over the natives by that of the government and government-supported native institutions. They had worked on behalf of annexation but had never foreseen the kind of administration that Gordon established. At first, Sir Arthur had moved warily in challenging Wesleyan authority because he recognized in Rev. Frederick Langham, the head of the Wesleyan mission, a powerful potential antagonist. Langham occupied "very much the position of one of the political bishops of the Middle Ages"[170] and controlled an organization among the Fijians that allowed him greater knowledge of events throughout the colony than Gordon's government could at first gain. The Governor sought always to avoid a head-on collision with the mission because he respected its power and admired its civilizing influence upon the natives. Nevertheless, he could not allow the missionaries to continue exercising authority beyond the spiritual sphere. Although Sir Arthur knew that many of his innovations, like the Bose vaka Turaga and the industrial schools, were, as Thurston said, "poison to men of the Rooney-Langham stamp,"[171] he still proceeded with them. As government became firmly established, Gordon did not refrain from replying tartly to missionary criticism. On one occasion he answered Langham, who had protested against certain native customs allowed by the Governor as immoral and destructive of religion, by saying "I am . . . convinced that the cause of religion is not lastingly promoted by making men feel 'like pigs fenced into a pig stye' though such restraint may for a time secure an outward good

[167]Minutes by Herbert and Kimberley on Gordon to Secretary of State, 27 Oct. 1879, enclosing clipping from *Fiji Times*, 22 Oct. 1879, giving an account of the Governor's speech to the colonists, PRO CO 83/20.

[168]Des Voeux, *My Colonial Service*, I, 407. Vanity doubtless also played its part in this performance.

[169]The Roman Catholic mission, claiming only about 10 per cent of native Christians, had but a small fraction of the power of the Wesleyan.

[170]*Fiji*, I, 164.

[171]Thurston to Gordon, 24 Jan. 1881, Stanmore Papers, 49204. The industrial schools were sponsored by the government but built and manned by natives. See below, p. 225.

appearance."[172] Nevertheless, Gordon did not win a complete victory in the "cold war" with the Wesleyan mission. Several months after the Governor's departure Thurston was lamenting that "the chief drag upon the progress of the Native Coach is the presence in Fiji of the great political & trading concern of John Wesley & Co."[173]

Gordon's native policy met opposition even within his government. Some objected to any restriction on native purchases of liquor because it reduced revenue and slowed the pace at which the native population would otherwise be diminished. Others, especially the lawyers, wished to replace native laws and customs by English laws and customs. The policy of supporting native institutions, law, and authority "had no stronger opponents" than Chief Justice Hackett and Attorney-General de Ricci.[174] Neither man lasted long in the service of Gordon's administration. Gorrie and Garrick, who succeeded them, were more elastic in their views, although Gorrie had his doubts concerning the propriety of the Bose vaka Turaga and the ability of native magistrates to administer the law.

Within the council the chief supporters of the Governor's policies were John Thurston and Dr. MacGregor. MacGregor's high character, prodigious energy, and great common sense made him an excellent councillor and administrator. Skilful as a physician and surgeon and broadly humanitarian he was one of the most respected and well-liked men in the colony. Gordon placed great reliance upon his friendship, support, and administrative capacity. Thurston was undoubtedly more hated by the settlers than any other man in Fiji, but for reasons all to his credit. As the leading member (though not prime minister) of King Cakobau's government he had objected to the white settlers taking over complete control of the government and the land from the natives. He had repressed European outrages against Fijians and had tried to uphold the constitution against white subversion. Thurston's ability and resourcefulness placed him far above the other Europeans in Fiji, and for this also the settlers hated him. For the first three years of Gordon's administration colonial hatred, Colonial Office suspicion, and Sir Arthur's doubts of Thurston's political honesty kept him in offices of second rank. While Thurston smarted under this treatment and resented

[172]Gordon to Langham, 29 June 1880, Stanmore Papers, 49245.

[173]Thurston to Gordon, 21 March 1881, Stanmore Papers, 49204.

[174]*Fiji*, I, 199. Hackett refused to take up his duties as chief justice if any native were allowed to retain a title as "Native Judge." Gordon had to give in rather than bring about a cessation of legal processes in the colony. Hackett also opposed Gordon's land policy saying that he regarded it as the duty of the Lands Commission on all occasions to make good a white man's claim wherever a legal or plausible *excuse* for doing so could be found. (Gordon to Selborne, 22 May 1880, *Fiji*, IV, 307.)

the higher salaries of some of his administrative colleagues he performed his duties flawlessly. In 1878 his perseverance brought its reward when Alfred Maudslay, who had succeeded Havelock as colonial secretary, went to England. Gordon then defied colonial antipathy to Thurston and gave him the appointment.

Other members of the council were often useful but Thurston and MacGregor made themselves indispensable both to Gordon and, later, to Des Voeux. Without their support within the council, that of Wilkinson, Le Hunte, and Carew among his field officers, and that of Cakobau, Ma'afu, and the Roko Tui Bau among the chiefs, Sir Arthur would have found his native policy extremely difficult, if not impossible, to execute. The shortage of competent European field officers was the chief weakness in Gordon's native policy, as, after his departure, a shortage of competent chiefs became its major fault. Ma'afu died in 1881, Cakobau in 1883, and others among the older chiefs soon after. Some of their successors, more worldly and Europeanized, abused their offices. This, rather than a change of government policy, probably accounts for the supersession, at the end of the century, of a large part of the authority of the chiefs by that of European officials.

The Colonial Office supported Gordon's native policy. Carnarvon opposed any indiscriminate application of English law to the natives, preferring to respect their "customs & social usages . . . so far as is compatible with natural equity, morality & order."[175] Although native law, native tax, and native councils made "rather a large pill [for the Colonial Office] to swallow," nevertheless, Herbert told Gordon, "we have swallowed it bravely in order to give you the chance you desire of proving that you can govern the natives instead of killing them off."[176] No doubt humanitarianism strongly influenced the Colonial Office's acceptance of these policies, but there were other motives. Native self-government and native law administered by natives were cheaper than European administration would have been. Furthermore, as Fuller wrote a few years later, "our hopes of avoiding native wars are bound up in the retention of the Tribal system in Fiji, & not in undermining the quasi-feudal system which exists in the W[estern] Pacific. . . . Truth is not absent from the allegation that if they had acknowledged this principle a little more in New Zealand there would have been less bloodshed & fewer complications."[177]

[175]Malcolm's minute on Gordon to Carnarvon, 27 Dec. 1875, PRO CO 83/6. The supreme court ordinance of Fiji, drawn up by Sir J. Pauncefote, left Gordon free to apply as much or as little English law to Fiji as he saw fit.

[176]Herbert to Gordon, 9 June 1876, Stanmore Papers, 49199.

[177]Fuller's minute on George Anderson, M.P., to parliamentary under-secretary Ashley, 8 Aug. 1884, PRO CO 83/39.

From the first the Colonial Office regarded Gordon's policy as an experiment. The minutes on the Governor's dispatches suggest that the natives' capacity for self-government surprised the Colonial Office. Fuller spoke of the "high degree of common sense among the Chiefs . . ." and of the Fijians as "a wonderful people for managing their own affairs."[178] Meade observed that "the chiefs in council seem to be a very shrewd set of men and understand exactly what they want."[179] Most of the staff believed Gordon deserved much credit for his native policy. Fuller wrote of it in 1878 as "the most satisfactory part of Sir A. Gordon's administration" adding that "he seems to have won the confidence of the chiefs & through them ruled the people."[180] Malcolm thought the Governor had been "wise to take advantage . . . of the material of a social system already existing."[181] Herbert, Carnarvon, and Hicks Beach were similarly approving. Two members of the staff, however, approved neither Gordon nor his native policy. Bramston rarely wrote an uncritical minute and Lowther never. Although the Colonial Office in general hoped that Gordon's policy would not check white settlement too much, Bramston and Lowther felt that the latter ought not to be checked at all. This was the basis of their disagreement with Sir Arthur. In addition Bramston revered precedent while the Government did not. Lowther disliked Sir Arthur and spoke of him as "the exceedingly vain Governor" and "the pretentious Prig who represents H[er] M[ajesty] in the Colony."[182]

Although no one in the Colonial Office, except Lowther and Bramston, and later Fiddes, disagreed very much with what Gordon was doing for and with the natives, everyone at one time or another did criticize his methods. For example the Office in general strongly approved his ordinance establishing the native regulation board and his regulations comprising the native code. The regulations had been "framed with care & skill [and were] avowedly intended to give form & precision to pre-existing native law & custom, modifying them only where modification seemed imperatively required."[183] Nevertheless the Colonial Office frowned when Gordon refused to obey its instructions

[178]Fuller's minutes on Gordon to Secretary of State, 25 Jan. 1878, PRO CO 83/16; and Thurston to Secretary of State, 3 Dec. 1885, PRO CO 83/42.
[179]Meade's minute on Des Voeux to Kimberley, 23 June 1882, PRO CO 83/30.
[180]Fuller's minute on Gordon to Secretary of State, 25 Jan. 1878.
[181]Malcolm's minute, 12 Sept. 1877, on Gordon to Carnarvon, 16 June 1877, PRO CO 83/13.
[182]Lowther's minute on Gordon to Secretary of State, 30 Nov. 1877, PRO CO 83/14.
[183]Malcolm's minute on Gordon to Carnarvon, 16 June 1877. For a summary of the native code see *Fiji*, II, 507–11.

to amend the ordinance so as to reduce the Governor's power over the native regulation board and when he failed to report new regulations in his dispatches, leaving the Colonial Office to find out about them from the *Gazette*. This latter practice, Bramston noted in 1881, was "not the sort of opportunity that ought to have been given [us]" but it was "quite characteristic of Sir A. Gordon. . . ."[184] Herbert and Kimberley agreed, but the former cautioned that "we must not say too much about the failure to report the Regulations as . . . we have had them regularly in the Gazettes & Sir A. Gordon would say that he concluded the Department did not fail to peruse the Colonial Gazette (as it should)."[185] Kimberley added, "the moral is: Examine Fiji Gazettes in future."[186]

Few of these criticisms of Sir Arthur's failure to observe protocol reached his ears. The Colonial Office realized that many of his sins resulted from shortages of printing and copying facilities. It also knew that as long as it approved his policies, and those policies worked satisfactorily, the advantage in debate over details of administration lay with the Governor. While Gordon remained in Fiji the Colonial Office offered no real criticism of his native system. Not until 1883 is there an intimation in the minutes on the dispatches from Fiji that anyone in the Colonial Office seriously thought of radical changes. In February of that year Fiddes believed "the time . . . inevitably will come, for a change in the Native System. . . ."[187] In August of the following year Herbert doubted "whether the policy, right in its original intention, of teaching the Fijians to govern themselves & tax themselves on tribal principles is not being injudiciously carried to a point at which it oppresses the native more than the opposite policy would do. . . . It seems deserving of consideration whether an independent inquiry into the whole condition of Fiji should not be instituted."[188] Lord Derby, who had become secretary of state late in 1882, discussed the question with Herbert and decided it would be "inexpedient to disturb the minds of the natives at the present moment. . . ."[189] The subject was dropped, and Gordon's native system remained intact until the death, in 1897, of his last disciple, Sir John Thurston. Much of Sir Arthur's system endured even beyond that time because as long as the Fijians retained

[184]Minutes on Des Voeux to Secretary of State, 21 April 1881, PRO CO 83/25.
[185]*Ibid.*
[186]*Ibid.*
[187]Fiddes' minute on Treasury to Colonial Office, 8 Feb. 1883, PRO CO 83/25. G. V. Fiddes was a Colonial Office clerk.
[188]Herbert's minute on Anderson to Ashley, 8 Aug. 1884.
[189]Derby's minute, *ibid.*

their lands, possession of which he had guaranteed them, they could not be entirely deprived of their independence.

IV. LAND AND LABOUR

In 1875 land and labour were vital matters to both Fijians and white settlers. Few Fijians wished to see more of their lands fall into the hands of Europeans and few desired to work on the white man's plantation for long months at low wages. Most of the settlers had come close to ruin during the disastrous collapse of cotton prices in the early years of the decade. Indeed, many had been ruined and had left Fiji after selling their land claims for what they could get. Those who remained required firm titles to the lands they occupied so that they might either sell their estates and leave the colony or begin cultivating new and more profitable crops. If the latter, they also needed a plentiful supply of cheap labour. Realizing the urgency of the settlers' plight Gordon gave high priority to an early solution of both their problems. Despite the penurious condition of the planters and of the colony itself he solved the labour question before he left Fiji. The land question, complicated by conflicting interpretations of the Deed of Cession and by Gordon's own stubbornness in safeguarding the rights of the natives, took longer to settle. Nevertheless, the majority of European claims and the basis of native tenure were decided by the time he departed for New Zealand.

Although Europeans[190] cultivated only some 16,000 acres they laid claim to more than 850,000 acres in Fiji, about one-fifth of its total area. Realizing that many of these claims were probably of dubious validity and wishing to protect the Fijians from exploitation, the Colonial Office intended to reserve to the Crown absolute power to settle the land question as it deemed fit. Lord Carnarvon had, therefore, instructed Robinson to obtain a completely unconditional cession of the islands. On landing in Fiji, however, Robinson had found that "persons whose interests were adverse to good government" had taken advantage of Carnarvon's speech in the House of Lords concerning the Crown's right to pre-emption in all lands "to excite distrust in the minds of both Europeans and natives. . . ."[191] He had thus felt obliged to insert a clause in the Deed of Cession (article IV) vesting in the Crown "the

[190]As a result of hard times and the political squabbles of the early seventies, the European population of Fiji had declined from about 3,000 in 1871–72 to some 1,650 in 1875 of whom 850 were men, 270 women, and 530 children. (John B. Thurston, *The Navigation and Trade . . . of the Fiji Islands . . .*, PRO CO 83/6.)   [191]Robinson to Carnarvon, 3 Oct. 1874, PRO CO 83/5.

absolute ownership of all lands not shown by those laying claim to them to be bonâ fide the property of Europeans or other foreigners, or not required for the maintenance and support of chiefs and tribes, leaving Her Majesty's Government to be the ultimate judge as to what lands have been fairly acquired by Europeans, and what extent is required for the support of the natives."[192] In explaining his action to the Colonial Office, Sir Hercules wrote that he could not avoid all specific reference to land without giving rise to charges of bad faith and that he could not insert any clause transferring to the Crown all lands irrespective of private ownership and the requirements of the tribes without lending colour to "the rumours of confiscation and spoliation of private rights which had been so industriously circulated."[193]

Herbert, in thinking that Robinson had been unwise to adopt "what is in fact a renewal of conditions as to land cession," had a presentiment of trouble. The Colonial Office nevertheless proceeded on the understanding that the Deed of Cession in no way restricted the power of the Crown to settle the land issue. Carnarvon's instructions to Gordon[194] left the latter no room to doubt his power, or more technically his government's, to settle the land question. According to orders he issued (on the day after his arrival in Fiji) a notice calling on all persons having claims to land to file them with the government before 31

[192]*Ibid.*

[193]*Ibid.* The actual wording of this clause (article IV) of the Deed of Cession is: "That the absolute proprietorship of all lands not shown to be now alienated so as to have become the bonâ fide property of Europeans or other foreigners, or not now in the actual use or occupation of some Chief or tribe, or not actually required for the probable future support and maintenance of some Chief or tribe, shall be, and is hereby declared to be, vested in Her said Majesty, her heirs and successors."

[194]Carnarvon to Gordon, 4 March 1875, PRO CO 83/5. These instructions stated that "(1) it should be declared that the whole of the land within the limits of Fiji . . . has . . . become absolutely and unreservedly transferred to the Crown, and that the Queen has the full power of disposing of the whole of the land in such manner as to Her Majesty may seem fit; having due regard to such interests as may be entitled to recognition under article 4 of that Instrument.

(2) that with the view of disturbing as little as possible existing tenures and occupations, and of maintaining (as far as practicable, and with such modifications only as justice and good policy may in any case appear to demand) all contracts honestly entered into before the cession, the Colonial Government, to which the rights of the Crown are delegated in that behalf, should forthwith require all Europeans claiming to have acquired land by purchase to give satisfactory evidence of the transactions with the natives on which they rely as establishing their title; and if the land appears to have been acquired fairly and at a fair price, should issue to the persons accepted after due enquiry as owners a Crown Grant in fee simple of the land to which they may appear entitled, subject to any conditions as to further payments and charges or otherwise which may appear just."

October if resident in the colony or before 31 December if resident elsewhere.[195] He had the legislative council pass an ordinance (3 of 1875) making it unlawful to commence or maintain suits respecting existing claims to land in any court of law in the colony. Again, according to instructions Sir Arthur appointed (30 October) a commission to investigate land claims. It began its work in December, under the chairmanship of the Chief Justice. Gordon considered its reports in executive council, reviewed the collected evidence, and with the advice of the executive council issued certificates of title. He could not at once issue Crown grants in fee simple because it was first necessary to have the boundaries of the properties surveyed and also to have a land titles ordinance passed. By March 1876 the commission had made progress, and Sir Arthur had issued 148 certificates of title.

Meanwhile lawyers in Fiji had disputed the Crown's right to settle land claims according to the principles laid down in Carnarvon's instructions to the Governor. They held that because article IV of the Deed of Cession recognized the existence of private rights to land acquired before cession, those rights could be determined only by a court of law and not by decision of the Crown.[196] Althought Gordon proceeded on the assumption that the lawyers erred, he nevertheless sought reassurance from Carnarvon. At the same time he warned that unless he adhered to the course prescribed "an amount of fraud upon the unfortunate natives will be sanctioned under the colour of law to which I should be most reluctant to be a party, and of which I should hesitate to be even a passive witness."[197] The Colonial Office missed the point of Sir Arthur's dispatch and after reiterating its policy told him that he had only to prepare and pass the necessary ordinances to give effect to that policy.[198] Gordon had to write again. This time the Colonial Office grasped the point, and Malcolm wrote to the law officers of the Crown for their opinion.[199] They replied that Lord Carnarvon's views were not "to a great extent incorrect," but were open to exception in two respects. First, the term *"bona fide"* meant only "without fraud or force." The fairness of the price, while an element in determining the existence of fraud, could not be taken by itself as determining the *bona fides* of the transaction. Secondly, owners

---

[195]These dates were later extended to 31 December 1875 and 31 March 1876 respectively, but Gordon accepted petitions from non-residents long after the latter date.
[196]Gordon to Carnarvon, 21 Aug. 1875, PRO CO 83/6.
[197]*Ibid.*
[198]Minutes, *ibid.*
[199]Malcolm to law officers, 19 April 1876, PRO CO 83/12.

of lands acquired *bona fide* before cession could not be compelled to accept grants of those lands from the Crown. "We think it is not competent for the Legislature of Fiji to enact that no right or title to land . . . shall be recognized in any Court of the Colony unless it is founded on a grant made by the Crown."[200] The legislature might make provision for the method of investigating claims, but such provision should deal only with procedure. "The claims should be adjusted upon the principles laid down in the Deed of Cession and upon those only."[201]

On receipt of the law officers' letter Malcolm minuted sadly: "The Law Officers will not uphold us in endeavouring to introduce the consideration of whether lands have been obtained '*at a fair price*' as well as 'fairly' as the proper interpretation of the terms of the deed of cession. In fact they will not authorize us to put any interpretation upon the deed but I presume hold that the Law Courts must interpret its meaning."[202] Therefore Malcolm thought it best to follow the Griqua Land precedent. The colonial government should pass an ordinance empowering the supreme court, or better, a special land court, to take cognizance of all pleas arising out of land claims and enact that a judgment of the court when made absolute should entitle the claimant to an indefeasible title and empower the governor to cause titles to be prepared and registered. He believed that if the court took a strict view of what constituted *bona fides* "the objects laid down by L[or]d Carnarvon . . . will be very nearly obtained."[203] A confidential dispatch in the sense of Malcolm's minute was then sent to Gordon.

Sir Arthur resisted giving final jurisdiction on land claims to any court. In his view a court, being confined to matters of fact, could not possibly serve the ends of justice. It could only reject or accept a claim in full. Many claims existed where, should a court decide on their enforcement, the natives would suffer and the government would face more dangerous political situations than in the highland rising in Viti Levu. Should a court wholly reject such claims many white settlers would experience hardship. To leave decisions to a court would entail not only hardship and expense but, because of appeals, long delays in effecting a final settlement of the land question. Moreover, claimants had been led to believe that if they complied with the call of the Crown and made good their claims they would at once receive an unquestionable title. They would have "good reason to complain of a breach of faith if they are compelled again to appear before a Court to prove the claims

[200]Law officers to Colonial Office, 3 Aug. 1876, PRO CO 83/12.
[201]*Ibid.*
[202]Malcolm's minute, 9 Aug. 1876, *ibid.*   [203]*Ibid.*

which have just been pronounced good by the Governor in Council."[204]
Furthermore, natives had not the knowledge, patience, or skill to conduct their own cases, and certainly not the money to employ counsel.
The Crown would be compelled to fight their cases for them and would
thus be brought into direct conflict with the Europeans.[205]

In January 1878 Gordon wrote to Herbert warning him that unless
the Colonial Office found "some means of overcoming the scruples of
the gentlemen of the long robe, and *substantially* adhering to the original
plan, the colony must go to pieces."[206] He continued:

> I am not given to screaming hysterics, but, I give you clear, deliberate, and
> emphatic warning that the course now proposed must at best entail an
> expenditure . . . perfectly ruinous, and that it would almost certainly involve
> us in an unjust, calamitous, and costly war.
>   . . . I should not view with complacency the conversion of a real success
> into a disastrous failure in order to satisfy legal pedantry. . . .
> The real question is whether the *intention* of the deed of cession (which
> cannot be disputed)[207] is to be followed, or the strict legal effects of its
> wording enforced without regard to the inevitable catastrophe such adherence
> to its letter must entail.[208]

Gordon thought he saw "a way out of this corner" that might satisfy the
lawyers and, since he would soon be going on leave, he asked Herbert to
prevent the Colonial Office committing itself "by act, word, or writing"
until he had arrived in England.[209]

A few weeks after his return to London he drew up a memorandum
reiterating all his arguments against changing the system. He ended by
suggesting an arrangement that he thought would satisfy nearly all who
desired bringing the law courts into operation without doing substantial
injustice either to the natives or to those settlers whose claims had
already been allowed.[210] Convinced of the validity of the Governor's
arguments, the Colonial Office asked him to submit a draft ordinance

[204]Gordon to Carnarvon, 9 Aug. 1877, *Fiji*, II, 553–57.
[205]*Ibid.*
[206]Gordon to Herbert, 22 Jan. 1878, *Fiji*, II, 704–5.
[207]Robinson assured Gordon that he "never contemplated that the investigation
into land claims would be made by a court of law . . ." and that "the view you
take is *precisely* what was in my mind at the time the deed of cession was being
framed. . . ." (Robinson to Gordon, 2 Aug. 1878, *Fiji*, III, 184.) Sir George
Innes, who drew up the Deed of Cession, wrote "I quite concur in the view he
[Gordon] takes as to the intention with which the 4th clause . . . was framed."
(Innes to Robinson, 29 July 1878, *Fiji*, III, 185.)
[208]Gordon to Herbert, 22 Jan. 1878.
[209]*Ibid.* By the end of June 1878, some 800 claims had been investigated. A
change of procedure at this stage would have thrown all of these "settled" claims
into the "unsettled" category.
[210]Private memorandum for Secretary of State, Sept. 1878, *Fiji*, III, 181–84.

embodying his suggestions. The main objects of Gordon's draft legislation were to provide for the indefeasibility of Crown grants and for rehearing of disallowed claims, and "to secure the native proprietors from the molestation which, without such protection, they would inevitably undergo from the reproduction in the courts of law of claims which have been disallowed by the Governor in Council. . . ."[211] Although the Colonial Office was fully prepared to accept the proposed ordinance it felt certain that the law officers would object to it as inconsistent with the Deed of Cession and thus beyond the competence of the Fiji legislature. It approved, therefore, when Sir Arthur enlisted his friend Lord Selborne, the former attorney-general (1863–65) and lord chancellor (1872–74), to help phrase the ordinance in such a way as to counter in advance such objections as the law officers might make.

When the law officers gave their opinion in May 1879, they admitted the legal competence of the legislature of Fiji to pass the ordinance. Although they did not offer an interpretation of the Deed of Cession they nevertheless urged as a matter of policy that the ordinance might later be contested on the ground of its inconsistency with the Deed of Cession. Gordon scorned "the possibility that such an interpretation might be placed by some parties upon the Deed of Cession. . . ." The intentions of the framers of the Deed, of those who executed it, and of those who accepted it were all perfectly clear.[212] He denied also the law officers' view that the interests of the Crown and of the European claimants of land were "clearly antagonistic" and that it was thus unjust for the Crown to be the judge of the *bona fides* of claims. In almost every case land that was not shown to be the property of Europeans was vested not in the Crown but in the natives. Therefore the Crown was justified in judging the *bona fides* of most claims. In the few cases where the Crown would become the beneficiary of a disallowed claim Gordon was perpared to leave the decision to the chief justice, the new legal member of the Lands Commission,[213] and one other independent and impartial person.[214]

Gordon's objections to the law officers' report on the ordinance were ably supported by Selborne. In a long memorandum the latter held that "the Crown is the fountain of Justice, and must be trusted . . ." and that "*any* mode of investigation which the Crown, acting in good faith, thinks most likely to result in a satisfactory and complete adjustment of all

[211]*Ibid.*
[212]Gordon to Colonial Office, 5 June 1879, *Fiji*, III, 318–21.
[213]Gordon had persuaded Victor A. Williamson to go to Fiji for a year as an extra member and legal adviser of the Lands Commission to help speed its work.
[214]Gordon to Colonial Office, 5 June 1879.

conflicting land claims in the Colony . . . is as much within its *moral* as within its legal competency."[215] Such investigation and adjustment embraced a wider field and required "a much broader equity and a more independent judgment, than is appropriate to the ordinary functions of any Court of Law." In Selborne's view, "any substantial deviation" from the procedure followed heretofore "would have a much more serious tendency to raise questions as to the good faith of the Colonial Government than any provisions in the proposed draft Bill. . . ."[216]

With Selborne's arguments and some minor revisions of the ordinance (to which Gordon consented) the Colonial Office overcame the scruples of the "gentlemen of the long robe." The ordinance then went into force and abolished any lingering uncertainty concerning the land question. The Crown-in-Council and not the courts would decide the *bona fides* of pre-cession transactions between natives and Europeans, and the Crown might apply as rigorous tests as it saw fit to determine what were *bona fide* transactions. Although the ordinance allowed the Crown to interpret the promises made in the Deed of Cession, it prevented the Crown from modifying them. Thus those promises became "inescapable commitments,"[217] which the Crown could not set aside for reasons of general policy as Carnarvon had originally contemplated.[218]

The discussions surrounding preparation of the ordinance had clarified the meaning of the Deed of Cession. In theory, but not in practice, such clarification strengthened the European claimant's position. The question of whether the transactions of Europeans had resulted in a *bona fide* acquisition of property had now to depend upon antecedent native titles, laws, and customs. In other words, the Crown would have to determine what the native system of land tenure had been before cession. It would then be able to determine the *bona fides* of the claims of Europeans and the extent of native lands.

Gordon was content. The Crown could not directly confirm the natives in possession of their lands because it lacked that absolute power of disposal upon which Carnarvon had insisted. Yet the Crown could effect the desired result indirectly because the system of native tenure made *bona fide* alienation extremely difficult. Just how difficult, it was not easy to say. Several theories existed concerning the system of native tenure. Some thought it feudal; some, tribal; and some, partly both. Most agreed that the chiefs had no right to alienate land without the consent

[215]Lord Selborne's "Memorandum on Fiji Land Claims," 4 June 1879, *Fiji*, III, 321–24.

[216]*Ibid*.   [217]Legge, *Britain in Fiji*, 188.

[218]See Carnarvon's instructions to Gordon quoted on p. 203, fn. 194.

of their people. Early in 1880 Rev. Lorimer Fison, who had devoted much study to the question, gave a public address in Levuka. He advanced the theory that Fijian land was tribal land and strictly entailed from one generation to another. It was thus completely inalienable. Gordon, who said at the meeting that he had already come to the same conclusion, gratefully accepted this view. It meant, if strictly applied by the Lands Commission, that no sale of land by natives to Europeans could be considered valid and that the Crown-in-Council would be able to disallow all claims put forward as of right. Actually, the Lands Commission employed much the same tests of the *bona fides* of transactions as it had before the passage of the ordinance or Gordon's acceptance of Fison's theory. The Crown-in-Council, however, in adjudging claims could consider justice and good policy almost as if it had the right of absolute disposal and could allow claims *ex gratia* on the basis of occupation. The final report of the Lands Commission[219] noted that out of 1,683 claims, 517 had been granted as of right and 390 *ex gratia* wholly or in part. In all, some 415,000 acres were granted compared with the 850,000 acres claimed. The reduction in the Fijian population resulting from the measles made it possible to confirm large amounts of land to Europeans. Since the latter had so few acres under cultivation they were liberally treated. They have no claim to sympathy in their subsequent complaints against the Lands Commission and Gordon.

Gordon's only reason for having insisted until 1879 upon Crown control over native lands had been that he saw no other way to prevent further alienation. He realized the disadvantage inherent in Crown control, for a successor might choose to follow a different policy and encourage alienation. By accepting native land customs, including the concept of inalienability, and codifying them in an ordinance, he might gain the end he had sought through Crown control and, at the same time, tie the hands of his successors.

The new land ordinance (21 of 1880) defined the native title and provided for its enforcement and for ascertaining and registering the boundaries of native lands. It further provided that all native lands should be inalienable except through the Crown and only then for public purposes. It allowed the Crown to inherit the land of an extinct *mataqali* (landholding group)[220] or to purchase the land of a *mataqali* much reduced in numbers; but if a *mataqali* increased in population the ordi-

---

[219]Enclosed in Des Voeux to Kimberley, 27 April 1882, PRO CO 83/29.

[220]There were (and are) two landholding groups in Fiji, the *mataqali* and the *tokatoka*. Fison, in error, identified the former as the chief group and the government recognized that group.

nance required the Crown to grant to it or purchase for it extra land. The ordinance allowed natives to give leases of land for periods not exceeding twenty-one years. It also contemplated the time when the common ownership of the *mataqali* might be split into individual ownerships but provided that even then alienation could not be effected for five years. "Were it otherwise," said Gordon, "experience, as in New Zealand, shows that the intending purchaser would bribe the natives to seek for the division of the lands while such a division was yet premature and inconsistent with the real wishes and true interests of the people."[221]

With the exception of the laws governing labour, Ordinance 21 completed the legislative structure Gordon felt necessary for his major objective in Fiji—to preserve and civilize the natives. Perhaps Sir Arthur was unduly optimistic over the effect that the ordinance would have upon Fijians. Rather than fostering change in their social organization it may have tended to halt a change already underway. It does not follow, however, that Fijians would have been more enterprising had the ordinance not been passed and they had been free to alienate such land as they wished. Nor does it follow that more rapid or different changes in their social organization would have benefited the natives, the Europeans, or the colony.

In recent years Gordon's land settlement has been criticized for having restricted development of the colony by leaving too little land for Crown sale to prospective settlers. Although Sir Arthur was "by no means impatient"[222] for rapid commercial and agricultural development of Fiji by Europeans, he was not blind to the financial benefits they would bring to the colony. He allowed Thurston to promote the sugar industry and agreed to sell Spence Brothers of Melbourne 400 to 500 acres of land and the Colonial Sugar Refining Company 1,000 acres in return for investing £20,000 and £100,000 respectively in sugar mills. The latter sale brought a query from Lord Kimberley, who asked why, if Fijian lands were inalienable, the Crown could sell 1,000 acres of *mataqali* land. Gordon replied that the sale had taken place before the passage of Ordinance 21. Furthermore, the establishment of the sugar factory was "a great object to the Colony at large, and to the natives of the locality. . . ." With the full consent of the latter and on payment to them of a fair price he saw no reason why the land should not have been

---

[221]Gordon's memorandum on Ordinance 21 of 1880, April 1881, *Fiji*, IV, Appendix A.

[222]Gordon to Carnarvon (private), 24 Dec. 1875, Carnarvon Papers, PRO GD 6/39.

sold.[223] Although these sales of land to, and investments by, commercial companies laid the basis for Fiji's future prosperity they were nevertheless isolated instances. Future investors who desired land would be compelled either to lease it from natives or acquire it from settlers.[224] Gordon looked to the settlers to supply land in the foreseeable future because they possessed a large area through the indulgence that he had accorded their claims and because many of them were unable to make the slightest use of the land they owned.[225]

Sir Arthur undoubtedly preferred that large companies or capitalists rather than a host of settlers with few resources should undertake the development of Fiji. He had seen how easily ordinary settlers succumbed to the vicissitudes of the market. Commercial companies would be more resistant to price fluctuations and better able to fulfil their obligations to their employees and to the state. Moreover the government could more easily enforce labour laws on companies than on small employers, because it had always to consider whether strict enforcement might not ruin the latter.

To appreciate the significance of Gordon's labour laws as part of his native policy they must be seen against the background of pre-cession recruiting and of the attitudes that settlers still showed toward the Fijian population. The early settlers cultivated their plantations with the help of the natives who lived on the land which the settlers had "bought" from them; but the settlers and natives soon fell out over the settlers' rights to the land. As a rule the planters then drove the natives away, burned their villages, and purchased labour from the nearest chief. This practice proved little better to the settlers than the first, because the natives were close to their villages and could spend too much time with their families and, if badly treated, could appeal to their chiefs. In the early sixties some planters began to import labour (collectively called

[223]Gordon to Kimberley, 28 March 1881, *Fiji*, IV, Appendix C; also PRO CO 83/25.

[224]After settlement of European claims had been completed in 1882 and after the boundaries of native holdings had been defined, only 82,215 acres remained as Crown land. (Legge, *Britain in Fiji*, 198.)

[225]"A few of the planters," Gordon had written in 1876, "are men of energy & character. Others have energy without character or character without energy. The majority have neither. They lead a miserable existence drinking gin when they can get it and yagona when they cannot, living with a greater or less number of Tokalau women, taking no trouble to make their surroundings less uncomfortable and complaining of the low price of cotton.

"It is probable that a more energetic set of men will succeed them once they can dispose of their lands, & it is to be much desired." (Stanmore Papers, 49199, f. 130–34.)

"Polynesians" in Fiji) from the New Hebrides, Line Islands, the Solomons, and other islands. Others reasoned that they too might have labourers at their mercy, and at lower cost, by recruiting them from distant islands within the Fiji group—the Yasewas Islands and the Ra and Ba districts of Viti Levu being the favoured areas. At first the planters did their own recruiting but soon found it convenient to purchase their labourers from recruiters whose methods, though effective, were inhuman. Nevertheless, at the height of the cotton boom the supply failed to equal the demand and the "Parliament of Fiji" imposed a poll-tax on all Fijian adults and provided that those who failed to pay it should be punished by imprisonment with hard labour "on the plantation of any one paying a certain sum to the Government."[226] Many Fijians fell victim to this law, and thousands more volunteered to work for those who would pay their tax. Prisoners taken in war against the hill tribes provided another source of slave labour until Commodore Goodenough forced their release. Robinson repealed the poll-tax. Planters then reverted to purchasing labour from the chiefs until they were stopped by Ordinance 2 of 1875. Yet recruiting by labour-agents, who employed lies, bribery, and other forms of cajolery, continued well into Gordon's administration.

When Sir Arthur arrived he found Polynesian immigration almost at a standstill because, with prevailing economic conditions, few planters could afford to return Polynesians to their homes or even support those whose indentures had been served. Still, the demand for Fijian labourers considerably exceeded the supply because the recent epidemic had killed so many of them. Although Gordon recognized the planters' need of labour and sympathized with their distress, he could not stomach the lightly disguised system of agricultural servitude that they wished to impose upon the Fijians. With his plans for the preservation and elevation of the native race he could agree to no more than that Fijians should work voluntarily for short periods on estates near their own villages. He favoured this arrangement and thought it should be encouraged. It was "a totally distinct and different thing from carrying people away from their districts for a long period,"[227] and would help develop skills and industriousness among Fijians. If labour of this kind should prove insufficient then planters would have to depend upon more expensive Polynesian and Indian labour. He was willing to do everything possible to help acquire that supplementary labour.

Gordon's first task in dealing with the labour problem was to send

[226]Gordon to Carnarvon, 12 March 1877, PRO CO 83/13; also printed in *Fiji*, II, 344–46.
[227]Gordon to Le Hunte, 14 Sept. 1877, *Fiji*, II, 606–7.

home the Polynesians who had served their indenture. Until that could be done, Fiji would find it extremely difficult to obtain new recruits. His second was to pass laws that would protect native Fijians from involuntary labour on the plantations. His third, when trade revived and the colony and planters could afford it, was to import Indians under the strict indenture system demanded by the Indian government.

The colony had already begun to send the Polynesians home before Gordon reached Fiji, Lord Carnarvon having authorized the government to spend £500 both in 1874 and in 1875 for this purpose. During 1875 about 600 were sent home[228] but the movement suffered delays through the difficulty of finding ships and because of the measles epidemic. In one sense, however, the latter eased the problem since 600 Polynesians died of the disease. Still, by the beginning of 1876, some 2,800 time-expired Polynesians remained in Fiji, many of them in dire straits. Most were gradually returned during the year through the government's advancing the costs although it could ill-afford them. The same course was followed during 1877, when nearly 1,600 more became eligible for repatriation. By January 1878, only 32 remained of those who had been entitled to return home in 1876 and only 700 required passages during the ensuing year.

In addition to aiding return passages Gordon also managed to provide funds to assist in introducing fresh Polynesian levies. In 1877 he placed £5,000 on the estimates for this purpose and in 1878, £11,400, partly for return passages but mostly for immigration. He rejected, however, a demand by the planters that he commit the colony in advance to spend £5,000 annually on Polynesian immigration. He also refused to increase the period of indenture from three to five years which the planters asked for in order to offset increased wages. The planters would have to pay going rates, he told them, or do without labourers.[229]

By 1879 the supply of Polynesians met the demand for long-term labourers, but now Sir Arthur began to hear reports of their ill-usage by certain planters.[230] An ordinance of 1877, based on ordinances in force

[228]The government had to pay not only passages but wages. It recovered immediately about one-third of the total cost, but it had to wait for the remainder, which was made a first charge on the estates of the employers concerned.

[229]Gordon's speech to the planters at Nasova, 26 Jan. 1878, *Fiji*, II, 693–704. The ordinance dealing with immigrant labour, passed in 1877, provided for a five-year indenture, but the Colonial Office had not allowed that section to come into operation. In any case Gordon did not wish to extend the term because it would then be necessary to provide for the introduction of women. This would overcome any financial advantage an extension might confer.

[230]Where a shortage of labour existed, planters usually treated their labourers well. Conversely, where labour was plentiful, planters sometimes treated their workers badly.

in Trinidad and British Guiana, had provided elaborately[231] for regulating the employment of immigrant labour, but with only an agent-general and a clerk Fiji's immigration department could not hope to enforce its provisions. The Governor had to depend for his information on occasional visits to plantations by the overworked magistrates and medical officers. Their reports, he told the planters on his return to Nasova in 1879, "for the first time, gave evidence of the existence in some places of a very unsatisfactory condition of things, and . . . of cases of labourers being habitually supplied with insufficient food, of their being lodged in improper dwellings, and of an entire want of medicine . . . followed by a heavy mortality."[232] He warned that he would do everything possible to check and punish such abuses by executive action, but asked that the planters themselves bring public opinion to bear "very decidedly and very harshly" on the offenders.[233]

Gordon's threat to take executive action was no idle one as a series of cases early in 1880 testified. Several overseers and planters, among them James Mason, a member of the legislative council, were successfully prosecuted for assaults on Polynesians.[234] Since there were relatively few further recorded cases of planters ill-treating Polynesians, it may be inferred that many took note of these incidents and acted more circumspectly, if not humanely, towards their labourers. Moreover, Gordon could exert some control over the planters through threats to halt immigration. He would have been reluctant to carry out such threats because a cessation of immigration would have led the settlers to turn more to Fijian labour, not merely for short-term contracts but for long-term ones. This development he wished to avoid. In any case the settlers who could not afford (or said they could not afford) immigrant labour constantly demanded that he "free" the Fijians to work on their estates. From the attitude of the settlers towards the Fijians he had no illusions as to the treatment he might expect the natives to experience if the planters ever got their way.

Gordon described the white population as a very heterogeneous mixture, containing men of both the "highest character" and the "utmost depravity." A large portion came from Australia and, being accustomed to "the lowest class of savages," had a contempt and hatred for

---

[231]Gordon was doubtless looking to the future and attempting to leave as nearly perfect a system as possible for his successors—a system which might be fully implemented as the colony advanced and could afford the requisite staff.

[232]Gordon's speech at Nasova, 16 Oct. 1879, *Fiji*, IV, 63–83.

[233]*Ibid.*

[234]See, for example, stipendiary magistrate (Taylor) to the Chief Justice, 15 Feb. 1880, *Fiji*, IV, 192–96.

Fijians.[235] Few saw any difference between the Australian blackfellow and the Fijian. They could not conceive that "a nigger" had any right to property[236] or that they themselves trespassed by turning their cattle loose in native gardens. Some simply wanted to exterminate the natives; others, to utilize them as serfs. The settlers from New Zealand held a higher opinion of the Fijians, but had learned to regard them as enemies. Almost without exception the settlers believed that the sole object of a native's existence was to work for the white man.[237] More than one planter "gravely proposed" that the government should make over to him the whole population of his district in return for certain charges to be undertaken by him.[238] In 1876 the Planters Association resolved that the government force each province to provide a stipulated number of labourers should planters fail to secure sufficient voluntary labourers.[239]

In an effort to prevent planters flogging and handcuffing their labourers and to curtail the unholy methods of the labour recruiters, Gordon passed ordinances in 1876 and 1877. Neither was especially rigorous. Neither sought to end recruitment of Fijian labour or to place limits on the number who might be taken from a district. Rather, they aimed at ensuring fair treatment both in recruiting and in employing the natives, and they restricted employment to a period not exceeding a year. Gordon felt that he might safely rely upon the chiefs and their councils to prevent over-recruiting. They would be reluctant to allow any large number of able-bodied men to be absent from their villages until their quota of the produce tax had been fulfilled. Most of the chiefs were as conscious as Gordon himself of the social dislocation which over-recruiting would bring to the villages. Moreover, by leaving this aspect of the labour problem to the natives themselves, Gordon could avoid charges by the planters that he was deliberately interfering with their supply of labour.

That Sir Arthur was justified in relying upon the chiefs is evident from the lively concern over the labour question that they revealed in the meetings of the Great Council. Said one chief at the meeting in 1875: "Men leaving their homes to work in other places causes both famine

[235]In 1885 the Australian *Handbook* observed that Fijians were "a cowardly, untruthful race, lazy and tricky" but that "with a very little management the white man could make them subserviently useful." (Quoted by Gordon in his diary, 18 March 1888, Stanmore Papers, 49264, f. 32.)

[236]One settler questioned Gordon as follows: "Does Your Excellency mean to say that if a native has got something we want, and are willing to pay him something for, we may not take it?" (Quoted by Gordon to Carnarvon, 24 Dec. 1875, PRO CO 83/6.)

[237]Stanmore Papers, 49199, f. 130–34.

[238]Gordon to Carnarvon, 11 July 1876, Carnarvon Papers, PRO GD 6/39.

[239]*Ibid.*, 8 Nov. 1876.

and much domestic evil."[240] In 1876 the chiefs resolved that not more than half of the unmarried men should be allowed to be away from their villages at one time. A year later the chiefs complained that the enticement of the men from their homes left their wives, children, and relatives in a "most bitter and pitiable condition—and . . . is the cause of the people being in a state of poverty and desolation." What they most desired, they said, was "that men should work for themselves . . . that they plant plenty, that they be in a position to furnish themselves with household necessaries, that their villages be kept clean and their houses in good repair. . . ."[241] By this time planters were complaining that they could no longer, even through bribes, persuade the chiefs to allow their villagers to engage to work on the plantations. The planters and the labour recruiters turned to other methods as the complaint of the chiefs in 1880 makes evident. Of the evils connected with labourers going to work outside their provinces the chiefs declared that: "If one measure is introduced to improve it, it is hardly tried until some other course is pursued [by the recruiters] which nullifies it. And now people are being taken by stealth on board the vessels by night—women and children— it is a source of vexation and trouble."[242] In 1881 the chiefs resolved that recruiting should cease and that, in future, plantation labour beyond the home district should be an entirely voluntary affair of the unmarried men and that they should be required to return home afterwards.[243] Their wishes received recognition in a new native labour ordinance about which Gordon, though no longer governor, had been consulted and which he highly approved.

Gordon certainly would have found it necessary to have legislated much more vigorously for the protection of Fijian labour had he not reduced settlers' demands for that labour by reviving Polynesian immigration and establishing the Indian indenture system in the new colony.

In addressing some two hundred planters on the day after he assumed the governorship, Sir Arthur suggested Indian immigration as a partial cure for the shortage of labour. The planters agreed, but the financial situation of the colony and of the planters made it impossible to proceed with the plan at the time. Although Gordon appropriated £7,000 in

[240]Notes of proceedings of the meeting of chiefs at Draiba, enclosed in Gordon to Carnarvon, 16 Feb. 1876, PRO CO 83/9.
[241]Chiefs' letter to the Queen enclosed in Gordon to Secretary of State, 25 Jan. 1878, PRO CO 83/16.
[242]Resolutions of the chiefs, enclosure no. 2 in Des Voeux to Secretary of State, 17 Feb. 1881, PRO CO 83/25.
[243]Resolutions of the chiefs, enclosed in Des Voeux to Kimberley, 23 June 1882, PRO CO 83/30.

1876 to aid both Polynesian and Indian immigration it was not until 1878, when financial prospects had improved, that he felt justified in sending Mitchell to India to make the necessary arrangements with the Indian government. In May 1879, the first shipload of nearly 500 coolies arrived in Fiji.

Sir Arthur had given Mitchell full power to negotiate with the government of India and to communicate directly with the Secretary of State. The government of Fiji had agreed to assume one-third of the cost of operating the system. These facts indicate how urgently Gordon regarded the extension of the Indian indenture system to Fiji. With the future of Polynesian immigration uncertain and agriculture again becoming profitable, he feared that, unless Indian immigration should begin immediately, he would not be able to withstand "the pressure which will be brought to bear upon the Government to consent to measures intended to coerce the native population of this Colony into an involuntary servitude, or at all events to wink at practices not consistent with fair dealing."[244] By such a step he might save the Fijians from serfdom.

Professor Legge has written that "the coolie system, together with the Pacific Island labour traffic in which Gordon encouraged the extension of the same kind of wage labour which he deprecated in the case of the native Fijian, must be regarded as a kind of human subsidy to his experiment in native rule."[245] In Gordon's view, however, the employment of natives as plantation labour, even on a well-defined and rigidly operated indenture system, would have worse consequences for Fijians and their society than the employment of either Polynesians or Indians would have for them or their societies. He believed it would destroy the Fijian society and throttle the emerging Fijian civilization in its childhood which, in turn, would lead to apathy and the disappearance of the Fijian race. The Polynesian societies were much more primitive than the Fijian and showed little of the Fijian capacity for civilization. Furthermore, the Polynesians were likely in any case to become plantation labourers and they might as well, perhaps better, come to Fiji than go to Queensland or elsewhere. At least Fiji, with its "severe" Crown colony government, presumably could afford them better protection than Queensland, where the government was subject to more direct pressure by the planters.

As for the Indians, their indentures were purely voluntary. They came from an older, more advanced, and much more populous civilization than the Fijian, one that would not be adversely affected by their

[244]Gordon to Secretary of State, 9 Aug. 1877, PRO CO 83/14.
[245]Legge, *Britain in Fiji*, 268.

departure. Besides, the government of India had power to withdraw the privilege of recruiting labour in India from any colony in which the coolies were badly treated. Finally, the Indian's individuality enabled him to be transplanted from his own country to another more successfully than a Fijian, with his strong communal feeling, could be shifted from his own island to another within the group. Although Gordon had seen in Mauritius the evils that could result under the indenture system, he had demonstrated in Trinidad how that system when properly administered could benefit Indians, planters, and colony alike. Indians and Polynesians doubtless were "a kind of human subsidy" to Fijian civilization, but they were not a human sacrifice. Had Gordon considered that they would become so he would have searched for a different way to secure time for the Fijians to make the difficult transition from fifteenth- to nineteenth-century culture.

Although immigration, especially Indian immigration,[246] solved Gordon's problem, it created new problems for the future. One aspect of the coolie system was that the Indian (having served a five-year indenture and five years as a free labourer) had the right to stay in the colony or to return home at the colony's expense. Some colonies, such as Trinidad, made land grants in lieu of return passages if the Indian desired. Over a period of time colonies making use of the indenture system usually built up a considerable population of free Indians. For those colonies with plenty of Crown land, there was no serious problem; but in colonies like Mauritius and Fiji it meant creating a landless proletariat. Gordon was alive to this disadvantage and had refused a suggestion by Layard and Carnarvon that Polynesians wishing to remain in Fiji be given land so as to retain them as labourers and cut the cost of return passages. The Governor had other reasons for not wishing Polynesians to settle in Fiji. Their non-return would make recruiting more difficult, and as they were, in his opinion, less intelligent and less advanced than the Fijians they would retard the latter's advance in civilization.[247] By contrast, the presence in the colony of the intelligent, individualistic, and money-hungry Indians might well stimulate the Fijians to more rapid advancement. The disadvantages of their presence would have to be endured for the sake of the overwhelming advantages it presented.

Gordon certainly never foresaw the day when the Indians would outnumber the Fijians. Nor did he foresee the political problem that an Indian majority and continuing Fijian control of most of the land would

[246]By 1891 there were over 2,200 Polynesians and nearly 7,500 Indians in Fiji. (Morrell, *Britain in the Pacific Islands*, 396.)
[247]Gordon to Carnarvon, 23 Sept. 1876, PRO CO 83/10.

create. No man, however, can forecast the results of his acts half a century into the future. Neither can any man solve all problems for all time, for it is in the nature of things that every solution creates a fresh problem. Sir Arthur accomplished what he intended: to save the Fijian race from extinction and to secure for it at least a generation in which to make the transition from mediaeval to modern times. Undoubtedly he over-estimated the speed at which Fijians would advance. Perhaps he made native institutions too resistant to change by breathing more life into them than he intended. Perhaps, also, he slowed native "progress" and the economic development of the colony through his land and labour policies. Yet few social experiments have come closer to success or been more deserving of it than Gordon's Fijian experiment. If community happiness rather than progress be the criterion, then certainly his native policy was eminently more successful than the alternatives would have been.

V. LINGERING FAREWELL TO FIJI

Throughout his governorship of Fiji Gordon gave much thought to his own and the colony's future after the time should come for his departure. Fearful lest the Colonial Office should fail to support his policies and concerned that the less able and experienced man, who, he had been warned, must succeed him, would demolish the edifice he had so carefully and laboriously constructed, he often despaired, feeling that he worked in vain. Although conscious of the importance of his work and of the uniqueness of his Fijian experiment, ambition and a desire for public recognition of his worth led him to suspect that he might be wasting his talents amid the reefs and mangrove swamps of those obscure Pacific islands. Unrequited personal ambition, elation over the success of his experiment, and anxieties concerning its future prompted him to hatch schemes whereby he might obtain a government more obviously in the public eye than Fiji and, at the same time, retain some control over Fiji itself.

Lord Carnarvon's annoyance at Sir Arthur's suggestion in 1877 that he be appointed governor of New South Wales and retain the governorship of Fiji has already been noted.[248] Herbert, however, had favoured the idea and evidently Carnarvon came to take a kinder view of it later, for he was reported to have spoken to Sir Michael Hicks Beach in favour of it.[249] Certainly Herbert advocated the plan to Sir Michael

[248]See above, p. 177.
[249]Herbert to Gordon, 18 Dec. 1878, *Fiji*, III, 232.

Hicks Beach, but, though the latter thought well of it,[250] he appointed Lord Augustus Loftus, whose term in St. Petersburg had expired, instead of Gordon to New South Wales.[251]

Gordon did not much bemoan this failure because his term in Fiji still had more than two years to run. He returned to his government in the summer of 1879 with his ego at least temporarily restored by the D.C.L. conferred on him by Oxford and the Freedom of the City of Aberdeen that had been given him in recognition of his colonial service.[252] He was undoubtedly heartened also to find himself "openly designated . . . as eligible for . . . the Viceroyalty of India."[253] Then, too, Gladstone had pressed him with "extreme earnestness" to return to Parliament and "in no obscure language" had held out "strong personal motives" to persuade him.[254] Gordon was attracted because it would mean an end to separations from his family. Although he agreed with his brother Alex that he would succeed him in East Aberdeenshire in a few years, he rejected Gladstone's offer on grounds of public duty, personal fitness, and private interest. He felt that he ought not to leave his work in Fiji unfinished, that being accustomed to absolute command he would not make a good follower, and that he owed it to his family to qualify for his pension. He had also a superstitious reason for his refusal. He believed, with his friend Selborne, that to deviate from one's duty on one's own responsibility or on the opinion of others was to tempt the fates. A few months after his return to Fiji, he wrote to his wife, who had remained in England: "I wish I could think Gladstone right in thinking that the time has come for me to go home. If only they would settle the point by electing me to the House of Commons in my absence it would greatly simplify matters. I should accept that as an indication where my place lay."[255] This expression did not indicate that the aristocrat had suddenly come to believe that *vox populi* meant *vox Dei*. It meant only

[250]*Ibid.*

[251]Gordon later discovered the real reason why he had not got the post. Shortly after his return to England in 1878 his brother Alex and his nephew, the Earl of Aberdeen, had withdrawn their support from Disraeli's government. Because Sir Arthur was known to disapprove the Prime Minister's foreign policy, he was suspected of having influenced their change of political allegiance. Although Sir Michael had been friendly and had said that politics ought not to count "he was speedily taught other views on the subject." (Gordon to Selborne, 24 April 1881, *Fiji*, IV, 278.)

[252]Sir Arthur felt deeply gratified at having his name associated with those of such distinguished former honorary citizens of Aberdeen as his father, Sir Robert Peel, and Sir James Graham. See *Fiji*, III, 210a–19, for an account of the presentation and Gordon's speech in which he described the functions of a Crown colony governor.

[253]Rev. J. E. Moulton to Gordon, 9 April 1879, *Fiji*, III, 275–76.

[254]Gordon to Selborne, 1 Oct. 1878, *Fiji*, III, 187–88.

[255]Gordon to Lady Gordon, 7 Jan. 1880, *Fiji*, IV, 161.

that he wanted to be reunited with his wife and children. He owned it his duty to remain in Fiji and when he entered the last year of his normal term he sought to extend his time in Fiji or, alternatively, to continue as its governor and obtain that of an Australian colony as well.

Always pessimistic when deprived of his family, Sir Arthur gloomily pondered the future. Although certain that his Fijian experiment would succeed if continued long enough, he feared any one of many adverse forces might suddenly arise to destroy it. The smallest domestic incident at home might "outweigh Fiji and all its concerns almost without a thought." His successor, although holding "the justest views and the most philanthropic feelings," might lack his own "instinct and sympathy" for dealing with the natives. Most disturbing of all, what if Lord Kimberley should return to the Colonial Office? Lord Carnarvon and Sir Michael Hicks Beach had supported him "most handsomely," but Kimberley's "narrow and unimaginative cast of mind would not allow him to take in the state of matters [in Fiji] or the sort of policy it requires."[256] "Oh," he exclaimed to Lady Gordon, "how I should like to keep this place for a few years longer, provided I could do so without your living away from it, until I had brought out clearly the success of my system."[257]

Although Gordon rejoiced on public grounds at the Tory defeat in the spring of 1880 he feared that, "by a curious infelicity," the incoming of a government containing so many of his strong personal friends would be disastrous to himself.[258] He hoped that Lord Derby or W. E. Forster would become secretary of state for the colonies; but no such luck. Kimberley it was. Lord Kimberley, Gordon lamented to his wife,

does not in the least understand me. He is thoroughly official, and he will replace me at the end of my six years, just as he did Sir Hercules Robinson in Ceylon. And I have no great belief in "influence" being of much use. "Put not your trust in princes" is a text which includes Prime Ministers and Lord Chancellors, and indeed in this case I am not sure that their interposition would not do more harm than good, for Lord K[imberley] when in office before showed some jealousy of my intimate relations with Gladstone, and is just the sort of man to *not* do a thing, all the more because he is asked to do it.[259]

Despite Gordon's lack of trust in princes, he requested Selborne, the new lord chancellor, to speak to the Prime Minister about his plan to be made governor of New Zealand, or Victoria, or New South Wales and

[256]Gordon to Marchioness of Salisbury, 29 March 1880, *Fiji*, IV, 245–47.
[257]Gordon to Lady Gordon, 5 June 1880, *Fiji*, IV, 316.
[258]Gordon to Selborne, 22 May 1880, *Fiji*, IV, 305–7.
[259]Gordon to Lady Gordon, 5 June 1880. This was unfair to Kimberley and Gordon probably did not believe the latter part himself.

to continue to direct *la haute politique* of Fiji through an administrator. He asked Selborne to have a word with Kimberley on the subject if an opportunity offered. He also wrote to Kimberley explaining why he felt his continued supervision of Fiji was absolutely necessary and how it might be accomplished. He would be willing to stay beyond his normal term rather than see strange hands employed in the work he had begun. He would most prefer to be appointed to an Australian colony, retain the governorship of Fiji, visit it once a year, and govern through the Colonial Secretary (Thurston) as administrator. His second preference would be to return home and have Thurston, after acting for a period as administrator, succeed him as governor. His third choice would be for Arthur J. L. Gordon to succeed him at any time after the expiry of his term.[260]

This letter containing such a clear exposition of Gordon's desires could not have reached Kimberley before he made up his mind to appoint Sir Arthur to New Zealand without at the same time allowing him to retain Fiji. The Secretary of State certainly knew Gordon's wish on this point because Herbert had explained it to him.[261] He had, however, to make an appointment to New Zealand quickly as Sir Hercules Robinson was about to leave and Kimberley and those of his colleagues "specially interested" in Gordon (presumably Gladstone and Selborne) decided that "it would not be well to place Fiji directly under the Governor of any one of the larger Australasian Colonies."[262] Kimberley told Gordon that he had appointed Des Voeux to succeed him and had "explained to him that you will exercise a general superintendance over Fiji native affairs."[263] Kimberley hoped in this way to retain

[260]Gordon to Kimberley, 15 June 1880, *Fiji*, IV, 331–33. Sir Arthur also considered Le Hunte as a possible successor in Fiji but did not mention him to Kimberley. Le Hunte, of course, was still quite young but he was able and good with natives although not quite as good as A. J. L. Gordon. (Gordon to Lady Gordon, 26 June to 9 July 1880, *Fiji*, IV, 340–41.)

[261]Herbert to Gordon, 13 Aug. 1880, *Fiji*, IV, 465.

[262]*Ibid*. Gordon probably would have agreed with this sentiment had any other governor of an Australasian colony than himself been given control of Fiji.

[263]Kimberley to Gordon, 11 Aug. 1880, *Fiji*, IV, 464. It is clear that the Colonial Office had been disposed to give Gordon more authority over Fiji than simply a general supervision over native affairs because Kimberley at first offered Des Voeux the lieutenant-governorship of Fiji at a salary of only £3,000. This would seem to imply that Des Voeux would not exercise a final authority over any facet of Fiji's administration. Des Voeux, who was in London at the time, had just been gazetted governor of the Bahamas at £2,200 and he refused the lieutenant-governorship of Fiji. An hour or two later Kimberley sent him a message offering him the governorship at £4,000. Des Voeux accepted. Apparently the title meant more to him than the money; and as he had been gazetted governor of Bahamas and had strong influence with the cabinet and with Hartington, Granville, and Derby outside it, he could scarcely have accepted a mere administratorship or lieutenant-governorship.

the advantage of Gordon's "experience in the way of advice and general direction. . . ."[264]

Gordon, while awaiting an answer to his letter to Kimberley, had consoled himself with the reflection that, now that he had passed the half-century, it was time he gave up caring for vanities. Yet he felt uneasy when, late in August, he learned from an Auckland newspaper[265] of his appointment to New Zealand. The paper printed only the bare announcement. His first sensation was one of relief that he need no longer worry about his fate. His next was joy at the prospect of reunion with his family. His third was alarm lest he had not retained Fiji. His last was the "very comforting reflection" that he did not much care because at all events, he told Lady Gordon, "we shall . . . be together again very shortly and uncertainty is over. I either go to New Zealand if I keep this government too, or I at once go home. . . ."[266]

But Gordon did "care," and "uncertainty" was not over. A fortnight later he received a telegram from the Colonial Office that informed him of Des Voeux's appointment as governor of Fiji, and of his own appointment to New Zealand with "superintendance" of native affairs in Fiji. "This is a catastrophe . . .," he wrote. "I am very unhappy about it all— very. I have . . . [a] physically sore, *beaten all over* feeling. . . ."[267] It was bad enough that the Colonial Office had failed, apparently, to implement his long prepared plan; but for it prematurely[268] to have appointed such a man as Des Voeux to replace him in Fiji was too much. Des Voeux was "a very inefficient man," a "loyal lieutenant . . . [but] an incompetent chief, wholly lacking in the powers of application, the strength of will, the calmness of judgment which are all indispensable to avert ruinous failure."[269]

Gordon knew Des Voeux well enough and had heard enough from Thurston, MacGregor, Gorrie, and Le Hunte during the year when Des Voeux had acted as governor to make these assertions. He could forecast quarrels between Des Voeux, whose temper was quick and violent, and the leading officers of the government. He could predict wholesale resignations among those officers. He himself, close by in New Zealand—to which he felt compelled to go because he had been appointed—would receive constant letters from his former officers and

[264]*Ibid.*

[265]Appropriately, perhaps, Solomons, the editor of the *Fiji Times*, brought the paper to Gordon. The rotund little Jew bustled up to the Governor's residence with it, panting and, doubtless, beaming with joy.

[266]Gordon to Lady Gordon, 20 Aug. 1880, *Fiji*, IV, 417.

[267]*Ibid.*, 5 Sept. 1880, 425.

[268]Gordon's term had still about six months to run.

[269]Gordon to Selborne, 7 Sept. 1880, *Fiji*, IV, 430–32.

would have to be a passive witness to the disintegration of the administration he had so carefully constructed.[270] Was there no way out? Surely "superintendance of native affairs" implied control. He sought enlightenment from Kimberley, whose letter,[271] purportedly explaining his telegram, had been ambiguous. As a matter of fact the Colonial Office had no information to give him because it had not defined, even to itself, what "general superintendance of native affairs" meant, nor how it could be implemented. Time had pressed. "General superintendance" had seemed a conveniently vague phrase which might not infringe too greatly upon the incoming Governor's authority nor entirely exclude that of the outgoing Governor. After all, the two were friends. Surely their former co-operation would guarantee a *modus operandi* satisfactory to both. So must the Colonial Office have reasoned if it thought about the arrangement at all. If so, it failed to count on Des Voeux's pride and on Gordon's concern for Fiji. Each interpreted the phrase to suit himself. Des Voeux in his autobiography wrote: "It was evident that whatever might be the nature of the supervision of native affairs which had been offered to Sir Arthur Gordon, it could not include any form of control [although] in its usual meaning 'supervision' certainly implied 'control,' and I feared that he might have regarded the offer . . . in this sense. . . . It was not without a certain trepidation that I regarded the prospect of our meeting."[272] Gordon certainly did regard "superintendance" or "supervision" as implying control. He could not see how Fijian native affairs could be separated from other Fijian business, nor did he find it easy to understand "a general superintendance" unless with some degree of authority.[273]

Gordon could not count on communications permitting the Colonial Office to clear the ambiguity from the arrangement before he was due to leave for New Zealand. During the few weeks that remained to him in Fiji he made a mighty effort to complete as many of his plans as possible. Ever since news had reached him of Kimberley's return to the Colonial Office he had had his sloop of state under full sail. He now fired the engines. In June he had still hoped to settle all the remaining land claims before leaving Fiji, to move the capital to Suva, to pass legislation related to native land tenure, and to begin the establishment of native industrial schools. Now the change of capitals would have to wait. Nor

---

[270]*Ibid.*

[271]Kimberley to Gordon, 11 Aug. 1880 (received 10 Oct.). Herbert's letter of 13 Aug., which was a little less oracular than Kimberley's, did not reach Gordon until much later because Lady Gordon had forgotten to send it.

[272]Des Voeux, *My Colonial Service,* II, 5–6.

[273]Gordon to Kimberley, 11 Oct. 1880, *Fiji,* IV, 465–66.

could all remaining European claims be decided, although at least those upon which the commission had reported could be studied, heard, and decided and his successor left with a clean desk. Gordon regarded the ordinance (21 of 1880) relating to native lands[274] as far too important to be left to Des Voeux, and he reported its passage to Kimberley the day before he left Fiji. Sir Arthur called it "one of the most important Ordinances . . . passed by the legislature of Fiji . . . the result of five years' careful thought and enquiry. . . ."[275] He thought its subject so vital that had he not been on the point of departure he would have wished to consider it for another year or two before legislating.[276] A law to provide for the establishment of native industrial schools was also desirable and could be rushed through before he relinquished power.

Native industrial schools were Wilkinson's brain-child, but Thurston and Gordon heartily approved of them and the council of chiefs devoted much time and thought to the subject. Gordon later said that the ordinance was almost wholly the Great Council's work. The schools were intended to "improve and extend the knowledge and powers of [the] people as a race . . .," not to turn students into would-be white men.[277] "We should," wrote Wilkinson, "simply aid . . . [the Fijians] to work out for [themselves] . . . an indigenous civilisation . . ." and not try to "force a foreign civilisation upon them without reference to their mental capacity or natural surrounding and consequent requirements arising out of climate, immemorial time-honoured and admirably suited customs."[278]

Of this final period of intense activity Gordon wrote:

Life with me here is almost always carried on at high pressure, but during the last six weeks it has been such as I could not have borne for a much longer time. Constant meetings of the Legislative Council to pass Ordinances that I desire to become law before I leave; sittings of the Land Court to deal with appeals; sittings of the Executive Council late at night and extending

[274]See above, pp. 209–10.
[275]Gordon to Kimberley, 15 Nov. 1880, *Fiji*, IV, 498.
[276]*Ibid*.
[277]Wilkinson's report enclosed in Des Voeux to Secretary of State, 28 July 1881, PRO CO 83/26.
[278]*Ibid*. The first industrial school was established at Yanavai in Vanua Levu in 1881. Wilkinson, who took charge of the work, reported that all the labour and materials had been provided by the natives at no cost to the government. He outlined the objects of the school and the lines along which it should be run. His report showed that his thinking leaned even more than Gordon's towards maintaining the native way of life. Despite Sir Arthur's fears that Kimberley would neither understand nor sympathize with his native policy, the Secretary of State considered Wilkinson's report "singularly interesting & full of good sense." (Kimberley's minute, 12 Nov. 1881.)

to the small hours of the morning to consider Land Claims; masses of administrative work to get through while still the chief, have occupied every moment. . . .[279]

By 9 November it was finished. Sir Arthur's last day at Government House was a sad one.

I have taken leave of all the objects animate and inanimate that are dear to me,—the houses I have built; the green *rara* that I have so cared for; the trees that I have planted; my pet exotics; the camphor tree, already well grown; the promising mahogany trees; the sandal-wood trees, still mere saplings; the flourishing mangoes, approaching maturity, but the fruit of which I shall never eat or see; and, above all, the men who have served me so faithfully and well in various capacities, and my native guard, noble-looking fellows, most of whom I know by sight and name. It is a lovely evening; the oleanders, the thunbergias covering the bank on which the house is built and climbing up the stays of the verandah, and the gorgeous crotons in the centre bed, glow in the fading light,—a fair scene, and largely of my creation.[280]

The next morning he sailed for Mualevu in the Lau Islands to open his last Bose vaka Turaga. He took Gorrie with him determined to show him what a Bose was really like so that the Chief Justice should no longer "indulge in suspicions bred of his own fancies and nourished by malicious misinformation."[281]

Gordon, in his address to the chiefs,[282] reviewed what had been accomplished since the Bose had last met. He then asked the chiefs to examine carefully steps to reduce the death-rate and to regulate plantation labour, and to consider whether the law forbidding sale of spirits to natives should not be extended to include themselves. Next he announced his appointment to New Zealand, noting that he retained "control and supervision" over native affairs. His departure pained him deeply, he said, for his heart was the heart of a Fijian; but, he continued, "I am comforted by the thought that I shall still be able to prevent evil, and to suggest good measures, and by the knowledge that he who succeeds me, and who is already known to you, loves Fiji also, and is as resolved as I am myself to see that you suffer no wrong or harm." He advised the chiefs to trust Des Voeux as they had trusted him but warned them that their future rested largely with themselves. "If you are foolish and wilful . . . no man can keep you in prosperity; if . . . you are wise and prudent, there is nothing whatsoever to prevent your increase in numbers

[279]Gordon's diary, Nov. [1880], *Fiji*, IV, 500.
[280]*Ibid.*
[281]*Ibid.*
[282]He addressed the chiefs in Fijian as, by now, he usually did. His address is printed in English in *Fiji*, IV, 501–3.

and in wealth, and your retention of your proper influence and position."[283]

In reply the chiefs thanked him for the unity and prosperity he had brought them, the fatherly interest he had shown in the Fijian people, and (most significantly perhaps) the satisfaction and peace he had given them by the manner in which he had settled the land problem. When they first heard of his new appointment they had become "very small-hearted," they said, and although they remained in Council and were now a little comforted by his promise to "oversee and visit" them, they could discuss nothing. "We think only that you are leaving us, and our minds are exceedingly heavy. . . ."[284]

On the day of Gordon's arrival in Fiji the sun had shone for the first time in weeks. The day of his departure appropriately ended a spell of good weather. All the chiefs and a vast crowd of people stood patiently in the merciless downpour waiting to bid him farewell. He found it saddening to take leave of all his native friends.

There were many touching incidents, but the one thing that burnt into my memory for ever was the expression on Maafu's face. He knew that in losing me he lost his strongest external help to the maintenance of his better nature.[285] He spoke not a word, but held my hand with both his as though he could not let go his hold, and looked into my eyes, his face speaking,— sorrow, affection, respect, and something of reproach at my deserting him were all mingled there. And the pitiless rain came down. . . .[286]

It was Ma'afu who proposed, at the close of the Bose in January 1881, that the chiefs give Gordon a small island "as a testimony of our gratitude and appreciation of what we now enjoy . . . [and of] our regard for him, and our Queen who sent him." He made this suggestion because he felt that "our late Governor's name ought never to be separated from Fiji."[287] The chiefs decided to present to Sir Arthur the islets of Yagasa Levu in Lau and Toberua in Tailevu and requested the Queen's approval.[288] In March, Gordon, still with his heart in the islands, asked the Colonial Office whether he might accept this gift. Herbert approved,

[283]Extracts from minutes of the native council held at Mualevu, Nov. 1880 to Jan. 1881, *ibid.*

[284]*Ibid.*, 503–5.

[285]Ma'afu, before British intervention, had had ambitions of ruling Fiji. Thwarted, he had taken to drink, but he and his Tongans in the Lau Islands had loyally supported British rule. (Morrell, *Britain in the Pacific Islands*, 392.) Gordon had some success in persuading him to curtail his drinking but within a few weeks of Gordon's departure Ma'afu died.

[286]Gordon's diary, 16 Nov. 1880, *Fiji*, IV, 505.

[287]Ma'afu's address, 4 Jan. 1881, *Fiji*, IV, Appendix B, 513.

[288]The council of chiefs to the Queen, Jan. 1881, *ibid.*, 514–15.

but hoped Sir Arthur would not follow "the undesirable precedent of Sir George Grey, who resides on his Island of Kawau in New Zealand, & takes a part in public affairs which an Ex-Governor cannot take without injury to his own reputation, & to the public interests!"[289] Kimberley added: "I agree; but he [Gordon] will probably end his days as a Roko Tui."[290]

Gordon had been able to promise the chiefs that he would continue to safeguard the interests of Fijians because he had finally received an answer to his telegraphic query of 9 September concerning the meaning of "general superintendance" and whether it included an annual visit to Fiji and presidency of the native council and land appeals court.[291] Kimberley had answered that: "It is intended that you should retain as much control as the distance and your duties in N. Zealand will permit. I think [an] annual visit to Fiji will be practicable and that you will be able to retain substantial control over land appeals, and remain President of [the] Native Council."[292] Armed with this reasonably unequivocal telegram Gordon repaired to Auckland to meet Des Voeux. He found that Des Voeux had already given interviews to the Auckland papers in which he had asserted that he was entirely independent of Gordon as regards Fiji. Gordon was considerably annoyed at this statement and by Des Voeux's commission as full governor which he regarded as inconsistent with the position granted him by Kimberley's telegram.[293] Nevertheless, he held his temper and, said Des Voeux, was "most conciliatory."[294]

Althought Gordon saw and strongly criticized Des Voeux's faults he liked Des Voeux and got on with him well when they were together. He knew that Des Voeux greatly respected him and hoped this would prompt the new Governor to concede the control he wanted over native affairs. That he was right is demonstrated by the list of concessions made by Des Voeux in the joint memorandum that Gordon wrote and Des Voeux signed. According to the memorandum Des Voeux agreed to send to Gordon copies of important dispatches, copies of the reports of the native provincial council meetings, and the reports of and evidence taken by the Lands Commission. The last Gordon would have printed

[289]Herbert's minute on Gordon to Secretary of State, 25 March 1881, PRO CO 83/25.
[290]Kimberley's minute, ibid.
[291]Gordon's telegram to Kimberley, 9 Sept. 1880 (received 22 Sept.), PRO CO 83/23.
[292]Kimberley's telegram, 26 Sept. 1880, PRO CO 83/23.
[293]Des Voeux, My Colonial Service, II, 5–6.   [294]Ibid., 17.

before the executive council dealt with them. Des Voeux promised that appellate sittings (on land claims) of the executive council should be held during Gordon's annual visit and that in such sittings Sir Arthur should occupy the position of senior member of the council next to himself. Moreover, the new Governor agreed, if circumstances permitted, to communicate privately with Gordon before taking any important step on any of the following: changes in the land laws, increases in native taxation, serious alterations of the native tax system, measures specially affecting native interests, organization or management of the armed native constabulary, highland affairs, and appointments of roko tuis. Finally, Des Voeux consented to send Gordon the regulations submitted to the native regulation board before they were approved by the legislative council.[295]

The two governors, having reached a clear understanding, parted amicably. No sooner had Gordon returned to Wellington, however, than Des Voeux again issued a statement to the press saying that Sir Arthur's interference in Fijian affairs was limited to the right to offer advice, which he (Des Voeux) might disregard. Gordon remonstrated. "It is important," he wrote to Des Voeux, "that the natives should be fully aware that I have *not* deserted them and am still watching over them."[296]

Des Voeux proved unco-operative even after he had received a dispatch from Kimberley telling him that the Colonial Office wished to retain Sir Arthur's services in certain Fijian matters "in which his matured experience might be of assistance to yourself & advantageous to the Colony."[297] The dispatch went on to say that Gordon's "general supervision" as well as his substantial control "over land appeals" should continue and that Des Voeux should refer "all cases of special importance" for Gordon's opinion before taking action on them. Furthermore, Kimberley had decided that Sir Arthur should remain president of the native council because it was important that he should "in the first instance, at all events, retain as much control in native affairs . . . as the distance . . . & his duties in New Zealand will permit. . . ." Finally, dispatches on native affairs, both to and from the Colonial Office, were, in future, to be transmitted through Gordon.[298]

In January 1881 the Colonial Office received the Gordon–Des Voeux memorandum and Fuller minuted: "Not much is left for Mr. Des Voeux to control, but I believe he quite understood that such would be the

[295]Gordon–Des Voeux memorandum enclosed in Gordon to Kimberley, 27 Nov. 1880, PRO CO 83/23.
[296]Gordon to Des Voeux, 11 Dec. 1880, Stanmore Papers, 49246.
[297]Kimberley to Des Voeux, 12 Oct. 1880, PRO CO 83/23.
[298]*Ibid.*

case before he left London." Bramston thought the arrangement would not work and that it would delay winding up the land claims. Herbert agreed with Bramston, but Kimberley, except for the point which required land appeals to be heard during Gordon's annual visit, was at first disposed to concur in the agreement.[299] The office finally decided that Gordon would not be given copies of dispatches and reports of the provincial councils, but that they should be sent through him under flying seal. It also concluded that delays in settling land claims would result from adhering to the arrangement and proposed instead that Des Voeux should consult Gordon only on the difficult land cases involving the natives and should set down such cases for appeal during "such time as will coincide with [Gordon's] presence in the Colony, if known beforehand."[300] In the remaining points the Colonial Office concurred.

Sir Arthur was not prepared to accept this revision of the memorandum. He agreed with the flying seal arrangement, but insisted that when Des Voeux perforce had to send dispatches direct he should receive a copy subsequently. He refused to admit the justice of complaints regarding slowness in settling land claims. They were being settled more rapidly in Fiji than in New Zealand. He insisted that the reports and evidence on all land claims be sent to him, not merely the important or difficult ones, because all hinged upon one another. He would find it useless to see only a few. Finally he conceded that appeals might be heard in his absence as long as a sitting took place at the time he visited Fiji when the most important cases should be investigated. As matters now stood he could give advice only if asked, and if asked he was bound to give it. Des Voeux would ask it only if he desired to shift responsibility for unpopular decisions.[301] Bramston thought "we had better give in to this unreasonable despatch in the sincere hope that the Land Claims will really come to an end this year"; and Herbert thought Gordon's proposals ought to be accepted.[302] Kimberley agreed and a telegram was sent to Gordon making the required concessions.

Meanwhile, Sir Arthur, disgusted by his powerlessness in New Zealand and beset with fears for his beloved Fijians,[303] had asked to be

[299]Minutes on Gordon–Des Voeux memorandum, PRO CO 83/23.

[300]Kimberley to Gordon, 6 Feb. 1881, PRO CO 83/23.

[301]Gordon to Kimberley, 18 April 1881, PRO CO 83/25; Gordon to Herbert (private), 18 April 1881, Stanmore Papers, copy filed in 49218 with letters to Selborne.

[302]Minutes on Gordon to Kimberley, 18 April 1881.

[303]Thurston had written that native affairs, "the most important thing in the Colony," were not attended to. (Thurston to Gordon, 17 March 1881, Stanmore Papers, 49204.)

reappointed to Fiji. Kimberley refused. Such a move, he said, "would have an air of eccentricity and vacillation of purpose which would not redound either to your credit or mine."[304] Herbert added that things would "get out of gear if promotion which has been earned is not given and accepted," and he questioned whether one of the smaller colonies, however interesting, could be allowed indefinitely "to absorb the services of one of the greatest Governors."[305]

Both Herbert and Kimberley felt sympathy for Gordon's distress in New Zealand and offered him the governorship of Jamaica. Gordon refused. There were two positions that he really desired, both equally unattainable: the governor-generalship of India or the professorship of modern history at Cambridge.[306] The governor-generalship of Canada might have tempted him before his re-introduction to responsible government in New Zealand. Now Ceylon was the only other government under the Colonial Office that had any appeal for him. Jamaica, after Sir John Grant's reform administration, would not give him sufficient employment. It would not be thought by others to be a fair trade for New Zealand. Moreover, until he had paid his first visit to Fiji he could not "voluntarily break even the slight ties which still connect me with work in which my whole heart and soul and being have been and are so deeply interested."[307]

Sir Arthur looked forward to that visit with anxiety. Although, since the arrival of Kimberley's telegram making the concessions for which he had asked, he had become convinced that the Secretary of State wished him to exercise an effective supervision over Fijian native affairs, he was pessimistic nonetheless. Des Voeux had refused to regard the telegram as official. Furthermore, in eight months, he not once consulted Gordon on any matter and since February had sent no dispatches. To Des Voeux any supervision by Gordon was "a delusion . . . [whose] effect is simply to add trouble and embarrassment to a government in any case difficult enough." Nevertheless, he grudgingly assured Sir Arthur, "I shall do nothing to prevent your visit passing off smoothly and I hope it may—mistaken policy though I believe it to be . . . that you should have anything to say to anything in my government."[308]

Des Voeux's unco-operativeness arose in part from wounded pride and in part from his inability to ignore the diatribes of the *Fiji Times*.

[304]Kimberley to Gordon (private), 23 March 1881, Stanmore Papers, 49201.
[305]Herbert to Gordon (private), 25 March 1881, Stanmore Papers, 49201.
[306]Gordon to Lady Gordon, 28 April 1881, *Fiji*, IV, 284.
[307]Gordon to Kimberley (private), 27 March 1881, Stanmore Papers, 49246.
[308]Des Voeux to Gordon, 12 Aug. 1881, enclosed in Gordon to Selborne, 27 Aug. 1881, Stanmore Papers, 49218.

In August 1881 he complained to Kimberley that his "present position" was raising difficulties, and he enclosed extracts from that irresponsible paper to prove his point.[309] In minuting this dispatch Bramston said he would not be sorry to see Des Voeux left to himself. Herbert wanted to leave matters as they were for the present. Courtney, the new parliamentary under-secretary, thought the arrangement for Gordon's supervision ought to be terminated. Kimberley simply said "wait."[310]

Gordon visited Fiji late in September 1881. He had scarcely begun to consider land claims when he had to return to New Zealand because of the threat of a Maori War.[311] In one sense he felt his visit had been satisfactory because he found Des Voeux "as amenable as he usually is to the influence of our personal intercourse, and as friendly and pleasant as possible."[312] Otherwise it had not been successful. He left convinced that his supervision of native affairs was a sham and that his withdrawal had seriously affected the work of the government.

Gordon blamed himself. "I cannot but uneasily recollect," he wrote to Selborne, "that I *did* wish to clutch at *both* positions, and am therefore not wholly unresponsible. . . ."[313] Perhaps, after all, the arrangement for his supervision of native affairs had been a mistake and Des Voeux might improve once he felt completely independent. MacGregor seemed to think so. "Of one thing I make pretty sure," he told Sir Arthur, "that after you *leave New Zealand*[314] Mr. Des Voeux will be more willing to carry out your wishes than now."[315] No doubt Gordon's continued authority over Fiji galled Des Voeux who later described the arrangement as one in which "two archangels might be expected to disagree. . . ."[316] Yet since he had accepted it in both London and Auckland, he ought to have tried to make it work. It is easy to sympathize with Des Voeux, and it would be easy to excuse his conduct had he been a competent Crown colony governor. He was, however, as much out of his proper element in Fiji as Gordon was in New Zealand.

Perhaps Sir Arthur should have terminated the arrangement voluntarily when he found it working so unsatisfactorily both for himself and for Des Voeux; but, feeling bound by his promise to the natives, he clung to it. When he left New Zealand in July 1882, he paid Fiji a

[309]Des Voeux to Kimberley (confidential), 4 Aug. 1881, PRO CO 83/27.
[310]Minutes on Des Voeux to Kimberley (confidential), 4 Aug. 1881.
[311]See below, chap. VI.
[312]Gordon to Selborne, 30 Nov. 1881, Stanmore Papers, 49218.
[313]*Ibid.*, 6 Feb. 1882.
[314]Gordon contemplated resigning his governorship.
[315]MacGregor to Gordon, 21 March 1882, Stanmore Papers, 49203.
[316]Des Voeux, *My Colonial Service*, II, 20f.

final visit. It proved more satisfactory than the previous one. He participated in hearing and deciding nearly all the remaining land claims, and perceived that it would be easy to place native affairs upon their former basis. He sadly noted, however, the "capricious uncertain[ty] of Des Voeux's temper and purposes," the steady exodus of the abler public servants, and the lack of further progress with projects begun in 1880.[317] His resignation from New Zealand became effective in December 1882 and with it his official connection with Fiji finally ceased. He remained interested in the islands where he had made his mark until the end of his life. When Gordon died the council of chiefs voted that every native in Fiji should subscribe a shilling to erect a memorial in Suva in recognition of "the difficult and important work he performed in the early days . . . [and of] his love and consideration for us Fijians."[318] Nor have the Fijians forgotten him. As late as World War II they were still staging *mekes* in honour of "Gordon-Chief, who stretched out his hand and drew us upward."[319]

Lord Carnarvon's choice of Gordon as organizer and first governor of Fiji could scarcely have been bettered. Only a man with his broad humanitarianism could have satisfied the philanthropic impulses which had prompted the British government to accept sovereignty of the islands. Only a man with his energy and desire for personal authority could have exercised the benevolent despotism which was, at once, all Fiji could afford and what it required. Only a man with his administrative experience and with his knowledge of the attitudes of planters towards non-Europeans could have created the political forms and social relationships under which the Fijians could maintain a sense of independence and self-respect. Only a man with his intelligence and capacity for work could have solved the problems which a generation of near anarchy and the impact of a semi-civilized purse-poor white population upon the half-barbaric and half-Christianized intelligent native inhabitants had generated.

[317]Gordon to Selborne, 6 Sept. 1882, Stanmore Papers, 49218.

[318]Resolution passed by the council of chiefs, 23 April 1912, *Fiji*, IV, Appendix D, following 517.

[319]Professor Paul Knaplund to the author, 11 Dec. 1961, quoting a recent letter from Dr. Colin R. Lovell, Professor of History at the University of Southern California.

VI

NEW ZEALAND, 1880–1882

⚜

GORDON WAS SWORN in as governor of New Zealand on 29 November 1880. The next year and a half was one of the unhappiest periods of his public life. Unable to accomplish much for his beloved Fiji, and prevented by responsible government from devoting his abilities and energies to the betterment of New Zealand, he lived in constant frustration and restlessness.

After his experience of responsible government in New Brunswick he had vowed he would never again accept the governorship of a self-governing colony. Undoubtedly the prospect of saving a little of his salary in New Zealand after his financially unrewarding sojourn in Fiji influenced his decision to break that vow. So also did his anticipated reunion with Lady Gordon and the children. Yet together these were insufficient reasons. Nothing but a desire to prolong his control over Fiji would have induced Arthur Gordon to accept New Zealand.

He well knew that any attempt on his part to play a positive or openly influential rôle in New Zealand would lead only to his own exasperation and to resentment among the colonists. He could not see how he would be able to "effect anything or affect anything," he confessed to his old friend, Sir George Grey, two days before he was sworn in.[1] He hoped, nevertheless, that his experience, particularly with natives, and his proven ability would lead his ministers occasionally to seek his advice. He hoped, too, that public affairs would be quiet so that he could devote much of his time to Fijian affairs and to those of the Western Pacific High Commission to which he had been appointed in 1877.[2] These anticipations were to be largely disappointed. He found

[1]Gordon to Grey, 27 Nov. 1880, Stanmore Papers, 49246.
[2]This subject will be dealt with in the next chapter.

that he could not exert much control over native affairs in Fiji[3] and that, as high commissioner, he could not overcome the disadvantages of insufficient power and transportation. In New Zealand, public affairs were disturbed and, to Gordon, disturbing. His ministers failed to consult him on any matter whatever. Furthermore, they did not even keep him informed about public affairs. Gordon early realized that the powers of a governor in a self-governing colony had deteriorated even more than he had imagined during the fifteen years since he had complained that in New Brunswick he had been no more than a cypher.

Although, in the early sixties, the governor had not been allowed to attend cabinet meetings, the premier had nevertheless reported all cabinet business to him. Now, no hint of cabinet proceedings reached the governor. Then, he had been able to communicate freely with all his ministers. Now, he could communicate with them only through the premier. Although formerly the ministry had made final decisions, all questions had been freely discussed with the governor, whose opinion was heard, considered, and sometimes adopted. His opinion now counted for nothing and was never solicited. Twenty years earlier, no step that required the governor's approval had been taken until it had been formally submitted to him. The ministry now acted first and later advised him, as a matter of course, to approve its acts. Formerly, the governor had been the sole medium of official communication between the colonial and Imperial governments. Now, each large self-governing colony employed an agent-general in London having direct contact with the Colonial Office. The governor saw none of the agent-general's correspondence with the colonial government. Moreover, the governor's dispatches were no longer an affair between himself and the Colonial Office, because the colonial government had the right to see all ordinary dispatches and affected practically to dictate them. Since even confidential dispatches might eventually be printed for the Imperial Parliament and be seen by the local ministry, the governor had either to be discreet even in what he wrote confidentially or to face the wrath of his constitutional advisers. The governor no longer commanded the militia, nor was his formal approval required for any matter relating to the armed forces.[4] In short, the governor's position had become wholly nominal and social, and his duties "purely perfunctory"[5] (except when,

[3]See above, pp. 228–32.
[4]Gordon to Selborne, 20 May 1881, Stanmore Papers, 49218. The imposition of military discipline on the constabulary and armed volunteers required the governor's formal sanction.
[5]Gordon to Secretary of State, 13 Sept. 1881, PRO CO 209/240.

in a political impasse, he might employ the royal power of selecting a prime minister).

Although Gordon had little official power as governor of New Zealand, he did have some unofficial power. It was founded on his personal influence with Gladstone, Selborne, and one or two other members of the Imperial cabinet, and on New Zealand's admitted sensitiveness to public opinion in England. Thus, if he were to threaten to resign in circumstances unflattering to his ministers he might, possibly, exert some control over them.

If newspaper opinion be any guide, New Zealanders themselves did not fully understand how small a rôle the governor now played in public affairs. In commenting on Gordon's appointment the *New Zealand Times* deplored the removal of Sir Hercules Robinson at a time when the country was experiencing a financial crisis and was facing trouble with the west coast natives. It charged the Imperial government with having simply consulted its own interests. Hinting that the self-governing colonies should be allowed to choose their own governors, the *New Zealand Times* noted, that, as matters stood, "any scion of a noble house, gifted with no special mental powers or administrative ability may be sent out to rule over an important colony like New Zealand, and repair his shattered fortunes by saving money out of his munificent salary. . . ." New Zealand had survived splendidly during the interval between Robinson's departure and Gordon's arrival when the Chief Justice had acted as governor. The *New Zealand Times* suggested that the Imperial government was unwittingly teaching New Zealand that it did not need a governor. Yet, the same newspaper failed to see that, if New Zealand did not need a governor at all, it scarcely needed one with special intelligence and administrative ability. It hoped, rather, that the men chosen to govern the colony would possess "high ability, large minds, and first-class administrative powers." Sir Arthur Gordon was said to be such a man. He had come at a good time. The worst of the depression had passed; the natives were quieter. He should find his position easy and comfortable.[6]

A life of ease and comfort held no attraction for Gordon. He remained sufficiently a Lowland Scot to consider work a virtue.

The fact that the Governor has "absolutely nothing whatever to do in the way of business" which one of my predecessors, Lord Normanby, in writing to me mentions as constituting one of the main attractions of the place is to me just the reverse. It is not without a sense of degradation that I find

[6]"New Zealand News Summary" for Nov. 1880, *New Zealand Times*, 3 Dec. 1880, PRO CO 209/239.

myself highly paid, well housed and well fed, for performing the functions of a *stamp*. . . . We are no longer in the earlier days of responsible government when the Governor though powerless still exercised a sort of traditional influence.[7]

Once a week there was an executive council meeting attended by the Premier, the Governor, and one other cabinet minister. The clerk read the captions of papers. The Premier then advised Gordon to approve them and handed him a pen. Gordon then wrote "appd. A.H.G."—total time elapsed, fifteen minutes. In Sir Arthur's first six months of office the Premier never spoke to him of public affairs, and the Governor never saw any of the other ministers except at dinner. As a rule he had no communication with them except through the Prime Minister. Two or three times a week Gordon received batches of papers to sign, as many as six hundred a day. Decisions on them had already been taken, and he had only to sign them. It was understood that no reasons were to be given the Governor for the ministerial advice. Most of the important matters did not require his signature, and he learned about them only through the newspapers. Gordon found John Hall, the premier, a pleasant man and was generally on good terms with him; but Hall made no secret of his belief that if he discussed any matter with the Governor the public would consider that he had betrayed his trust.[8]

Gordon conceded that a governor with his experience ought to find a way to exert some influence over his constitutional advisers. But how could he unless the ministers gave him an opportunity to express his opinion before they acted? Local politicians were perfectly aware of the governor's potential influence and took care to prevent him gaining knowledge of their plans. The press and its readers regarded the governor as a costly puppet. At Riverton the mayor called for three cheers for Hall and one cheer more for the Governor, which, said Gordon sourly, "accurately enough recognized the true position."[9]

At the opening of Parliament in 1881, Gordon was asked if he would continue the custom of acknowledging the welcome traditionally accorded a newly arrived governor. He therefore inserted a sentence in the throne speech describing his reception as "cordial and respectful." The ministry objected to the word "respectful." Gordon said that he would not have used it had he known the word would be distasteful, but that he would not withdraw it since he would be admitting that he had not been respectfully received. In any case the Queen's representative was

[7]Gordon to Selborne, 2 Jan. 1881, Stanmore Papers, 49218.
[8]*Ibid.*, 23 April 1881.
[9]*Ibid.*, 20 May 1881.

entitled to respect. The ministry's reply was to throw out the whole sentence and drop the custom. Hall told Gordon that, as a man, he might be entitled to the highest respect, but asked whether Gordon seriously thought that the people could respect "such an official as the Governor is with us," that is, a mere rubber-stamp.[10]

The *Sydney Morning Herald* remarked that governorships in Australian colonies had become sinecures, which were defensible only on the ground that they provided for worn-out public servants. Gordon considered this an accurate description of the governorship of New Zealand. He himself was still in his prime, eager to do hard and important work. He resented what his holding the office of governor of New Zealand implied: that he was worn-out and fit only for a soft job.[11] As usual Sir Arthur showed no reluctance in letting the Colonial Office know how he felt. No one in England, he complained, realized the position that the governor in fully self-governing colonies had come to occupy. Herbert, who had been premier in Queensland twenty years earlier, was, Gordon told him, "misled by recollections." Others were led astray partly by preconceived ideas and unreal analogies with the position of the Sovereign in England, and partly by the natural reluctance of most governors to admit, even to themselves, how utterly useless they were. They "either delude themselves . . . that their ministers are only carrying out the exact measures they themselves would have adopted; or they . . . try to persuade themselves, and others, that their 'indirect influence' is considerable, and that they are largely contributing to the progress of the coach when in fact their poor little wheel is spinning and buzzing, idly, round and round in the air."[12]

The Colonial Office did not receive Gordon's complaints about his lack of power without critical comment. Herbert noted that the duties of a governor under responsible government were apparently altogether distasteful to Gordon but, he added, "they exist nevertheless and are anything but 'perfunctory'."[13] Lord Kimberley added, "it is singular that a man of Sir A. Gordon's ability should be wholly unable apparently to understand the position and functions of a Governor in a Constitutional Colony. He probably supposes that the duties of the Sovereign of this country, apart from social influence, are equally 'perfunctory'."[14]

[10]*Ibid.*, 18 June 1881.

[11]Gordon to Herbert, 18 April 1881, copy enclosed in Selborne correspondence, Stanmore Papers, 49218.

[12]*Ibid.*

[13]Herbert's minute, 25 Oct. 1881, on Gordon to Secretary of State, 13 Aug. 1881, PRO CO 209/240.

[14]Kimberley's minute, 26 Oct. 1881, *ibid.*

Gordon was thoroughly aware of the influence that permanency and the hereditary principle gave the Queen and he understood the position and functions of a governor of a constitutional colony fully as well as Kimberley and the realities of the situation much better than Kimberley. Although Gordon was justified in deploring the failure of the officials in the Colonial Office to see things as they were, they may be forgiven for occasionally being angry with him. There are few in positions of authority who enjoy hearing home-truths from subordinates. Despite private impatience, however, the Colonial Office tried to avoid offending Gordon. It sent him only gentle and oblique remonstrances and attempted to reassure him concerning the importance of his office. Herbert, for instance, wrote:

> I quite understand how vexatious it must be to an experienced and successful *administrator* to sit by and affix his "stamp" to administrative acts which he sees to be unwise or feels to be wrong. But do not you too sternly decline to see that other side of the question which I see in possibly too strong a light?
> A Crown Colony is greatly benefited by a strong and fearless administration, but when the six years of such administration are completed it may have to go through six "lean years" under incompetence. . . . It is therefore comparatively speaking a limited boon to a Crown Colony to give it a first rate Governor, though it is our duty to do always the best that circumstances permit.
> But it is of the greatest possible importance at the present moment to place Governors of high standing and ability in the Great Responsible Governments. Among the many excellent men now administering Governments there are, as you know, very few whose training has specially qualified them for Parliamentary work. . . . Therefore, if I am right in believing that our best available men are necessary for the Responsible Governments if the Colonies are to continue satisfied with their present relations, am I not bound to wish that you could with satisfaction to yourself take the helm of a Responsible Government?[15]

Gordon failed to see any logic in placing a man of great ability in a situation where he could do little and a man of little ability in a position calling for the exercise of great responsiblity. He had to have work to do. Unlike some of his predecessors he was incapable of whiling away the time. Sir Hercules Robinson had amused himself with horse-racing, Normanby by shooting and card-playing, and Sir James Ferguson— although unable to endure his position for much more than a year—by yachting. Gordon studied German and went riding in the hills, but he was ill at ease. "He was never meant," wrote Lady Gordon, "to be a Constitutional Governor. . . . He is so miserable. . . . The sooner we get

[15]Herbert to Gordon, 12 Sept. 1882, Stanmore Papers, 49201.

away the better. . . ."[16] "He is not very well, and I don't think the place suits him. I would a hundred times sooner be in Fiji myself."[17]

Even the much-praised climate and scenery of New Zealand failed to please the Gordons. Neither Sir Arthur nor Lady Gordon liked Wellington, where the wind blew almost constantly. Lady Gordon quoted with approval Lady Robinson's opinion that the capital was "the most depressing and foul place" she had ever seen.[18] Government House was most convenient and comfortable, "but the taste of it all is too dreadful. It is so pretentious."[19] The nature-conscious Governor thought New Zealand scenery had been extravagantly over-praised due partly to "the American habit of the people to deal freely in super-latives," partly "to the tendency to self laudation so common in the colonies, & indeed in all narrow societies," and partly, also, "to the ordinary tourist impulse to admire to *order*."[20] Gordon admitted that the country had "*some* pretty scenery," but in general he found the landscape "*utterly* bare, and unspeakably dreary." Even in the mountain regions the hills had "the great artistic fault of rising in one unbroken slope from base to summit, losing all the intricacy, mystery, and variety that are given by successive ranges of gradually increasing height."[21]

Socially and politically he was equally disappointed. In by-gone days New Zealand had had "more gentlemen in public life . . . than . . . any other constitutional Colony." Few were left now, and Parliament was mainly composed of "drunken, ignorant, corrupt boors as in the other Colonies." If New Zealand's political descent had been rapid so had its social descent. The great work that had been accomplished during the first twenty years of the colony's life had been undone during the last twenty.

Hardly the smallest vestige remains of Bishop Selwyn's work. From none do you hear more bitter and savage anti native talk than from the clergy. . . . But it is not only in the utter shipwreck of the native church that one sees a painful change. With the exception of one or two, the Bishops who have taken the place of Selwyn and Hobhouse and Abraham, and Williams, are men of quite another stamp: not gentlemen, not learned, not active, and I am almost tempted to add not Christians, so bitter and narrow are they in their sayings and doings. One is quite startled by the pervading tone of unbelief. All religion is carefully proscribed in schools except Sunday schools,

[16]Lady Gordon to her sister Jane [Ryan], 10 April 1881, Stanmore Papers, 49229, f. 120.
[17]*Ibid.*, 10–22 May 1881, f. 127.
[18]*Ibid.*, 7 June 1881, f. 133.
[19]*Ibid.*, 10–22 May 1881, f. 122.
[20]Gordon to Lady Sophia Palmer, 13 Aug. 1881, Stanmore Papers, 49221.
[21]*Ibid.*

and in Dunedin there is more than one *infidel Sunday school* where the children are brought together to be taught on that day, "moral and civic" duties, and be lectured on superstition, and the absurdities of Revelation. The railway book stalls all teem with infidel literature. . . .

It is not a pleasant picture. . . .[22]

The Gordons' general gloom was slightly relieved when they eventually met "one or two rather nice persons" in Wellington and when they made excursions to the South Island, where they found the climate "quite perfect" and the people agreeable.[23] Sir Arthur, moreover, was not insensible to the solid advantages of £5,000 a year, which allowed him to save his private income.[24] These were small compensations to Gordon for whom "the sole *satisfaction* in being a Governor is the knowledge that one is working to benefit large masses of men, and the only *pleasure* is the sense of power conferred by directing the labours of willing and able instruments."[25] New Zealand afforded him neither.

Although Gordon's appointment to New Zealand neither portended Colonial Office interference on behalf of the Maoris against the New Zealand government nor recognized his special knowledge of natives, it was nevertheless to be expected that, as a result of his Fijian experience, he would pay close attention to native affairs in New Zealand. His fame had gone before him, and everyone in the government knew where his sympathies would lie should further hostilities develop between Maori and European. This fact by itself was sufficient for the ministry to regard him with suspicion from the first and to prejudice gravely any chance he had of persuading his ministers to adopt a non-aggressive and conciliatory policy towards the Maoris.

There were rumblings of trouble when Gordon arrived in New Zealand. Looking for a way out of the current financial crisis and consequent unemployment, the New Zealand government had decided to settle more people on the land. Little was available in the South Island, but much remained to be settled in the North—always provided that it could be taken from the Maoris. The Treaty of Waitangi had once stood in the way, but the New Zealand government had been granted control of land policy and native affairs. It had already confiscated the

[22]*Ibid.*

[23]Lady Gordon to Jane [Ryan], 7 June 1881, Stanmore Papers, 49229, ff. 137, 139.

[24]Gordon drew the same salary in New Zealand as he had during his last three years in Fiji. In Fiji, however, he had felt compelled to use part of it to support his administration. In New Zealand Gordon's travelling expenses and living costs were lower than in Fiji.

[25]Gordon to Lady Sophia Palmer, 13 Aug. 1881.

lands of Maoris who had fought against the Crown during the Maori wars and, in 1862, it had passed an act repealing the Crown pre-emption clause of the treaty. Settlers took advantage of the act to purchase tracts of land directly from the Maoris. Boundary disputes between whites and natives inevitably followed. Furthermore, the government at the time of the confiscations had promised loyal natives ample reserves of land. It had not kept its promise. Loyal Maoris thereupon began entering and cultivating so-called "Crown" lands and interfering with government surveyors and road makers by pulling up stakes and building fences.

The trouble spot was Parihaka, the headquarters of Te Whiti, a Christian chief[26] who had been loyal to the government in the past wars. The government met native interference by arresting those who caused it. Te Whiti ordered his followers not to resist arrest, and as each group of them was arrested more volunteers took their places. During 1879 about 170 Maoris were arrested at Parihaka. Forty were tried and sentenced to prison for three months, and the other 130 were retained in custody without trial. By October 1880, all were still in prison, the 40 because the bond they had been required to post for future good behaviour had been set too high, the others because their trials had twice been postponed by acts of the New Zealand Parliament.

Meanwhile, in October 1879, the government headed by Sir George Grey had fallen and been succeeded by one led by John Hall with the notoriously anti-Maori west coast politician John Bryce as his minister of native affairs. The new ministry quickly arrived at a definite, though two-sided, native policy. On the one hand, it appointed the West Coast Commission to investigate land claims in the disputed area and to make recommendations for settling them. This action probably reflected the feeling of moderates in the ministry who felt that the Maoris had genuine grievances arising from unfulfilled promises by previous governments. On the other hand, the new government decided to continue the penal acts against the Parihaka Maoris, a decision which should be attributed to the extremists led by Bryce who aimed either at weakening Te Whiti's resistance to the government's attempt to take his land or at baiting him into an overt act which could excuse confiscation.

The commission got to work quickly and issued its three reports between March and August 1880. It emphasized that the Maoris had real grievances and recommended that all individual grants made to the

---

[26]Those who coveted Te Whiti's lands claimed he was a religious fanatic whose Christianity was adulterated by paganism. Although it would be strange indeed had Te Whiti's religion been entirely free of ancient native beliefs, the charge of fanaticism against him cannot be made to stand. His actions were not those of a fanatic but of a mystic.

Maoris be confirmed and that two additional blocks of 25,000 acres, one in the Waimate plains, the other at Parihaka, be awarded to a former rebel chief and to Te Whiti respectively as compensation for any remaining claims. At the same time it made it clear that the government should take the remainder of the land in the area. The government, however, delayed putting the recommendations into effect, and Te Whiti, who had refused to give evidence before the commission, refused also to risk open conflict with the government or to complaisantly abandon his lands. Instead, he and his followers countered the ministry's moves by petitioning the Imperial Parliament for release of the prisoners. They chose the notorious Charles Bradlaugh, M.P., to present their petition because "he, at least, was not a Christian."[27]

At the end of September 1880 Bradlaugh wrote to the Secretary of State for the Colonies reviewing the case and protesting against the continued imprisonment of the Maoris. In minuting on this letter Mercer, one of the clerks, noted that Bradlaugh had correctly stated the facts, and he added:

It may reasonably be questioned whether the circumstances justified this practical suspension of the Constitution. But the fact seems to be that the New Zealanders have been to some extent demoralized by the habits which the necessities of former occasions first thrust upon them of investing their Government with strong arbitrary powers to meet native difficulties. The Act of 1863—the prototype of the Bill of 1880, established martial law in the disturbed districts, but it was justified by the declared warfare that was proceeding. The Disturbed Districts Act was also passed at a revolutionary period. But the Maori Prisoner's Bill of 1880 has no such excuse. There is no war. There is no resistance. The old measures are repeated although there is no recurrence of the old occasions.[28]

The Colonial Office thought that to oppose the act would be too extreme a measure, but it hoped circumstances would soon permit release of the prisoners. It ordered Gordon on his arrival in New Zealand to report on the imprisonments and on the land disputes which had led to them.

It is extremely doubtful whether the Colonial Office meant for Gordon to do more than send a perfunctory dispatch covering a report from his ministers. But momentarily happy to have something to occupy his attention, he conscientiously examined the whole Parihaka dispute and sent the results of his work to Kimberley on 26 February 1881. Meanwhile, in December 1880, he had appointed Sir William Fox, a former

[27]Quoted by Gordon to Lady Sophia Palmer, 13 Aug. 1881.
[28]Mercer's minute, 11 Oct. 1880, on Bradlaugh to Secretary of State, 30 Sept. 1880, PRO CO 209/239.

New Zealand premier who had been a member of the West Coast Commission, to inquire further into land claims and to survey the native reserves so as to avoid future disputes. He also sent Captain Knollys to Te Whiti to arrange a meeting at which the Parihaka dispute might be settled. Neither Hall nor Bryce wished to hold such a meeting. Both preferred a show-down. Gordon prevailed upon Hall to agree that, before taking any action against the chief, he would allow time for the meeting to be arranged and for deliberate discussions. Te Whiti, however, distrustful and obstinate, treated Knollys rudely and refused the proposed meeting. This action allowed Bryce, who had meantime completed his preparations for "measures of active hostility against Te Whiti and the natives of Parihaka,"[29] to place his policy before the cabinet, but he failed to carry it and resigned. W. Rolleston, a "just & fair man"[30] favourably disposed to the Maoris, succeeded him. This ended the danger of armed conflict for the time being, and six months later the Maori prisoners were released. On receipt of the telegram announcing Bryce's resignation, Herbert minuted: "I hope this may be taken to indicate that the New Zealand Government has determined not to press matters against the Maoris so far as Mr. Bryce had desired; and not that Sir A. Gordon has insisted too far against the policy of his ministers."[31] The former was the fact. A majority of the cabinet regarded a war as either unjust or inexpedient, but according to Gordon the pro-war minority had been large and had included the Premier.[32]

With the Governor and Premier holding diametrically opposed views on native affairs a clash between them was only a matter of time. The occasion came in mid-May 1881 when Gordon's February report (in an open dispatch to Kimberley) on the Parihaka incidents and imprisonments of 1879 was made public. Gordon had painstakingly surveyed the background of the dispute, noted both Maori and government actions, and frankly stated his opinion that "the Maoris appear . . . to have been

[29]Gordon to Kimberley, 12 Jan. 1881, Parl. Pap., 1882, XLVI [C-3382], 106–13.
[30]Gordon to Selborne, 29 Jan. 1881, Stanmore Papers, 49218.
[31]Herbert's minute, 25 Feb. 1881, on Gordon to Secretary of State (confidential), 31 Dec. 1880, PRO CO 209/239.
[32]Gordon to Kimberley (confidential), 12 Jan. 1881, PRO CO 209/240; Gordon to Selborne, 11 Jan. 1881, Stanmore Papers, 49218. Gordon may have been mistaken in his estimate of the size of the minority and in his belief that Hall was included in it. There is little evidence that anyone save Bryce wanted war *at this time*. Hall and others certainly believed that they should make war on Te Whiti if, after a decent interval, he should not peacefully submit. It was mainly a question of when, not whether. Gordon may have been misled concerning Hall's attitude by the several concessions which the latter had made to Bryce over the previous three months to prevent his resigning.

substantially in the right, although undoubtedly wrong in the mode they took to assert their pretensions." Te Whiti had never "borne arms against the Crown, and he and others in the like situation are undoubtedly entitled to the full enjoyment and possession of their lands, even if situated in confiscated territory." Gordon had also criticized the government for its framing of the laws and noted especially the infliction on natives of penalties of two years' imprisonment for "being suspected of 'an intention to commit' an illegal act."[33]

The Hall ministry resented the Governor's criticisms as well as his failure, for more than two months, to show the ministers the dispatch containing his opinions. The Premier sent him a sharp note of protest, followed a few weeks later by a memorandum accusing him of errors in matters of fact and in the conclusions he had drawn. The ministry had been unable, for example, to see the ground for the Governor's conclusion that the Maoris had been "substantially in the right" in the dispute about fences. Moreover, the ministers believed that Gordon's report had been calculated to mislead the Secretary of State. On 12 July Gordon replied that "after a full consideration of the points urged in Mr. Hall's memorandum, and a very careful re-perusal of the documentary evidence" he saw no reason "in any important particular" to alter or modify the conclusions at which he had previously arrived.[34] He had been duty bound to state the opinions that he truly held and to relate the facts as they appeared to him to have occurred.[35]

Hall now claimed that the ministry had the right to see the Governor's confidential dispatches before they were sent to the Colonial Office. He further claimed that the Governor's dispatches ought to contain no information but that supplied by the ministry. Gordon resisted both claims. Unable to shake the Governor on either point and fearful lest the government's chances be injured in the approaching elections should Gordon's confidential dispatches become public, Hall requested the Colonial Office to delay publication of papers relevant to the Parihaka dispute should they be requested by the Imperial Parliament. Kimberley and Herbert agreed. Herbert suggested that if Parliament asked for the papers the Colonial Office should say that they would be delayed pending receipt of further communications from New Zealand. When these arrived the Colonial Office should then say that they contained matter not directly related to the question at issue and were therefore unsuitable

[33]Gordon to Kimberley, 26 Feb. 1881, Parl. Pap., 1882, XLVI [C-3382], 124–25.
[34]Gordon to Hall, 12 July 1881, Parl. Pap., 1882, XLVI [C-3382], 138–40.
[35]Ibid.

for publication.[36] Kimberley promised to delay publishing the papers unless pressed and then to forewarn the New Zealand ministry.[37]

Gordon realized that, since there was no question of the ministry not having the support of the House and the country over the Parihaka affair, he would ultimately have to accept its decision concerning further action against Te Whiti or resign. He hated the prospect of having his name associated in the public mind with government measures that he considered would almost inevitably be unjust. While touring the South Island in March 1881, he thus took pains to make his position quite clear. He assured the public that, despite his long experience of despotic power, he had not forgotten how to be a constitutional governor. Although he willingly placed his knowledge of natives at the service of his advisers, he stressed that he had no control over native affairs. Authority belonged to his ministers. Whatever policy they embarked upon would be theirs and theirs alone.[38] In sending a newspaper report of this speech to the Colonial Office, Gordon undoubtedly intended to impress upon the Secretary of State the facts that the long years since his governorship of New Brunswick had not impaired his understanding of responsible government and also that he disapproved of active measures against Te Whiti.

For a short time in mid-1881 it appeared that native troubles might be over. The new Native Affairs Minister was sympathetic to the Maoris. Fox had completed a survey of the Waimate plain and had set aside a large continuous native reserve and other smaller ones. Thus, according to Mercer of the Colonial Office, "the Government have made amends for any harshness or injustice wh[ich] might be attributed to the various Maori Prisoner's Acts."[39] (One may wonder how it is possible to make amends for an injury by doing something that should have been done in the first place.)

The period of calm was brief. With an election in the offing, the government felt impelled to heed the demands of the land-grabbers. Early in September it confiscated Te Whiti's land "up to the very gates of his fortress."[40] Within a few days settlers purchased 10,000 acres at prices ranging from three to four pounds an acre for farm land and thirty-five to eighty pounds for half-acre town lots. "This," exulted the

[36]Minutes on Gordon to Secretary of State, 16 July 1881, PRO CO 209/240.

[37]Herbert's minute, 22 Aug. 1881, minute paper 123/81, PRO CO 537/122. The papers were not published until 1882.

[38]Southland Times, 18 March 1881, clipping enclosed in Gordon to Secretary of State (confidential), 26 March 1881, PRO CO 209/240.

[39]Mercer's minute, 26 Sept. 1881, on Gordon to Secretary of State, 13 Aug. 1881, PRO CO 209/240.   [40] The Times (London), 25 Oct. 1881.

correspondent of the London *Times*, "is the real solution of the Native difficulty."[41]

Compelled to accept ministerial advice Gordon could do nothing except write a confidential dispatch to the Secretary of State informing him of the circumstances. For all the good that he did he might as well have saved his ink. Courtney, it is true, called it "an ugly business." It was plain, he thought, that the New Zealand government, in the past, had determined to let Te Whiti have all the Parihaka sector from Mount Egmont to the sea, but that, after permitting him to enjoy it for some years, the government had then changed its mind. It had begun constructing a road cutting off the seaward half of Te Whiti's land and was "now going to justify" its conduct through Te Whiti's protests. "It is a purely colonial question," Courtney concluded, "but we must be on our guard."[42] Kimberley added: "It is, as Mr. Courtney says, a purely colonial question, and we have long established the policy of not attempting any interference with the N[ew] Zealand Gov[ernmen]t whose jealousy of the slightest interference is extreme. Hitherto they have managed the native question with singular prudence and success."[43] The previous history of the New Zealand government's handling of native affairs and the unwarrantable ultimatum issued to Te Whiti on 19 October[44] (the Colonial Office had been informed by telegram of the ultimatum before Kimberley's minute was written) make it difficult to regard the Secretary of State's sentence as anything but "singular" itself. For Kimberley to accept the "ugly business" at Parihaka because he could do nothing about it was one thing. To condone it on the ground that a native policy, which had led to war in the past, had been "hitherto" prudent and successful was quite another. The events of the next few months, however, were to modify slightly Lord Kimberley's indulgent view of New Zealanders and their handling of native affairs.

Although Te Whiti made no attempt to resist by force the government's theft of his land, Gordon felt a little uneasy about his projected visit to Fiji. He had planned this visit for September 1881 and had sought and obtained Kimberley's approval. He also sought that of his ministers. A few months earlier they had refused to allow him to go to Auckland to receive the royal princes on their tour of New Zealand because the House was still in session.[45] Gordon therefore asked Hall

[41]*Ibid.*
[42]Courtney's minute, 28 Oct. 1881, on Gordon to Secretary of State (confidential), 9 Sept. 1881, PRO CO 209/240.
[43]Kimberley's minute, 31 Oct. 1881, *ibid.*   [44]See below, p. 250.
[45]Lady Gordon to Jane [Ryan], 10–17 July 1881, Stanmore Papers, 49229, f. 144.

whether his absence in Fiji would cause any injury to the public service. The Premier replied that "no serious inconvenience will result from His Excellency's departure for Fiji on the 12th instant." On the day Gordon left he suggested that he could postpone his visit, but Hall told him that "there was no cause whatever" for a postponement.[46] The Premier had even consulted the opposition and Gordon quoted one of its leaders as having said it was "not of the smallest consequence whether the nominal Governor was in New Zealand or Fiji, so long as the true Governor [the Premier], . . . remained in New Zealand. . . ."[47] With these assurances Gordon left for Auckland on 12 September and sailed for Fiji the next day.

In view of the events of the next few weeks it is highly probable that the government was glad to be rid of him and to have the pliable Chief Justice, Sir James Prendergast, acting in his stead. Although wifely pride may have accounted in part for Lady Gordon's judgment that the ministers "are very much afraid of him, and that as long as he is here he exercises some sort of check upon them more than he himself allows,"[48] the happenings of September and October 1881 suggest that she was right. No sooner had Gordon got well away from New Zealand's territorial waters than the government decided to force a show-down with Te Whiti, whose fence-building had continued to interfere with government road construction. Rolleston having failed to persuade Te Whiti to cease his obstruction, the government declared that it now faced such a threatening situation that it felt compelled to increase the constabulary. It made this announcement on 15 September, only two days after Gordon left Auckland. Two days later Te Whiti, in his monthly address to his followers, made remarks which the government chose to regard as incitement to violence.[49] On 21 September it enrolled the Taranaki settlers in the New Zealand armed forces, and the Minister of Defence asked for and got a credit of £100,000 for the war that the government considered almost inevitable.

[46]The correspondence between Gordon and Hall relating to Gordon's proposed trip to Fiji is to be found in Parl. Pap., 1882, XLVI [C-3382], 165, and 1883, XLVII [C-3689], 44–46.

[47]Gordon to Kimberley, 13 Sept. 1881, Parl. Pap., 1883, XLVII [C-3689], 45–46.

[48]Lady Gordon to Jane [Ryan], 15 Nov. 1881, Stanmore Papers, 49229.

[49]There is no agreement as to what Te Whiti actually said because his remarks were either ambiguous, misreported, or garbled in translation. It is clear, however, contrary to the most recent article on the Parihaka affair (D. K. Fieldhouse, "Sir Arthur Gordon and the Parihaka Crisis, 1880–1882," *Historical Studies Australia and New Zealand*, X, 1961, 30–49) that the deterioration of the situation began with the government's announcement of 15 September to which Te Whiti's speech was a reaction.

Hall's next move is significant. Before Gordon's departure for Fiji Hall had questioned Gordon's right to resume the governorship on his return.[50] He now persuaded Prendergast to ask Kimberley for the law officers' opinion on the question. The Prime Minister would have been singularly ill-informed had he not known that Gordon's leave was entirely regular and that a governor normally resumed his full powers after his return to a colony. Why then did Hall indulge in this remarkable bit of intrigue? The only reasonable explanation seems to be that he was afraid that Gordon might get wind of the government's preparations for war and return to frustrate them. Aware that the law officers were often tardy in providing opinions, he hoped, perhaps, to prevent temporarily Gordon's resumption of office by holding that the question was *sub judice*. In any case, Kimberley replied promptly that Prendergast's commission would lapse on Gordon's return.[51] Perhaps it would not be unfair to the Hall government to infer that while it had planned to take advantage of Gordon's absence to conclude the issue with Te Whiti (Hall had invited Bryce to rejoin the cabinet on 24 September), Kimberley's promptness forced it to rush matters before Gordon could return. This view is borne out by Hall's sudden decision within a week of receiving Kimberley's telegram to send Te Whiti an ultimatum as Bryce had long wished him to do.

Word of the government's actions of 15 and 21 September reached Gordon on 4 October through the New Zealand newspapers and through his private secretary, F. P. Murray. No member of the government wrote to him on the native question or, indeed, on any subject. Murray, who acted as secretary to Prendergast in Gordon's absence, perhaps felt the ambiguity of his position and merely hinted at what had taken place. Sir Arthur abandoned his Fijian business and hurried to Wellington as quickly as the slow H.M.S. *Emerald* could take him. Word of the Governor's departure from Fiji and of the arrival of his ship in New Zealand waters reached Wellington well before the *Emerald* docked on the evening of 19 October. Murray told Prendergast on the morning of the 19th that the Governor was expected that evening. Hall was similarly informed.[52] Late in the afternoon Prendergast instructed Murray to call an executive council meeting for eight o'clock that night. Despite the imminent arrival of the Governor, the "emergency" meeting convened between eight and nine o'clock. It reinstated Bryce as minister of defence

[50]Gordon to Kimberley, 17 Sept. 1881, PRO CO 209/240.
[51]Kimberley's telegram, 30 Sept. 1881, in reply to Prendergast's telegram of 27 Sept. 1881, Parl. Pap., 1883, XLVII [C-3689], 46.
[52]For Murray's evidence see Parl. Pap., 1883, XLVII [C-3689], 57; and G. W. Rusden, *History of New Zealand*, III, 399.

and native affairs and sanctioned his programme for dealing with Te Whiti. On advice of the ministry, Prendergast signed a proclamation giving Te Whiti two weeks to evacuate Parihaka or face eviction by force. The proclamation was rushed to the printers that night and distributed early the following morning. Bryce dashed off to Parihaka to deliver it to Te Whiti.

Although the *Emerald* reached Wellington about two hours after the council meeting the Governor did not disembark until nine the following morning. Learning what had taken place the previous evening, he at once summoned the council and demanded that the ministry submit to him a full written account of its proceedings. The ministers were furious at this show of authority but complied. On the same day Gordon telegraphed Kimberley to ask whether the administrator's commission lapsed when the governor arrived within the territorial waters or only when the governor actually landed.[53] Two days later he telegraphed again to say that he would have refused his consent to the measure adopted by the government. He would not share responsibility for the consequences of these measures which, if the acts of the administrator were held to be valid, could not be recalled. He would resign rather than consent to war. Not wishing to embarrass the Secretary of State by resigning, he asked whether he might be granted leave or an exchange with either the governor of Ceylon or the governor of Cyprus. If granted leave he hoped to spend some months on High Commission affairs and in winding up the Fijian land claims. Should he find resignation necessary he urged that Kimberley not remove him from the high commissionership or the executive council of Fiji. If allowed to continue in those offices he would require only his expenses.[54]

Herbert, in minuting on these telegrams, wrote: "The Governor when within the territorial waters had technically returned to the Colony, and it was a weak piece of sharp practice for the ministers (having heard that the ship was coming in) to induce the Acting Governor to re-appoint a minister to whose views the Governor was known to be decidedly opposed."[55] Herbert could not see what Gordon hoped to attain by his query. The Governor "seems to imagine that he can work Responsible Government on some not acknowledged principle."[56] Courtney observed that: "The case is emphatically one for the *personal* decision of Sir Arthur Gordon. He has constitutionally the right to attempt to change

[53]Gordon to Kimberley, 20 Oct. 1881, PRO CO 537/122.
[54]*Ibid.*, 22 Oct. 1881.
[55]Herbert's minute on Gordon's telegrams of 20 and 22 Oct. 1881.
[56]*Ibid.*

his ministers if he disapproved of their advice. If he finds a change impossible he is constitutionally bound to act upon their advice, at least until he can be relieved."[57]

The Colonial Office's telegraphic reply to Gordon followed Courtney's minute and added that, with the existing crisis in New Zealand, the Secretary of State could not grant him leave; that no possibility existed for an exchange of governors with Cyprus or Ceylon but an exchange might be made with Jamaica; and that the question of the high commissionership and Fiji must be reserved until after Gordon had made his decision about resigning. Most important from Gordon's viewpoint, however, was the intelligence that the administrator's acts were held to be valid until the governor had actually resumed office[58] and that the governor had no responsibility for acts done in his absence either by the ministry or the administrator.[59]

Had the Colonial Office decided that Prendergast's acts were invalid, Gordon would have been compelled to validate them, or resign, or attempt to change his ministers. Since the last alternative would not have succeeded he would have resigned. He would have resigned also had the Colonial Office decided that the governor was responsible for acts performed in his absence. As matters stood, he could continue to hold office with a clear conscience. Should the government's ultimatum to Te Whiti result in war, however, Gordon decided that he would resign in protest.

Ignored by Te Whiti the ultimatum expired on 5 November. Bryce led a force of two thousand armed volunteers and constabulary into the "fortress" of Parihaka.[60] Te Whiti had ordered his people to offer no resistance. To Bryce's obvious displeasure his men were met, not by defiant Maori warriors, but by a crowd of women and children carrying five hundred loaves of freshly baked bread. Bryce forbade his men to accept the bread, ordered the riot act to be read, and conducted a vigor-

[57]Courtney's minute on Gordon's telegram, 22 Oct. 1881.

[58]This ruling apparently contradicts Herbert's judgment. The point evidently turned on whether Prendergast knew of Gordon's arrival in New Zealand waters. Almost certainly Prendergast knew of Gordon's imminent arrival but he assured Gordon that he did not know of his actual arrival in the colony. Technically, this was probably true. Gordon at least affected to believe him and, in his telegrams of 20 and 22 October, told Kimberley that he believed Prendergast had not been aware of his arrival. Sir Arthur also informed the Colonial Office that the Attorney-General (Whitaker) held the administrator's acts to be valid.

[59]Kimberley to Gordon, 24 Oct. 1881, PRO CO 537/122.

[60]Gordon did not have to give formal approval for the movement of the force to Parihaka although he had to sanction the imposition of military discipline upon the force. For obvious reasons he felt it better that the men should be under military discipline than not.

ous search for arms. His men greatly damaged native houses but found few guns. Te Whiti, his brother-in-law and co-chief, Tohu, and several hundred of their followers were arrested. Te Whiti and Tohu were charged with treason. In the days that followed, the village was cleared of its two thousand inhabitants, and many of their homes were destroyed and their crops damaged.

The New Zealand public approved the measures taken against Te Whiti and his followers, if one can judge by the reaction to Bryce's speech shortly after the "invasion" of Parihaka. "The most tumultuous applause" greeted Bryce's statement that, had any resistance been offered to Te Whiti's arrest, every native in Parihaka would have been put to death on the spot.[61] Some whose avarice had made them blood-thirsty even regretted that the Maoris had not offered resistance and that war had not followed. The influential *New Zealand Times* observed editorially on 2 December that:

> The work of dispersing the natives at Parihaka is proceeding with quite as much celerity as can be reasonably expected. . . . The fact that they offer a perfectly passive resistance adds somewhat to the tediousness of their dispersal. It is impossible to use any severely coercive measures with people who assume the characteristics of dumb driven cattle, and compel those in authority to remove them almost bodily from the land they have so long and unprofitably encumbered.
>
> By-and-bye, when the members of each tribe have been deported to their own homes, and all traces of Parihaka have been destroyed it will be seen whether or not the lesson now being taught the natives will have a lasting effect. Some hazard the opinion it will not. . . . We scarcely think any serious apprehensions need be felt on this score. . . . There will be no shepherd permitted to call together the dispersed flocks.
>
> Before the present summer has passed away many broad acres of land, as yet scarce trodden by the foot of European will be thrown open for settlement. . . . In following out the line of action which [he has] . . . the Hon. John Bryce has well gauged the Native disposition. He has assumed an authority which they understand, and to which they submit sullenly and unwillingly, no doubt, but with the evident conviction that resistance would be useless . . . and that their only choice is to submit to the inevitable. This has been brought about in no slight degree by the display of armed force. . . .[62]

Had the editor been a little less diplomatic he would have said: "It is a pity the natives are so submissive. They would be much easier to get rid of otherwise. However, force has triumphed and they will not again resist our efforts to acquire their land."

[61]Gordon to Selborne, 31 Dec. 1881, Stanmore Papers, 49218.
[62]*New Zealand Times*, 2 Dec. 1881, filed with Parl. Pap., 1882, XLVI [C-3382], 194.

Only the *Lyttelton Times* consistently opposed the government's harsh native policy and supported the Governor's attempts at conciliation. On the day after the ultimatum was issued the editor asserted that Gordon's "first appearance in the Colony produced the only gleam of good sense we have had in the native question. Before his light the insane fire of Bryce paled, and eventually went out. As soon as he got safely off to Fiji, embers . . . were raked together and, after some little delay, the old flame was once more re-kindled, and made at last to burn more fiercely than ever."[63] After the arrest of Te Whiti and Tohu, the editor of the Lyttelton paper commented that they had "committed the one sin which of all sins cannot be forgiven by our present rulers: They have refused to give up the inheritance of their fathers."[64]

In confidential dispatches Gordon forcefully criticized his government's actions. He admitted the popularity of the Parihaka "invasion," but the more he studied the history of the west coast question the more he doubted the soundness of the popular view. Had he been in the colony on 19 October he would not have signed the proclamation against Te Whiti without ascertaining "whether the responsibility of advising me to refuse to do so would be assumed by any leading member of the legislature." He had not had this opportunity, however, and since his return to the colony had simply done his "constitutional duty, in opposition to [his] own wishes and contrary to [his] own judgment."[65]

Gordon made perfectly clear to the Colonial Office his opinion that the whole Parihaka incident had been disgracefully unjust and that war had been avoided only by the forbearance of Te Whiti. To the Colonial Office the facts that war had not broken out and that the government's policy had succeeded were sufficient. It was not inclined to question the justice of that policy. Courtney did feel it providential that "we are not bound to express an opinion on the conduct of the New Zealand Government." Kimberley added, however, that it was "fortunate also that we have not to deal with these native questions, which the colonists understand and manage much better than we can at this distance. . . ." With obvious satisfaction Bramston observed that "the ministry knew what they were about better than Sir A. Gordon or *The Lyttleton Times*."[66]

Any lingering belief that the Treaty of Waitangi still possessed mean-

[63]*Lyttelton Times*, 21 Oct. 1881, Parl. Pap., 1882, XLVI [C-3382], 176.
[64]*Ibid.*, 9 Nov. 1881, 219.
[65]Gordon to Kimberley, 3 Dec. 1881, Parl. Pap., 1882, XLVI [C-3382], 266–68.
[66]Minutes, 19 and 20 Dec. 1881, on Gordon to Secretary of State (confidential), 22 Oct. 1881, PRO CO 209/240. The Colonial Office had received news of the Parihaka invasion and the arrest of the chiefs long before these minutes were written.

ing was certainly dispelled by the reaction of the Colonial Office to the Parihaka steal and to subsequent efforts in Britain to prevent repetitions. In June 1882, the Colonial Office made its attitude public. At that time the parliamentary under-secretary stated categorically in the Commons that land in New Zealand lay "entirely within the province of the Colonial Parliament and the Colonial Government."[67] Until then the Colonial Office, in conformity with its promise to the New Zealand Parliament,[68] had delayed producing the papers relevant to the Parihaka dispute and had answered parliamentary questions about the dispute in vague and general terms.

Kimberley showed himself completely unsympathetic to the Maoris. He rejected a plan put to him by a number of members of Parliament to guarantee to the Maoris possession of their hereditary lands. He rejected the memorial of a delegation of Maori chiefs who journeyed to London to present it to the Queen. This memorial was vainly supported by the Aborigines Protection Society, prominent members of Parliament, Bishop Selwyn (formerly bishop of New Zealand), and Bishop Suter (of Nelson, New Zealand). The Secretary of State finally, in August 1882, told the Maori chiefs and their supporters that: "The management of the land of New Zealand was absolutely handed over to the New Zealand Government, and the Queen was advised by the ministers of the Colony with regard to these matters, and not by himself, as there could not be two governments for one country. It had been decided . . . that the affairs of New Zealand should be managed in the colony rather that in Downing Street."[69]

With such a complete abdication by the Colonial Office of the Crown's responsibility for native lands it was scarcely to be expected that the Secretary of State would intervene to end the illegal imprisonments that had resulted from the land dispute at Parihaka. For six months Te Whiti, Tohu, and a number of their followers lay in prison awaiting their trial for treason. Even the pro-government *New Zealand Times* complained of Bryce's failure to bring them to trial.[70] When, finally, the prisoners were tried the judge threw out the case against them on the ground that their arrest had been illegal. But the ministry was afraid to give Te Whiti and Tohu their freedom in case they might bring a court action against the government for recovery of their lands and so expose the weakness of the government's case, or use their liberty to

[67]H. of C., *Debates*, 1882, ser. 3, CCLXX, col. 1585.
[68]See above, p. 245.
[69]Parl. Pap., 1882, XLVI [C-3382], 291.
[70]*New Zealand Times*, 2 Dec. 1881.

stir the Maori tribes to rebel. A rebellion was not beyond the bounds of possibility because the Parihaka affair had demonstrated to the Maoris that they could no longer depend upon the Imperial government to maintain them in possession of their lands. Happy with the success of the Parihaka incident as an election dodge, and content with the portion of the native reserve that they had obtained, most of the ministers were now disinclined to risk a Maori war.

The government therefore brought charges of sedition and inciting to violence against the two chiefs, and in July 1882 it passed the "West Coast Preservation Bill," which provided for their imprisonment without trial. Gordon, having obtained a copy of the draft, wrote a blistering commentary on it before it went to the House. It was not a bill of general or permanent application, but one which affected solely the liberty, property, and future prospects of two individual British subjects. Proved necessity, wrote Gordon, was the only excuse for such legislation. No proof had been furnished by the government that necessity existed; only the word of the ministers had been offered. The government had not alleged that the ordinary courts were incompetent to try the prisoners for the offences with which they were charged. It had produced no evidence of the prisoners' guilt. Gordon warned the House that it would make a grave error if it did not demand such evidence before taking on itself a judicial character and deciding that individuals had been guilty of crimes that they denied, and then proceeding to restrict their liberty and to ruin them financially.[71] There was, continued the Governor,

probably no precedent in Parliamentary history of the passage of an Act affecting individuals by name in life, limb, or liberty, without opportunity being given to those whom it affects to defend themselves. No such legislation against individuals has been resorted to in England since the attainder of Sir John Fenwick, nearly 200 years ago; no such legislation has been even attempted since the Bill of Pains and Penalties against Queen Caroline; but even in the worst days of English history the right of self defence has been unchallenged.[72]

In short the two Maoris were to be considered guilty until proved innocent. Meanwhile, they were to be denied all opportunity of giving such proof. Only one reason seems possible for this legislation: the government feared the questions that would be asked in a court of law concerning its policy in the Parihaka affair. It was, as one observer

[71]Gordon's commentary on West Coast Preservation Bill, 1882, Stanmore Papers, 49206, ff. 199–202. Te Whiti and Tohu were finally released in March 1883, and Te Whiti rebuilt Parihaka.
[72]Ibid.

put it, "a land swindle on a large scale."[73] It is perhaps worth noting that, by the time this legislation came before the assembly, Fred Whitaker had become prime minister. According to Gordon, Whitaker was "notoriously the largest land purchaser and jobber in New Zealand and [one] who has had the astuteness to give shares in his speculations to the leading opposition members."[74]

During the last two months of 1881, Gordon almost daily contemplated resigning. By the end of the year he had decided to leave New Zealand in mid-January and to stay in England to edit his father's papers, unless offered an appointment that he would not think it right to decline, such as Ceylon or an Indian presidency. He felt that by staying in England he might be better able to protect his Fijian experiment, and, while a member of the colonial service, he might avoid being compelled to testify concerning native policy in New Zealand, Queensland, and the Pacific. "I should be *most* unwilling to do this, for I believe it would do no good, and would undoubtedly do me great harm; but I cannot but feel some doubt whether the conviction that I *must* speak, and that I sin if I forbear, may not some day possess me with overmastering force."[75]

Suddenly, however, Gordon decided to remain for a few months longer. Politically, affairs were quiet, and Parliament would not meet until June. He needed a year or two more to be eligible for a pension, and he did not wish to undertake a new appointment that he might well dislike. At the end of the year, too, he and his family had gone for a long visit to the South Island, where they were happily installed at Christchurch. Here, for the first time since his arrival in New Zealand, Gordon enjoyed himself. He delighted in the open country and each morning before breakfast walked half a mile to bathe in the river. He was, his wife said, like a different man, so happy and cheerful, away

[73]Dr. R. H. Bakewell to Gordon, 17 July 1882, Stanmore Papers, 49239, ff. 175–80. For a detailed and pro-Government account of the Parihaka affair see Fieldhouse, "Sir Arthur Gordon and the Parihaka Crisis." The author excuses the government's policy on the grounds of the land-hunger of its followers, Te Whiti's exceptional resistance to that policy, and the fact that the policy worked. But he neglects to note a number of pieces of evidence which place the affair in a somewhat different light. The most significant are: (1) the government's absolute lack of right to any of Te Whiti's land; (2) the government's announcement of 15 September 1881 (see above p. 248 and fn. 49); (3) the approach of a general election and the government's desire for an issue or a record which would be popular; and, finally, (4) Hall's intrigue concerning Gordon's right to resume the governorship on his return from leave (see above p. 249).

[74]Gordon to Selborne, 20 Jan. 1882, Stanmore Papers, 49218.

[75]*Ibid.*, 31 Dec. 1881.

from the daily annoyances and worries of Wellington. He even went to receptions and chatted easily with everyone he met, in contrast to his unsociable behaviour in the capital. The Canterbury people liked him and were proud of having the Governor among them and of his interest in their cathedral.[76]

This pleasant idyll came to an end early in April when John Hall resigned the premiership because of illness. At first Gordon suspected that, because disagreements had recently divided the cabinet, Hall's plea of illness was only an excuse. The Premier, however, was truly ill. Gordon might have been expected to rejoice in Hall's resignation because the relationship between the two men had been far from smooth. They had disagreed sharply concerning native affairs and, more than once in the months since Parihaka, each had expressed dissatisfaction with the other's behaviour. In early January 1882, in answering the Governor's protest at not having been informed of the appointment of Sir Henry Parkes to represent New Zealand in the United States, Hall noted that his recent dealings with Gordon had left him with the impression—an impression which had become stronger since Gordon's return from Fiji— that the Governor "did not wish to enter into New Zealand questions in which he was not officially called upon to take a part." Hall was sorry if his impression was incorrect but, he concluded, "I cannot take any blame to myself. . . ."[77] A few days later Gordon took Hall to task for the foregoing and other remarks. The governor, Gordon wrote, could reasonably expect to be told of any important step taken by the ministry, even if that step were not a matter for his formal approval. How else could he do his duty of reporting to the secretary of state? He should not have to obtain his information from the newspapers. He did not ask to be consulted. Except on matters affecting imperial interests, it was up to the ministry to consult him or not as it saw fit.[78] Evidently Hall had made some remark about how much easier he had found it to consult Sir Hercules Robinson than to consult Sir Arthur, because Gordon told the Premier that "no relative estimate of the personal qualities of my predecessor & myself sh[oul]d 'preclude' your asking of me what you w[oul]d have asked of him." Showing his deep resentment at Hall's imputations the Governor tartly concluded:

That I do not possess the winning manners of Sir H. Robinson no one can be more painfully aware than I; that he is my superior in ability may be

[76]Lady Gordon to Jane [Ryan], 24 Feb. 1882 and 17 March 1882, Stanmore Papers, 49229.
[77]Hall to Hon. Major Atkinson (telegram), 6 Jan. 1882, Stanmore Papers, 49206, ff. 93–94. Atkinson was colonial treasurer.
[78]Gordon to Hall, 9 Jan. 1882, Stanmore Papers, 49246.

very probable; but I cannot admit that I am less careful to discharge with conscientious exactness the obligations of my office. . . . It is most clearly my duty, if consulted . . . to consider the question proposed to the best of my ability, and form the most careful judgment. . . . I have never given you any cause whatever to suppose that I should hesitate to do this, and I must, most emphatically, protest against any suggestion that, when desirous to communicate with me, you are deterred by reluctance on my part to be consulted; or by indisposition to afford the government any assistance in the conduct of public business which it may be in my power to give.[79]

Nevertheless, despite such exchanges, Gordon was sorry, for two reasons, to see Hall resign the premiership. First, he felt duty-bound to delay his departure from New Zealand, prepatory to his own resignation, in order to see a new ministry through its first session.[80] Secondly, he considered Hall superior to most colonial politicians, having "some qualities which are not too common among men in political life in New Zealand, and the loss of which will not . . . be without disadvantage to public interests."[81] He felt, he told the retiring Premier, that were his own stay in New Zealand to be longer he would "often have cause to remember . . . the courtesy and good temper you have always shewn in our personal intercourse, and which I shall always recollect with gratitude."[82]

The election had been fought a few weeks earlier, but the new House had not met before Hall resigned. Bryce had resigned before Hall and the other ministers shortly after. Party lines being not yet sharply drawn in New Zealand, it was impossible to tell which of the parties or politicians might command a majority in the legislature when it convened.[83] Two of the former ministers (Dick and Johnston) told Gordon that they retained their freedom of action, that is, that they would or would not support the new premier depending upon who might be selected. The retiring ministry did not advise Gordon whom he should call upon to form a government; nor did Gordon seek its advice. Hall told him unofficially that he thought Fred Whitaker could reconstruct the old cabinet.

Gordon probably wished to avoid calling upon Whitaker because he suspected him of being the real purchaser of thousands of acres of

[79]Ibid.

[80]Lady Gordon to Jane [Ryan], 17–22 April 1882, Stanmore Papers, 49220.

[81]Gordon to Hall, 4 April 1882, Stanmore Papers, 49246.

[82]Ibid. Gordon recommended Hall for a knighthood.

[83]Gordon complained in a letter to Gladstone of the absence of "distinct political parties." (Gordon to Gladstone, 5 May 1882, quoted by Knaplund, "Gladstone-Gordon Correspondence, 1851–1896," Transactions of the American Philosophical Society, new ser. LI, pt. IV, 1961, 86.

supposedly inalienable Maori lands. According to the act of 1862 the Maoris could sell their lands only with the consent of the governor, but, said Gordon, the ministry *"always* advised" him to give his consent. In a single day he had been advised to consent to the sale of 130,000 acres, mostly to the same obsure people who, he felt sure, were acting as "a blind" for Whitaker.[84] Before calling on the former Attorney-General, Gordon therefore asked Sir George Grey what strength he thought he might have in the new House. Grey apparently replied that he did not think he could count upon a majority. Gordon then concluded that, since it was impossible to say which party had a majority, the benefit of the doubt should be given to the retiring ministry. He sent for Whitaker, who accepted the invitation and succeeded in forming a cabinet that won the confidence of the House when the legislature convened.

Whitaker naturally resented the Governor's consulting Grey even though Gordon had not asked Grey to form a government. Gordon, no doubt, expected this reaction, because his long friendship with Grey had already led to rumours that he sought and listened to Grey's advice behind the backs of his ministers. Inured to unjustified attacks and false allegations, Gordon had not been deterred by possible unpopularity from the course he believed right. He remained unperturbed by Whitaker's resentment.

At least one New Zealand historian has called Gordon's consultation with Grey "a grave constitutional blunder."[85] Even if Gordon had called upon Grey to form a government, it would be difficult to see how his action could have been more than a mistake in judgment. He had a perfect right to call upon any elected member to undertake to form a government whether or not he had been advised officially by the retiring ministry. The political situation that faced him was unusual. His procedure was constitutional and, in the circumstances, sensible.

Sir Arthur Gordon's connection with the new ministry was brief and mutually uncongenial. He delayed his departure from the colony only long enough to see it safely launched upon its first session of Parliament. In June he sent his family to Sydney. He himself sailed for Fiji to complete hearings on the land claims on which little progress had been made since his hurried departure the previous October. His last weeks in New Zealand were marred by acrimonious disputes with his ministers over the content of his dispatches, his selection of enclosures, and his right to send reports to the Secretary of State without first sub-

[84]Gordon to Selborne, 20 Jan. 1882.
[85]William Gisborne, *New Zealand Rulers and Statesmen, 1840–1897*, 212.

mitting them to his ministers. These quarrels arose from the fact that the Colonial Office had finally printed for Parliament some of his confidential dispatches on the native lands question, and his ministers, ever sensitive to English opinion, objected to the criticisms of the government that they contained. Whitaker accused Gordon of misreporting the facts in his dispatches and of having unfairly selected enclosures.[86] He protested against the Governor's refusal to alter dispatches. He and his colleagues believed, they said, that Gordon's actions were calculated to impair the relations that ought to exist between a governor and his ministers.[87] Gordon refused to submit. He did not think it his duty, he told Kimberley, to shrink from expressing his honest opinion in reporting to the Colonial Office.[88]

Shortly after his departure from the colony more of his dispatches were printed for Parliament. Again his ministers protested that the dispatches were unfair and should not have been sent without the approval of the ministry. Again Gordon pointed out that the dispatches in question were confidential and that the governors of self-governing colonies were expressly prohibited from showing such dispatches to their ministers.

Gordon left New Zealand with but one regret: that he had ever been been connected "however passively, with the working of this government, and the spoliation of the Maoris.[89] Although he had hated his post from the beginning, he had striven always to do his constitutional duty and to prevent as much injustice as his powerlessness allowed. He quitted the colony hated by his ministers for having (as they believed) exceeded his authority, and reproached by his friends for not having opposed himself to his ministers more vigorously. One old friend, Dr. R. H. Bakewell,[90] justly blamed him for prolonging without trial the imprisonment of Te Whiti and Tohu. "It seems to me," he told Gordon, "that in yielding to the advice of your ministers you made one of those mistakes which can rarely be made more than once in a man's career, because he so rarely gets the chance of making them twice."[91] Bakewell thought Gordon should have defied his ministers. In all likelihood they

[86]Gordon did, in fact, enclose an unduly large number of clippings from the *Lyttelton Times* as compared with clippings from papers that supported the government.

[87]Knaplund, "Sir Arthur Gordon and New Zealand, 1880–1882," *Pacific Historical Review*, XXVIII, 1959, 172.

[88]Gordon to Kimberley, 15 June 1882, Parl. Pap., 1882, XLVI [C-3382], 284.

[89]Gordon to Selborne, 20 Jan. 1882.

[90]Bakewell had served under Gordon in Trinidad and had been living in New Zealand for some years.

[91]Bakewell to Gordon, 17 July 1882, Stanmore Papers, 49239, ff. 175–80.

would not have resigned because of their anxiety that the whole Parihaka transaction should not come before the Imperial Parliament. Had an open quarrel resulted and had the Colonial Office not supported Gordon, he could have resigned.

What a splendid position you would have been in! Defending the liberties of the subject . . . resisting a tyrannical democracy in its attempt to rob a minority belonging to an inferior race . . . ! You would have been . . . in this island, at least, the object of something more than veneration and respect. . . . At Home unquestionably you would [have] gained immense prestige. People . . . would have hailed with delight the ex-Colonial Governor who had been bold enough to defy the Colonial Government and displease the Col[onia]l Office, for the sake of doing right, and defending the natives in the enjoyment of their property.[92]

Bakewell feared that a precedent had been established for keeping people in prison without trial.

We have no other shield from the tyranny of a democracy, than the vague traditions of English freedom, each year becoming vaguer. . . . and, until this act of Your Excellency's the hope that the Representative of the Crown might in the last resort interpose.[93]

Twenty years earlier Gordon would undoubtedly have attempted to pit himself against his ministers and colonial opinion. Then, the Colonial Office probably would have backed him. Times had changed, however, and he had grown more cautious. Moreover, he realized that he could hope for no support from the Colonial Office under Kimberley. Had he followed the course plotted, after the event, by Bakewell, his career in the colonial service would have ended abruptly. Realizing that he could do nothing to effect the release of the Maori prisoners, he had followed a less heroic but more discreet course. He had accepted ministerial advice and had then awaited a time, when his departure could cause no embarrassment to the New Zealand government or to the Colonial Office, to withdraw quietly from the scene.

Gordon did not announce his resignation publicly. Since he had six months' leave coming to him his resignation would not become effective until December 1882. Nevertheless, it was general knowledge that he did not intend to return. While his departure was regretted by many, especially in the South Island, the New Zealand Times undoubtedly reflected the general feeling of the colony when it fervently wished that "where next he sojourns he may be better appreciated. He does not understand New Zealand, and could not, even if he would, identify himself in sympathetic freedom with a free and independent

[92]*Ibid.*   [93]*Ibid.*

community. . . . His remaining in this colony would have made but the most insignificant variation in the progress of legislative business— his absence, in point of truth, may possibly lead to expedition in such respect."[94] These comments were too much even for Kimberley. By this time, he had become more than a little soured on New Zealanders because of the avarice and injustice they had displayed toward the Maoris. He wondered

what the *New Zealand Times* thinks that "sympathetic freedom with a community" means! From another part of the paper I should guess it meant no sympathy with any coloured man and freedom for the white man to oppress the coloured man as he pleased.

Sir A. Gordon has no doubt shown his sympathy with the coloured races at times injudiciously, but he has done good work in Fiji and it may not have been altogether without use that he has had the courage to tell some unpleasant truths to the New Zealand colonists. In this country the feeling is with him rather than with the colonists.[95]

Sir Arthur Gordon made no claim that he had accomplished anything during his administration of New Zealand. Instead, he considered that his time, energy, and ability had been utterly wasted. Eighty years later it is hard to disagree with his judgment. It is harder still to see how, apart from forcing a show-down with the government over the imprisonment of Te Whiti and Tohu, he or any other governor could have done more good or prevented more evil. Economic self-interest, traditional fear of the Maoris, and political immaturity combined to produce a democratic tyranny that no politician, no matter how just, moral, or liberal, dared defy, and against which no governor, however courageous, could hope to fight with any prospect of success.

During the next generation New Zealanders matured politically. No longer self-conscious about their autonomy they felt less need to demonstrate their independence of the Imperial Parliament or to throw the governor's powerlessness in his face. Liberalism began to graft itself to New Zealand democracy. Moreover, the colonists discovered that, despite a rapid growth in their numbers, they had more than enough land. Their realization of this fact and their loss of fear of the Maoris, whose numbers continued to decline, brought about a revolution in New Zealand's attitude to the Maoris. "Measures were taken for the rehabilitation of that noble race . . . which twenty years earlier would have gladdened the heart of Sir Arthur Hamilton Gordon."[96] It may

[94]*New Zealand Times*, "Monthly News Summary" for July 1882, PRO CO 209/241.
[95]Kimberley's minute, 4 Sept. 1882, *ibid.*
[96]Knaplund, "Sir Arthur Gordon and New Zealand, 1880–1882," 172.

be that Gordon's "unpleasant truths" concerning native affairs played a part in starting that revolution, but the reasons for changes in public opinion are too hard to establish to allow one to form any definite judgment.

Gordon's greatest accomplishment as governor of New Zealand was to force the Colonial Office into a greater understanding of how white settlers treated native peoples unless checked by Downing Street and a strong governor. In this connection it is well to recall that Gordon had to deal with a Colonial Office much changed from the days of Lord Glenelg, James Stephen, and the Evangelicals, when the Colonial Office regarded the protection of the natives as its first duty. The forties saw the beginning of a generation of laissez-faire during which "a hands-off the colonies" policy was accepted. Humanitarianism slept, to be roused briefly by the Jamaica rebellion of 1865 and by Carnarvon's tenure of the Colonial Office during the middle seventies. It showed an alarming tendency to doze again whenever the Liberals held the reins of office. Gordon's strictures on the New Zealand government's native policies stirred Kimberley from his customary acceptance of the doctrine that "white is right," and helped to harden the Colonial Office's disposition to safeguard the Fijian experiment and to lead it to think twice about bowing to Australiasian demands for annexation of islands in the Western Pacific.[97]

On leaving New Zealand Gordon hoped for an end to his Pacific frustrations. He could scarcely have been more mistaken. They began again almost at once. Although his Fiji visit was fairly satisfactory, he found on landing at Sydney, where he was to rejoin his family, that he and a hundred fellow passengers would have to spend three weeks in quarantine. His personal servant, a Fijian, had a rash that the health officers diagnosed as smallpox. The chief medical officer admitted that the Fijian did not have smallpox, but as he himself was soon to enter politics he felt the publicity he would gain by showing severity to a governor would stand him in good stead. Gordon bore his incarceration with good humour and would not allow Lady Gordon to send things to him because he did not wish to fare better than the four companions with whom he shared quarters. Nevertheless, the experience did nothing to raise his opinion of Australians who, he later observed, "[are] worse than . . . Americans, for they have all the offensive qualities of the American without his redeeming points of ability, decision, & humour."[98]

[97]See below, chap. VII.
[98]Gordon to Sir Arthur Havelock, 27 March 1902, Stanmore Papers, 49207.

Gordon arrived in England early in the autumn of 1882. Although, at fifty-three, still at the height of his powers, he had no expectation of early re-employment. He had given up New Zealand before half his normal term had expired. Moreover, he had several times refused the governorship of Jamaica that had been pressed upon him by both the Secretary of State and the Prime Minister. He had spurned these offers even though he knew "all that is involved in refusing the advice of any Prime Minister, and especially of Gladstone, who resents with a strangely *personal* feeling (as I know by long experience) any resistance to his will or difference from his opinion."[99] Finally, Lord Kimberley, whom Gordon regarded as his enemy, still held the Colonial Office.

Yet Gordon was too active and too able and experienced a man in a service never overburdened with talent to be allowed to remain idle for long. Only a few weeks after his return to England, Lord Kimberley (despite his personal feelings perhaps) offered him the plum of the colonial service—the governorship of Ceylon. "The offer was made in the handsomest manner," Gordon exulted, "and I expressed, I hope, all fitting acknowledgments."[100] He did not sail for Ceylon at once. His leave had not yet expired and he had to complete much business connected with the Western Pacific High Commission before he could leave England.

[99]Gordon to Selborne, 5 Nov. 1881, Stanmore Papers, 49218.
[100]*Ibid.*, 21 Nov. 1882.

VII

GORDON AND THE WESTERN PACIFIC ISLANDS

❧

I. APPOINTMENT AS HIGH COMMISSIONER AND CONSUL-GENERAL OF THE WESTERN PACIFIC

DURING THE LAST three years of Gordon's governorship of Fiji he had also been high commissioner and consul-general for the Western Pacific. Even when transferred to New Zealand he retained both offices: the high commissionership under the Colonial Office and the consul-generalship under the Foreign Office. He continued to hold these appointments during the interval between his resignation as governor of New Zealand and his departure late in 1883 to take up his new post as governor of Ceylon. During much of this interval Gordon was occupied as a royal commissioner charged with reporting upon the operation of the High Commission.[1] He spent the remainder of his time in tendering both solicited and unsolicited advice on New Guinea affairs to the Colonial Office and to his friends in the Cabinet.

The Western Pacific High Commission, as finally established in 1878, was designed to enable the Imperial government to control British subjects in those Western Pacific islands not governed by a civilized power, and to put teeth in the Pacific Islanders Protection Act, which had been passed in 1872 to stop Britons from kidnapping islanders for work on plantations in Fiji and Queensland especially.[2] This act had not been applied to Fiji because in 1872 Britain extended recognition to King Cakobau's government; but annexation in 1874 had solved the

[1]Commodores Hoskins and Wilson, both of whom had recently commanded the Australian station, were the other members.

[2]For the origins of this act see Owen Parnaby: "Aspects of British Policy in the Pacific: The 1872 Pacific Islanders Protection Act," *Historical Studies Australia and New Zealand*, VIII, no. 29, Nov. 1957, 54–65.

problem there. Prompted partly by economic and partly by political reasons, the Australasians urged further annexations. Disraeli's government, however, had no more intention than Gladstone's of annexing more territory. Other ways of curbing the lawlessness of British subjects and protecting the natives of the islands had to be found. Carnarvon therefore sponsored the Pacific Islanders Protection Act of 1875, which provided the legal basis for the establishment of the High Commission. Through this the Crown might exercise authority over British subjects in those Pacific islands lying outside the jurisdiction of a civilized power in the same manner as if the Crown had acquired power and jurisdiction by cession or conquest. Carnarvon decided to confer consular authority, and jurisdiction in the High Commission Court, on the governor of Fiji to whom a commission would be issued under an order-in-council for which the Act of 1875 made provision.[3]

Although the idea of giving the governor of Fiji special authority over British subjects in the New Hebrides, the Solomons, and other islands in the Western Pacific had originated in the Layard-Goodenough report on Fiji, the title "High Commissioner for the Western Pacific" was probably Gordon's suggestion. Worried lest his friends and colleagues agree with Gladstone and Cardwell in considering his acceptance of Fiji a step down, Gordon sought to enhance his position by combining the high-sounding office of high commissioner with his governorship.

The term "High Commissioner" had a familiar ring to Gordon, who, fifteen years earlier, had been secretary to Gladstone, high commissioner to the Ionian Islands. Furthermore there were existing precedents, for the governors of Cape Colony, the Gold Coast, and the Straits all held jurisdiction as high commissioners or consuls-general over territories beyond the borders of their colonies. Gordon visited the Colonial Office on 6 November 1874, the day when Herbert first recorded the plan for conferring special extraterritorial powers on the governor of Fiji, and it is likely that Sir Arthur suggested the title then. Although Carnarvon did not make him the formal offer of Fiji until late November the project had been under discussion for months. The Secretary of State wanted Gordon for Fiji. A formal overture and Gordon's acceptance of it depended on Carnarvon's capacity to offer Gordon acceptable terms. As far as Gordon was concerned those terms had to include the assurance of the high commissionership. His wife later wrote that he

---

[3]The origins of the Western Pacific High Commission have been carefully examined by W. D. McIntyre in an article entitled "Disraeli's Colonial Policy: The Creation of the Western Pacific High Commision, 1874–1877," *Historical Studies Australia and New Zealand*, IX, no. 35, Nov. 1960, 279–94.

"would never have accepted this Government [Fiji] except with that promise."[4] Gordon himself stated that "I was promised in writing that, if I would start [for Fiji] without the Commission, which I had declared to be essential, and without the promise of which I declined to go to Fiji, it should be sent after me immediately, and would probably overtake me at Sydney."[5]

Gordon expected that his commission would confer power upon him not only to control British subjects in the Western Pacific area and to suppress kidnapping but also to treat with native rulers and even to accept certain cessions of territory if offers should be freely made as in Fiji. According to Gordon, Herbert told him just prior to his departure that he should "as quietly as possible secure the annexation of the Navigators and Friendly Islands[6] to Fiji at the earliest possible period."[7] There is no reason to doubt Gordon. Herbert had been premier of Queensland and he sympathized to some degree with the Australian fear that, unless Britain undertook further annexations in the Pacific, other nations would take the islands and thus threaten Australian interests and security. Initially at least, Herbert saw the High Commission as a means of Britain's "quietly acquiring paramount influence among the Islands."[8] He was, however, sufficiently realistic to understand that in areas outside Samoa and Tonga, perhaps, it would be necessary to make haste slowly. "Further annexation will come at the proper time," he told Carnarvon in May 1875, "but to tell the world . . . that we *now* contemplate it would be to defeat the object. . . ."[9] Herbert's statement implies that although annexation was not to be one of the immediate purposes of the High Commission it was, in Herbert's mind, one of its ultimate but hidden purposes. He would hardly have written to Carnarvon in this strain unless the latter in some degree shared the feeling that further annexations were either desirable or inevitable.

Carnarvon was at first prepared to allow Gordon to deal with native chiefs,[10] and in May 1875 used publicly the phrase "commander of

[4]Lady Gordon to Mrs. Ryan, Whitsunday 1876, *Fiji*, II, 39.
[5]*Fiji*, II, 408.
[6]Samoa and Tonga.
[7]*Fiji*, II, 407.
[8]Herbert's note for Carnarvon, 5 May 1875, filed with Vogel to Carnarvon, 4 May 1875, PRO CO 30/6/47.
[9]*Ibid.*
[10]This is borne out by a letter from Meade to the Under-Secretary of State for Foreign Affairs dated 26 Jan. 1876. Meade wrote: "Lord Carnarvon is inclined to think that the steps being taken for the appointment of a High Commission to repress such outrages [as the recent murder of Captain King by the natives of the New Hebrides] render further reports to Parliament unnecessary, unless in very special cases." (PRO CO 83/12, Foreign Office.)

these tribes" to describe part of the high commissioner's duties.[11] Nevertheless, although he may have considered some further annexations as both inevitable and desirable, he saw suppression of kidnapping and lawlessness by British subjects as the high commissioner's most urgent duty. In order to obtain Foreign Office agreement to establish the Commission and to appoint the commissioner, Carnarvon was prepared to curtail the authority of the high commissioner to deal with native rulers and to accept offers of territorial cessions.

The Foreign Office was most reluctant to confer extraterritorial authority on the governor of Fiji. Although Lord Derby, the foreign secretary, was willing to consider such proposals, the permanent officials were jealous of any Colonial Office infringement of Foreign Office authority and dreaded increased responsibilities. Fearing lest the title "High Commissioner" be taken to mean the establishment of a British protectorate over the Pacific islands they tried to substitute for it the title "Special Commissioner." The Foreign Office believed that the appointment of a high commissioner endowed with consular powers might be regarded by other countries as a step to further annexations. These countries might then be tempted to begin annexing islands themselves. If they acted on this assumption, Britain would be forced to annex more territories to protect her own and Australasian interests. To remove this danger the Foreign Office refused to allow the high commissioner the power to negotiate with native chiefs or to accept cessions of territory. It eventually agreed to giving the high commissioner the additional office of consul-general because in this office his dealings with native rulers and the representatives of foreign states would come under Foreign Office control.

Foot-dragging by the Foreign Office, legal hair-splitting by the law officers, and penny-pinching by the Treasury combined to delay until August 1877 the issue of the order-in-council appointing the Governor of Fiji as high commissioner. It might not have passed then, had not Gordon sent Alfred Maudslay home with authority to tender the Governor's resignation of Fiji if his commission were not immediately forthcoming.

The two-year delay proved embarrassing to Gordon. Everyone knew that he was to be high commissioner and natives and British subjects alike constantly appealed for his intervention in their disputes and problems. He looked in vain for his commission by every mail. In the meantime, powerless to act, he watched the increasing chaos in Samoa, the growing German influence in Tonga, and the continuing lawlessness

[11]*The Times*, (London), 3 May 1875.

of British subjects elsewhere in the islands. During the interval, moreover, any opportunity that might have existed for quietly annexing Samoa and Tonga slipped away. "In 1875," wrote Gordon twenty years later, "the annexation of Samoa could have been effected with the greatest ease. That of Tonga would have involved more difficulty, but it might, I believe, have been accomplished. Much confusion, much bloodshed, and much inconvenience would have been thus avoided. . . ."[12]

Sir Arthur correctly attributed the delay to interdepartmental "jealousies and petty routine considerations."[13] He noted especially the unwillingness of the Foreign Office to allow a Colonial Office official to be a consul or to conduct Foreign Office business. The bitterness of his feelings is patent in his conclusion that "the fate of these island populations was a matter of very small importance, or rather of none at all, in Downing Street."[14]

Two considerations underlay Sir Arthur Gordon's anxiety for the prompt issue of his commission. In the beginning his desire for personal prestige was undoubtedly paramount. Not only would he have a high-sounding title but, with the authority that he and Herbert (and evidently Carnarvon[15]) had first considered attaching to his office and that for months he expected would be given him, he would also possess definite power over a wide area of the Pacific. Besides if he could annex Samoa and Tonga to Fiji, he would have an important governorship in public estimation. After some months in the Pacific, where he observed the prevailing chaos, particularly in Samoa, his desire for prestige took second place to his desire for power so that he might promote the welfare of the island peoples. Gordon always found difficulty in remaining a bystander when confronted with human suffering. Thus the delay in the issue of his commission frustrated him, and its limitations of his powers when he finally received it bitterly disappointed him.

To say, as the most recent writer on this topic has said in an otherwise admirable article, that Gordon "misunderstood the purposes of the Western Pacific High Commission"[16] is to over-simplify matters. Gordon was no wild-eyed jingoist. Never at any time did he believe in indiscriminate annexation or in the High Commission as primarily an instrument for the promotion of British interests in the Western Pacific. He did approve Maudslay's statement of December 1876 that "during

---

[12]*Fiji*, II, 407f. See also Gordon to Waterfield, 2 Sept. 1891, in which Gordon said: "I was near getting powers in 1875 which would have saved much trouble in the Pacific." (Stanmore Papers, 49252.)

[13]*Fiji*, II, 408.

[14]*Ibid.*

[15]See p. 267, fn. 10.   [16]McIntyre, "Disraeli's Colonial Policy," 289.

the first few years of the existence of the High Commission . . . there are two matters to be attended to: the extension of British influence in these islands, and the prevention of their annexation by any other power...."[17] It is clear from the context, however, that by "these islands" Maudslay meant Samoa and Tonga, for he added "I cannot but think that the annexation of Samoa or Tonga—especially Tonga—by any other power would be anything but a severe blow to Fiji."[18] When Gordon arrived in the Pacific, he certainly hoped to annex both groups. He continued to feel such action to be desirable. Moreover, when a goldrush to New Guinea appeared likely to develop late in 1878, he could see no way in which the situation might be met except by small-scale annexations of territory in the immediate vicinity of such settlements as might be established.[19] In 1880 Gordon won the Imperial government's consent to the annexation of Rotumah to Fiji.

These, however, were the only annexations which Gordon proposed as high commissioner. In each case special circumstances prompted him. Tonga and Samoa lay close to Fiji. Internal dissension might well bring foreign intervention and annexation, which could weaken Britain's control over Fiji. Fiji was particularly vulnerable to Tonga's influence because the eastern islands of Fiji contained a large Tongan population and much intermarriage had taken place between the Fijian and Tongan aristocracies. Foreign possession of Rotumah would also pose a threat to Fiji. Moreover, if that island were to be annexed to Fiji, from which it could easily be governed, the oppression of the Roman Catholic native minority by the Wesleyan native majority could be ended. As for New Guinea, Gordon regretted that he could see no solution to the situation likely to develop there except annexation; but he wished to confine annexations "within the narrowest possible limits."[20] Unless Britain undertook some annexations in New Guinea, the high commissioner, under his existing powers, would not be able to protect the native population. Australians, who would comprise most of the settlers, would claim to be American subjects (a claim that would be difficult to disprove) and thus place themselves beyond his jurisdiction. The Australian colonies ought not, he thought, to be asked to share the cost of governing the annexed territories because the Australian attitude to "blacks" ruled them out as proper governors of native peoples. "The grant of money by a Colony could not possibly be disassociated from the exercise of some control over its expenditure on the part of the Colony granting it [and] it is not, I think, desirable to place the control

[17]Maudslay to Gordon, 11 Dec. 1876, *Fiji*, II, 241.   [18]*Ibid.*
[19]Gordon to the Colonial Office, 22 Nov. 1878, *Fiji*, III, 220–23.   [20]*Ibid.*

of relations between settlers and natives in the hands of local Colonial Ministers, responsible to a parliament in which one of the interests concerned is exclusively represented."[21] Gordon also saw the threat to Australian security that would be posed by the eastern portion of New Guinea falling under the control of a foreign power; and when such a threat later developed from Germany he was again willing to consider annexation, but not by the Australian colonies.

Gordon did not object strongly to other powers making annexations where native governments failed to maintain order and where existing British or colonial interests would not be threatened by such action.[22] At the same time he did not actively desire such annexations because he could not hope that Germany, France, or the United States would attempt, as he had in Fiji, to govern the natives through their own agency or for their own benefit. He might avert foreign annexations by curbing disorder in the Western Pacific islands and thus limit pretexts for foreign intervention. He therefore sought to make the High Commission as effective as possible. Late in 1876 he had Maudslay work out a scheme for the efficient functioning of the High Commission which Maudslay presented to the Colonial Office in September 1877, just after the passage of the order-in-council.

This plan called for the appointment of deputy commissioners in Tonga, Samoa, the New Hebrides, the Solomons, and, eventually, in the Gilbert, Marshall, and Caroline chain. Herbert labelled the plan "as usual much too grand,"[23] not because it was inconsistent[24] with the purpose for which the High Commission had been established but simply because he knew that the Treasury would not approve the expenditures which the plan would entail. The Imperial authorities had no objections to the growth of British influence, as distinct from sovereignty, and Herbert had no objections to some increase in the latter depending on the time and circumstances.[25] How else than by some such plan as Gordon's and Maudslay's could the High Commission function efficiently? Gordon could not spare much time from Fiji and, even so, he was dependent for transportation on the commodore of the Australian station, who could not always spare a vessel at the proper time. The

[21]*Ibid.*

[22]"The extension of influence by Germany or other European Powers, in other parts of the Pacific, might be regarded by us not only without jealousy or apprehension, but with absolute indifference . . . ," Gordon wrote in 1880. (Gordon to Foreign Office, 31 July 1880, copy enclosed in Gordon to Colonial Office, 31 July 1880, PRO CO 83/22.) See also quotation below, p. 286.

[23]Maudslay's memorandum, 18 Sept. 1877, PRO CO 83/15.

[24]McIntyre, "Disraeli's Colonial Policy," 289.

[25]See p. 267.

High Commission, despite the many other disadvantages from which it suffered, undoubtedly would have enjoyed greater success had there been five or six deputy commissioners to seek out, arrest, and try offenders against the Pacific Islanders Protection acts. The Commission did operate most successfully in the Navigators and Friendly groups to which the Colonial Office appointed deputy commissioners.

It is incorrect to allege that Gordon misunderstood the purposes of the High Commission either because, before receiving his commission, he proposed limited annexations or because he put forward a plan for the efficient operation of the High Commission. It is true that, during the two years between Gordon's departure from England and the passage of the order-in-council, the Imperial government had considerably modified its original intentions respecting the High Commission. Gordon, however, had not been kept fully informed; and if he continued to think in terms of the agreement concerning his powers which (he had every reason to believe) had been concluded before his departure from England,[26] it was scarcely his fault. Once he received his commission he saw immediately the limits of his powers and the records do not suggest in any way that he misunderstood or exceeded his powers.

Early in 1878 his commission arrived. It directed him to implement the Act of 1875 by making regulations for the government of all British subjects in the Western Pacific and to issue licences for the control of the labour traffic. It ordered him to constitute a court having cognizance of all offences committed by British subjects within his jurisdiction.[27] It also allowed him to prohibit any British subject dangerous to peace and good order from living in any part of the Pacific for two years, and to remove such a person from the island on which he resided. Gordon's commission defined the area of his jurisdiction as the Friendly and Navigators islands, Union, Phoenix, Ellice, Gilbert, Marshall, Caroline, Solomon and Santa Cruz islands, Rotumah, New Guinea (east of the 143rd meridian of east longitude), New Britain and New Ireland, the Louisade Archipelago, and all other islands in the Western Pacific[28] not within the limits of the colonies of Fiji, Queensland, or

[26]See Gordon's statement to Kimberley (16 July 1881) that early in 1875 it was intended that he should receive extensive and exclusive powers with respect to British subjects, superintendence of the labour trade and of the intercourse with native tribes. (Paper no. 23, *Correspondence Respecting the Natives of the Western Pacific*, Parl. Pap., 1883, XLVII [C-3641], 411–610.)

[27]A supplementary order-in-council in 1879 allowed the high commissioner to sit alone as a judge where the assistance of a judicial commissioner was unobtainable.

[28]The limits of the Western Pacific were not defined.

New South Wales and not within the jurisdiction of any civilized power. In all, Gordon had an area of some nine million square miles of land and water over which to exercise control as high commissioner. To operate the High Commission during its first year the Treasury agreed to the sum of £5,000.[29]

When Gordon received his high commissionership he also received his appointment as consul-general with authority over the same area. The decision of the Foreign Office to give Gordon consular jurisdiction arose from an earlier decision to appoint a new consul at Samoa.[30] The Foreign Office resolved on this Samoan appointment despite Lord Derby's promise to the Colonial Office that no new consuls would be appointed within the jurisdiction of the proposed High Commission and despite the fact that Gordon had been given to understand that he would be free of any competing authority. Gordon's first intimation of this action by the Foreign Office was the arrival at Levuka near the end of 1876 of the appointee, E. A. Liardet. Gordon was indignant at this "breach of faith, and at having the conduct of affairs in which I was so nearly interested taken out of my hands."[31] Nevertheless, he decided to make the best of Liardet and work through him. This arrangement did not prove easy because (according to Gordon) Liardet

was a man wholly unfit for any official position, hopelessly puzzled-headed,[32] inaccurate if not untruthful, and wholly without tact or judgment. . . . The clerks in Downing Street had evidently instilled into him that he was not to admit any Colonial Office interference, and instead of wishing to avail himself of my experience (as he was a little later only too eager to do), his sole object in desiring to ascertain my wishes was to afford him an opportunity of acting in opposition to them.[33]

Liardet failed to comply with Foreign Office instructions to send his dispatches through Gordon under flying seal. He authorized a deputation of Samoan chiefs to visit Gordon in Fiji where they asked to be taken under his protection. Gordon had no authority to comply with this request nor with an appeal from Liardet for his intervention in the

[29]Since the High Commission did not come into operation until February 1878 and since Gordon was on leave in England for much of that year, expenses amounted to only £3,000. The Treasury took the opportunity to reduce the vote for 1879 from £5,000 to £3,000. Several years passed before it could be induced to restore the original sum. A Treasury officer once said that the Treasury's duty was "not to pay but to refuse to pay." (Stanmore Papers, 49266.)

[30]The consulate at Samoa had been vacant for some time.

[31]*Fiji*, II, 424.

[32]Little over a year later Liardet died of a brain disease. Probably his incompetence (which is obvious from the correspondence appearing in *Fiji*, II and III) was attributable to his illness.

[33]*Fiji*, II, 424.

Samoan civil war that broke out in July 1877.[34] Although Sir Arthur gave Liardet good advice whenever the latter gave him an opportunity, the Consul lacked the ability to profit by it. Both the Foreign and the Colonial Offices began to take alarm at the increasingly serious situation in Samoa.

Aware of Gordon's annoyance at the appointment of the Samoan consul and his disgust with the appointee, the Colonial Office at first attributed the Gordon-Liardet impasse to a clash of temperaments. Malcolm, who was undoubtedly the wittiest member of the Colonial Office staff and enjoyed coining pungent phrases even at the expense of accuracy, wrote: "No man can serve two masters especially when one of them is Sir A. Gordon. . . . "[35] Carnarvon thought "it may be reasonably hoped that we shall not in future have to deal with two persons of such peculiar temper at one & the same time."[36] Nevertheless, the Secretary of State agreed with Herbert that the experience had demonstrated the dangers that could flow from divided jurisdiction.[37] He authorized Herbert to suggest to the Foreign Office, first, that Gordon be made consul-general and, secondly, that a deputy commissioner be appointed at Samoa who should also be consul and should report through Gordon in both rôles.

The Foreign Office agreed to the first proposition but suggested that its own official, the consul at Samoa be named deputy commissioner. The Colonial Office gave in reluctantly. Herbert recorded his dejection: "I am not hopeful as to the practical success of the High Commissonership. The F[oreign] O[ffice] partly through antipathy to Sir A. Gordon & partly through a desire to get & keep patronage, seem determined to maintain their officers in a position which will encourage them to oppose the High Commission."[38]

Despite its victory in preventing the Colonial Office from exercising any political jurisdiction in the Western Pacific, the Foreign Office nevertheless took months to prepare Gordon's instructions as Consul-

[34]Herbert considered that Gordon had acted "prudently and . . . avoided committing H. M. Govt. to any responsibilities." (Herbert's minute, 20 July 1877 on Gordon to Secretary of State (confidential), 25 April 1877, PRO CO 83/13.)

[35]Malcolm's minute, 2 Aug. 1877, on Foreign Office to Colonial Office, 23 July 1877, PRO CO 83/15. Gordon was not yet Liardet's "master."

[36]Carnarvon's minute, 12 Aug. 1877, ibid.

[37]Herbert's and Carnarvon's minutes, ibid.

[38]Herbert's minute, 18 Sept. 1877 on Foreign Office to Colonial Office, 8 Sept. 1877, PRO CO 83/15. The only basis for the Foreign Office's antipathy to Gordon seems to have been its suspicion that he might seek to supplant the authority of its consuls. Gordon was on friendly terms with Lord Derby and had never indulged in controversy with the permanent officials unless, perhaps, in 1875, over his powers as high commissioner.

General. The Colonial Office was understandably annoyed. Malcolm believed the Foreign Office "to be actuated by an unworthy suspicion of the C[olonial] O[ffice]."[39] Herbert noted that "Sir J. Pauncefote [under-secretary at the Foreign Office] is apparently acting under the instructions of the Consular Department who cannot understand the question and also have a spite against Sir A. G[ordon]. He need not be so weak as to give up his judgment to them."[40] Carnarvon lamented the "interminable controversy" with the Foreign Office, which seemingly did not appreciate the expediency of getting an early settlement.[41]

Although the danger of renewed civil war in Samoa and Liardet's appeals to Gordon for help did not prompt the Foreign Office to hurry Gordon's commission as consul-general, they did prompt it to suggest to the Colonial Office that Gordon be told to visit Samoa to protect British lives and interests. The Colonial Office knew that Gordon favoured annexing Samoa to Fiji should the Samoans spontaneously agree, and it believed with Gordon that, since the Navigators were richer than the Fijian islands, annexation would reduce the cost to the mother country of the colony of Fiji. Yet the Colonal Office also thought it unwise, at the present juncture, to extend the Queen's sovereignty in the South Seas.[42] It was thus not at all sure that Gordon ought to visit Samoa. Malcolm warned that: "We should be putting ourselves very much in his hands if we suddenly ordered him to go . . . & gave him a ship of war to go in. He might, unless he got special instructions think that this was an intimation to him to take up a 'strong" policy."[43] Herbert, who had changed his mind since 1875 respecting the annexation of Samoa, thought Gordon should go but should not lend himself to schemes of annexation.[44] Carnarvon was not convinced

[39]Malcolm's minute, 12 Dec. 1877, PRO CO 83/15 (Foreign Office), minute paper 14661.
[40]Herbert's minute, *ibid.*   [41]Carnarvon's minute, *ibid.*
[42]Gordon to Secretary of State (confidential), 25 April 1877, and minutes, PRO CO 83/13.
[43]Malcolm's minute, 20 Oct. 1877, PRO CO 83/15 (Foreign Office), minute paper 12998.
[44]Herbert's minute, *ibid.* Herbert's attitude to the annexation of Samoa and Tonga from 1875 to 1880 was not consistent. He approved of it in 1875, opposed it in 1877, and, in September 1879, wrote: "It is very unfortunate that at this moment, when the nations are taking what they require in the Pacific, Australia is just of an age which precludes her from similar prompt & effective action in the Navigator, Friendly Islands, & other places which we will not take & hold for her." Hicks Beach added: "If Australia fulfils the expectations of her friends she will some day be strong enough to take all she may want in these seas!" (Minute on Pauncefote to Herbert, 11 Sept. 1879, CO 537/136.) It may be suggested that Herbert's changes of front were dictated by changing circumstances in the Pacific and perhaps by who happened to be secretary of state.

that he could quite count on Gordon's tact "in what may be a very delicate affair," but he believed Sir Arthur should be allowed to go. "The order . . . should not be imperative—he s[houl]d be allowed an option in case he considers it inexpedient to go—and the caution suggested [by Herbert] should be very strict."[45]

Gordon, however, had no intention of going to Samoa until he had his full powers as high commissioner and consul-general in his hands. These reached him early in the new year and, at the beginning of February 1878, he set out for Samoa in H.M.S. *Sapphire*. The Foreign Office had meanwhile cleared the ground by recalling Liardet.[46]

II. SAMOA

Gordon found Samoa a confused place. The Americans, Germans, and British all had interests in Samoa. Although less numerous than the British, the Germans had the largest investment through the Hamburg trading firm of J. C. Godeffroy and Company, whose manager, Theodore Weber, was also German consul. The British held the next largest interest and the Americans, the smallest. Griffin, the American consul, acted as unofficial adviser to the Taimua and Faipule,[47] a faction that had emerged from the 1877 civil war as the *de facto* ruling party of Samoa. A numerous minority disputed its authority, however, and the threat of renewed civil war hung over the country. Indeed, the leaders of the defeated Puletua party were still in refuge in the grounds of the British consulate. Both the American and the British consuls had been intriguing to expand the influence of their countries—the latter, at least, contrary to his instructions. The German consul had been seeking to promote the interests of his company. None was willing to trust or co-operate with the others to safeguard foreign lives or property. The Taimua and Faipule, without awaiting an answer to their 1877 application for a British protectorate, had sent their secretary to Washington to ask for an American protectorate; but what they meant by a protectorate was merely protection and support against their political opponents.

[45]Carnarvon's minute, 31 Oct. 1877, PRO CO 83/15 (Foreign Office), minute paper 12998.

[46]Liardet died in Samoa on the day Gordon's ship reached port.

[47]The *Taimua* comprised fifteen chiefs, and the *Faipule* consisted of representatives elected by the people. Together they formed the Samoan equivalent of the United States Congress—not surprisingly, perhaps, since the remodelled constitution that created them had been the work of the American filibuster, Colonel Steinberger. (Morrell, *Britain in the Pacific Islands*, 217.)

Since Samoa was so politically divided, Gordon realized at once that "the time was not propitious for any immediate annexation"[48] and that only close co-operation between the three consulates could restore some degree of order. He had several objectives in visiting Samoa. He wished to hold a high commissioner's court to try a number of charges against British subjects;[49] to return the formal refusal of Her Majesty's government to the Samoan application for protection; to establish harmony between the three consulates; to obtain from the Samoan government rights for British subjects equal to those granted other foreigners; to arrange for the settlement of the indemnity levied on the Samoan government for the *Barracouta* affair in March 1876;[50] to get a written guarantee for the personal safety of the Puletua refugees; to recognize the Taimua and Faipule as the *de facto* government and help it establish an administration able to end the prevalent anarchy and misrule; and finally, if possible, to set up a municipal government in Apia, the chief town, whose area of jurisdiction should be respected as neutral in the event of renewed civil war.

At first the Samoans appeared co-operative, but, after a few days, negogiations stalled. It became evident that Griffin, who professed to have nothing to do with Samoan politics, had forbidden the Taimua and Faipule to agree to anything. Gordon had no alternative but to seize the Samoan government schooner *Elizabeth* in partial satisfaction of the *Barracouta* claims and return to Fiji.[51]

Except for establishing good relations with Weber and showing by his seizure of the *Elizabeth* that Britain would not be ignored, Gordon had to admit that his first visit to Samoa almost wholly failed. Yet he believed that he had laid the foundation for future success.[52] After returning to Fiji, he sent Maudslay to Samoa as acting deputy commissioner and acting consul. With the threat of the *Sapphire*'s guns, Maudsley was able to extract a guarantee for the safety of the Puletua chiefs from the Taimua and Faipule and to collect the remainder of the *Barracouta* indemnity. Because Griffin had promised that he would prevent the British collecting the indemnity, his failure greatly weakened his influence with the Samoans.

[48]*Fiji*, III, 29.

[49]Judge Gorrie who accompanied him and who had been appointed chief judical commissioner undertook this task.

[50]See Morrell, *Britain in the Pacific Islands*, 218, for a brief account of this episode in which three sailors from H.M.S. *Barracouta* were killed by Samoans.

[51]For a full account of Gordon's visit to and negotiations in Samoa, see *Fiji*, III, 30–58, especially Gordon to Derby, 4 March and 2 April 1878, 50–58.

[52]*Fiji*, III, 45.

After a few months Gordon sent Maudslay to Tonga and appointed R. S. Swanston to Samoa as deputy commissioner and acting consul. Although Swanston was by no means a wholly suitable man he did know Samoan and was the best man Gordon could spare. Until the Foreign Office appointed one of its own men as consul, Swanston followed a successful neutralist policy and avoided trouble.

During Gordon's leave of absence (mid–1878 to mid-1879) the American farce slowly played itself out in Samoa; the Taimua and Faipule gradually lost ground and King Malietoa's[53] party, which was pro-British, became dominant. When Gordon, on his way back to Fiji, landed at Samoa in August 1879, he found a completely different situation than the one he had left in 1878. All the foreign representatives and the captains of the American, German, and British men-of-war now agreed to recognize Malietoa as the *de facto* ruler in place of the Taimua and Faipule. Malietoa readily assented to negotiate with Gordon a treaty (which the Foreign Office had empowered Gordon to make) similar to those which the Taimua and Faipule had recently signed with the United States and Germany. The King also agreed to the formation of a municipal government for Apia, which should be controlled by the consuls and representatives of the three European communities. The treaty was signed on 28 August and the convention for establishing the municipality of Apia on 2 September.

In December 1878 a British resident in Samoa had written to Gordon prophesying that "the fruit will be ripe in August, and the knife of annexation would then easily cause it [Samoa] to fall into the basket."[54] Nevertheless, Sir Arthur was startled when, two days after signing the treaty, Malietoa and a large body of chiefs called on him and offered the unconditional cession of Samoa to Great Britain. In describing the situation to Lady Gordon, Sir Arthur wrote:

It is curious with what clearness, rapidity, and decision mental operations are carried on at a moment of crisis. I have felt this before, at the time of the Trent alarm, at the threatened Fenian invasion of New Brunswick, and during the Colo war [in Fiji]. I had now to make up my mind while Malietoa was making the very short speech accompanying his offer. My thoughts ran thus. "This is a great temptation. This is what I have desired and worked for for the last two years. It would be good for the Samoans, good for Fiji, and I believe useful to Imperial interests, but of that, of course, the Imperial Government must judge. Is it possible to accept, and risk the chances of suc-

---

[53]There were two Malietoas in Samoa. The younger Malietoa had been deposed in 1876. In 1879 he renounced his claim to the throne in favour of his uncle, the elder Malietoa and the one referred to here.

[54]Houstoun to Gordon, 24 Dec. 1878, *Fiji*, III, 483–85.

cess? No. The fatal pledge given by the Samoans to the German Government shown me by Weber stands in the way. I might possibly have even been able to get over that had Malietoa been in undisputed possession of the whole of Samoa, but he is not. Though we have all recognized him, the Taimua and Faipule still exist, and such a breach of faith on Malietoa's part would give the Germans a ground of which they would at once avail themselves for breaking with him and taking up the other faction, possibly— probably—with armed assistance. I must refuse, but I will do so in such a way as not to preclude the consideration of the offer by the three Powers interested. Shall I while refusing give Malietoa an English adviser? No, I have not the man available. Done now, it would excite jealousies it is desirable to quench. It will come more naturally out of the working of the Convention." And in this sense I replied, decidedly refusing the proffered gift, but undertaking to bring it before the European Governments. As soon as Malietoa and his Court were out of the house, I hurried down to the German Consulate, where I knew the Consuls were sitting on Municipal business, being anxious that no distorted report of what had happened should reach them before they heard it from myself. They were somewhat amazed, and at first somewhat ruffled, but less so than I expected, and I think they appreciated my action, both in declining the offer, and at once communicating to them the whole transaction without a grain of mystery or reticence. I felt I had confirmed the lead I had obtained. . . .[55]

Before leaving Samoa, Gordon, with the consuls, made an unsuccessful attempt to reconcile the Taimua and Faipule to the new order by offering them a guarantee of protection. Before the month was out they renewed the civil war and desultory fighting continued until the end of the year, when Malietoa triumphed. In the meantime, during a three-day visit to Samoa, Gordon established friendship with the new German Consul-General (Zembsch) and ironed out differences that had arisen in setting up the municipality of Apia.

Samoan affairs now appeared fairly settled. Unfortunately, however, Malietoa, whom Gordon had advised "not to attempt to play off one Power against another, . . . to be moderate and forbearing in his treatment of those who had been his adversaries; and always to remember . . . the welfare of his people . . . ,"[56] chose, rather, to persecute his former opponents. His government proved nearly as ineffective as that of the Taimua and Faipule. The King evidently realized his shortcomings and the inability of his government to rule Samoa to the satisfaction of the white settlers. These reasons prompted him to ask that Britain, the United States, and Germany consult together as to the future of Samoa and decide whether it would be expedient that one of them should assume direction of the government. Should their

[55]Gordon to Lady Gordon, Sept. 1879, *Fiji*, IV, 18–19.
[56]Gordon to Salisbury, 15 Sept. 1879, *Fiji*, IV, 22–25.

answer be in the affirmative he insisted that the Samoan government should choose to which power the cession should be made. He made it clear to Gordon that his government desired to cede Samoa only to England.[57]

Gordon supported this request in a dispatch to Salisbury in March 1880. He stated that the Samoans were convinced of their inability to manage their own affairs, that the country could easily be ruled from Fiji at little additional cost, that the interests of the natives would be best served by the establishment of British authority, and that the acquisition of Samoa would be desirable and eventually remunerative. He pointed out, however, that unless annexation took place with the cordial good will of the other interested powers, it would have no advantage to Britain. He suggested that France[58] and the United States be asked to appoint commissioners who, with the German Consul-General and himself, might "examine into the true state and real wishes of the country, and prepare a joint report for the information of our respective Governments on which the ultimate decision of these Powers might be based."[59]

The Foreign Office asked the British ambassador in Berlin for his opinion. He replied that some confidential interchange of views and explanations between the British and German governments should take place before the appointment of commissioners. He thought the present moment favourable because Bismarck, who was disgusted with the German Parliament for throwing out his bill guaranteeing Godeffroy's Samoan South Sea Trading Company, might be willing to drop "the Samoan scheme" altogether. The British ambassador asked that immediate confidential overtures be made to Count Münster, the German ambassador, because, should Berlin bankers succeed in a few days in forming a new Samoan company, they might enlist Bismarck's protection, in which case he would "never give the consent of Germany to the annexation of Samoa by England."[60] The Foreign Office sent the ambassador's letter to the Colonial Office, which threw cold water on the scheme. Herbert wrote: "The annexation of the Navigators Islands with the consent (if obtainable which is at least very doubtful) of the other Powers interested in the Pacific, might perhaps lessen our expenses and our difficulties in that part of the world; but I presume that

[57]*Ibid.*, 25–27.

[58]France had almost no interests in Samoa although there was a small French Roman Catholic mission.

[59]Gordon to Foreign Secretary, 1 March 1880, PRO FO 58/168.

[60]Lord Odo Russell to Granville (confidential and immediate), 4 May 1880, PRO CO 537/136.

the question is altogether out of the field of practical politics, & therefore not worth discussing.[61] . . . The present tripartite protectorate is probably all that is practicable."[62] Kimberley added: "I quite agree. We have got quite enough on our hands already."[63] This ended such chance as there may have been for British annexation of Samoa and for the establishment in those islands during the next twenty years of peace, order, and economic prosperity.[64]

Sir Arthur Gordon paid a last visit to Samoa in August 1880 to exchange treaty ratifications with Malietoa and to deal with a disreputable New Zealander named Hunt, whom Malietoa had appointed as his chief secretary, adviser, and sole guide. Hunt's bad advice had almost completely alienated the King and the consuls. The latter considered Hunt a threat to peace and order and demanded that Gordon remove him from Samoa. They also wished to depose Malietoa and recognize the Taimua and Faipule. Gordon agreed to order Hunt to leave[65] but advised the consuls to "make the best of old Malietoa."[66] Bad as it was, the King's government was slightly better than the anarchy of the acephalous Taimua and Faipule. Gordon and the consuls decided, however, to minimize as far as possible the support to be given the King because "unless we are ready to face all the difficulties of a protectorate . . . , the less we interfere in the internal affairs of the country the better."[67]

In November 1880 old Malietoa died and was succeeded by the less popular younger Malietoa. For the next three years "lethargy rather than anarchy prevailed; but there was no governance as Europeans understood it."[68] Until 1883 Gordon, who transferred to New Zealand in November 1880, exerted from a greater distance what influence he could to maintain the harmony that prevailed among the consuls.

Although for five years Sir Arthur had undoubtedly prevented much disorder and bloodshed in Samoa and had impeded American and German intrigues, he felt dissatisfied. He had been unable to accomplish

[61]Perhaps because Gladstone and Kimberley were back in office. Contrast with Herbert's minute, fn. 44 above.

[62]Herbert's minute, 18 May 1880, on Russell to Granville, 4 May 1880.

[63]Kimberley's minute, 19 May 1880, *ibid.*

[64]For an account of the disorders and international rivalry in Samoa to its partitioning in 1900 see Morrell, *Britain in the Pacific Islands.*

[65]Hunt later launched two unsuccessful suits for damages against Gordon for this action, one in Fiji, the other in New Zealand. The Treasury fought the second case for Gordon.

[66]Gordon to J. H. Graves (British consul in Samoa), 20 July 1880, *Fiji,* IV, 376.

[67]Gordon to Granville, 13 Sept. 1880, *Fiji,* IV, 424–25.

[68]Morrell, *Britain in the Pacific Islands,* 225.

annexation which was the one thing that could have secured peace and prosperity to the Samoan people and, at the same time, improved the financial position of Fiji, reduced Britain's difficulties in Polynesia, and enhanced his own prestige. He could hardly reproach himself for his failure. The doctrinaire opposition of the Imperial government to annexation proved too strong. Had he taken the one opportunity which had presented itself on the occasion of Malietoa's offer of cession in 1879, his action almost certainly would have been repudiated by both the Foreign Office and the Colonial Office.

III. TONGA

As strongly as Gordon had felt about Samoa he felt even more strongly about Tonga. Annexation of the latter by Germany would present much greater dangers to Fiji and to Britain's influence in the Pacific than the annexation of Samoa by either the United States or Germany. Encouraged by the Wesleyan missionary, Shirley W. Baker, German influence was strong and increasing. Baker, the real ruler of Tonga, was in the pay of Weber, the manager of Godeffroy and Company. Poor and unhappy as the Samoans were by reason of their chronic political anarchy and consequent disruption of trade, the Tongans were even worse off. As religious mentor and medical adviser to King George Tubou, Baker had won tremendous influence over him and had transformed the constitutional monarchy, which he himself had practically created in 1875, into a lightly veiled dictatorship that reflected his own will. By this means he imposed a series of socially restrictive laws on the Tongan people to the detriment of their health and happiness, and extracted from them such large missionary contributions that they had to mortgage their crops at a fraction of their value to Godeffroy and Company. In short Baker was one of those "ecclesiastical robbers," as Herbert once called an element among the Wesleyan missionaries in the South Seas.[69]

A series of "mellifluous interchanges of thought"[70] between Gordon and the King paved the way for Gordon's first visit to Tonga in 1878. Baker was absent in New Zealand—"fortunately," said the King, for had he been in Tonga he would somehow have contrived to prevent the King conferring with Gordon.[71] Gordon was thus able to win the King's

---

[69]Herbert's minute, 20 May 1876, PRO CO 83/12, f. 189.

[70]Fuller's minute, 29 Jan. 1878, on Gordon to Secretary of State, 29 Nov. 1877, enclosing copies of correspondence with the King of Tonga, PRO CO 83/14.

[71]Gordon's account of his meetings with the King, *Fiji*, III, 100–2.

confidence and to obtain a promise that the social laws would be relaxed. He found the King willing to grant the High Commission Court the same power of summoning Tongan witnesses as the Tongan Supreme Court and eager to sign a treaty with Britain similar to that which Tonga had signed with Germany in 1876. The King was quite obviously glad of Gordon's presence as high commissioner and consul-general because it would partially offset Baker's power over him.

The relationship between the King and Baker reminded Gordon of that between King Louis XIII and Richelieu. "He writhes under his tyranny, but cannot and will not shake it off."[72] Although the King disliked Baker and hated his Europeanizing system, gratitude for long and faithful, if not good, service and fear of political anarchy and his own death[73] should Baker be removed kept him under the missionary's thumb. He believed that Baker was ruining the country but until Gordon's visit had seen no alternative. Now, with England's influence to balance Germany's and Gordon's advice to counteract Baker's, he thought "Tonga may live—yes, Tonga may live—Tonga will live."[74] King George Tubou later referred frequently to Gordon's April visit "as a new departure in the history of the country."[75]

Shortly after his 1878 trip to Samoa and Tonga Gordon went home leaving Maudslay in Tonga as vice-consul and deputy commissioner. While in England, Sir Arthur persuaded the Foreign Office that Britain's interests necessitated the reduction of German influence in Tonga. Salisbury was easily convinced that "we should do all we can to keep the Germans off Tonga."[76] Gordon suggested that the Germans should be warned off. Salisbury doubted whether this would work.

No power really attends to a warning that they must keep their paws off any particular place. They promise but they don't perform; and the fact of having exacted the promise makes subsequent interference more difficult, as it has the effect of openly doubting their sincerity. More effect is produced by dealing with each pretension or encroachment as it arises. . . . But the real remedy is to increase your own power there. . . . If we leave any room in the heart of Tonga for a second affection, Messrs. Godeffroy will fill it.[77]

[72]Ibid.
[73]Baker had made the King believe that he would surely die without Baker to prescribe for him.
[74]King George to Ma'afu quoted by Gordon, Fiji, III, 101.
[75]Maudslay (acting consul-general and deputy commissioner for the Western Pacific, and vice-consul at Tonga) to Foreign Office, 23 Jan. 1879, PRO FO 68/164.
[76]Salisbury to Gordon, 13 June 1879, Fiji, III, 315.
[77]Ibid.

Salisbury authorized Gordon to negotiate a most-favoured-nation treaty with Tonga and told Count Münster, the German ambassador, that Tonga lay so close to Fiji that Britain could not "bear any predominance there of any other Power. . . ." Münster "professed the entire acquiescence of Germany in this view, and said the Pacific was large enough for both of us. . . ."[78] Sir Arthur was thus able to return to the Pacific with some assurance that Germany posed no immediate threat to Tonga and with authority to secure Britain's position by treaty.

Meanwhile Maudslay, who had arrived in Tonga in mid-June 1878, some three weeks after Baker's return, tried to hold the fort against Baker's attempts to regain his prestige. The Tongan parliament met for the first time free of Baker's pressure and, in accordance with the advice of Gordon and Maudslay, modified Baker's harsh laws. The King signed an interim agreement which had been negotiated by Gordon and which was to regulate Tongan-British relations pending the negotiation of a regular treaty. The Tongans found pleasure in their unwonted freedom to "talk about things like Tongans"[79] and in the fact that Maudslay's presence kept the low whites in order. At first Baker was subdued, probably because the Sydney Conference of the Wesleyan mission had privately taken him to task over the complaints lodged against him by Gordon. He contented himself with forecasting grim times for Tonga, making disparaging remarks about Gordon and Maudslay in his sermons, and winning to his side the King's grandson, Wellington Gu, the most Europeanized member of the royal family. Through the latter he attempted to prevent the King signing the interim treaty. Maudslay investigated Baker's mission extortions with a view to giving the Sydney Conference solid evidence on which to act against him. Baker retaliated by suspending from church appointments natives who gave Maudslay information. He forged a new alliance with Weber who visited Tonga in October 1878, and satisfied all the warrants of distress issued against natives for mission debts. Gratitude to Baker for relieving Tongans of their debts persuaded many to forgive him his past misdeeds and to resume their former allegiance to him. Fear drove others back to the missionary fold. Convinced that Maudslay's failure to do "something to Baker"[80] indicated that Baker had recovered his old power, many Tongans dared oppose him no longer. Maudslay then wrote two long dispatches to Salisbury[81] and a letter to Gordon[82] de-

[78]*Ibid.*, 17 June 1879.
[79]Maudslay to Gordon, 8 Aug. 1878, *Fiji*, III, 393–95.
[80]*Ibid.*, 28 Oct. 1878, 480–83.
[81]Maudslay to Salisbury, 23 and 24 Jan. 1879, *Fiji*, III, 503–10.
[82]Maudslay to Gordon, 25 Jan. 1879, *Fiji*, III, 510–16.

scribing Baker's missionary exactions, his control over government business, and his dealings with and support of the Germans. Gordon forwarded Maudslay's letter to the Sydney Conference, which decided to recall Baker because his usefulness in the Tongan mission was at an end. It also decided to send a commission to Tonga to investigate Maudslay's charges against him.

Meanwhile Gordon had returned to the Pacific, and in November 1879 he visited Tonga to negotiate a definite treaty similar to that signed with Samoa. With Baker again absent in New Zealand Gordon's visit passed off without unpleasant incidents. The terms of the treaty allowed twelve months for an exchange of ratifications. The months passed, and Gordon received no word from the Foreign Office, which in 1880 passed from Salisbury's to Granville's hands. Gordon feared that the diliatoriness of the Foreign Office would give the King, who was once again under Baker's influence, an excuse for not ratifying the treaty.

The Sydney Conference, as a result of its investigation of Maudslay's charges, had reduced Baker to an unpaid supernumerary and given him permission to rest a year in New Zealand. It could not, however, forbid him to visit Tonga. The secretary wrote Gordon saying that because "we are really trying to do God's work . . . I can trust God to interpose and help us."[83] The secretary's trust was evidently misplaced, for Baker had no intention of paying Tonga only a brief visit. Returning in June 1880 he took up residence in the mission house, resumed preaching in Zion Church, and, by securing from the King appointments as foreign minister and comptroller of the revenue, established himself as the dictator of Tonga. He proceeded to levy heavy taxes, to support German interests, to oppose the treaty with England, and to re-enact the former harsh laws respecting sex, drink, and sports.

Gordon could have prohibited Baker residing in Tonga, but he hesitated to invoke this power for two reasons. First he was reluctant to do anything which might harm the Wesleyan mission in the Pacific, whose work on the whole he approved. Secondly, he feared lest Baker's removal might introduce a period of anarchy in Tonga. On the theory that a bad government is better than none he allowed Baker to remain. Nevertheless he was not disposed to let him go on unchecked, and with Baker, Hunt, and various other adventurers in the Pacific islands in mind he proposed to Granville that British subjects be required, under penalties, to obtain licences before taking service under any native chief or king.[84] This proposal, however, concerned the long term. The

[83]Rev. B. Chapman to Gordon, 12 March 1880, Fiji, IV, 232–34.
[84]Gordon to Granville, 19 July 1880, enclosing draft regulation, Fiji, IV, 372–74.

question of the treaty was urgent. Should the treaty not be ratified no bar would exist to the grant by the King of exclusive trading privileges to the house of Godeffroy or to the virtual establishment of a German protectorate over Tonga.[85]

Gordon was prepared to take strong action to ensure ratification. He wrote to Granville:

You are possibly aware—at all events some of your colleagues are, . . . how repugnant to me, as a matter of good taste and good feeling as well as of policy, is the bullying of a small, semi-civilized, semi-barbarous state.

You must, therefore, give whatever weight is due to . . . my reluctant but decided conclusion that we cannot allow the King of Tonga to refuse to ratify the Treaty he has already agreed to without not only a loss of repute in the Pacific generally—a matter to which we might perhaps afford to be indifferent—but without a serious and perhaps dangerous diminution of the Queen's authority over her native subjects in this colony [Fiji].

If they see that she can be "snubbed" with impunity by the King of Tonga (and in native eyes the refusal to ratify will be a gross insult) they will begin to doubt her power, and I need not say the consequences of such a doubt are not easily calculated. . . .

There is not a single German naval officer on the station who is not working eagerly for the annexation of Samoa and Tonga, and . . . Mr. Baker's advice to King George not to ratify the treaty has been backed up by something like a threat from Captain Chuden of the [Imperial German ship] "Nautilus." So far as I am concerned I should be inclined to say, "Let the Germans annex what they please, and exercise influence where they please *except* in *Tonga*," for that is practically to annex and exercise influence over a large part of Fiji.[86]

Granville neither accepted Gordon's suggestion concerning licences nor hurried sending the treaty. Gordon was forced to ask King George Tubou for an extension of the ratification period. The King at first refused, and only the accidental presence of H.M.S. *Alert* and warnings by John Thurston (whom Gordon had sent as his personal representative) of Her Majesty's certain displeasure persuaded him to consent. Not until July 1882, when Gordon visited Tonga after leaving New Zealand, were the treaty ratifications exchanged.

Baker had meanwhile consolidated his position with the King and his grandson[87] and had been appointed premier. He had little success,

---

[85]Gordon had recently discovered that Baker had accepted the Order of the Red Eagle (some accounts say Black Eagle), third class, from the German government. Baker's action was contrary to the law prohibiting acceptance of foreign decorations without the permission of the Imperial government.

[86]Gordon to Granville, 3 Aug. 1880, PRO FO 58/168, *Fiji*, IV, 394–95.

[87]The King's son, David Uga, had died in New Zealand in 1880 and the return of his body to Tonga served as Baker's excuse to revisit the islands.

however, in making himself popular with Tongans generally. They feared and hated him. They groaned under the severe laws and heavy taxation which he had imposed. Many refused to plant crops, saying they would rather go hungry than have most of their produce go for taxes. In 1881 Baker regulated the times and places at which cricket (which had become popular over the previous two or three years) might be played. The natives declared that unless they could play where and when they chose they would not play at all. H. F. Symonds, the British vice-consul, thought it worth noticing that since the general introduction of cricket, petty pilfering and stealing (which the natives did not consider crimes but only exciting pastimes) had been comparatively unknown. He added that, at a meeting to discuss the new law, one man had exclaimed, "so we must give up cricket and take to stealing again[!]"[88]

Matters came to a head when a large number of representative Tongans met to complain of Baker and to petition the King for redress of grievances. The King was conciliatory, but said he would retain Baker in office. He advised the petitioners to go home and not to interfere in politics again. They took his advice, but Baker attacked them violently in his newspaper. They met to reply to him. The government then summoned ten of the leaders on charges of high treason. The magistrate found them not guilty, but warned them that if they offended again they would be hanged or banished. They then got up a petition containing 1,500 signatures asking Gordon to remove Baker from Tonga. The government arrested fourteen of the men, threw them into prison without charges or trial, kept them in irons, and heaped other indignities on them. The King, urged by Baker, said he intended to hang some of them. In forwarding a petition from a dozen Europeans asking for Baker's removal, the Vice-Consul warned of rebellion if the King went ahead with his plan.[89]

Since Gordon was about to visit Tonga to exchange the treaty ratifications, he was able to intervene. He had several talks with both the King and Baker pointing out that he could and would, if forced, remove Baker from Tonga. The prisoners having, in the interval, been charged with high treason, he stressed that they had been guilty at most of sedition. Convinced that Baker had intended to maintain his authority by "the most forceful measures," Gordon spoke strongly to him telling him

[88]PRO FO 58/173, f. 101.
[89]Symonds to Gordon (confidential), 6 Jan. 1882, enclosed in Gordon to Foreign Office, 28 Jan. 1882, and Symonds to Gordon, 20 March 1882, enclosed in Gordon to Foreign Office, 22 May 1882, PRO FO 58/177.

"how much odium he would justly bring upon himself, and how grave a responsibility he would incur, if he,—a minister of religion,—caused, or allowed, men to be put to death for the offence of seeking to remove him from his office . . . , and how futile it would be for him to attempt . . . to shelter himself under the plea that any such measure would be an act of the King, and not his own."[90] He further indicated to Baker that, in becoming the lawgiver and virtually irresponsible head of the executive of an independent state, he had obtained a position of usefulness attained by few but, at the same time, had assumed responsibiilty for the state's future welfare or disaster.[91]

Sir Arthur left Tonga convinced that he had saved the prisoners' lives but certain that Baker would rule Tonga as long as the King lived. "Were Mr. Baker dispossessed of power at the present moment," Gordon advised the Foreign Office, "the government must fall into the hands of some lower and more unscrupulous foreign adventurer, or . . . anarchy must at once ensue."[92] He hoped that the warning and fatherly advice he had given Baker would induce him to act more judiciously in future. This hope was to be disappointed. Baker was shrewd enough to realize why Gordon had not removed him from Tonga. He believed that future high commissioners would not remove him either.

Despite the worsening of Baker's tyranny[93] none of Gordon's immediate successors as high commissioner found that the advantages of removing him outweighed the dangers. In 1887 Sir Charles Mitchell even condoned Baker's action as prosecutor in the trial of six Tongans, who were sentenced to death for having made an attempt to assassinate him.[94] It was not until 1890, three years before the King's death, that Thurston, as high commissioner, ordered Baker to leave Tonga for two years.

Considering the limits of Sir Arthur Gordon's authority over Tonga he had done well. The High Commission Court had gone far to settle disputes between whites. The treaty (together with the decline of German influence after the failure of Godeffroys) had helped to guarantee the independence of Tonga and had ensured that Germany would have no influence in Fiji. The impact of Gordon's prestige upon the internal affairs of the country had served, though briefly, to lighten the burden of missionary exactions and to rekindle in Tongan hearts an appreciation of personal freedom and the joy of life. Nevertheless, we may question Gordon's wisdom in not removing the reprehensible Mr. Baker.

[90]Gordon to Foreign Office, 15 July 1882, PRO FO 58/177.
[91]*Ibid.*
[92]*Ibid.*
[93]For a brief account see Morrell, *Britain in the Pacific Islands*, 323–26.
[94]The sentences were carried out.

IV. THE HIGH COMMISSION IN OTHER AREAS OF THE WESTERN PACIFIC

It should be stressed that the reasons why the High Commission and consul-generalship worked reasonably well in Samoa and Tonga were that both groups had deputy commissioners with consular authority normally resident in them and that Gordon in Fiji was close enough to intervene personally when the occasion warranted. In most of the area under the High Commission, however, the order-in-council was, said Gordon in 1883, "practically powerless for good. . . ."[95]

Concerning the prevention and punishment of crime this comment was very nearly accurate. A few offences had been detected and punished, and possibly many others had been prevented out of fear for the consequences.[96] Still, the number of crimes prevented, or detected and punished, was probably negligible. Shortages of staff and money and Gordon's lack of time and transportation were obvious reasons. Even without these disabilities a provision of the order-in-council requiring a month's notice of a prosecution and the commencement of proceedings within three months of an alleged offence would normally have rendered this aspect of the high commissioner's work nearly futile.

Although the secretary of the Aborigines Protection Society credited Gordon with having exerted "every effort which wisdom or humanity could suggest . . . to secure substantial justice for the labourers,"[97] it is hard to see that Sir Arthur could have done much to regulate the Pacific labour traffic. As high commissioner he was required to superintend that traffic. The Colonial Office had no sooner given him this power with one hand than it had taken it away with the other by conferring authority on the governors of all the Australian colonies to issue licences to labour traders and to make regulations to govern the traffic. The governors in those colonies had to obey their political masters who were, at least in Queensland,[98] those who profited from the labour trade.

[95]*Report of a Commission appointed to enquire into the working of the Western Pacific Orders in Council and the nature of the measures requisite to secure the attainment of the objects for which those orders in council were issued*, Parl. Pap., 1884, LV [C-3905], hereafter cited as *Report of a Commission . . . into the working of the Western Pacific Orders in Council*. Although Commodores Hoskins and Wilson acted on this commission, it can be taken for granted that Gordon was the author of the report and that the others simply appended their signatures. Gordon spoke of it to Selborne as "My Western Pacific Report." (17 Nov. 1883, Stanmore Papers, 49218.)

[96]*Ibid.* Gordon had earlier written of this aspect of the High Commission's work as "far from useless" with "not a few offences" having been detected and punished. (Gordon to Kimberley, 16 July 1881, Parl. Pap., 1883, XLVII [C-3641], paper no. 23.)

[97]F. Chesson to Derby, 12 Sept. 1883, copy in Stanmore Papers, 49201.

[98]Besides Fiji, Queensland was the largest importer of Polynesian labour in the Pacific.

Des Voeux noted the case of a frustrated captain of a Queensland labour vessel who burned three native villages in the Lachlan Islands as well as the copra factory of a German whom the captain suspected of being the cause of his failure to obtain recruits. The facts at the captain's trial indicated that the Queensland authorities had been largely responsible for the outrages. Furthermore the Queensland Agent-General of Immigration had written to the captain: " 'There is only one comfort, you did nothing dishonourable or that you need in the least be ashamed of.' "[99] Des Voeux also called attention to the fact that the Queensland authorities had allowed a recruiter who had been dismissed for habitual kidnapping to be engaged by another Queensland ship.[100] Rev. D. Macdonald speaking at Melbourne in 1883, although noting a recent improvement in the labour traffic, nevertheless considered it "a blood blot on the name of Great Britain."[101] In 1880 Kimberley feared that "we have . . . a traffic which differs in little but name from slave trade. . . . It is the old African story over again."[102]

Gordon certainly believed that his regulation and supervision of the labour traffic had been "almost wholly and absolutely inoperative. . . ."[103] Five years after the inauguration of the Western Pacific High Commission, Gordon, Hoskins, and Wilson found that the labour trade continued to suffer from kidnapping and the purchase of recruits from chiefs; cajolery, misrepresentation, and breaches of promise by recruiters; total disregard by recruiters of tribal, chiefly, and family authority; recruitment of women for immoral purposes; failure of labour vessels to return labourers to their own islands or villages on expiry of their contracts;[104]

[99]Des Voeux, *My Colonial Service*, II, 91.   [100]*Ibid.*

[101]Reported by Melbourne *Argus*, 17 July 1883, extract printed in Parl. Pap., 1884, LV [C-3863], 12.

[102]Kimberley's minute, 21 Oct. 1880, on Gordon to Secretary of State, 16 Aug. 1880, PRO CO 83/23. The draft dispatch in reply quoted Kimberley's words, but Fuller minuted: "I doubt whether Lord Kimberley intended [these words] to be embodied as containing an admission not hitherto allowed. . . . Philanthropic societies . . . wd. be likely to fasten on them, if these papers are ever moved for & printed."

[103]Gordon to Kimberley, 16 July 1881.

[104]On 8 Nov. 1882 the Melbourne *Argus* noted that the labour vessel *Roderick Dhu* had landed some of her "return boys" at Paala, where they were immediately killed and eaten by the inhabitants, and that the *Helena* had landed three boys at Apii, where they met the same fate. (Copy filed in Stanmore Papers, 49239, f. 224.) Commodore Wilson observed that unless a returning labourer was landed not only on his own island but at his own village, "he is sure to be consigned to slavery, if not death, as well as the forfeiture of his hard-earned store of trade, in return for his three years of labour and expatriation. . . . Not infrequently . . . the unfortunates are landed anywhere, and have been seen gesticulating and wild with despair, as the boat pulls away. . . ." (Quoted by Justice Higinbotham in a speech at Melbourne reported by the Melbourne *Argus*, 17 July 1883.)

harsh treatment of, and heavy mortality among, recruits both at sea[105] and on the plantations; and, finally, the trade in firearms, which led to depopulation.[106] Commodores Wilson and Hoskins agreed with Gordon in thinking that the whole labour traffic should be prohibited unless its evils could be checked.[107] They believed the abuses could be eliminated by creating five districts in the islands to the west of Fiji each under a deputy commissioner who should be *ex officio* vice-consul. In addition the high commissioner should have a steam yacht which he could make available to each deputy commissioner for an annual inspection of his district. Each deputy commissioner should have a small sailing boat for shorter journeys. Regulation of the labour trade should be brought wholly under Imperial authority.[108]

The royal commissioners had further suggestions for the more efficient functioning of the High Commission. They recommended amending the order-in-council to allow the high commissioner a freer hand and to enable naval officers to bring offenders before the High Commission Court. They advised separating the High Commission from the government of Fiji and establishing High Commission headquarters in New Guinea. Finally, they recommended that the high commissioner–consul-general should report to one department only, whether Colonial Office or Foreign Office.[109]

Gordon and his colleagues warned that most of their suggestions, if put into practice, would require increased expenditure. This was just what the Colonial Office wished to avoid. Indeed, the Colonial Office under Kimberley had already attempted to rid itself entirely of responsibility for the high commissionership. In 1880 Herbert suggested giving the High Commission to the Admiralty when Gordon should cease to hold the office. Grant Duff, the parliamentary under-secretary, supported the idea. Kimberley believed it would be quite unprecedented and doubted whether the Admiralty could exercise the high commissioner-

[105]Harsh treatment did not occur in the traffic to Fiji after the beginning of 1880 when new and stringent regulations went into effect in that colony. See MacGregor's report, 19 May 1880, enclosed in Gordon to Secretary of State, 13 Sept. 1880, PRO CO 83/23.

[106]*Report of a Commission . . . into the working of the Western Pacific Orders in Council*, 20–24.

[107]*Ibid.*

[108]*Ibid.*, 27–28. Such regulation would entail employing better government agents and paying them partly from Imperial funds; requiring every colonial labour vessel to report to the deputy commissioner of the district to acquire a licence and an agent before recruiting, and to return afterwards to report before proceeding under heavy securities to its destination. Vessels returning labour would be forced to follow a similar procedure.

[109]*Ibid.*

ship.[110] Nevertheless, early in 1881, he made the suggestion to the Admiralty. Sir Cooper Key, the first sea lord, dismissed it abruptly telling Kimberley that the commodore of the Australian station already had enough on his hands and that the appearance of a naval officer as judge, jury, and executioner would be objectionable.[111] Herbert thought the Admiralty's refusal was based on an "imperfect understanding" of the whole question. "They do not know how the High Commission would work if properly administered by a naval man. . . ." He considered its failure to accept the responsibility "unfortunate," and since he felt that handing the High Commission to the Foreign Office would not be to anyone's advantage, he advocated "the entire & summary abolition of the High Commissionership."[112] A year later Herbert wrote to Gordon that although Gordon had done good work under adverse conditions he did not believe there would be any advantage in appointing a successor because it had been impossible to give the high commissioner the legal powers or ways and means to make his office thoroughly effective.[113]

With such defeatist views the Colonial Office was unlikely to welcome the practicable Gordon-Hoskins-Wilson report. Indeed, according to Gordon, Bramston indicated "very plainly that he was displeased with my Western Pacific Report and that we 'ought' to have reported in favour of handing over Pacific Affairs to the Australian Colonies."[114] Faced with this attitude Gordon never expected the report to be acted upon, and late in 1883 he resigned his high commissionership and departed for Ceylon in deep gloom over the future of the Pacific natives whom "I feel as though I had deserted, and who I have shewn when properly managed to be capable of much self government and by no means inevitably doomed to extinction."[115] Nevertheless he did not give up the fight. Turning to personal influence as always, he wrote to Gladstone, Selborne, and Derby,[116] urging resistance to Australasian ambitions in New Guinea and elsewhere in the Western Pacific. Lord Derby did nothing to lighten Gordon's heart. "We will do what is possible to protect native rights and save the existing population; but . . . there is only one ending possible. . . . All my observations on the temper

[110]Minutes 26 and 28 Aug. 1880, PRO CO 83/24, minute paper 13097.
[111]Sir Cooper Key to Commodore Wilson quoted by Gordon to Selborne, 13 Aug. 1881, Stanmore Papers, 49218.
[112]Herbert's minute, 23 June 1881, on Des Voeux to Kimberley, 24 Feb. 1881, PRO CO 83/25.
[113]Herbert to Gordon, 12 Sept. 1882, Stanmore Papers, 49201.
[114]Gordon to Selborne, 17 Nov. 1883, Stanmore Papers, 49218.
[115]Ibid.
[116]Lord Derby succeeded Kimberley as secretary of State for the colonies in December 1882.

and tendency of the colonial mind lead me to the conclusion that within the next generation or two we in England shall have nothing to say to Australasian affairs."[117]

Gordon based his antipathy to the Australasians and his opposition to the extension of their authority over the Western Pacific islands upon several considerations. He had direct experience of their crass and inhumane attitude to the culturally advanced Fijians and Maoris. He knew about the Australian policy to exterminate the primitive Australian "black-fellow"[118] and about the depredations (especially Queensland-ers') in the labour trade among the islands. Gordon deplored the failure of the Australian governments to regulate recruiting or properly to protect plantation labour. He resented the omission of some of the Australasian governments to publish (until 1879) the 1878 order-in-council and thus recognize him as high commissioner. To add injury to insult the Australians had then vigorously and unfairly denounced him as high commissioner for failing to protect whites against native out-rages.[119] The *Sydney Morning Herald* fully illustrated Australian mis-understanding of the High Commission's powers and objects:

The business entrusted to the High Commissioner was that of seeing that justice was done all round . . . but it can hardly be said that it has had this effect among the Natives. The aim of Sir Arthur Gordon's policy has been to curb the excesses of the whites rather than those of the blacks. The assump-tion is that the Natives of the South Seas are in danger of being victimized by unscrupulous traders. It can hardly be said that the assumption has been a groundless one. . . . But although the conduct of the traders may extenuate the atrocities of the Natives it can never justify them. . . . Those that know them best tell us that the bulk of them kill because killing is a delight.[120] In this congenial occupation they have been encouraged rather than re-strained by the policy of the British authorities. . . .
The reason . . . is partly that the authorities in England are not sufficiently concerned about the Natives of the South Seas to encourage a vigorous

[117]Derby to Gordon, 4 Dec. 1883, Stanmore Papers, 49201.
[118]"At this moment," Gordon wrote to Selborne in 1881, "the Govt of Queens-land, with full approval of the overwhelming majority of people is pursuing a system worthy of the Spaniards in the worst West Indian days." (30 Nov. 1881, Stanmore Papers, 49218.)
[119]Gordon had no authority whatever to punish natives of the Western Pacific for offences against whites. Should those offences amount to acts of war the navy could take reprisals. All Gordon could do was to give advice as to the nature of the punishment should the navy ask for it.
[120]This was a slander against the natives as A. N. Murray (a missionary of the London Missionary Society who had spent forty years in New Guinea) testified when, on 3 Dec. 1880, he wrote to the *Sydney Daily Telegraph* that "in the vast majority of cases the outrages committed by Natives are occasioned by the conduct of foreign visitors." (Printed in Parl. Pap., 1883, XLVII [C-3641].)

policy in regard to them, and partly that there is still a feeling in England that the misconduct of black races must be corrected not by canon [sic] balls, but by Christian philanthropy. This feeling is as strong in the House of Commons as it is in Exeter Hall.[121]

When the Australian Inter-colonial Conference at Sydney in 1881 made similar imputations against Gordon, he made what Kimberley called an "able refutation" of them,[122] pointing out that he was being criticized for not exercising a jurisdiction that he had been forbidden to assume, that he had no control over the ships of the Australian station, and that the High Commission had not been instituted to protect whites from natives. He asked why Australians did not understand the well-recognized principle that those who freely took their lives in their hands forfeited the right to the support of the state whose protection they had left.[123]

Added to the foregoing counts against the Australasians was Gordon's apprehension that if they were successful in taking control of much of the Western Pacific his Fijian experiment must inevitably perish. He had "so much experience of the almost incredible weakness of the C[olonial] O[ffice] in giving way to noisy demands, and of the great indifference felt as to the fate of natives . . ."[124] that he could not avoid fearing the Australians might get their way. In 1880 Queensland had been allowed to annex the islands of the Torres Strait and to dispose of the lands of many natives. In April 1883 Queensland sent an agent to New Guinea to proclaim as British territory the portion of the island not under Dutch ownership. Aware of the "relief from all responsibility [for New Guinea] which annexation by a self-governing colony would bring" to the Colonial Office,[125] Gordon reacted vigorously. He wrote to Glad-

---

[121]*Sydney Morning Herald*, 7 Dec. 1880, Parl. Pap., 1883, XLVII [C-3641], paper no. 13.

[122]Kimberley to Gordon (private), 19 May 1881, Stanmore Papers, 49201.

[123]Extracts from a memorandum by the High Commissioner for the Western Pacific, 26 Feb. 1881, printed as paper no. 14, Parl. Pap., 1883, XLVII [C-3641]. Although Kimberley privately called Gordon's memorandum a "complete answer" to the Australians (Kimberley to Gordon [private], 19 May 1881), he did not say this publicly. Instead, he told the Australian Conference that he was conferring with the Admiralty as to the best mode of dealing with the problem of native atrocities. It was probably in deference to the Australians that Kimberley proposed that the Admiralty take over the high commissionership which Gordon interpreted as an attempt by the Secretary of State to deprive him of the high commissioner-ship. (Gordon to Selborne, 13 Aug. 1881, Stanmore Papers, 49218.)

[124]Gordon to Selborne, 12 Dec. 1883, Stanmore Papers, 49218.

[125]*Ibid.*, 16 April 1883. "I am not at all pleased," wrote Gordon to Selborne on 21 April 1883, "by the bias which has been shewn all along at the C.O. in favour of Queensland—and, . . . of the labour trade,—and which has gone far to render my efforts as High Commissioner nugatory." (Stanmore Papers, 49218.)

stone, Derby, and Selborne protesting strongly against Queensland's action and calling for its repudiation.

Queensland's proposal, Gordon informed Gladstone, raised two distinct questions: should New Guinea be annexed at all, and, if so, should it form part of Queensland? Gordon believed that the Imperial government ought to answer "no" to both.

To assume (unasked), the sovereignty of several millions of savage and semi-civilized natives, seems to me undesirable; because (as L[or]d Derby in former days phrased it), England has already black subjects enough; it seems to me somewhat immoral; because we shall . . . take from them their independence, & I fear . . . other, & perhaps dearer, rights; it seems to [me] impolitic; because, no consent being given, it is probable that there will . . . be resistance . . . which will be styled "rebellion," and suppressed by force; and it seems to me unfortunate at the present moment; as absolutely shutting our mouths in the way of remonstrance . . . to the proceedings of France in the way of annexation.

But even if . . . it were thought necessary for political reasons . . . that New Guinea should be taken possession of by the Crown, I should still more earnestly protest against its being placed under the control of the government of Queensland, than which I can hardly conceive any government more unfit for such a task.[126]

Several circumstances, Gordon continued, disqualified the government of Queensland from exercising dominion over native races. Queenslanders took their idea of "the nigger" generally from their own extremely primitive aborigines. The habit of regarding natives in Queensland as vermin had given the average Queenslander "a tone of brutality and cruelty" in his dealings with "blacks."

I have heard men of culture and refinement, of the greatest humanity and kindness to their fellow whites . . . , talk, not only of the *wholesale* butchery . . . , but of the *individual* murder of natives, exactly as they would talk of a day's sport, or of having had to kill some troublesome animal. This is not the spirit in which to undertake the government of native races.[127]

Moreover, since the chief industries of Queensland required black labour, Queensland would use New Guinea for recruiting without restrictions except those its Parliament chose to impose;[128] and the labour traffic

[126]Gordon to Gladstone, 20 April 1883, copy enclosed in Gordon to Selborne, 20 April 1883, Stanmore Papers, 49218. This letter is printed in full in Paul Knaplund's article "Sir Arthur Gordon on the New Guinea Question, 1883," *Historical Studies Australia and New Zealand*, VII, no. 27, Nov. 1956, 328–33.
[127]*Ibid.*
[128]Commodore Hoskins wrote to Gordon to say that Warner, a partner with Sir Thomas MacIlwraith, the Queensland premier, in an enormous estate in Northern Queensland, had told him that the annexation of New Guinea would be their "salvation" as they would be able to get whatever labour they wanted. (Gordon to Selborne, 11 June 1883, Stanmore Papers, 49218.)

being then a coasting trade, the Imperial government would not be able to interfere with it in any way.

> You are engaged at this moment in . . . an endeavour which commands my heartiest & most thorough sympathy—to extend local self government in India. . . . Will the same hands . . . deliberately make over the millions of New Guinea . . . to the absolute control of those who will despise—use— and destroy them?
> I do not know that I have ever felt more strongly, or more deeply, on any question, and whether I think of you as the foremost statesman of the time, or simply as a friend whom I love and venerate, I am equally anxious that the consummation of what seems to me an iniquity should not be associated with your honoured name.[129]

To Selborne, to whom he had sent a copy of his letter to Gladstone, Gordon wrote:

> If with our eyes open, we permit an enormous wrong to be done, which cannot be done without our consent, we are morally responsible for what follows. . . . We shall not be free from guilt, if we give our consent to what is tantamount to handing over the millions of New Guinea to destruction. . . . If we do this thing "the Lord God of recompenses will surely requite."[130]

Averse to imperial expansion, Gladstone and Selborne welcomed and used Gordon's arguments.[131] Lord Derby, the irresolute colonial minister, was less responsive. A large section of the British press including *The Times*[132] was applauding Queensland's action and Ashley and Herbert, Derby's parliamentary under-secretary and permanent under-secretary, and several other members of his staff supported it.

[129]Gordon to Gladstone, 20 April 1883.

[130]Gordon to Selborne, 7 May 1883, Stanmore Papers, 49218.

[131]Selborne thought annexation of New Guinea would be "impolitic . . . and also morally unjustifiable, if it were done without demonstrable necessity and without that sort of invitation and concurrence, on the part of the principal native tribes or their rulers which we had in the case of Fiji." (Quoted by Morrell, *Britain in the Pacific Islands*, 250–51.) Gladstone agreed. Selborne and Gladstone probably did not know that (as the New Guinea missionary W. G. Lawes had told Gordon) New Guinea had numerous tribes and few powerful chiefs. This fact, however, scarcely rendered their argument concerning the immorality of annexation invalid because Lawes had also said that labourers could be obtained in New Guinea only "by force or deceit, not otherwise." (Gordon to Selborne, 11 June 1883, quoting a letter from Lawes to Commodore Erskine.)

[132]*The Times* accepted the annexation as a *fait accompli* although it suggested that New Guinea should be governed by all the Australian colonies rather than Queensland. Gordon, who sent a letter to the editor signed "D. C. L." which appeared on 15 May 1883, thought this might be a little better but not much. In his opinion all the Australian colonies had equally low views of "the nigger" and all would be equally interested in acquiring native lands. "It is at *Sydney* & at *Melbourne*, not in Queensland, that the greatest indignation is felt & expressed against me for the steps I took to secure the native rights to land in Fiji." (Gordon to Selborne, 7 May 1883.)

The weeks passed without a decision by the British government. Gordon fretted. Delay could only add to public conviction in Britain and Australia that Britain would acquiesce in the annexation and Queensland would rush forward with preparations for occupation. He pressed the Colonial Office, if it considered annexation inevitable, to place New Guinea under the high commissioner and to designate New Guinea as his headquarters. On 11 June he met his old enemy Sir Charles Dilke, who told him of Herbert's observation that the proposition the Colonial Office intended to make to the cabinet was substantially Gordon's.[133] Selborne, Northbrook, and Herbert all assured Gordon that it had been decided to repudiate Queensland's proclamation. Nevertheless, Ashley announced in the Commons a few days later that no decision respecting the annexation had been reached. In the circumstances Sir Arthur found this announcement inexplicable. His fears found no relief until July when Lord Derby told the House of Lords[134] that the annexation had been repudiated and informed Queensland that her action had been "most unjustified" and that, even if annexation had been justified, the territory would not have been allowed to become part of Queensland. Derby observed that the opinion of the Australian colonies that New Guinea should be brought under British rule had great weight with Her Majesty's government. He hoped that the Australian colonies together would finance the policy which they wanted the Imperial government to follow, should Britain feel it right to adopt such policy. On behalf of Britain he offered to strengthen the naval force on the Australian station if Queensland would furnish a reasonable sum to place one or more deputies of the high commissioner on the New Guinea coast. "A protectorate thus gradually established over the coast would be capable of meeting the principal requirements of the case for some time to come. . . ."[135] Except for the point concerning Queensland's financial contribution (which Gordon opposed on the ground that this would allow Queensland to exercise some control over New Guinea) this proposition was consistent with the plan Gordon had suggested to the Colonial Office.

[133]Dilke later wrote: "On June 12th, 1883, there was hatched a scheme for the partial annexation of New Guinea, which had been prepared by the Chancellor [Selborne], Mr. Gladstone, and Sir Arthur Gordon, of Fiji and New Zealand fame. On the 13th a Cabinet decided to go slowly in this matter, and they went so slowly that we lost half of our half of New Guinea to Germany and almost lost the whole of it." (S. Gwynn and G. M. Tuckwell, *Life of Sir Charles Dilke*, I, 536.)

[134]Derby's House of Lords speech of 2 July 1883, House of Lords, *Debates*, 3rd ser., CCLXXXI, cols. 14–19.

[135]Derby to the Acting Governor of Queensland, 11 July 1883, Parl. Pap., 1883, XLVII [C-3691], paper no. 21.

Herbert had once observed that "when money is in question they [the Australians] generally retire with dignity in favour of the British tax payer. . . ."[136] If the Imperial authorities counted on the Australians beating a dignified retreat at this time they were to be disappointed. At the convention of representatives of the Australasian colonies in Sydney in 1883, the colonies were unanimous concerning the necessity of annexing New Guinea. Queensland, Victoria, and New Zealand favoured contributing toward the expense. In July the agents-general for New South Wales, New Zealand, Queensland, and Victoria wrote to Lord Derby attempting to show that the High Commission had failed, that there was real danger of foreign annexations, which would damage Australasian interests and imperil Britain's strategic position, and that unless some foreign power took the Western Pacific islands Britain eventually would have to occupy them. "The same impelling power, not of mere desires but of events, which induced the Imperial Government to do at last in Fiji what they so often refused, is constantly at work, and incessantly being renewed and strengthened with regard to the Western Pacific."[137] Britain should intervene in the interests of civilization. The Australasian colonies were, said the agents-general, taking steps to act in concert and to contribute to the cost of what they were asking Britain to do.

In reply,[138] Lord Derby noted that there was less uncertainty about the claims of foreign powers in the Western Pacific than the agents-general had suggested. Samoa and Tonga were independent states. Fiji and Rotumah were British. France and Britain had an understanding respecting the New Hebrides. New Caledonia and the Loyalty Islands were French. New Britain, New Ireland, the Solomons, and Santa Cruz Islands lay far from Australia and were not suitable for white settlement. Lord Derby, however, had been much impressed by the strength and unanimity of the Australasian demands. He was now prepared not only to act with respect to New Guinea in accordance with the terms of his 11 July letter to the government of Queensland, but to consider "any similar definite proposal" respecting other islands that the Australasian colonies might wish to make to him.[139]

Gordon's relief at the repudiation of Queensland's annexation of New Guinea was brief. Throughout the summer and autumn of 1883 "annexation fever" continued to rage in Australasia. Victoria asked for

[136]Herbert to Gordon, 4 May 1875, Stanmore Papers, 49199.
[137]The agents-general to Lord Derby, 21 July 1883, Parl. Pap., 1883, XLVII [C-3814], paper no. 18.
[138]Colonial Office to the agents-general, 31 Aug. 1883, Parl. Pap., 1883, XLVII [C-3814], paper no. 39.
[139]Ibid.

the annexation of the Solomons, New Hebrides, and other groups. Some of the discontented Fiji planters demanded annexation to New Zealand or to one of the "free" Australian colonies. The government and legislature of New Zealand talked of going to "the assistance and responding to the wishes of the people of Fiji."[140] A bill was introduced into the New Zealand legislature to authorize the government to negotiate with the chiefs or people of any Pacific islands and to receive them into union with New Zealand.[141] Sir Arthur could not believe that "our government will have the weakness—I had almost said the criminality—to listen to such a proposal . . ." but New Zealand's offer to take over the Fiji debt was doubtless a tempting bait.[142] Moreover, Lord Derby had been "seized with new terrors as to the necessity of 'pleasing' the Australian agitators . . .,"[143] and "a strong undercurrent in favour of the filibusters" pervaded the Colonial Office.[144] Strengthening Gordon's fears was the fact that Queensland agents continued to remain in New Guinea to which no deputy commissioner had as yet been sent.

Still, Gordon continued to be consulted by Gladstone on Pacific affairs. This gave him an opportunity to exercise some influence over the Imperial government's course in that region. Late in September Gladstone's private secretary sent Gordon letters from Derby and Lord Normanby[145] concerning the Australian "annexation fever." The Prime Minister wanted Gordon's "diagnosis of the disease."[146] Gordon stated what he thought were the causes and made suggestions for reducing the fever:

The Australian agitation for sweeping annexations in the Pacific is . . . to a great extent unreal, and does not reflect the genuine feelings of the working and thinking part of the community.

In so far as the desire is genuine, it is in a great degree due to a real, though unreasonable, fear of the influx of criminals into Australia from convict stations, which foreign powers *may* hereafter establish in the Pacific, and to a strong *jingo* feeling, in which a vague sentiment that it is a fine thing to extend Australian dominion is combined with great ignorance of actual facts. But, in addition to those influenced by these rather hazy views, are two powerful classes, who have a direct interest in annexation, and who work on the passions and prejudices of those who have none. I refer to the sugar growers of the north, and the ship owners engaged in what is called the island trade. These are both very powerful interests, which every Colonial

[140]Gordon to Selborne, 13 Oct. 1883, Stanmore Papers, 49218.

[141]*Ibid.* Thurston and Gordon believed the reason for this bill was to be found in the New Zealand Attorney-General's (Fred Whitaker) financial relations with Shirley Baker of Tonga.

[142]*Ibid.*   [143]*Ibid.*, 1 Oct. 1883.

[144]*Ibid.*, 17 Nov. 1883.   [145]Governor of Victoria.

[146]Sir Edward Hamilton to Gordon, 21 Sept. 1883, quoted by Knaplund, *Gladstone's Foreign Policy*, 101–2.

politician will seek to consolidate and propitiate, if he can do so without offence to other sections of the community.[147]

Gordon saw no reason "for the present" to resort to extreme measures although he agreed with Thurston in fearing that "this Jingo fever . . . will urge Foreign Powers to take action upon what as yet have been only half intentions with them."[148] He believed that the High Commission, if improved in accordance with the recommendations contained in the report that he was about to forward to the Colonial Office,[149] would furnish "all the requisite machinery for exerting as much control over British subjects . . . and influence over natives . . . as it is at present desirable to exercise or assume."[150]

Gordon's letter had the effect he desired. Although Gladstone was prepared to consider Australian annexation of New Guinea should the Australian colonies form "some kind of political union,"[151] he was looking for arguments against Britain undertaking annexation on behalf of the Australians. Armed by Gordon he rejected Lord Derby's late autumn conclusion that "as regards New Guinea we cannot hold out against the demand for a protectorate."[152] Gordon himself left England in November. While at home he could often "anticipate mischief" by a word to Gladstone or Selborne, but he could not do this from Ceylon. He begged Selborne to keep a vigilant eye on Pacific Affairs and to re-member that " 'masterly inaction' just now, means simply letting the colonies and labour traders do as they will. If after our report [on the High Commission], nothing is done, those who do nothing will in fact have taken very momentous action."[153]

Although none of the Australasian colonies had as yet voted any money, Lord Derby, in May 1884, stated that if they would supply £15,000 he would immediately appoint a high commissioner or a deputy commissioner to New Guinea, give him large independent powers, and furnish him with a staff and transportation. Queensland and Victoria agreed to guarantee the sum and Derby, influenced by Bismarck's rejection of "the Australian Monroe Doctrine in the South Pacific," recommended to the cabinet the establishment of a formal British protectorate over eastern New Guinea. The cabinet took more

[147]Gordon to Gladstone, 8 Oct. 1883, printed in full by Knaplund, "Sir Arthur Gordon on the New Guinea Question, 1883," 328–33.

[148]Thurston to Gordon, 12 Aug. 1883, copy enclosed in Gordon to Selborne, 13 Oct. 1883.

[149]See above, pp. 290–91.   [150]Gordon to Gladstone, 8 Oct. 1883.

[151]Gladstone to Derby, 19 May 1883, quoted by Knaplund, Gladstone's Foreign Policy, 104.

[152]Derby to Gladstone, 7 Dec. 1883, ibid., 108.

[153]Gordon to Selborne, 17 Nov. 1883, from Port Said, Stanmore Papers, 49218.

than a month to decide. Meantime Germany, from secretly and carefully prepared positions, made her move to annex New Britain and the north coast of New Guinea east of Dutch territory. It is unnecessary here to follow the subsequent Anglo-German negotiations[154] which in 1886 resulted in the demarcation of their respective spheres of influence and in Australia's disgust and anger with the mother country.

It is possible to assert that Gordon's arguments to Gladstone and Selborne against Australasian expansionism contributed to the cabinet indecision that allowed Germany to occupy so much of the Western Pacific[155] and in particular so much of New Guinea. If Gordon misjudged German intentions in the Pacific, so too did the British government misjudge them. Robert Meade of the Colonial Office was "nobody's fool." Yet even he heard nothing of the German intention although he was visiting Berlin officially when the German flag was hoisted in New Guinea. Although it is easy after the event to say that Australasian fears of foreign intervention were justified, the fact is that the Australians had no special sources of information.[156] Furthermore, they had no special claim to New Britain, which, at the time, lay outside Australia's vital strategic sphere and in which the Germans had built up a considerable trading establishment. Indeed, Australasian jingoism[157]

[154]See Marjorie G. Jacobs' article "Bismarck and the Annexation of New Guinea," *Historical Studies Australia and New Zealand*, V, no. 17, Nov. 1952, 14–26; and Morrell, *Britain in the Pacific Islands*, 254–62, for summaries.

[155]It should not be forgotten, however, that Bismarck was in a position to blackmail the British government by threatening to side with France over Egypt.

[156]The only clue to German intentions was the reference by deputy Bamberger (in the German Budget Commission late in June 1884) to the von Hansemann plan to buy land in northern New Guinea and this did not necessarily presage the founding of a German colony. (Jacobs, "Bismarck and the Annexation of New Guinea," 19.) The Foreign Office noted the alleged intended purchase and, in mid-September, passed the information to the Colonial Office. Mercer thought the news might be a reason for Britain adopting a decided attitude toward southeastern New Guinea. Fuller minuted: "If this news is really true, Australia would never forgive this Office." Herbert, however, proposed to rely on Gladstone's recent announcement that the southern shore of New Guinea would come under British protection and on Germany's recognition of the "natural desire" of Australians that the south shore should be under British control. (Minutes on Foreign Office to Colonial Office, 17 Sept. 1884, PRO CO 537/136.)

[157]Germans were doubtless a little disturbed at statements, such as the following, which emanated from the Australian press: "The spirit of enterprise is too deeply implanted in the heart of the Anglo-Saxon to ever allow his restless nature to remain in quiescence while there are new lands to conquer, or new sources of commerce to open up . . . ," and, "we are the Colonists *par excellence* of the world, . . . French may be the language of courts and diplomatists, English is that of enterprise and action. These islands lie at our very doors, we have but to stretch out our hand and they are ours. . . ." (Extracts from the *Sydney Daily Telegraph* and the *Evening News* respectively [late 1880 or early 1881], included in paper no. 13, Parl. Pap., 1883, XLVII [C-3641].

and (as Morrell has observed[158]) the activities of the Queensland labour traders probably forced the hand of the Germans in New Britain. Once they had decided to consolidate themselves there, the north coast of New Guinea was of nearly as much strategic value to them as they admitted the south coast was to Australia. Moreover, the Australians had none but a strategic right to any part of New Guinea and only a similar right to the southeastern portion. Over this Britain had established an unchallenged protectorate in the closing months of 1884, and had appointed Major General Sir Peter Scratchley as special commissioner. The Australians were to furnish the cost of the protectorate and also a council of advice that Gordon, who admitted he found it difficult to write with moderation on the subject of New Guinea, said would be a "council of dictation."

On the way to Australia and New Guinea Scratchley visited Gordon in Ceylon. Gordon took pains to explain his views on governing native peoples and found the Special Commissioner responsive. Sir Arthur, nevertheless, believed that the Australian governments who were to pay the piper would also call the tune. He remonstrated to Selborne:

> You have really done exactly that which you said you would not do: made over the millions of New Guinea to the tender mercies of the Australian mob. I entertain a very strong opinion as to the moral character of this step which I am willing to believe is only adopted because it is believed to be "necessary." Oh! that you could see how wholly unnecessary such departure from right is, and how little respect is really due to the pothouse politicians of Australia, who on such matters may be very safely ignored![159]

For various reasons the administration of New Guinea turned out much more favourably than Gordon anticipated. The Queensland election of late 1883 had brought Sir Samuel Griffith's Liberal party to power. The new government strengthened recruiting regulations in 1884. In 1885, as the result of the atrocities committed by six Queensland labour vessels in New Guinea waters in 1884, it passed a bill which, in effect, provided for abolition of the labour trade after the end of 1890.[160] Victoria's protest that Special Commissioner Scratchley's duties as deputy commissioner were partly imperial persuaded the British government to provide £18,000 for a ship to serve as his headquarters. Finally, Griffith's pleas and the German occupation of northeastern

[158]*Britain in the Pacific Islands*, 255.

[159]Gordon to Selborne, 5 Jan. 1885, Stanmore Papers, 49219.

[160]I. D. McNaughtan, "Colonial Liberalism, 1851–1892," *Australia: A Social and Political History*, ed. Gordon Greenwood, 127. The act prohibited the negotiation of further labour contracts after the end of 1890.

New Guinea led Derby to substitute the Queen's sovereignty for the protectorate.[161]

Scratchley reached New Guinea in late August 1885, but died before the end of the year. Gordon mourned his death. In losing him and Wilson[162] he had lost the two men who, after Thurston and MacGregor, best understood and appreciated his views on native policy and were most determined to carry them out.[163] Scratchley had, said Gordon, done his work in the same manner and spirit as he himself would have, so far as "thwarted in Australia and neglected in Downing St. he was allowed to do any work at all."[164] He feared that Scratchley's successor might prove less scrupulous concerning native interests. He worried unnecessarily. Although for the next year and a half the administration of John Douglas (a former premier of Queensland on whom as the most experienced man on the spot the mantle of special commissioner had fallen) cared little for such interests, July 1887 saw the selection of William MacGregor, Gordon's friend and Fiji helper, as first administrator of British New Guinea.

MacGregor had sought the post. In June 1886 he had written Gordon:

> The lessons I have learned from you are I feel lessons that fit me better for administration, especially of the particular kind required in New Guinea than for anything else. Then I could put into practice many of the principles which I believe are founded on a high sense of justice. . . . It seems to me therefore that my duty would be to plant your school in New Guinea if I can obtain that appointment. . . .
> It is time that some of the young men of your school, who think they understand it, who certainly believe in it, got into the lines of administration. . . .[165]

The fact that MacGregor preached Gordon's maxims on native government before the Australian Federal Council and that the Australian governments still found him acceptable as administrator indicated a growing sense of responsibility, a deeper understanding, and a greater humanity among Australians. Perhaps, after all, Gordon's ten-year advocacy of native rights had fallen upon fewer deaf ears than he had thought. If so, his sojourn in the Pacific had not been as vain as so many

[161]Morrell, *Britain in the Pacific Islands*, 261. Queensland, on behalf of all the Australian colonies, was to guarantee administrative expenses, supervise the expenditure, and see that the administration was conducted on principles meeting general approval. (Morrell, 407.)

[162]J. C. Wilson had recently retired as commodore of the Australian station.

[163]Gordon to Selborne, 31 July 1886, Stanmore Papers, 49219.

[164]*Ibid.*, 4 Jan. 1886.

[165]MacGregor to Gordon, 5 June 1886, Stanmore Papers, 49203.

of his letters indicate he believed it.[166] Certainly MacGregor's eleven-year administration of New Guinea bore most of the hall-marks of the Gordon system. Although a man of remarkable intelligence and independent judgment, MacGregor adopted most of the fundamental Fiji ordinances, adapting them, where necessary, to the different circumstances of New Guinea.[167] In 1889, for example, he established a native regulations board and a system of district courts on the Fijian model and, in the following year, formed a native constabulary. In writing to Gordon concerning his projected native employment ordinance of 1892, he called it the most important work he had done for a long time. He promised Gordon a copy of the draft ordinance telling him that he would see "how the doctrines of the Gordon school are applied in it. That will not surprise you: but the mere fact of its being highly appreciated by the Government of Queensland will shew you that, after all, Queensland may not be so bad as represented."[168]

Arthur Gordon's influence in the Western Pacific thus lived on through the application of his principles of native government in New Guinea, first through MacGregor and then through the latter's successor G. R. LeHunte, another of the young men from Fiji. After LeHunte's retirement came a short interval before the appointment of J. H. P. Murray, whose thirty-two year administration drew heavily upon the policies and administrative system established by MacGregor. Gordon's influence also endured in the High Commission. For most of the decade and a half after he gave up the office, two more of his disciples, Des Voeux (1883–85) and Thurston (1887–97), held it. Of course the High Commission's geographical scope narrowed after the Anglo-German demarcation of 1886. Moreover, the Colonial Office made no serious attempt to effect the recommendations of the Gordon-Hoskins-Wilson report, which had aimed at increasing the efficiency of the High Commission.

[166]For example in 1884 he exclaimed: "How I wish now that I had never gone to Fiji at all in 1875 . . . !" (Gordon to Lady Sophia Palmer [Dec. 1884], Stanmore Papers, 49221.)

[167]See Morrell, *Britain in the Pacific Islands*, 409–22, for a summary of MacGregor's administration of New Guinea. Students of British Empire history can look forward to Professor Roger Joyce's biography of MacGregor which is in course of preparation.

[168]MacGregor to Gordon, 13 Oct. 1890, Stanmore Papers, 49203. In one important particular Gordon's Fiji experiment could not be extensively applied in New Guinea. As a rule, New Guinea chiefs had much less authority than Fijian chiefs and could not, therefore, fulfil the rôle in native self-government that the Fijian chiefs did.

VIII

CEYLON, 1883–1890

❧

"WHAT LUXURY my work here is to me after New Zealand!" exclaimed Gordon soon after his arrival in Ceylon. "It is work of great interest and it is real."[1] For many years he had desired appointment to this rich, populous, and important colony which offered an ambitious and energetic governor scope for his talents, opportunity for the exercise of almost unlimited power, and a position "important enough to be free from the element of the ridiculous which . . . is supposed to attach to a Colonial Governorship."[2] He had been quick to accept the challenge of ruling Ceylon.

When Gordon arrived in Ceylon he found it less neglected than he had found Trinidad and Mauritius, the other long-established Crown colonies he had governed. Ceylon's size, population, and importance ensured it a fairly unbroken succession of capable governors. Nevertheless, much needed to be done. Most important were, first, to re-establish the ancient irrigation system in order to provide means of raising native living standards and, secondly, to extend the system of transport to encourage the colony's exports. Ceylon's economy had recently suffered a severe blow from decreased coffee production because a leaf disease had destroyed a large proportion of the coffee trees. More roads and railways were needed so that new areas could be opened to tea cultivation and tea planters could be given cheaper access to the ports.

[1]Gordon to Mary Gladstone, 25 Dec. 1883, in L. M. Phillipps and B. Christian, *Some Hawarden Letters*, 161.
[2]Gordon to Selborne, 12 Dec. 1883, Stanmore Papers, 49218.

Under ordinary circumstances, neither rejuvenating the island's irrigation system nor extending its transport facilities would have presented difficulties to an energetic and determined governor such as Gordon. In 1884, however, Ceylon's circumstances were far from normal. For several years the world depression had been crippling her trade and reducing her income. Moreover, an excessive annual contribution for defence reduced still further the money available for the public works that would increase the island's productivity and eventually improve its economy.

Gordon knew about Ceylon's most pressing needs before he left England. Although he had formulated tentative plans for his administration—especially for speeding irrigation works—he realized that, in view of falling revenues, he could not immediately act energetically. During his first few months in office he was content to acquaint himself with the island and its administrative system. With an area of some 25,000 square miles and a population close on three million, Ceylon required a more elaborate administrative system than the smaller Crown colonies. The island was thus divided into several provinces each ruled by a lieutenant-governor or government agent assisted by a number of subordinate officers. The efficiency of this system depended upon the quality of the provincial administrators and upon how closely the governor supervised them. In Fiji Gordon had selected his own assistants and had over-seen everything. Ceylon could not be governed in such a personal fashion. Although Gordon did not attempt to change the administrative system he supervised it closely and tried to secure more energetic and efficient men for the civil service. His attempts to raise the quality of the civil service were to lead him into a long and, at times, bitter controversy with the Colonial Office over methods of appointing officials.

As time went by, Gordon discovered other facets of the colony's life that required reform: the administration of justice, the make-up of the legislative council, and the method of controlling the so-called "Buddhist temporalities." These were to be important reforms, but none so great as Gordon's revival of irrigation works or his extension of the road and rail system. These were vital to the colony's future.

Gordon had just begun to put his irrigation and railway plans into operation when he came face to face with a financial crisis that forced him to postpone them until he had dealt with it. He was at Nuwara Eliya[3] on 3 May 1884 when he heard by telegraph that the Oriental

[3]The governor's summer residence in the hills.

Bank had suspended payments. The Oriental Bank had been forced to take this action because land values, upon which it had speculated heavily, had dropped spectacularly on account of the worsening depression.

Normally a bank failure would not have seriously harmed the colony. Depositors and shareholders would have lost money and perhaps a few businesses would have gone bankrupt, but there would have been no other damage. With the Oriental Bank, it was a different matter. There were but three banks in Ceylon, only two of which were banks of issue, and the Oriental Bank's currency made up 80 per cent of all the notes in circulation.

Gordon returned at once to Colombo where he found the situation deteriorating rapidly. The Oriental Bank's suspension of payments had made its notes valueless and had shaken popular confidence in all paper currency. These developments had led to an almost entire cessation of trade, to pressure on the remaining bank of issue, the Chartered Mercantile Bank, to convert its notes to silver, and to a refusal by traders to sell rice except for silver. Since silver was in short supply in Ceylon, rice for estate workers became almost unobtainable. Moreover, the Postmaster-General had forbidden postmasters to cash post office orders because of the shortage of silver in the colonial treasury.

Gordon immediately summoned the bank managers to meet him. They proposed that the government of Ceylon guarantee Oriental Bank notes circulating in Ceylon, amounting to some Rs 3,200,000.[4] In return they undertook to accept Oriental Bank notes at face value. A delegation from the Chamber of Commerce made a similar proposal. Sir Arthur considered the consequences. If he refused the guarantee, public distrust of notes would be intensified, the demand for silver would doubtless bring down the Chartered Mercantile Bank, and the government itself might well have to suspend payments. The distribution of rice would probably come to a stop, resulting in want, misery, and possibly food riots. Finally, there would be general dislocation of trade. If he gave the guarantee, the government of Ceylon would be required to make up the difference between the amount that the Oriental Bank would eventually pay on its notes and their face value. At worst this would amount to Rs 3,200,000, a sum which, in the long run, could be retired without difficulty, although many desirable and cherished projects would have to be abandoned. Gordon preferred the "definite risk, the limits of which were ascertainable, to the grave certain, and

[4]The pound equalled 12 rupees in 1885 in Ceylon.

yet graver uncertain risks. . . ."[5] He gave the guarantee. Public confidence was largely restored and within two days ten-rupee notes were passing in private trade with only a few cents discount. On 9 May Gordon wrote that the immediate danger was over[6] but that it would soon be necessary to tell the public when the notes would be paid in full. He proposed to Lord Derby that the Oriental Bank notes be redeemed by notes of government issue. He believed this to be the only measure which would thoroughly and permanently restore confidence.

By guaranteeing the Oriental Bank notes, Gordon was assuming responsibility that was not his to assume and that, by the Royal Instructions and by a special circular dispatch (18 August 1875), was expressly reserved for the home government. Although he rarely missed an opportunity to extend his responsibilities, in this case there was neither conscious nor unconscious self-aggrandizement. With the colony deep in a financial crisis, he had no time to ask the Secretary of State for instructions. Even if he had overcome the difficulties of conveying all the relevant information by telegraph to the Colonial Office, the decision would not have been made by his own chief (now Lord Derby) but by the Lords of the Treasury. It was doubtful that they could have decided quickly, and almost certain that, had they done so, they would have advised against giving the guarantee.

Gordon's action caused surprisingly little consternation in the Colonial Office. Meade wrote a long minute criticizing Gordon for not having made the Chartered Mercantile Bank share in the guarantee. He admitted, however, that it was difficult to tell at a distance whether the Governor's decision had been justified.[7] Herbert thought that it might have been fortunate for Ceylon that Gordon had not given the home government the chance of rejecting his proposal to guarantee the notes "as we should, I suppose, most probably have done." He added: "I am disposed to be thankful that the colony has escaped the panic which I think would have arisen and gone to great lengths among the ignorant native community. . . . I would therefore avoid . . . any overconfident declaration or any sharp answer on this matter." Nor did Lord Derby feel justified in criticizing Gordon. The latter, wrote Derby, could not have telegraphed the case in sufficient detail and "we should have

---

[5]Gordon to Derby, 9 May 1884, PRO CO 54/554.
[6]*Ibid.*
[7]Meade's minute on Gordon to Derby, 7 May 1884, PRO CO 54/554. Meade noted that a recent request by the acting Governor of the Straits Settlements to be allowed to guarantee Oriental Bank notes had been refused without disastrous results but that the Oriental Bank's notes in that colony had comprised less than 10 per cent of the total circulation.

probably refused his application. . . . If his prompt action has saved the colony from great trouble and disturbance, I am not inclined to find fault with its irregularity."[8]

The Treasury felt less disposed to be tolerant. It criticized Gordon for not making greater use of the telegraph, for not requiring the leading merchants, persons of standing in Colombo, and the Chartered Mercantile Bank to join in the guarantee, and for failing to take control of the silver reserve (Rs 1,100,000) of the Oriental Bank through arrangement with the local manager. The Governor did not seem to have been aware of the grave objections to his action: "The effect on the conduct of banking business in Crown Colonies is so likely to be pernicious that the act [of guarantee] cannot be approved even if it be not condemned. The gravity of the step is so great that it may not improbably require a detailed examination of the currency in each Crown Colony for the purpose of safeguarding a possible repetition of it."[9] The Colonial Office sent a copy of the letter containing these remarks to Gordon, Derby saying that, to some extent, it embodied his own views.

Gordon replied that he did not think he deserved criticism in view of the way in which things had turned out. Besides, the Treasury did not know the colony or what it would have faced had he not acted as he had. Gordon's executive council supported him and dealt with the Treasury's specific criticisms. It noted that, even after some months and its reception of full information, the Treasury still did not understand the gravity and urgency of the crisis, thus proving that telegraphing details would not have worked. The council added that an association of bankers and merchants to guarantee the notes would have been of little use since orientals trusted only the government. Furthermore, said the council, the local manager of the Oriental Bank had no authority or power to allow the government of Ceylon to use the silver reserve even had he been willing.[10]

Under the circumstances criticism of Gordon's decision seems justified on only one point. He could and should have forced the Chartered Mercantile Bank to assume partial responsibility for the guarantee. But this is a small matter, especially in view of the fact that the Oriental Bank, when it finally settled its affairs, paid its creditors nineteen shillings on the pound.

The Governor's decision in the crisis of 1884 led to a permanent

[8]Herbert's and Derby's minutes respectively on Gordon to Derby, 7 May 1884.
[9]Leonard Courtney (Treasury) to Herbert, 13 Sept. 1884, PRO CO 54/556.
[10]Memorandum of the executive council of Ceylon enclosed in Gordon to Derby, 18 Nov. 1884, PRO CO 54/555.

change respecting the issue of paper currency in Ceylon. Gordon had suggested establishing an issue of government notes to replace notes of private issue in order to restore confidence permanently. Hitherto the Treasury had preferred private to state note issues.[11] It had no intention of reversing its policy merely because of inconvenience. "My Lords," wrote one of its officials, "do not think that the failure of a bank in Ceylon, and the natural but perhaps exaggerated alarm of a Governor not specially versed in economic subjects justify a reversal of a policy founded on approved authority."[12] Now, however, there were other considerations which made a change in policy inevitable. By sanctioning the guarantee of the Oriental Bank's notes, Lord Derby had admitted the principle of state liability for private issues. The government had thus entered a partnership in which it was required to bear the losses but was unable to share in the profits of its speculative partner. The latter would be encouraged to take unwarranted risks without fear of consequences. The Treasury believed that catastrophes like that of the Oriental Bank failure were likely to recur and that "timid Governors" would find in the precedent of Ceylon an easy escape from embarrassment. "With such a prospect before them My Lords must review their position. . . . State liability for so-called private issues being once admitted the . . . argument for private issues becomes untenable. My Lords therefore . . . agree . . . that it is advisable to establish a State issue in Ceylon. . . ."[13]

Owing to Gordon's prompt and responsible behaviour Ceylon emerged from its financial crisis with a sounder currency and without marked hardship to its people or much damage to its credit. Furthermore, although the crisis forced Gordon to postpone his plans for restoring irrigation works, the delay was brief compared with what it would have been had he failed to guarantee the currency. In the meantime he could take steps to reduce Ceylon's military contribution and thus make more funds available for his irrigation projects.

II. FINANCE AND PUBLIC WORKS

Anticipating the financial difficulties ahead of him in Ceylon, Gordon, several months before his departure from England, had proposed a large reduction in Ceylon's contribution to the cost of maintaining a military establishment on the island. In 1883 this contribution amounted to Rs 1,240,000 or, at the prevailing rate of exchange (Rs 10.7 to the

---

[11]There were two exceptions: Mauritius which issued its own notes in all denominations and Hong Kong which issued $1.00 notes.
[12]Courtney to Meade, 28 Aug. 1884, PRO CO 54/556.   [13]Ibid.

pound), slightly more than £116,000. Gordon thought it impossible, in justice to the people of Ceylon, to reduce other expenditures while this burden remained untouched. He argued that the *per capita* rate was higher than in any other colony, that the amount was out of proportion to the resources of Ceylon, and that it was admittedly in excess of the requirements of the colony. He further alleged that the amount of the contribution had been set in boom times. It should now be reduced and fixed for five or ten years, taking into consideration the financial position of the colony.[14]

As a result of this letter and conversations between Gordon and Meade, the Colonial Office, which had long held Ceylon's contribution to have been excessive, decided to appeal to the Treasury for a reduction. Gordon was asked to consult his council and to feel out public opinion in Ceylon as soon as he could after his arrival. Meanwhile, the Treasury suggested to the War Office that the military force in Ceylon be reduced from a battalion to a wing of a regiment; if this were to be done a corresponding reduction would be made in the colony's military contribution.[15]

After consulting his council Gordon proposed a reduction to Rs 500,000 annually for a five-year period and, the end of that time, the negotiation of a new agreement for the next period.[16] The Colonial Office supported this suggestion and got a rebate of Rs 240,000, beginning in April 1884. Arguing that Ceylon should not pay simply the cost of the troops necessary for its internal security but also whatever it could afford towards its external security, the Treasury fixed the cost of the colony's internal security at Rs 516,000. It offered Ceylon a choice, for the five years beginning with 1885, of paying Rs 600,000 unconditionally or Rs 516,000, a sum which might be increased by a naval contribution after its finances improved. The colony chose to pay the former sum.

Gordon observed that the Treasury's alternative offer had implied that colonies should make contributions for general imperial purposes. He warned that if this principle were adopted, it

would make a very new departure in English Colonial policy and an abandonment of what has hitherto formed one great superiority of the English over the Dutch system of Colonial Government—vizt, that the revenues of the colony were expended on the colony. . . . If once the principle be established, it will be difficult to put a limit to its application, and . . . the great temptation to the Financial authorities at home to pare down the sums

[14]Gordon to Derby, 25 Aug. 1883, PRO CO 54/551.
[15]Treasury to Colonial Office, 13 Dec. 1883, PRO CO 54/550.
[16]Gordon to Derby, 4 Feb. 1884, PRO CO 54/552.

allowed for the purposes of Colonial Government and . . . to increase the amount of tribute . . . would grow with its indulgence.[17]

The Colonial Office concurred, and made clear to the Treasury that the colony by paying Rs 600,000 did not admit the principle of colonial contributions for imperial purposes. As for the difference between Rs 516,000 and Rs 600,000 the Treasury was told, not very politely, to suit itself what to do with it.[18]

This ended the matter for the time being; but as the five-year period drew to a close and as the colony's finances recovered, negotiations began for a new agreement. Although an agreement had not been reached before the end of 1889, the War Office nevertheless asked Ceylon to accept an increase for 1890 on the ground that the garrison had been augmented. When Gordon and his successor, Sir Arthur Havelock, proved that this was not so, the War Office withdrew from that position and asked for £50,000 for 1890 instead of Rs 600,000, complaining that the rupee had fallen in value during the 1885–89 period. When the Colonial Office pointed out that the agreement had called for the payment of Rs 600,000 and had said nothing about the value of the rupee, the War Office then contended that the correspondence in 1884–85 implied that the sum of Rs 600,000 was fixed on the assumption that it would yield £50,000. Bramston of the Colonial Office agreed but added that the correspondence clearly showed that "the bargain was made in Rs—and there is no suggestion that the colony would have been let off for less than Rs 600,000 if silver had risen instead of falling."[19] The War Office got its £50,000 for 1890.

Gordon had predicted both this result and a further increase in Ceylon's contribution when, at the end of the five-year period, the Colonial Defence Committee again considered the matter. He had charged that the whole question would be practically decided by the War Office alone. This the Colonial Office denied. Gordon retorted that he had been intimately associated with the business of government long enough to learn how such committees as the C.D.C. were appointed and how they worked. The C.D.C. was composed of one member from the Treasury, War, and Colonial Offices. The War Office representative, Gordon wrote,

knows nothing, and probably cares nothing, about the local wants of the island, or its people; his business is to look to measures for its defence. The Treasury member knows as little as the Military member about the wants

[17]Gordon to Derby, 26 Feb. 1885, PRO CO 54/558.
[18]Colonial Office to Treasury, 27 March 1885, PRO CO 54/558.
[19]Bramston's minute, 25 Oct. 1890, minute paper 20839, PRO CO 54/591.

of the Colony, and is naturally anxious to throw on it any burden . . . which will relieve the Imperial Treasury. Practically therefore he is ready to support the Military Member. . . The Colonial Office member who is aware of the need of large expenditure on works which will augment the revenue or benefit the social or physical condition of the people, is consequently in a permanent minority, and the decision arrived at is practically that of the military authorities.[20]

It is perhaps unnecessary to remark that the Colonial Office did not send this part of Gordon's dispatch to the War Office without extensive paraphrasing. Edward Fairfield, a principal clerk, considered that "one who aspires to be a peer like Sir Arthur Gordon should pay greater respect to the Standing Order of the House of Lords inculcating abstention from 'sharp and taxing speeches.' "[21]

Late in 1890 the Colonial Defence Committee made its decision. Ceylon's military contribution was to be £70,000 in 1891 with increases of £10,000 a year until 1894 when the amount would be £100,000. In the Colonial Office gloom and misery prevailed. Lucas darkly observed: "This means an end to good feeling in, and development of Ceylon for years to come." Fairfield warned that "there seems to be an opinion that the unofficials [in Ceylon] will all resign. If so, those at the Straits and possibly those at Hong Kong may follow suit. Thus the Eastern Colonies will be all in a blaze at once." Herbert added dejectedly: "We are beginning to 'reap the whirlwind.' "[22]

Gordon had meantime completed his term and had returned home; but he did not give up the fight. He discussed the matter with the Colonial Office staff. The Colonial Office was "seeking to *abate* the claim" of the War Office, he told his successor (Havelock), but it would inevitably fail. It was offering "grumbling resistance," but it always gave way. (Who knew this better than Gordon?) The War Office was aware of "the full squeezableness of the Colonial Office."[23] Gordon thought there would be no injustice in making "*all* colonies pay a *moderate fixed* percentage of their revenue for Imperial purposes. . . ." It would, however, be wholly impracticable because it could be done only by an Imperial act of Parliament, which would have the same effect in Canada

[20]Gordon to Lord Knutsford (formerly Sir H. T. Holland), 23 April 1890, PRO CO 54/586. Knutsford was secretary of state for the colonies January 1887–August 1892. He had been raised to the peerage some months after becoming secretary of state. I have, however, referred to him as Lord Knutsford throughout this chapter.

[21]Fairfield's minute, 13 May 1890, *ibid.*

[22]Minutes by Lucas and Fairfield, 12 Dec. 1890, and Herbert, 13 Dec. 1890, on Treasury to Colonial Office, 11 Dec. 1890 (Treasury 24091), PRO CO 54/591.

[23]Gordon to Havelock, 27 Feb. 1891 and 19 Nov. 1894, Stanmore Papers, 49207.

and Australia as the Stamp Act had had in the United States. If those colonies were to be excluded it would be manifestly unjust to apply the idea in the few colonies "where might is still right."[24]

The Colonial Office did not inform Sir Arthur Havelock officially of the new arrangement until July 1891, when it stated that it had reluctantly been forced to agree to the plan. The dispatch included a historical sketch alleging that the Imperial government had always contemplated that, when finances permitted, the colony should pay the whole of its military expenses. No longer was much of a force needed to maintain civil order. It was now a matter of protecting Ceylon and its coaling station from sudden attack in time of war, and a question of why Ceylon "like other countries" should not provide for its self-defence.[25] The Ceylon Association in a letter signed by its president, Sir W. H. Gregory (a former governor), questioned the accuracy of some of the Colonial Office's statements. It denied that the Imperial government in 1801 had ever contemplated requiring Ceylon to pay for its external defence. Ceylon was *not* "like other countries." It was a dependency. Self-governing colonies should pay for their own defence because in those colonies and in Britain the cost of defence was a voluntary burden. "All that an Englishman holds dear is involved in defence of his country against foreigners." Most of the Ceylonese, however, cared little which foreigner ruled them. "The defence of Ceylon is the defence of English supremacy against the substitution of that of some other European power; it is not the defence of an independent nation."[26]

In the opinion of Lucas this was "an exceedingly able letter—written no doubt by Sir Arthur Gordon." Nothing was to be gained by trying to answer the arguments—"Some of them are unanswerable."[27] Fairfield, whose fears of a revolt of the unofficials in the Eastern Colonies had been unrealized, bravely added: "I don't think we need be too effusive in answering this. Ex-Governors drawing pensions, do not act in a becoming way when they turn agitators and aggravate the situation by smart writing."[28] If Gordon composed this letter, and there seems little doubt from its phrasing that he did, it was his last appearance in the controversy. Although he had lost the war, he had won a five-year respite for Ceylon and had saved approximately £250,000, which could be applied to projects of more direct benefit to the colony.

[24]*Ibid.*, 13 Feb. 1891.
[25]Sir W. H. Gregory, president of the Ceylon Association, to Under-secretary of state, 17 Nov. 1891, minute paper 22401, PRO CO 54/598.
[26]*Ibid.*
[27]Lucas's minute, 23 Nov. 1891, *ibid.*
[28]Fairfield's minute, 23 Nov. 1891, *ibid.*

Gordon found two other ways in which to save money for the public works that he considered vital to the economy. First, he opposed completion of the harbour at Colombo and, secondly, he reformed the system of road building and maintenance. In 1885 the Colombo Chamber of Commerce proposed that the colony complete the port facilities at Colombo by building a northern arm to the breakwater. The Colonial Office favoured the project, believing that it was in the interests of the colony and that it would soon produce an income sufficient to relieve the general revenues. Although the depression was reducing Ceylon's trade (the annual value declined from Rs 96,000,000 in 1879 and Rs 98,000,000 in 1880 to Rs 77,000,000 in 1884 and Rs 75,000,000 in 1885), the business of the port of Colombo was actually expanding. It appeared likely that the proposed new facilities would soon pay dividends. Gordon shared that view but felt that irrigation, railways, and roads would benefit larger areas and populations and for that reason should take priority over the breakwater. Since the colony could not afford all, Gordon therefore resisted the pressure of both the Colombo merchants and the Colonial Office, and the colony did not undertake the harbour extension during his governorship.

The system of road maintenance in effect in Ceylon was the usual one in British colonies and former colonies of Britain during the nineteenth and early twentieth centuries: compulsory statutory labour or, in lieu thereof, payment of a commutation fee. When Sir Arthur Gordon arrived in Ceylon he found the system collapsing. Many people evaded both labour and fee. Attempts to deal with them through the regular courts involved a great waste of time and money through issuing orders, certificates, warrants of distress, summonses, and warrants of arrest. The number imprisoned had increased from 2,566 in 1875 to 8,129 in 1878, and to 15,283 in 1883, but these prisoners accounted for only a small fraction of defaulters. "The lesson that was being inculcated [wrote Gordon] . . . was, firstly, a general familiarization with imprisonment, which was fast tending to disassociate all feeling of disgrace from that punishment, and secondly, a direct incitement to the people to disregard their obligations, seeing that such dishonesty would, in the vast majority of cases, entail no penalty. . . . It would be difficult . . . to devise a more effective method of sapping the morality of the people."[29]

Gordon's solution to the problem was an ordinance ensuring adequate punishment for defaulters by substituting thirty days hard labour for six days with or without hard labour, and guaranteeing certain and prompt

[29]Gordon to Secretary of State, 31 Dec. 1884, PRO CO 54/555.

punishment by placing power in the hands of the chairmen of the local road committees. The chairmen were all ex-magistrates with experience of the law. The Governor recognized that lodging both executive and judicial power in the same hands tended toward arbitrary government. Nevertheless, he felt that his new system would be less arbitrary in practice than the existing one in which there was no judicial inquiry and, for the most part, no trial. The Colonial Office agreed with Gordon that the ordinance although objectionable in principle would doubtless work satisfactorily in practice; but it warned him to keep a close eye upon its operation. In 1888, Wingfield of the Colonial Office drew attention to the measure's great success[30]—how great may be seen from Table IV.

TABLE IV*

Year	No. performing work or paying commutation	No. remaining in default	No. imprisoned	No. unaccounted for
1883			15,283	
1884	372,786	103,771		
1885	441,121	46,567	3,470	13,771
1886	443,160	21,925	1,883	6,869
1887	462,266	15,250	2,653	

*Figures appear in minute paper 11238-87, PRO CO 54/571, and minute paper 18425-88, PRO CO 54/579.

In addition the ordinance induced a healthier respect for the law, reduced the work of the police and courts, saved the colony a considerable sum of money—Rs 150,000 according to Gordon—and brought improvements in the roads.

To work towards re-establishing the irrigation system was undoubtedly the most socially and economically beneficial project which any governor of Ceylon could have set himself. The ancient irrigation system of Ceylon, based on great reservoirs or tanks, had broken down sometime in the Middle Ages. The canals had become clogged, and by the beginning of the nineteenth century all that remained of the once great system were the small village tanks located on rivers and streams. These were kept up through the communal labour of the whole village, which was turned out by the chief on certain days. After 1832, when the Imperial government called this communal effort "forced labour" and forbade the chiefs to call out the villagers, even these local water works decayed. The Imperial government was mistaken in its belief that self-

[30]Wingfield's minute, 1 Oct. 1888, minute paper 18425, PRO CO 54/579.

interest would prove sufficient to induce the villagers to repair the works voluntarily.

Coincidentally with the order against forced labour, a commission of inquiry, headed by Sir William Colebrooke, recognized the expediency and duty of restoring the ancient but abandoned tanks and canals. Later, in 1846, a report by Sir J. E. Tennent emphasized Britain's duty to help restore irrigation. Nothing of consequence was done, however, until Sir Henry Ward's term as governor of Ceylon (1854–60). In 1855 Ward recommended a grant of £50,000 for repairs to irrigation works. This was agreed upon and a further sum was voted the following year. By 1858 these expenditures had produced a striking effect at and about Erikamam in the Eastern Province, and the Secretary of State sanctioned a further large grant for irrigation. But Ward's term was expiring and work ceased. Nothing was done during the administration of Sir C. J. Macarthy, but Sir Hercules Robinson (1865–71) pressed irrigation work forward with new vigour. By 1870 Robinson was able to report that seven works of considerable size had been completed and that sixteen others were in progress or had been sanctioned. Robinson's policies were further developed by Sir William Gregory (1872–77). Gregory restored the almost abandoned works of the North Central Province and planned to restore annually from 120 to 150 village tanks, partly by government aid and partly by the labour of the villagers themselves. He also rebuilt the great tank of Kanthalai in the Eastern Province and that of Tissamaharama in the Southern Province.[31] By the eve of his departure from Ceylon he had drawn up plans for the restoration of still another great tank, that of Kalawewa in the North Central Province. Little was to be accomplished however, during the next seven or eight years.

The irrigation programme had one great weakness. It depended for its funds upon an annual vote of the legislative council. In good years the council always voted a fair sum, but when depression came irrigation was one of the first items in the budget to be cut. Any reduction in the services to the European community raised so much clamour and opposition that even a strong government was reluctant to face them. The vote for irrigation, however, could be reduced or abandoned without unpleasantness. Although great harm might thereby be done to the native population and to the future revenues of the colony, natives could be counted upon to bear their trials stoically, and damage to the revenues

[31]Kanthalai tank was unsuccessful in attracting population to its vicinity because the district had been deserted for many years, perhaps for centuries. The Tissamaharama tank proved to be a stimulus to production because there were already many people living in the area at the time of its restoration.

did not become immediately apparent. Thus, during the administration of Sir James Longden (Gregory's successor and Gordon's predecessor), the work of restoring tanks and waterways faltered. Longden was aware of the importance of the work, but his lack of initiative ("Wait-a-bit-Jemmy" he was called) and the advent of the depression resulted in smaller and smaller annual votes for irrigation until, in 1881, no money was voted at all.

The Colonial Office was very much alive to the desirability of restoring the irrigation system of Ceylon. "The works," wrote Lord Kimberley to Longden, "are undertaken in the interests of the native population. . . . It must not be forgotten that whilst their wants are greater than those of other sections of the community, they are perhaps less likely to be brought to the notice of the Government."[32] In response to Lord Kimberley's urging, Longden in 1883 reluctantly increased the vote for irrigation to Rs 160,000, some Rs 77,500 more than for 1882. Of this sum, Rs 100,000 were to be spent on new works.

Before Gordon left England, he suggested to the Colonial Office that this money might be expended more profitably if Rs 20,000 were to be spent on new small works and Rs 80,000 set aside to pay the interest on a loan sufficiently large to restore the Kalawewa tank. He had discussed his plan with Gregory, Robinson, and Longden, and all thought it good. The Colonial Office agreed, Lord Derby minuting: "I like this notion of Sir A. Gordon's. It is sound in principle and we may say so. . . ."[33] Yet the scheme was not to be realized at once.

The failure of the Oriental Bank with the attendant increased financial responsibility of the government of Ceylon halted the Kalawewa project for a short time. Gordon was unwilling to delay for long and in the autumn of 1884 he pressed the Colonial Office to authorize a loan of Rs 300,000 to proceed with the restoration of Kalawewa. This request would certainly have been refused, despite the Secretary of State's reluctance to reduce expenditures which affected native interests, had it not been that the Oriental Bank was able to pay off 95 per cent of its debt. Even then, Herbert and Derby, although agreeing that a loan could not be avoided, allowed Gordon to raise only Rs 200,000. In 1886 another Rs 100,000 was added to the loan and in 1887 a final Rs 65,000. The latter year saw the completion of the great Kalawewa tank.

The restoration of Kalawewa was a spectacular project, as was the

[32]Quoted by Meade in his minute, 15 Sept. 1883, on Gordon to Secretary of State, 25 Aug. 1883, PRO CO 54/551.
[33]Derby's minute, 19 Sept. 1883, ibid.

reconstruction of the elaborate irrigation works of Dhatu Sen.[34] Both left to posterity monuments to Gordon's earthly passage.[35] Yet he worked just as hard on unspectacular projects, the responsibility for whose realization would in a few years be forgotten although the benefits which they conferred would continue for generations. Even in the villages, he restored old and created new tanks and canals.

To provide an adequate water supply was basic to Gordon's plan to improve village life. Those who believed that education must come first and all else would follow were wrong. "There is," he wrote, "a material education due to physical improvements which must precede learning. No advantage can attend a hasty attempt in the first place to set down a school in some miserable fever-stricken village. . . . It is an excellent thing to cure people of diseases but it is better to prevent their falling ill."[36] First the jungle had to be cleared, the place made accessible, and water provided. Then, when people had been taught to live, the schoolmaster could begin.

In pursuit of these objects Gordon evolved a new system for carrying out irrigation works which would avoid the pitfalls of past schemes. In 1887 he created a central irrigation board and provincial irrigation boards and devoted one-quarter of the revenue from the paddy or grain tax to repairing, improving, and constructing irrigation works. The central irrigation board, of which the governor would be a member, would select the projects to be undertaken from among those proposed and would lay down the principles upon which they were to be carried out. The provincial boards were to be administrative bodies seeing to the actual construction work. They were to be composed of office-holders at first, but gradually native people were to be added to them. Devoting a quarter of the annual proceeds of the paddy tax to irrigation would ensure that funds would always be available for irrigation independently of a grant from the legislative council. He did not intend that this fund should relieve the council of voting funds for irrigation purposes. He wished, rather, to make certain that work on irrigation should continue in the event that hard times disposed the council to refuse funds. Gordon

[34]The Kalawewa tank was built originally by King Dhatu Sen who ruled Ceylon in the fourth century A.D. The dam was 6 miles long, 200 feet thick at the bottom, and 40 or 50 feet high. The main irrigation canal (the Bodi Ela) leading from it was 57 miles long. The system began to fall into disrepair about the eleventh century.

[35]Gordon approved the carving of a bas-relief of himself upon the wall of the restored tank and was doubtless pleased when the natives came to look upon it as a god. (Phillipps and Christian, *Some Hawarden Letters*, 165 fn.)

[36]Gordon to Derby, 11 Nov. 1884, enclosing message to legislative council, PRO CO 54/555.

reasoned that since irrigation was conducive to grain growing it would be appropriate that the money should come from the grain tax, and since the natives paid most of the grain tax they should get some return for their money.

The ordinance containing these plans was passed unanimously by the council and went into operation in 1887. The Colonial Office agreed with the scheme. Lucas, for example, maintained that "the proceeds of the paddy tithe, paid as it is by natives, cannot be more appropriately laid out than in repairing the tanks on which the paddy crops so much depend."[37] It is worth noting that the council did not use the existence of the new fund as an excuse for failing to vote funds. Indeed, the vote for irrigation in 1888 was Rs 446,000 as compared with Rs 361,000 in 1887. Fortunately for Ceylon the council took this attitude—although not without concessions[38]—because shortly after Gordon's departure from the colony the paddy tax was replaced by a land tax, much to Gordon's disapproval.[39] His special guaranteed annual fund for irrigation thus disappeared. Nevertheless, his central and provincial irrigation boards continued to function until replaced about 1906 by a separate irrigation department.

Much was done to provide irrigation work for the villages during the three years Gordon's scheme was in effect. The villagers themselves built and maintained the bunds or dykes, being allowed to substitute their labour for taxes, and the government provided the masonry and the sluice gates in the dams and supervised all the work. "By this wholesome kind of bargain," Lucas noted, the natives were gradually getting their tanks into order. He found it interesting to observe that, although the abolition of the old custom of forced labour had been most fatal to irrigation, the revival of the village council system which Gordon had promoted had given irrigation new life. "In other words, Ceylon, worked under its old native customs, was a well irrigated land, and the people only prosper by being governed with due regard to those customs."[40]

Gordon's promotion of village councils and his provision of adequate supplies of water had excellent results. Native health improved; thus medical costs to the government tended to decrease. The supply of rice increased; thus famine could be prevented and relief costs reduced. The population of the irrigated areas grew. That of the North Central

[37]Lucas's minute on Gordon to Secretary of State, 29 Dec. 1887, PRO CO 54/573.
[38]See below, pp. 321–24.
[39]Gordon to Havelock, 13 Feb. 1891, Stanmore Papers, 49207; and Gordon's memorandum, 7 Aug. 1890, attached to minute paper 2712, PRO CO 54/591.
[40]Lucas's minute on Gordon to Knutsford, 8 Feb. 1890, PRO CO 54/586.

Province, for example, showed a gain of nearly 14 per cent in the decade of the eighties as compared with under 4 per cent in the seventies.[41] That province also produced a greater revenue.[42]

Gordon did not attain his objectives without difficulty. Lack of competent engineers often delayed work on the village tanks. The poor financial condition of the colony, which persisted until the middle of his administration, and the want of enthusiasm for irrigation on the part of the European community were other stumbling blocks. "That which I take most interest in and work hardest at [wrote Gordon] is irrigation, about which nobody else *except the native cultivators* . . . takes any interest at all—this is speaking generally for there are not a few Government officers really earnest in the work, but there is no sympathy from the press or the European public."[43] The legislative council did vote funds for irrigation purposes, but not out of any enthusiastic or philanthropic spirit. It provided money because the unofficial members believed that, by showing their willingness to support irrigation for the benefit of the natives, they might more easily obtain government funds for the railway extensions they desired.

If Gordon found no great disposition in Ceylon, outside official circles, to promote irrigation, he found backing in the Colonial Office. For a time after the Oriental Bank failure it did refuse to authorize the loan for the Kalawewa project, prompting Gordon to complain of "the niggardliness of the authorities at home"[44] and of "the ineptitude of the C.O. which only seeks to shelve questions instead of solving them."[45] At all other times, however, it enthusiastically approved his irrigation plans and frequently complimented him. For example, a dispatch to Havelock, Gordon's successor in Ceylon, concluded: "I take the opportunity of informing you how highly Her Majestys' Government appreciate the persevering manner in which Sir Arthur Gordon pressed on the great and beneficent work of irrigation and of expressing their confident hope that you will carry on his work in the same spirit as that by which he was actuated."[46]

There can be no doubt that irrigation was the most pressing need in Ceylon during Gordon's administration, or that it was his chief interest and care. Yet the governor of a Crown colony has responsibility for

[41]Gordon's diary, 1891, Stanmore Papers, 49226, f. 8.
[42]Lucas's minute on Gordon to Knutsford, 8 Feb. 1890.
[43]Gordon to Waterfield, 15 May 1887, Stanmore Papers, 49251.
[44]*Ibid.*   [45]*Ibid.*
[46]Secretary of State to Havelock, 9 May 1890, copy to Gordon, PRO CO 54/586.

seeing that the just desires and needs of all sections of the community are fulfilled and that all interests are kept in some semblance of balance. The tea and coffee planters in Ceylon could hardly be expected to look favourably upon the annual expenditure of fairly large sums on irrigation, which benefited them little, whilst their own interests went unattended. Nor were the prospects bright that the legislative council, where the planting community was represented and commanded some sympathy even among the official members, would continue voluntarily to vote annual sums for irrigation purposes unless attempts were made to accede to the planters' legitimate demands. Of course the governor, commanding an official majority, could force the council to pass any measure whatever; but most governors endeavoured to maintain harmony in their councils and to avoid using their majorities. Some, like Sir Henry Barkly in Mauritius, went much too far in this direction, either betraying their duty or failing to see where it lay.[47] Others like Gordon attempted to maintain harmony but not at the expense of duty or principle. Gordon, therefore, having benefited the native population by providing funds for irrigation to the limit of the colony's engineering facilities to use them, saw no reason, when Ceylon's financial condition began to improve, why something could not be done to aid tea and coffee growers.

For some years that group had wanted an extension of the railway to the planting districts in order to convey their produce to the coast more safely, more quickly, and more cheaply. The proposed line was to run from Nanoya, the existing terminal, to Haputalé, a distance of about twenty-five miles, to tap a new tea growing district which contained a large native population. The cost was estimated at about £500,000. At the commencement of Gordon's administration the colony clearly could not afford to service such a debt. Not until 1885, after Gordon had overcome the Oriental Bank crisis and had reduced Ceylon's military contribution, did he place the railway project before the Colonial Office. He felt confident not only that the line would encourage production, but that it would earn a profit which could be used to finance other needed public works.

Before Gordon's arrival in Ceylon, the Colonial Office had considered and rejected the project as a public work and had even refused to allow it to be built by a private company. The Secretary of State therefore gave a decidedly cool reception to Gordon's proposal that the Ceylon government undertake construction of the railway. The Colonial Office criticized the Governor for having revived the planters' waning hopes.[48]

[47]See chap. IV.
[48]Minute paper 12411, 1885, PRO CO 54/559.

Lucas believed him to be guilty of sharp practice because he had coupled his proposal to extend the planters' railway with a scheme to extend the coastal line from Bentola to Galle. The latter extension of some twelve miles would depend mainly on native passenger traffic for its revenues. Lucas thought that Gordon had supported the Bentola to Galle line only to forestall Colonial Office objections to building the Nanoya-Haputalé line which would solely benefit the planters.[49] Although Colonel Stanley, the new secretary of state,[50] agreed to withdraw the prohibition against private construction of the Haputalé extension, he still objected on several grounds to its being undertaken as a public work. The line would cost too much in view of the financial circumstances of the colony, and its ultimate success could not be considered as beyond all doubt. Other public works including irrigation, completion of the defences of Colombo, and extension of the breakwater at Colombo should take precedence over the railway.

In June 1886, Gordon dealt with these objections. The first was based upon the dire predictions of 1882, when it was anticipated that Ceylon would have a deficit of Rs 500,000 rising to Rs 1,000,000 by 1885. This had not occurred. Rs 600,000 annually had been saved by reducing the colony's military contribution and a further Rs 300,000 had been saved over a two-year period through the new system of road maintenance. Rather than a deficit in 1885 there had been a surplus despite the fact that public works costing Rs 500,000 had been built and paid for. Gordon agreed that the financial condition of the colony still required "a vigilant eye and a firm hand to keep clear of danger," but he could see "no reason for apprehension, or for the exercise of a niggardly parsimony."[51] As for the second objection, he argued that "the success of no human undertaking can be said to be absolutely free from a certain degree of doubt. The chances of failure are almost always numerous and if we allow ourselves to dwell on them too exclusively, they may go far to make the success of any proposal appear well nigh hopeless." In the present instance he considered that there was "such a probability as determines most of the actions of life, that the enterprise will prove not only remunerative, but handsomely remunerative. . . ."[52]

Gordon agreed with the Colonial Office that constant attention should be paid to irrigation. He argued, nevertheless, that irrigation works were

[49]*Ibid.*
[50]Sir F. A. Stanley was secretary of state for the colonies from June 1885 to February 1886.
[51]Gordon to Granville, 23 June 1886, PRO CO 809/32. Granville was secretary of state for the colonies from February to August 1886.
[52]*Ibid.*

proceeding as quickly as the surveyors and supervisory staff available to the colony permitted and that the railway would not decrease the sums voted for irrigation nor interfere with any work contemplated. Moreover, the council would not *"voluntarily"* accept larger votes for irrigation while the railway remained unbuilt. Regarding the proposed northern breakwater at Colombo, Gordon, his executive council, and all members of the legislative council maintained that it could not be compared with the railway as a stimulus to production. Finally, he had no hesitation in saying that, whatever claim to precedence the fortification of Colombo might possess, there was no probability that the legislative council would admit that claim as long as the Secretary of State considered its cost an obstacle to the building of the railway.[53] A month later Gordon followed up this argument with a dispatch in which he estimated that the railway would pay 8 per cent on its capital. He had already had a loan ordinance passed without waiting for the Secretary of State to sanction the project.

Annoyed with the Governor, the Colonial Office staff disagreed with his estimates of the railway's earnings and complained that he had forced the Secretary of State's hand by passing the loan ordinance. They believed that Gordon had pitted class against class in Ceylon by promising the railway to the planters in return for their support of irrigation to benefit the natives. The Colonial Office was also disturbed by Gordon's warnings of obstruction in the legislative council. Nor did it feel that the planters would long be satisfied with the proposed extension. Lucas believed that the planters deserved much consideration, but he did not think their interests compared with those of the native masses. Meade added: "Hitherto we have fought this preposterous proposal [for the railway] singlehanded but now we have a good deal of outside support— Sir W. Gregory and his friends in England—and in the Colony a newspaper[54] which the governor does not allow us to see and the two native members of council." Meade advocated delaying tactics, to which Herbert and Stanhope, the secretary of state, agreed.[55]

It is interesting to see the implied accusation by the Colonial Office that Gordon was sacrificing native interests to those of the planters. To anyone with the slightest knowledge of Gordon's record, such an accusation was patently absurd. Indeed, it should never have been entertained in the Colonial Office, particularly by such well-informed men as Lucas

[53]*Ibid.*

[54]*Ceylon Times.*

[55]Minutes on Gordon to Secretary of State, 27 July 1886, PRO CO 54/565, minute paper 15124. Edward Stanhope was secretary of state for the colonies from August 1886 to January 1887.

and Meade. But perhaps Gordon, from Fiji and New Zealand, had succeeded beyond expectation in teaching the permanent officials to respect and consider native interests.

Gordon continued, despite delays and rebuffs, to press for the railway extension, and Captain Ommanney, Lucas, and Meade continued to write unfavourable minutes concerning the project.[56] Sir Cecil Smith[57] and G. T. M. O'Brien,[58] who were both in England in the spring of 1887, argued strongly in favour of the plan and of Gordon's estimates. O'Brien wrote to Gordon in May saying: "They gave me your admirable further despatch on railway extension at the C.O. . . . . Even the hostile Lucas is touched with its ability, and I am not without hopes that it may produce its effect."[59] Finally, early in 1888, after receipt of another able dispatch[60] from Gordon the Colonial Office capitulated. Construction began almost at once. When completed, the railway proved a financial success.

Gordon had no difficulty in obtaining Colonial Office consent to a vote of the Ceylon government for Rs 200,000 for the Bentola to Galle coastal line. Even though he had not sent plans or estimates, Fairfield minuted, "we should not be obdurate," and approval was given immediately. The line was opened to traffic early in 1890. Although other factors were involved, the chief reasons for the changed attitude in the Colonial Office were the increasing prosperity of the colony and the fact that this line would serve a large native population.

III. CONSTITUTIONAL, LEGAL, AND ADMINISTRATIVE REFORMS

Not much escaped Gordon's experienced eye. He saw the need for changes in the legislative council, the civil service, the administrative and the legal machinery, and the treatment of the native population. Before his term expired he managed to infuse all these phases of the colony's life with a greater degree of justice, honesty, and efficiency.

As a Crown colony, Ceylon had a legislative council containing an official majority. The council consisted of eight official and six unofficial members. Of the latter, three were European: one represented the

[56]Gordon to Secretary of State, 29 March 1887, and minute paper 7398, PRO CO 54/570.

[57]Sir Cecil Smith was the lieutenant-governor of Ceylon.

[58]George Thomas Michael O'Brien, C.M.G. (1889), G.C.M.G. (1894). Appointed writer in Ceylon (1867), rose to acting colonial secretary, became auditor-general (1891), colonial secretary of Cyprus (1891) and of Hong Kong (1892–95), was appointed governor of Fiji (1897).

[59]O'Brien to Gordon, 13 May 1887, Stanmore Papers, 49207.

[60]Gordon to Secretary of State, 16 Jan. 1888, PRO CO 54/576.

planters, one the merchants, and the other the general interests of the 5,000 Europeans in the colony. Of the native unofficials, one was Sinhalese representing a population not much under 2 million, one was Tamil representing approximately 700,000 people, and the other represented the Eurasian, or burgher, element of some 18,000. This arrangement was perhaps unfair in that it gave the Europeans over-representation on the basis of population although this was partly offset by the fact that the Europeans accounted for the greater portion of the island's production. More unfair, however, were the lack of representation for the 200,000 Kandyan-Mohammedans and the under-representation for the Sinhalese.

To remove these inconsistencies was not a simple matter. Gordon wished to add a Kandyan and another Sinhalese to the council. But he knew that this move would annoy the Europeans, particularly because the Kandyan would have to be a Ratamahatmeya, or village headman, who was in receipt of a government salary and who would thus be looked upon by the unofficials as an addition to the official membership of the council. To avoid this difficulty, Gordon rather weakly suggested the appointment of another European unofficial. The Colonial Office told him to go ahead and appoint a Mohammedan and a Sinhalese, plus two more officials in order to maintain the proportion between officials and unofficials on the council. Gordon carried out the order but asked that appointment of another European unofficial be reconsidered at a later date. As it turned out Gordon need not have worried about the Kandyan Ratamahatmeya being regarded as an official because he showed himself to be a vigorous opponent of the government. In any case the Colonial Office was not disposed to reopen the question although Fairfield, who was often somewhat acid in his minutes, commented, "we might give him another European as a thorn in his side in the person of Mr. Wall [perhaps Gordon's severest critic in Ceylon], the Editor of the Independent."[61] Had Fairfield's suggestion by any chance been acted upon Gordon would doubtless have resisted it, not because of personal objections to Wall but, as he had told the Colonial Office a year or two earlier, because "if the Governor does his duty, and notwithstanding the apparent tendency of the present day to assume that no public officer will do his duty unless fettered by inelastic rules making independence of judgement or action impossible, . . . it should be presumed that he will . . . endeavour to nominate a truly representative man. If so, he has better means of ascertaining who such men are than

[61]Fairfield's minute on Gordon to Secretary of State, 4 May 1889, PRO CO 54/583.

any one else in the Colony. . . ."[62] "Or," he would have added, had he thought it necessary, "than anyone in the Colonial Office."

One other constitutional development of interest took place during Gordon's régime. Encouraged by the "National Association," as the Agricultural Association of Ceylon had recently styled itself,[63] one or two of the younger unofficial members of the council began, in 1889, to oppose the Governor on all occasions as a matter of principle. Early in the new year the National Association followed this up by petitioning Gordon to allow official members of the council full liberty of speech and free votes, to appoint unofficials for seven-year instead of three-year terms, to allow any member of the council to propose money votes, and to refrain from appointing office-holders to unofficial seats.[64] Gordon rejected all of these demands except the second; he increased the term to five years. The Colonial Office agreed.

During Gordon's administration, reform of the colony's civil service and legal system was much more prominent than constitutional reform. Sir Arthur was usually critical of the colonial civil services, an attitude which can be explained by his concept of administration. He believed it essential in colonies of mixed population like Ceylon that the governor "should really govern, and . . . that this should be understood and recognised by the people at large."[65] Such personal government brought him into closer contact with colonial civil servants than a governor who allowed them to rule the colony by themselves. It was thus to be expected that Ceylon's civil service should come under his scrutiny immediately.

From the first Gordon expressed disappointment with the civil service. There were some good men, some clever men, any number of conceited men, but most were of the "very narrowest and most redtapeish style of thought."[66] A year later he wrote: "I *never* in the course of my long experience, have had a set of officials who, though honest and well intentioned, were so far below mediocrity as those in Ceylon."[67] The higher offices seemed to be at the favour of Lord Wolseley, who had successfully nominated three men for high appointments. Gordon felt that in two cases Wolseley "must have been prompted by a desire not to

[62]Gordon to Secretary of State, 29 March 1887.

[63]Lucas thought he saw a parallel between this transition and that in Ireland, where "the 'Land League' [had] developed into the 'National League'. . . ." (Marginal note on Gordon to Knutsford, 29 Jan. 1890, PRO CO 54/586.)

[64]Gordon to Knutsford, 18 Feb. 1890, enclosing petition of National Association of Ceylon, PRO CO 54/586.

[65]Gordon to Knutsford, 29 Jan. 1890.

[66]Gordon to Lady Sophia Palmer, 18 Jan. 1884, Stanmore Papers, 49221.

[67]Gordon to Selborne, 14 Feb. 1885, Stanmore Papers, 49219.

have his friends any longer employed about himself."[68] The lower ranks were as bad as the higher, and it was not long before Gordon began complaining to the Colonial Office about the method by which civil servants were recruited.

To some officers of the colony, Gordon's advent came as a breath of fresh air. He had begun his administration with his customary energy. He travelled extensively about the island encouraging, advising, driving, congratulating, or provoking the officials, whichever seemed most appropriate. Some caught his spirit and energy. O'Brien, the acting colonial secretary, testified in 1885 that:

> I have found peculiar gratification in working under you, both because I felt that you trusted me, and because I knew that such work as I might be able to do would be utilised by you to good advantage. There has never since I came to Ceylon [1867] been so much important work accomplished . . . in so short a time as during your administration, and I consider myself exceptionally fortunate in having been connected with it. With any other Governor that I know of it would not have been possible.[69]

Writing the year after Gordon's departure, F. H. Price[70] said, "I was asleep years ago when you came to Ceylon; and it was you who woke me, gave me an impulse to work, and inspired in me a taste for something more than my frivolous interests in the days before I had the good fortune to serve under you."[71] A few weeks after Gordon's retirement, H. Wace, clerk of the legislative council, wrote: "It is difficult to realize . . . that I can no longer write to you for the advice and assistance that you always so freely gave me. I shall much value the time of service here under you."[72]

Despite the personal admiration, affection, and devotion to duty that Gordon inspired in many of his officers, many more objected to being forced out of the pleasant ruts which they had filled for years and in which they might normally have expected promotion solely by seniority. They protested against Gordon's penchant for filling openings with younger but more competent men, or, if such were not available, for appointing men from outside the covenanted civil service. They objected also to his failure to take men from their ranks for executive or "treasury" offices. It was not long, therefore, before the Colonial Office

[68]Gordon to Selborne, 18 Sept. 1884, Stanmore Papers, 49218. Garnet Joseph Wolseley (1833–1913), the well-known army commander and military reformer, who was created Baron Wolseley in 1882.

[69]O'Brien to Gordon, 11 Sept. 1885, Stanmore Papers, 49207.

[70]F. H. Price, assistant government agent, Kegalle, and formerly office assistant, Anuradhapura.

[71]Price to Gordon, 19 Dec. 1891, Stanmore Papers, 49266.

[72]Wace to Gordon, 1 June 1890, Stanmore Papers, 49265.

began receiving complaints from the civil service about the methods which Gordon used.

The Colonial Office supported Gordon against the complaints respecting promotion by merit rather than by seniority. On one occasion, when the Office was considering an adverse reply to such a grievance, Fairfield thought that "we might add something cheering to the effect that the best thing for the . . . members of the Civil Service to do would be to spare no effort towards attaining a higher level of efficiency in their work, and thus render it unnecessary for the Gov[ernmen]t to depart except rarely from the rules of seniority in selecting officers for the higher offices." Lord Knutsford, then secretary of state, thought Fairfield's advice sound but "hardly 'cheering' to the memorialists."[73] There were times, however, when the Colonial Office balked and refused to allow Gordon to appoint men outside the civil service to the higher posts. These were skirmishes and were not directly related to the main issue of civil service reform. Here a running battle developed between the Colonial Office and Gordon which lasted throughout his régime.

There were two main problems. The first was to work out some method by which natives of Ceylon, regardless of origins, might enter the civil service of the colony. Both the Governor and the Colonial Office wanted to make this possible. Although Gordon at first believed that it would not be a difficult problem to solve and promised to suggest a plan, he found, as he became better acquainted with the colony and occupied with many other matters, that a solution was not as easy as he had anticipated. Months and years passed and still Gordon's plan was not forthcoming. Although the Colonial Office itself had no suggestions to offer, it was understandably impatient and pressed the Governor for his plan. Gordon was either unable or unwilling to forward it until the end of his term.

The chief obstacle to the natives' entering the civil service of the colony was the system, adopted by the Colonial Office in 1880, which required candidates to enter by open competition in London. In May 1890, Gordon finally proposed that Ceylonese youths desiring entry to the covenanted civil service should be allowed to write examinations in Ceylon at the same time and in the same subjects as in England. He did not expect this proposal to be adopted, nor did he take it very seriously because he had no respect for "the efficacy of examination as a test of administrative ability."[74] Rather, he proposed as an alternative that

[73]Fairfield's and Knutsford's minutes on Gordon to Secretary of State, 28 May 1889, PRO CO 54/583.
[74]Gordon to Secretary of State, 7 May 1890, PRO CO 54/587.

deserving Ceylonese be admitted to the covenanted service (except to executive posts not under supervision) on the basis of proven ability. He further proposed a few more lucrative appointments of natives to the so-called clerical service and a few new appointments of native headmen of a superior grade. Subject to the approval of the secretary of state, the governor should, he thought, "exercise unfettered right of selection from natives who had achieved a certain standing or experience."[75] The Colonial Office rejected the plan believing that its acceptance would mean the "absolute breakup of the Service."[76] The problem was therefore allowed to stand over for his successor's attention.

The second problem connected with civil service reform derived from the question of whether Gordon would be compelled each year to accept a certain number of cadets (successful candidates in the open competition held on behalf of the Eastern Colonies) instead of following his practice of keeping posts open for a long time or filling them locally on a temporary or acting basis. There were disadvantages either way. Adherence to the cadet scheme meant that the colony would have a surplus of civil servants, promotion would be slow, and the younger men would become disgruntled and lose their keenness and efficiency. Doubtless, the alternative had the advantage of being more efficient in the short run, especially under a vigilant governor like Gordon; but, as Lucas noted in 1885: "It leaves a colony dependent for good or bad government on the whims or caprices of a single man—and it hampers succeeding governors with the bad bargains of their predecessors. . . . It is especially fatal in a large colony like Ceylon, where administration to be efficient must be uniform and systematic."[77]

Lord Derby favoured the existing cadet system which he believed had worked well.[78] He forced Gordon to accept a few cadets each year and thus to maintain the system, at least in theory. Nevertheless, the Governor had his way in practice. He followed obstructionist tactics, arguing against the method of cadet selection and failing to keep the Colonial Office informed of the number of vacancies in the civil service. During the later years of his term he received a degree of support for his point of view from Sir Robert Herbert and Lord Knutsford, although the junior members of the Colonial Office maintained their opposition.

Such support as Gordon obtained within the Colonial Office on civil service matters was given because, more often than not, he could provide

[75]Ibid.

[76]Lucas's memorandum, 16 June 1890, ibid., minute paper 9816.

[77]Lucas's minute on Gordon to Secretary of State (telegram), 17 June 1885, PRO CO 54/559.

[78]Derby's minute, ibid.

convincing arguments to bolster his opinion and because, as Herbert put it, "the idiosyncracies of individual Governors often compel us to subordinate principles in some degree to the necessity of getting the best practical results for the time being."[79] Confirmation of this statement may be found in the discussions within the Office on another matter closely related to the civil service: Gordon's proposal to divide the Western Province. The reaction in the Colonial Office was immediate. The junior officials criticized Gordon for disrupting the system in order to increase his own power. The senior officials considered the case Gordon made and took his predilection for centralization into account.

Ceylon was divided into provinces, each administered by government agents or sub-governors. Gordon wished to divide the Western Province because it was too large for efficient administration even by an active man, which the incumbent was not. Moreover, two districts, being Kandyan, were not naturally a part of the Western Province and were being neglected. These were quite legitimate reasons. With his wide knowledge of the local scene and the support of his executive and legislative councils, the planters, and the people of the districts concerned, the Governor was entitled to expect the approval of the Colonial Office. Instead, Lucas, who seems to have been the staunchest supporter of "system," argued long and strenuously against the proposal or, perhaps it would be truer to say, against the Governor.

Sir Arthur Gordon likes personal government; he does not want a system of strong and well paid men in the provinces. . . . It seems to me . . . that you must try to keep in full force this provincial system which has worked so well. . . . One governor and another can do a great deal but after all it is a sound system which is the real object to be worked for. . . .[80]

A few months later Lucas again attacked:

It is obvious that Sir A. Gordon will if possible have his way about this as about other points, and not make any compromise, if he can help it, to meet objections from this side. . . . It is therefore probably almost useless to reiterate objections or urge new ones. Nevertheless I submit the following: . . . that the work at the centre—the Colonial Secretariat—has been enormously increasing, and must be further increased by creating another centre with which correspondence will be carried on. . . . The reason why I write rather persistently about this [Gordon's] proposal is because it means increasing the work at the centre and gradually breaking up rule through the government agents.

[79]Herbert's minute, 10 May 1888, on Gordon to Knutsford, 14 March 1888, PRO CO 54/577.
[80]Lucas's minute, 1 Nov. 1888, on Gordon to Knutsford, 9 Oct. 1888, PRO CO 54/579.

Given a governor who prefers centralization and personal superintendence to a system in which there are several sub-governors, and it is obvious
that he will try and substitute the former for the latter.[81]

Lucas, joined by A. A. Pearson, one of the clerks, advocated delay until
Gordon's term had expired.

Lucas overlooked two points. If Gordon had intended to destroy the
system by sub-dividing the provinces, he would hardly have waited
until nearly the end of his term before commencing. The secretariat's
work expanded not only through Gordon's liking for "personal superintendence" but also because, as an able, energetic, and imaginative
governor, he greatly enlarged the scope of governmental activities and
closely supervised his subordinates' work.

The higher officials in the Colonial Office, while agreeing that Lucas's
objections had weight, did not fall in with his delaying tactics. Herbert
thought that "we should yield" to the Governor's wishes and Knutsford
agreed. Yet the latter wished Gordon to understand that he was giving
way because the executive council and the interested local groups wished
it.[82] As Lucas had foreseen, Gordon got his way.

One of the thorniest and least rewarding tasks which Sir Arthur
Gordon had to face was the improvement of the institutions connected
with the law and the administration of justice. His attempts at reform
were not wholly successful and met with some criticism both locally and
in the Colonial Office.

In Ceylon in the 1880's, law enforcement and the dispensing of
justice were erratic. Murder, theft, and destruction of produce were
common crimes. (During 1886 and the first half of 1887, 140 persons
were tried for murder, and in 1888 82 persons were found guilty of
culpable homicide.) Bribery and corruption were rife in the attorney-
general's office. The judges of the supreme court, although all trained
lawyers, were men of the old school with great reverence for minute
technicalities which resulted in ludicrous miscarriages of justice. The
judges of the district courts, chosen from among those in the civil
service who were too stupid to hold executive offices, were the laughing
stock of the country.[83] Police magistrates and constables were often
young men, fresh out from England, untrained in the law and lacking
local experience or knowledge of a native language. Prison discipline
was notoriously lax.

[81]*Ibid.*
[82]Herbert's and Knutsford's minutes, 6 and 7 Nov. 1888, *ibid.*
[83]Gordon to Selborne, 24 April 1884, Stanmore Papers, 49218.

Gordon's first move was to pass an ordinance allowing the lash to be inflicted for theft or destruction of produce. This was sanctioned by the Colonial Office, but only because "a philanthropist so careful of the good treatment of natives as Sir A. Gordon"[84] had strongly recommended it.

Murder, of course, carried the death penalty, but judging from the number of murders committed during the 1880's it was not an effective deterrent. An officer from India attributed the prevalence of murder in Ceylon to gambling, drunkenness, quarrels about property, and unrestricted immigration of bad characters from India.[85] Certainly, none of these factors was altogether new in Ceylon. Why then the increased number of murders? Part of the answer lay in the rapidly changing economic condition of the colony. Ceylon experienced the whole economic cycle from boom to depression to recovery during the eighties, and the strains imposed upon its polyglot population must have been great. There was undoubted merit also in Gordon's assertion that the increase in crime, including murder, was partly due to the imperfections of the judicial system, such as uncertain punishment. Although it is questionable whether the mere existence in law of prescribed penalties prevents crime, it is reasonable to assume that many potential criminals are deterred if they are certain of punishment.

Two cases serve to illustrate the difficulties in the path of justice in the colony during the eighties. On one occasion, a Sinhalese was tried and convicted of forgery. He appealed, although there was no doubt of his guilt. The indictment, however, had used English words and figures to describe the forgery which had been committed with Sinhalese figures. The man went free even though the indictment had been interpreted to him word for word in Sinhalese. The judges would not even allow a new trial. This procedure was hardly logical, for if, on the one hand, the accused could then plead *autrefois acquit*, his appeal should not have been allowed. If, on the other hand, the offence was not the same, the trial of the accused on what was, in the eye of the bench, a different charge should not have been refused.[86] The other case concerns a man who had been convicted of murder and sentenced to death a number of years earlier but whose sentence, for no very good reason, had been commuted to twenty years imprisonment. He escaped. A search party found him asleep. He resisted arrest, wounded the gaol guard, and fatally stabbed a constable. The judge strongly charged the jury to

[84]Herbert's minute, 22 May 1885, PRO CO 54/558, minute paper 8916.
[85]Knutsford to Gordon, 14 March 1890, PRO CO 54/586.
[86]Gordon to Selborne, 24 April 1884.

acquit the man on the ground that he had been suddenly awakened from sleep and "merely did what any of us would have done under similar circumstances." The jury nevertheless found the prisoner guilty of homicide, whereupon the judge sentenced him to two years and told him that had he himself been on the jury he would have acquitted him.[87]

There was little a governor could do to prevent such occurrences beyond keeping the Colonial Office informed so that, when the occasion offered, better judges might be appointed. The Colonial Office hoped that some of the judges would soon retire and that one at least could be induced to retire on pension. It could only express regret at these miscarriages of justice.[88] It was little wonder that Sir Arthur's opinion of the judges was unflattering, but he was not, as the Colonial Office for a time felt, so "notoriously hostile" toward them that his judgment was warped.[89] For example, Gordon, who considered the jury system to be unsuited to Ceylon, agreed with the judges to recommend that in all but capital cases the accused might elect to have his case tried by a judge. This limited jury system was sanctioned and, together with the new penal code and law of criminal procedure enacted in 1883, tended to simplify the work of the courts. By 1887 Gordon was able to see an improvement: more convictions were being obtained and fewer frivolous and false charges were being laid. In addition the criminal work of the supreme court had been lightened without much increasing that of the district courts because many cases which formerly went to trial were now being dealt with summarily in magistrates' courts.

Not all miscarriages of justice were those in which too much leniency was shown. Sometimes individuals were wrongly convicted or were given sentences too severe for the circumstances of their crimes. In such cases Gordon used his discretionary power as governor to remit or reduce the sentence. In 1885 the *Ceylon Observer*, charging him with having remitted sentences without consulting the judges, remarked that "discretion" was not his strong point. It warned that his experience of political and administrative "hot water" in the West Indies, Mauritius, Fiji, and New Zealand was likely to be repeated in Ceylon.[90] On an earlier occasion when one of the clerks in the Colonial Office had suggested that Gordon be told that he had acted judiciously Meade had minuted: "we never express opinions on questions of this kind and if

[87]Gordon to Secretary of State, 23 May 1887, enclosing and commenting upon two reports from the Attorney-General respecting the administration of justice, PRO CO 54/571.
[88]Minutes, *ibid.*
[89]Minutes on Gordon to Secretary of State, 19 June 1885, PRO CO 54/559.
[90]*Ceylon Observer*, 17 Feb. 1885, filed with paper 9305, PRO CO 54/562.

the Secretary of State saw grave reasons to doubt the Governor's discretion all he would do would be to remind him that he took a great responsibility in deciding to interfere with the sentence in the exercise of his discretion."[91] Nevertheless, after the *Observer* had positively stated that Gordon habitually pardoned prisoners without reference to the judge who had presided at the trails, Meade considered that some inquiry should be made. Herbert pointed out, however, that the governor was not required to consult the judge except in remitting capital sentences and warned that "Sir A. Gordon will be down upon us if we question his proceedings without good grounds."[92] The Colonial Office decided to send a confidential circular dispatch to all governors instructing them to ask for a report by the chief justice before remitting a capital sentence. Because Gordon considered that his long and varied experience had conferred upon him judgment equal if not superior to that of most colonial judges, he probably did not relish the new instruction, but since it was sent as a circular he did not take it as a personal reproof. Two years later a letter to the editor of one of the Ceylon papers charged that the Governor's leniency in remitting sentences had led to an increase in crime. Yet there is no reason to suppose that he ignored the instruction to consult the chief justice before commuting capital sentences. There is some evidence, however, that the chief justice did not always concur.[93] Gordon, himself, did not believe that he had been more lenient than previous governors although privately he rather enjoyed his new reputation. It was "a novel sensation and rather flattering" to one who had "usually been assailed as too sternly rigorous."[94]

Perhaps the most serious obstacle to the proper administration of justice in Ceylon during the early years of Sir Arthur Gordon's rule was corruption in the Crown law offices. Before Gordon had been many months in the colony, he had come to believe that bribes were systematically and habitually taken by most of the Crown counsel, who in Ceylon discharged the office of grand jury. He established a commission of inquiry which worked under great difficulties: records "disappeared," as did some witnesses, and other witnesses found themselves being sued or prosecuted.[95] The commission, reporting in April 1885, revealed "a state of corruption which one would have thought utterly impossible in any British Colony. . . ."[96] It alleged "a wide-spread if not universally

[91]Minutes on Gordon to Derby, 8 April 1884, PRO CO 54/553.   [92]*Ibid.*
[93]Minutes on Gordon to Knutsford, 24 Jan. 1890, PRO CO 54/586.
[94]Gordon to Thring, a newspaper editor in Ceylon (private), 16 Dec. 1887, Stanmore Papers, 49246.
[95]Gordon to Selborne, 25 March 1885, Stanmore Papers, 49219.
[96]DeRobeck's minute, 27 May 1885, PRO CO 54/558, minute paper, 8917.

prevailing belief in the existence of corruption in the Department of the Attorney-General,[97] and of frequent miscarriages of justice in consequence."[98] Bribery was rampant. "Large sums have been expended in the belief that they were applied for the purpose of influencing members of the Department."[99] The commissioners believed that they had had only glimpses into the working of the department, but that these glimpses were "an indication of what has not yet been brought to light, and we have no belief that we have gone near sounding the depths. . . ."[100]

The commission of inquiry had a salutary effect upon the attorney-general's department, albeit only a few heads fell owing to the extreme difficulty of obtaining evidence and to the failure of the Colonial Office to back the Governor in a case arising out of the inquiry. The commissioners had reported a man guilty of lying in giving evidence before them and of having accepted a bribe. Gordon deprived him of the honorary rank he held, and the road committee of the province (which was not a government body) dismissed him from his job. Because the man was well-to-do and had influential friends in Ceylon and England, he persuaded the Colonial Office to order the Governor to restore his rank and the road committee to re-employ him. Gordon was in England in the autumn of 1885 and saw a draft dispatch to this effect on the evening of his departure for Ceylon. He remonstrated and left England considering resignation. Matters of this nature were usually left to the governor's discretion; indeed, it was unnecessary for the Secretary of State to express any opinion as Gordon's action had not required his confirmation. The effect of such a reversal would be to lower the Governor's prestige and to encourage corruption. The man in question presently died. Although the Secretary of State had, in any case, decided to reconsider, the episode had an unhealthy effect. In future the Governor was bound to be cautious unless he had a clear-cut case.

Prison discipline was the final weak spot in the administration of justice. The chief difficulty arose from the amalgamation of the offices of inspector-general of police and inspector-general of prisons which had been carried out as a depression measure on the understanding that the offices would again be separated if the prisons suffered by it. The officer in charge, although still too young to be pensioned, had passed

[97]The Attorney-General himself was not implicated; he was only incompetent. Gordon summed him up as a former Seychelles magistrate, above suspicion but useless.

[98]Report of the Commissioners enquiring into Corruption in the Judicial Establishment of Ceylon, enclosed in Gordon to Derby, 25 April 1885, PRO CO 54/558.   [99]*Ibid.*   [100]*Ibid.*

the peak of his efficiency and proved incapable of discharging both offices. Prisons and prison discipline had fallen into "a disgraceful state."[101] That Campbell, the inspector-general, was too young to be retired and could not afford the reduction in salary which would have resulted from being deprived of one of his offices was no excuse for Gordon's failure to carry out the separation although it may be considered an extenuating circumstance. What Gordon did was to appoint a one-man commission to report upon the reorganization of the police force and prisons. The report, with Gordon's comments, reached the Colonial Office after Gordon's retirement and the reorganization devolved upon his successor.

Sir Arthur Gordon was at his best in dealing with the native inhabitants of the colonies. Unlike many governors he had a warm sympathy for them and their problems and a tolerance for their culture. Realizing the psychological impact of western cluture upon them and believing that native institutions must eventually crumble before the assault of occidental civilization, he wished the change to take place slowly and gradually. Could the transition be spread over a generation or more, the shock would be lessened and friction between government and governed kept to a minimum. For that reason Gordon maintained the old native system of local government whereby native headmen ruled the villages, mostly without pay.

This ancient system had begun to break down in the area most affected by European culture, the western and southern maritime districts. It had been suggested that all headmen should be paid by the government, but Gordon believed that, because it would be impossible to pay them all, their number would have to be reduced. Such a move, he said in opening the legislative council in 1889, would convert the headmen into paid servants and agents of the central government and compel the creation of a new system of local government that would have no hold on the native mind. Furthermore, it would not be as cheap, efficient, or easy to control as the one in operation, and it would be regarded as the mere creation and instrument of alien power. He hoped, instead, "to preserve as long as possible, a system which enlists all natural local influences in support of authority . . . and which shields the Government to a great degree from direct friction with those it governs."[102] For these reasons Sir Arthur decided to take no action to

[101]Lucas's minute, 5 Aug. 1890, PRO CO 54/587, minute paper 11639.
[102]Gordon's speech to the legislative council, Oct. 1889, enclosed in Gordon to Knutsford, 31 Oct. 1889, PRO CO 54/584.

bring purely local government under the central government's control.

The difference between Gordon's tolerant and helpful attitude toward the natives and that of the lesser officers was amusingly demonstrated in 1884 when the Inspector-General of Police prohibited native processions. Gordon reversed the order. The Inspector-General then observed that:

> Many of the inhabitants of Ceylon are very fond of processions, induced thereto by vanity and ostentation; and their processions accompanied by fireworks, rumtumming, and other loud and barbarous sounds, and by large strange forms, of startling color, have often blocked the thoroughfares, obstructed traffic, frightened horses and cattle and seriously disturbed and annoyed sick and nervous and busy people.
>
> Now it is a group . . . who seek to go dancing about the streets for days together, chained and painted like tigers, and accompanied by native drums and crowds more or less large. Now it is the same people, carrying a painted tomb in memory of Hassan and Hoosain though most of the mummers are not themselves Mohamedans at all. Now it is a marriage party spending more than a year's income in foolish display—and very often it is a procession got up by one or two crafty priests, or quasi religious or charitable persons, with the object of collecting crowds and extorting money.
>
> Such processions . . . we have always kept down as much as possible. . . .[103]

He asked the Governor to reconsider his ruling. Gordon replied:

> What I wish strongly to express is my entire disapproval of perpetual petty meddling, which is just what the Police most delight in. It is the constant interference in the affairs of daily life by the Government that is so much felt and resented, though obeyed, and this interference it is the object of a wise government to minimize. Here in Ceylon, as in many other places ruled by us, the people admit they have security and justice, but complain that life has no amusements. Of course, "danger" and "obstruction" should not be allowed to exist, but I think a very large tolerance should be given to the amusements, habits, and familiar customs of the people. It is not only to religious and grave processions that I wish tolerance shown. . . . It is not their [the police] office to cure peoples' "vanity," or suppress any manifestation that is peaceable, legal, and not attended with *grave* public inconvenience.[104]

In forwarding this correspondence to the Secretary of State Gordon added: "It is no part of the duty of the Government or of the Police, to interfere with harmless usages, simply because to Western ideas they seem foolish. . . ."[105]

[103]Inspector-General of Police to Gordon, enclosed in Gordon to Derby, 29 Aug. 1884, PRO CO 54/554.
[104]Gordon to Inspector-General of Police, 5 April 1884; PEO CO 54/554.
[105]Gordon to Derby, 29 Aug. 1884.

Another demonstration of Sir Arthur's concern for natives and their institutions was his reform of what were called the "Buddhist temporalities." When Ceylon came under the Crown, the government took over control of the estates of the Buddhist church, but in the 1840's the British authorities withdrew from their position of control and assigned these vast estates to the Buddhist priests. At that time it was recognized that the government ought to provide the Buddhist church in Ceylon with a sound working constitution, but the difficulties had always proven too great. In the intervening years before Gordon went to the colony, great and scandalous abuses had prevailed in the priests' management of the church's estates. The priests, contrary to their ordination laws, had meddled in worldly affairs and had become corrupt.

Gordon believed that, as long as management of Buddhist religious estates remained unreformed, Britain had not fulfilled her obligations to two-thirds of the inhabitants of Ceylon.[106] He began to work on the problem in 1884 and four years later proposed a solution. He rejected the suggestion that the government should confiscate the estates, arguing that, since the British had removed all the former checks on maladministration and had put nothing in their place, the Buddhist community should first have a chance to wipe out corruption. If his plan failed then the estates might be confiscated. The scheme which Gordon and the Attorney-General drew up was based on one that had worked well in India. It transferred church estates to local trustees controlled by committees and ensured a strict audit of the accounts under the direction of the judicial authority. A bill incorporating these points was passed early in 1889 with the unanimous support of the unofficial members of the legislative council.[107]

Some opposition to the measure had developed both inside and outside the council. A legislative subcommittee which sat on the bill weakened it in certain respects, an action which drew from Gordon the comment that it was marvellous "how hard it appears to get the idea of religious equality practically realized."[108] The bill was opposed by some of the Buddhist priests who were being deprived of temporal power, by some Christians who considered it an official recognition of Buddhism, and by some who did not wish to have Buddhism relieved of the bad odour which the scandals had given it. The opposition was much less than Gordon had expected, however, and he reported the passage of

[106]*Ibid.*

[107]Gordon to Knutsford, 14 March 1888, PRO CO 54/557, and 19 April 1889, enclosing ordinance, PRO CO 54/582.

[108]Gordon to Attorney-General Grenier, 3 March 1889, Stanmore Papers, 49246.

the bill to the Secretary of State with pardonable pride. The Colonial Office, pleased that someone had at last solved a seemingly insoluble problem, was congratulatory.[109]

Gordon showed his interest in native culture and welfare in other ways. He saw to it that hospitals were built in areas which had not previously enjoyed such service. He patronized native art. He repaired the great Abhayagiria Dagoba, carried out excavation at Anuradhapura, and took measures to care for those ruins. He visited many areas in Ceylon never before visited by a British governor, and bore with admirable patience the long and elaborate welcoming celebrations with which he was greeted everywhere he went.

IV. GORDON'S POPULARITY AND SUCCESS

Arthur Gordon was undoubtedly more popular in Ceylon than he had been in any other colony except, perhaps, Trinidad. The inhabitants certainly appreciated his interest and care. When the end of his term approached, both Sinhalese and Tamils sent memorials to the Secretary of State asking that the Governor's term be extended. Neither memorial had any effect since the Colonial Office had already decided to extend his term by six months, but both were impressive. The Sinhalese memorial was signed by 122,000 men of property who were able to sign their names, and the Tamil by over 16,000 men, among them the leading members of the Tamil community. Lord Knutsford assured Gordon of Her Majesty's government's high appreciation of "this well deserved recognition of the exceptionally valuable services which you have been able to render to Ceylon,"[110] and of his own pleasure at "this proof that you have won the confidence of the Tamil as of the Sinhalese members of the community."[111]

Gordon's popularity with the native peoples is beyond question; but what of his popularity with the planters and the commercial community of Europeans and burghers? His speedy action on the failure of the Oriental Bank assured him initial favour with those groups, and in 1884 he was presented with an address by the legislative council in addition to the ordinary one in reply to the speech from the throne. This performance was "quite unprecedented," and despite Gordon's professed disregard for popularity ("I have never sought popularity, and rarely

[109]Minutes on Gordon to Knutsford, 19 April 1889.
[110]Knutsford to Gordon, 8 Oct. 1889, PRO CO 54/583.
[111]Draft dispatch in reply to Gordon to Knutsford, 14 Sept. 1889, PRO CO 54/584.

obtained it. . . ."),[112] he found the experience agreeable. "It is a great pleasure," he wrote to Lady Sophia Palmer, "to feel that one has done some good, but the pleasure is certainly enhanced when instead of grumbling or opposition one meets with recognition on the part of those served."[113] His popularity was short-lived. He lost the approval of the planters when he successfully resisted their claim that he be their servant instead of their master, their desire to subordinate the affairs of the Sinhalese and Tamils to their own interests, and their wish to devote the revenues of the colony to the improvement of the planting districts.[114] He was able to purchase their co-operation only by his advocacy of the Nanoya-Haputalé railway extension. He forfeited the good opinion of the commercial men in 1885 when he failed to support their petition for the completion of the harbour at Colombo.

His stock seems to have risen on his return from a short holiday in England during 1888. In his absence public business had come almost to a stand-still. His energy and determination had been missed. Many were glad to have him back, although one of the newspapers, commenting on the rumour that Gordon might receive a peerage, had the bad taste to remark that he was "hardly fit for a place among the Peers, but the position is one which no lady could more fitly and conspicuously adorn than Lady Gordon."[115] "Such impertinence!"[116] exclaimed Lady Gordon. Sir Arthur himself tended to ignore colonial newspapers, considering most of them beneath his notice and that of the Colonial Office as well. More than one minute by the staff of the Colonial Office suggests that Gordon, contrary to the rule which required governors to send home newspapers representing all sections of any importance in the community, sent regularly only the paper which most nearly reflected his own opinion.[117] In Ceylon that paper was the *Observer*. The leading opposition papers were the *Examiner, Times,* and *Independent*. No doubt Gordon felt that opposition opinions would reach the secretary of state more easily than his own.

As long as he had the necessary power (as he had in Ceylon) to do good work, lack of popularity did not perturb him. "The consciousness," he told the legislative council in 1888, "that one has been able . . . to

[112]From report of speech by Gordon in legislative council, enclosed in Gordon to Secretary of State, 31 Dec. 1888, PRO CO 54/579.

[113]Gordon to Lady Sophia Palmer, 11 Nov. 1884, Stanmore Papers, 49221.

[114]Gordon to Selborne, 24 April 1884, Stanmore Papers, 49218.

[115]Lady Gordon to her sister Jane [Ryan], 18–20 May 1888, Stanmore Papers, 49229.

[116]*Ibid.*

[117]For example, see Johnson's minute in PRO CO 54/575, minute paper 4681.

increase the food supply of a large number of people, to make their hard conditions of life somewhat lighter to them, and to throw some cheerfulness and light into the homes of men who have never seen, and who will never see one, and who do not know one's name, and will feel no gratitude whatever towards one, is to me far more than any popularity. . . ."[118] Although the editor of the *Independent* thought that Gordon had "succeeded in irritating every important community in the island,"[119] Sir Arthur, nevertheless, left Ceylon in May 1890 as an esteemed and popular governor. Throughout the colony there were no discordant notes. Many public meetings were held and all testified to the benefits that he had "conferred on the island in general and on their district in particular."[120]

The Colonial Office staff felt that Gordon's administration had been remarkably successful although it expressed criticisms of some of his particular practices. It accepted, probably correctly, the allegation made by Wall[121] that the Governor had shown favouritism in some of his appointments. It complained, justly, that he was often late with estimates and reports.[122] On the whole, however, its comments were approving. Early in 1889 Lucas wrote that he thought Ceylon had "been singularly well pushed along during very difficult times," and some months later he minuted, "this is the last opening address [to the legislative council] of a governor who has done a great deal for Ceylon. . . . Acknowledge and add that Lord Knutsford is regretfully reminded . . . that the colony which has so largely benefitted by his services will shortly lose them." To this Fairfield added: "But is glad to think that his good work will be remembered—or something cheerful to that effect" and Meade said: "Yes, cheer up."[123]

V. PRIVATE LIFE AND DEPARTURE

Sir Arthur Gordon's public life in Ceylon was happy. Occasionally he suffered frustrations, but he enjoyed power and work and had plenty of both. Privately he was less contented. His son entered Winchester in the

[118]Report of speech to legislative council enclosed in Gordon to Secretary of State, 31 Dec. 1888.
[119]Gordon to Knutsford, 14 Aug. 1889, PRO CO 54/583.
[120]Testimony of Sir William Gregory quoted in Gordon's diary, 7 July 1890, Stanmore Papers, 49265.
[121]Gordon to Knutsford, 14 Aug. 1889.
[122]Gordon composed slowly, his travels about Ceylon took time, and his leaning toward personal government necessitated an increased local correspondence. For these reasons he was often late in submitting information to the Colonial Office.
[123]Minutes on Gordon to Knutsford, 31 Oct. 1889, PRO CO 54/584.

autumn of 1884 and had been left in England when Gordon sailed for Ceylon. This was their first long separation, and they were to be apart for most of the time until Sir Arthur's retirement. The latter's desire for home thus became much stronger than formerly. Then, in December 1888, Lady Gordon fell ill. On the twenty-first Sir Arthur was "anxious about her," on the twenty-second the doctors made him "very anxious." By the thirty-first the doctors were unanimous that she be sent to England. The Gordons sailed on 2 January, reached Aden on the ninth, Brindisi on the seventeenth, and Malta on the nineteenth. Lady Gordon was too ill to proceed. She died on the twenty-sixth of a "creeping paralysis."[124] She was buried in Malta, and Sir Arthur later (1895) had a chapel built there in her memory.

Gordon did not go on to England but, accompanied by his son and daughter, returned to Ceylon. His son could stay but a few weeks, and, after Lady Gordon's sister Madeleine, who had earlier paid the Gordons a lengthy visit in Ceylon, refused Sir Arthur's request that she come to Ceylon as companion to his daughter, he felt he had to send his daughter home. He was thus left alone during his last year in the colony.

Lady Gordon's death affected her husband deeply. His external life continued as before, and he was able to attend fully to business; his health did not suffer, nor did he lose interest in things around him or in political affairs in England. But all was different "at all times and in all ways."[125] For some weeks he could not unburden his heart even to his closest friend, Lord Selborne, who also had recently lost his wife. He tried several times to answer Selborne's letters but "both brain and hand refused to perform." In March he finally wrote: "A sort of vacuity seems to possess me. . . . I find my mind filled with vague images, and losing itself in memories. . . . I find a most real support from the thoroughly intimate *knowledge* that *absence* is not *loss* . . . [and] that this is an absence free from all anxiety, which could not be said when I was in Fiji, or Mauritius, or New Zealand, and my wife in England."[126] As time went by Sir Arthur felt his wife's death even more. On the anniversary of that event he observed to Selborne how strange it was that people should speak of time as a consoler. "A year has gone since my wife left me, and the sense of want and a void is far greater than it was in the earlier days of her loss."[127]

These last eighteen months in Ceylon were unhappy but they were

[124]Gordon's diary, Stanmore Papers, 49265.
[125]Gordon to Selborne, 18 March 1889, Stanmore Papers, 49219.
[126]*Ibid.*
[127]Gordon to Selborne, 26 Jan. 1890, Stanmore Papers, 49220.

not typical. There had been better days spent travelling about the island observing native customs, investigating ruins, seeing new and strange sights. Three gubernatorial residences, Queen's House (Colombo), The Pavilion (Kandy), and Queen's Cottage (Nuwara Eliya), also afforded Gordon variety. He preferred Kandy to Colombo, although he enjoyed the endless succession of vignettes afforded by the latter. To a keen amateur botanist and a lover of nature with a sensitive eye for beauty, Nuwara Eliya presented special attractions, contrasting as it did the old-fashioned English garden of Queen's Cottage with a view of wild nature in the surrounding hills. There, also, the Governor could be alone with his family and his secretary or aide, official duties could be pushed into the background temporarily, and he could vegetate. Partially off-setting such pleasures was the fact that Gordon had the leisure to miss his son more, to grow more homesick, to worry because his "day of action" was rapidly passing (or so it seemed to him) and to long for the opportunity of doing something more useful and permanent than he could do in Ceylon. Still, it was a pleasant rustic life that Gordon enjoyed at Queen's Cottage: "The air is sweet with orange blossoms and roses and mignonette, and musical with bees, and, here and there, a bird. All is bright, and tranquil."[128]

In August 1889, Gordon was notified that his successor was to be Sir Arthur Havelock. He received this news with mixed feelings. He himself was to remain until May 1890 to wind up such important matters as he wished, and since both his children were now in England he was eager to return home. There was therefore no question of his being replaced before he wished to be. Yet Havelock's appointment caused him some pain. The fact was that Gordon's pride was hurt. He had introduced Havelock into the colonial service only fifteen years before, and he felt humiliated that "my former A.D.C." should in that "comparatively short time, and at the age of 42 attain, without, (I think,) abilities exceeding my own,—a position which it took me twenty-two years to reach, at the age of 54!" He was ashamed of this feeling, but he could not help experiencing it, and twice transgressed his father's "supplementary commandment: 'Thou shalt not make ill-natured comments concerning others'."[129] To Lady Sophia Palmer he wrote that Havelock was "not a man of remarkable ability, or extensive knowledge or special force of character,"[130] and shortly after leaving

[128]Gordon to Selborne, 25 March 1885, Stanmore Papers, 49219.

[129]*Ibid.*, 19 Aug. 1889.

[130]Gordon to Lady Sophia Palmer, 8 Oct. 1889, Stanmore Papers, 49223. That this estimation of Havelock may not have been completely without foundation is indicated by Sir William Gregory's statement that "I doubt whether he is a

Ceylon he noted in his diary: "Havelock is an actor, insincere, selfish and a humbug. . . ."[131]

Despite this feeling Gordon telegraphed to the Colonial Office that he rejoiced to learn that Havelock had been named as his successor. He assured Havelock that he felt it

> a great positive pleasure to know that I am to be followed by a man who will carry forward my own work and not destroy it; who has just and right views and is not afraid to act on them and to whom one can hand over the Colony with the knowledge that it will be governed by him with a view to its interests and welfare and not merely in such a way as may best secure a quiet time for himself. And oh! it is *such* a relief . . . to know that a gentleman and lady are coming here and not a mere office hack. . . .[132]

To Selborne he spoke of Havelock as having just and sound views, adding that he was quite sure that there was no one in the colonial service and few outside it whom he would rather have succeed him.[133] Havelock, he told Selborne's daughter, was "a gentleman, and an honest man, and considering what a scurvy lot, intellectually and morally, the general run of Colonial professional governors now a days are one might be thankful, even if Havelock were a much inferior man to what he really is, to be spared the infliction of a Pope Hennessy or a Sir Ambrose Shea."[134]

There is no ground for believing that these statements in praise of Havelock were less sincerely meant than the derogatory ones. Gordon's ambivalence is explained by his wounded pride at being succeeded by one so much his junior and by his joy that his successor would be, not a "professional," but a "gentleman" who would not overturn all he had done simply to demonstrate independence of mind.

In the end there were many dinners, speeches, and addresses which Sir Arthur found gratifying, but trying. He had begun to slow down. During the previous September he had been unable, for the first time, to complete one of his tours. Nevertheless, he left Ceylon feeling that there was still some work left in him and hoping that if he did not receive a peerage he might be appointed governor-general of India.

---

man who sees much further than the end of his nose" (quoted by Gordon in his diary, 7 July 1890, Stanmore Papers, 49265), and by the fact that Havelock, quite soon after his arrival in Ceylon, allowed the so-called paddy tax (which apart from votes of the legislative council, provided funds for irrigation) to be repealed despite Gordon's protests.

[131]Gordon's diary, 5 June 1890, Stanmore Papers, 49265.
[132]Gordon to Havelock, 20 Aug. 1889, Stanmore Papers, 49246.
[133]Gordon to Selborne, 19 Aug. 1889.
[134]Gordon to Lady Sophia Palmer, 8 Oct. 1889.

IX

RETIREMENT AND PEERAGE

❧

SIR ARTHUR GORDON was approaching sixty-one when he retired from the governorship of Ceylon. He had aged in the past three years. His beard had turned white, he had grown much stouter, and he had given up riding. Nevertheless, except for an occasional attack of fever, he enjoyed good health and did not consider his retirement from the colonial service a permanent departure from public life. Should no occasion for important public service appear, he would have an opportunity to publish a biography of his father, a work he deemed both a labour of love and a duty.

From time to time since 1871 Gordon had thought of retiring from the colonial field, but he had not seriously considered it until the end of his administration of Fiji. In 1878 Gladstone had pressed him "with, for him, extreme earnestness to return to Parliament at the next general election,"[1] an invitation which, for several reasons, Sir Arthur could not accept. Fiji was an important work in which he could not easily be replaced, and he had promised to return to it. Moreover, he had become so used to absolute command that he felt himself poorly prepared to act in concert with equals. Finally, he owed it to his family to serve the time necessary to qualify for a pension.[2]

During the last ten years of Gordon's colonial career he began to think more frequently and more seriously about retirement. He qualified for a good pension in 1886. The following year Fiji passed into

[1]Gordon to Selborne (private and confidential), 12 Oct. 1878, Stanmore Papers, 49217.
[2]*Ibid.*

Thurston's capable hands. In any case Gordon felt he could do more at home to safeguard Fiji than he could abroad. The eighties took a heavy toll of his friends and relatives and he sometimes feared that he would find himself a stranger in England unless he soon retired. Gordon had ascended the heights in the colonial service and, after Ceylon, any new colonial appointment could only be a step downward. His ambition, as yet unsatisfied, led him still to yearn for "employment of a really important character."[3] Would he not stand a greater chance at home of obtaining such employment? Moreover, as time passed, Gordon felt increasingly dissatisfied with the Colonial Office. Its growing "habit of shelving, rather than solving questions submitted to it, . . . [and] its disposition to deny all discretionary power, and to meddle in the minutest trifles . . ."[4] irked him more and more and prepared him to break his long-standing ties with it.

In Sir Arthur's gloomier moods he considered his life and work failures. His diaries, he noted in 1888, were

a record of a wandering and to a great extent a wasted life; and are full from end to end of unfulfilled intentions, disappointed hopes, unrealized projects, and unsatisfied ambitions. Few have started on a career in life with greater advantages than I did. Few have more wasted them, and thrown them away. In my juvenile folly I thought it rather fine to do so and "rest only on myself."[5] And it is chiefly by my own fault that I find myself, at 59, the obscure subordinate of the highly respectable gentleman [Lord Knutsford] whose father used to feel my pulse, and give me black draughts and pills.[6]

In his letters to Lady Sophia Palmer and her father, Lord Selborne, he prophesied the failure of his native policy and predicted the debasement and demoralization of the native peoples of the Pacific:

Granting, for argument's sake, that high motives and not lower ones, have been my spring of action, (which may perhaps be doubted) and granting that I have not, inasmuch as I have done all I could (if I have), really failed in the *performance* of my own work, and the discharge of my own duty, what then? The poor people whose rights I have striven to maintain, and whose existence I have tried to preserve, are not the less surely stripped of those rights or the less speedily trampled out of existence, and *this is* failure: —failure that cannot be repaired, and that is infinitely more saddening than any consequences to oneself of personal failure.[7]

He was not much comforted by Lady Sophia's assurance that "no life that has been an effort for service to God and man is or can be a

[3]Gordon to Selborne, 19 May 1887, Stanmore Papers, 49219.   [4]*Ibid.*
[5]This was not perhaps an altogether accurate interpretation of events.
[6]Gordon to Lady Sophia Palmer, 20 Oct. 1888, Stanmore Papers, 49222.
[7]*Ibid.*, 8 Oct. 1886.

failure . . ." or by her reminder that, although his "struggle for the weak against oppression and wrong, seems to have failed and the Pharisees and Scribes to have, as usual, got their way,"[8] he should not forget "that there is the apparent failure and crucifixion and triumph of evil, *before* resurrection and triumphant life."[9]

During the eighties Sir Arthur's ambitions revolved around securing a peerage, an Indian presidency, and even the governor-generalship of India. In 1880 his brother-in-law, George Shaw-Lefevre, informed him that he had heard that had Lord Ripon not accepted the governor-generalship of India Sir Arthur would have had the best chance.[10] Gordon never entirely despaired of securing that post until Lord Curzon's appointment in 1898. Lord Selborne sometimes chided him for his ambition. "But surely," Gordon rejoined, "it is not wrong, when one not only knows, but has proved by exercising it, that one possesses the power to govern—when one finds that in governing alone does one find satisfaction for all the higher faculties of one's nature, surely, I say, it is not wrong to desire, and to desire ardently, employment for those energies on a large scale, before the time comes for their loss or enfeeblement, before life closes on them idle and unused."[11] But as the decade advanced and his desire for home increased, Sir Arthur was more disposed to settle for a peerage and to find some useful work in the House of Lords.

There is little doubt that he would have received a peerage in Gladstone's "outgoing batch" in 1886, had it not been for the adverse publicity which he received arising out of the Bryce-Rusden libel case. There was, for a time, a possibility that Bryce would institute a suit against Gordon as well, because the latter had transmitted to the historian Rusden a memorandum written by Bishop Hadfield of New Zealand containing information, which Gordon said could be relied upon, concerning Bryce and his part in the Maori Wars. Rusden, Gordon charged, had embroidered the memorandum and published it without his consent. Gladstone wrote kindly, telling Sir Arthur that he had thought it unwise to proceed with the peerage as long as the possibility of further legal action existed. He assured him, however, that the wait would not be long as he would soon be back in power. Gordon fully admitted his indiscretion, but thought he had been heavily punished.

[8]The reference here is to the increasing control by the Australasian colonists of the natives of the Western Pacific.

[9]Gordon to Lady Sophia Palmer, 2 Sept. 1886, Stanmore Papers, 49222.

[10]Stanmore Shaw-Lefevre to Gordon, 18 Sept. 1880, Stanmore Papers, 49224, f. 287.

[11]Gordon to Selborne, 25 March 1882, Stanmore Papers, 49218.

Still, it had saved him some embarrassment. For the past few years he had been taking a closer interest in British politics and had concluded that he did not see eye to eye with Gladstone on a number of important subjects. Even though he had informed Gladstone of the limited extent of his support for his Irish policy, Gladstone had written back ignoring all differences of opinion. Gordon believed he would have been compelled to have refused the peerage as long as there was a chance that Gladstone was under any misconception.[12]

The following year Sir Arthur hoped he would be included among the Jubilee peers because he was, after Sir Hercules Robinson, the doyen of colonial governors. He thought this should give him claim to consideration irrespective of politics. He supposed, however, that his known intimacy with Gladstone would be fatal to his chances under the Salisbury government, although "as a matter of fact it would find in me a staunch supporter."[13] In the light of subsequent events, this statement of Gordon's requires some explanation.

In the first place, Sir Arthur had been long out of England and had lost much of that sense of party loyalty which comes from being a constant participant in the party struggle. Secondly, he was a Whig. He viewed with alarm the advent of democracy, which was being ushered in by the radical section of the Liberal Party to which Gladstone seemingly deferred. He felt in consequence an increasing charity toward the Conservatives "extending retrospectively even to Dizzy himself."[14] Gordon's letters during the eighties show his frame of mind: "The radicalism of the present day is running far ahead of my liberalism...."[15] "It seems to me that revolutionary changes are being hurried on by a vigorous minority, in entire opposition to the intelligent opinion of the country."[16] "The real fight of the future will be between old-fashioned ideas of property and some form of communism, I have no doubt whatever. . . . I wish I had Gladstone's sublime faith in the wisdom of the ignorant, the generosity of the selfish, and the nobleness of the mean. . . . Though it may take some time for them to learn their power, I cannot but think it will be used, and used as one would most naturally anticipate."[17] " 'The democracy' (when I was a boy they

[12]Gordon to Selborne, 31 July 1886, Stanmore Papers, 49219.

[13]*Ibid.*, 11 April 1887.

[14]Gordon to Mary Gladstone, 9 Jan. 1886, *Some Hawarden Letters*, 220. The full quotation is as follows: "As to *mere* party politics, I confess I feel every day a growing detachment from all parties and a great and increasing charity to all sides, extending retrospectively even to Dizzy himself."

[15]Gordon to Selborne, 25 March 1883, Stanmore Papers, 49218.

[16]Gordon to Lady Sophia Palmer, 18 Jan. 1884; Stanmore Papers, 49221.

[17]*Ibid.*, Dec. 1884.

talked of 'the mob') do not care for logic nor do eager party leaders."[18]
"I am perplexed and muddled, as to what one ought to anticipate, and
whether one should look with hope or fear to the future; remembering
that by 'future,' I am not referring to the Irish Question alone, but to
the maintenance of property, of the monarchical form of government,
and a few other trifles of a similar nature."[19] Although at one point
Gordon stated that he would have supported the extension of the
franchise in 1885, he was, by 1887, asking Selborne why that bill or
even that of 1867 had been necessary. "To me, far off, and dimly
seeing, *there* appears . . . to be the irrecoverable mischief."[20] What
bothered Gordon was the fact that the society in which he had reached
maturity, and which he knew and loved, was being destroyed in consequence of the spread of radicalism in the Liberal party. In 1886 he
hoped for a union of Whigs and Conservatives which might delay the
coming to power of radical democracy. After the formation of the
Salisbury ministry he was inclined to be sympathetic to it as the pre-
server of the traditional order, although his old affection for Gladstone
led him to adopt an uneasy neutrality.

Sir Arthur's opinion of Gladstone was undergoing revision during
these years. In 1868 he had written in his diary: "Whether one agrees
with him or differs from him one cannot but admire and love the *man*.
What a fine fellow he is really, and in some ways how simple[-]minded
notwithstanding all his subtlety of intellect."[21] In 1884 he noted that
"it has always been Gladstone's misfortune that he is more desirous
to persuade others that facts are as he wishes them to be, than to realize
what the facts are."[22] With reference to Gladstone's campaign of 1884
Gordon commented: "It is strange, it is lamentable, it is a fresh proof
of his powers of self deception, that he should fail to perceive that it
is the duty of a statesman to have and to avow opinions on great
questions of national policy. . . . To say that he will not assist the
formation of a national opinion as to the Crown, the Church, and the
House of Lords, by expressing his own . . . is to abdicate his position."[23]
He thought Gladstone was taking this line in order to maintain party
unity and so continue as prime minister. He contrasted this "petty, if not
immoral" procedure with the "far nobler" one of Sir Robert Peel who
had broken up his party "rather than leave great objects to take care of

---

[18]Gordon to Waterfield, 24 Jan. 1887, Stanmore Papers, 49251.
[19]Gordon to Selborne, 26 Aug. 1887, Stanmore Papers, 49219.
[20]*Ibid.*
[21]Gordon's diary, 22 Oct. 1868, Stanmore Papers, 49267.
[22]Gordon to Selborne, 24 April 1884, Stanmore Papers, 49218.
[23]Gordon to Selborne, 4 Jan. 1885, Stanmore Papers, 49219.

themselves. . . ."[24] He found it painful to see Gladstone "resort to the shifts and devices which he now . . . habitually uses." He did not care "to have to scrutinize the words of *any* Prime Minister, as if they were those of some sharp, shameless attorney, much less the words of a man one so honours."[25] Until 1887, Sir Arthur believed that Gladstone's aims "as pictured to himself [were] as lofty and noble as ever,"[26] but after Gladstone's Jubilee speech at Hawarden, in which he had said unkind things about royalty, Gordon was much shocked. He had hitherto thought that Gladstone had always "meant what he said, and said what he meant." He thought so no longer.[27]

The estrangement of his intimate friends, Lord Selborne and Lady Sophia Palmer, from Gladstone doubtless further weakened Gordon's confidence in the latter. Lady Sophia noted "the growing *hatred* among the upper and trades classes" for Gladstone,[28] and quoted Lecky as saying, "we have had enough of Mr. Gladstone's Genesis. I am longing for his Exodus."[29] She asked whether Wolsey's words about Henry VIII were not "curiously applicable to the G.O.M.: 'He is a prince of a most royal carriage and hath a princely heart; and rather than he will miss or want any part of his will, he will endanger the one half of his Kingdom.' "[30] By early 1890, Gordon, having read Gladstone's Manchester speeches, found himself doubting Gladstone's faith in himself. Those speeches indicated to him that Gladstone disliked and, in his heart, suspected the utility of the measures he recommended. "That," wrote Sir Arthur, "is dishonesty of a more vulgar and less subtle character than the dishonesty of which we have had cause previously to complain, or perhaps more truly, to lament without complaining. What a wise man my father was. . . . He said that G[ladstone] 'might one day lead the radicals.' "[31]

Gordon was of two minds about his return home. He was tired of exile, but reluctant to lose Gladstone's friendship. Gladstone, in Lady Sophia's words, had "bulled himself Infallible"[32] and would not be satis-

[24]*Ibid.* [25]*Ibid.*, 25 March 1885.
[26]*Ibid.*, 10 March 1886. [27]*Ibid.*, 7 Oct. 1887.
[28]Gordon visited England in 1888 and was much perturbed by "the marked and quite novel manner in which society has been cut in two by political differences. . . . You but rarely see man or woman in the houses of those of the opposite 'colour.' " At no former time had he seen "anything like the social division which now exists, and . . . I am old enough to remember the Repeal of the Corn Laws." (Gordon to Lord Dufferin, 27 July 1888, Stanmore Papers, 49247.)
[29]Lady Sophia Palmer to Gordon, 18 March 1886, Stanmore Papers, 49222. See also Philip Magnus, *Gladstone: A Biography*, 349.
[30]Lady Sophia Palmer to Gordon, 18 June 1886, Stanmore Papers, 49222.
[31]Gordon to Selborne, 4 Jan. 1890, Stanmore Papers, 49220.
[32]Lady Sophia Palmer to Gordon, [April ?] 1886, Stanmore Papers, 49222.

fied with less than absolute and unconditional acquiescence in his leadership and policies. Gordon knew that he could never follow Gladstone unconditionally. He decided therefore to avoid being beholden to him for a peerage and tried to secure the honour through the Salisbury administration. If he could obtain it as a reward for his colonial services, he would be in an independent position and able to support government or opposition as his conscience dictated. Despite the fact that Gordon approached Salisbury through his (Gordon's) nephew, George Hamilton, and through Lord Selborne, he was not included among the Jubilee peers (1887). Some months after his retirement from Ceylon (1890), he was again passed over even though Lord Knutsford urged Salisbury to recognize Gordon's thirty years of service. Apparently it was seriously considered on this later occasion but was finally rejected because the Queen did not believe his wealth (£100,000) great enough to support a peerage. Lord Salisbury wrote to Selborne:

> Sir Arthur is in error in discrediting the idea that the question of fortune has been of decisive importance. I have been *very* anxious to create a system of life Peers; but . . . the man who checkmated me was Gladstone—because he thought Life Peers would strengthen the House of Lords. But, if Life Peers are not allowed, then, with respect to men who have sons, the question of fortune becomes of great importance; and is looked upon in this light by all who have to do with this most repulsive duty.[33]

Gordon was disappointed. Feeling that he had "still vigour and strength enough for active usefulness . . . ," he regretted being laid on the shelf.[34]

In the meantime he had been twice approached to run for Parliament. In December 1890, he was asked by Lord Huntly, on behalf of the Liberal Unionists and Conservatives, to stand for West Aberdeenshire; but his age, his "old affection for Gladstone," consideration for his nephew, Lord Aberdeen, and "the general posture of affairs" dictated his refusal.[35] He wrote to Gladstone telling him of the offer. "I should like you to know that, in refusing, I have told those who asked me, that, even did I share their views, (which I do not), and had I not other reasons to disincline me to stand, nothing on earth would induce me to take a position in which I should find myself publicly placed among those who were acting in opposition to yourself."[36] In August of the following year his friend Waterfield asked him whether he would be willing to represent the University of Cambridge. This was attractive. If elected he would have an independent political position. He had no

[33]Salisbury to Selborne, 11 Aug. 1892, Stanmore Papers, 49220.
[34]Gordon to Selborne, 15 Aug. 1892, Stanmore Papers, 49220.
[35]Gordon's diary, 3 Dec. 1890, Stanmore Papers, 49265.
[36]Gordon to Gladstone, 11 Dec. 1890, Gladstone Papers, 44322.

university distinction except his Cambridge M.A. and the honorary D.C.L. which Oxford had given him in 1879, but be thought he might receive support "not likely to be given to any other liberal unionist."[37] He forwarded to Waterfield a statement of his position on the issues in which the university would be interested and authorized him to show it to the Senate. He was opposed to Church disestablishment in both England and Wales. He would give Ireland the largest degree of local self-government compatible with maintenance of the unity of the Empire. He could be described, he said, as "a Liberal not hostile to the present Government and wholly unfettered by pledges or engagements." The Salisbury government on the whole had administered the affairs of the Empire with wisdom and success, and although he did not vow allegiance to it he would take no step to contribute to its fall.[38] Sir Arthur, however, did not become a candidate (for reasons which are not clear) and the university elected two resident professors. In November 1892, he was "importuned to stand for East Aberdeenshire" and assured that he would be returned whichever side he took. He declined because it would have caused "unpleasantness and family quarrels," since had he stood for election he would have done so as a Unionist.[39]

Since his return from Ceylon Sir Arthur had paid at least two visits to Hawarden, in October 1890 and October 1891. His impression from the first was that Gladstone had adopted Scottish disestablishment and believed English disestablishment distant but certain. As for Ireland, both Gladstone and his son Herbert took "a low-pitched tone"; the Irish Parliament would only be a glorified county council.[40] The second visit took place a week or two after Gladstone's announcement of the "Newcastle programme." Gordon disliked it and went to Hawarden fearing that Gladstone might give him a cool reception. To his surprise, he had never before found him so affectionate and seldom more confidential. Gladstone was not astonished that Gordon did not like the "Newcastle programme"; he did not like it himself. It was all the fault of Lord Hartington and the Liberal Unionists; their secession had deprived the Liberal party of its moderate and conservative elements.[41] Gordon did not think he had ever felt Gladstone's kindness of manner more. Personal contact revived the old friendship and enabled Gladstone, whose magnetism and attractiveness were irresistible when he took the trouble to exert them, to regain some of his old ascendancy over

[37]Gordon to Selborne, 27 Aug. 1891, Stanmore Papers, 49220.
[38]Gordon to Waterfield, 1 Sept. and 2 Sept. 1891, Stanmore Papers, 49252.
[39]Gordon to Selborne, 17 Nov. 1892, Stanmore Papers, 49220.
[40]Ibid., 8 Oct. 1890.
[41]Ibid., 26 Oct. 1891.

Gordon—at least when they were together. Even so, Gordon was not pleased at Gladstone's victory in 1892. "If," he wrote, "the new Government remains in office three years, it will, I think, in that time have passed measures which will ensure the permanent ascendancy of the revolutionary party."[42]

Sir Arthur was now by conviction more nearly an ally of the secessionist Whigs and the Conservatives than of the Liberals. Habit held him to the Liberals. Friendship and family connections tore him both ways. Self-interest inclined him to the party in power. When the elections came on, he had not yet learned that he would not get his peerage from the Tories. He had known earlier of the Queen's objections, but until the government resigned in August, he thought that he had overcome her objections and that he might well be included in the defeated government's customary "outgoing batch" of peers. The letter that Gordon sent to Gladstone in mid-July, soon after the results of the general election were known, was therefore not a thinly veiled request for a peerage. Gordon wrote:

I think our long intimacy is sufficient to give me the right to offer you my humble tribute of satisfaction. . . . The possession of the office of Prime Minister is by no means a subject of unmixed congratulation; but it is a legitimate cause for congratulation, (and that unmixed with misgiving or anxiety), that you should enjoy the unique distinction of being called on a fourth time to fill that post. . . .

It is a stormy prospect that you have to look to, and I fear that Labour questions may raise even greater difficulties than Ireland. I have the strongest sympathies with the aspirations of labour, but . . . to me, "individualism" seems a necessary condition of true liberty. . . .

My object in writing is to assure you, once more, of my affection and sympathy. . . . Nor has that affection ever ceased or materially diminished, though at one moment [1859], it waned. For many years the thing I most craved for was to be a Secretary of State in a government of which you were the Head. That dream, like many other visions and ambitions, has long since died away; though, possibly, I might yet, as a Peer, some day, be of some obscure usefulness as an Under Secretary for the Colonies, or India, or in speaking for Home Rule.[43]

Gordon plainly wanted new employment. On his return from Ceylon he had settled with his son and daughter in the house he had bought in 1879, the Red House, Ascot. There he had finally begun work on the long-delayed biography of his father. By the summer of 1892 this task neared completion. Had his wife lived he might have withstood the prospect of idleness with greater equanimity; but with so little to take

[42]*Ibid.*, 8 Aug. 1892.
[43]Gordon to Gladstone, 18 July 1892, Gladstone Papers, 44322.

his attention and engage his energies he began to fret and to seek such employment as his political connections might obtain for him. This was the object of Sir Arthur's July letter to Gladstone. Gladstone, however, took it as a request for a peerage. He responded with an offer to carry out his former intention (set aside by the Bryce-Rusden trial) of making Gordon a baron.

Despite his obvious desire for a peerage Gordon did not seize upon this opportunity. Instead, he visited Hawarden and told Gladstone what had passed between himself and Salisbury on the subject. He told him also that had it not been for the Queen's objection he would now be in the Lords on the opposition benches and that he had too much knowledge of Gladstone's strained relations with the Queen to wish him to press on her a step to which she had objected a short time before. Gordon left Hawarden thinking the matter at an end.[44] He heard nothing more about it until mid-May 1893, when, on his way back from a visit to Italy and Malta, he received at Gibraltar the following letter from Gladstone:

I wrote yesterday [2 May] to Kimberley our leader in the Lords, to say that I thought of submitting your name to the Queen for a Peerage. He answers by enquiring "will he support the Government?" This is an enquiry to which I can easily answer for my own satisfaction. But as I am to vouch you to another I think I ought to do it only with your own direct sanction, and I daresay you will put me in a condition to do so.[45]

On 16 May Gordon replied by telegram: "My reply is yes," and by letter as follows:

You may safely assure Lord Kimberley that I shall . . . "support the Government." My own convictions, and my devotion to yourself alike prompt me to do so. In so saying however, I do not mean to pledge myself to the unhesitating and unfailing support, on all occasions and at all times, which is expected from those who are bound by the ties of office. As a matter of fact, it is very unlikely that I should give a vote contrary to your opinions or wishes, but, as a matter of self respect, I think I should say that on Colonial questions I can hardly be expected not to have opinions of my own, and that should questions really religious . . . come under discussion, my course must be guided by my conscience as it may at the time dictate.

As regards Home Rule, our conversation will [have] shewn you how cordially I accept it. I can hardly expect you to remember my letter[46] to

[44]Gordon to Selborne (secret), 25 May 1893, Stanmore Papers, 49220.
[45]Gladstone to Gordon, 2 May 1893, Gladstone Papers, 44322.
[46]In this letter, dated 28 March 1886, Gordon advocated Home Rule, "the more independent the Irish Parliament the better," with the exclusion of Irish members from Westminster.

you of 1886, before the Bill was introduced but you may possibly recollect my saying to you, only a short time ago, that I thought I could speak with some effect in its favour.[47]

Gladstone wrote on the 22 May, not in reply to the letter just quoted, which had considerably modified the unqualified "yes" of the telegram, but to the effect that he had proceeded with Gordon's peerage which would be in recognition of his colonial service. Sir Arthur on the twenty-fifth expressed his gratitude "for the recognition . . . of such public service as I may have rendered during my thirty years of colonial administration. . . ."[48] Gladstone then notified him that the Queen had given her approval.

Gordon was disturbed that Gladstone had neither replied to nor acknowledged his letter of the sixteenth. His position now was that he would accept the peerage as a reward for service, but he would not do so if it were understood to imply the surrender of his own views as to Home Rule and Disestablishment. His letter to Gladstone certainly had not promised support on the latter, but it clearly had on the former. He went to London to see Gladstone to make his position clear. The consequence was that the announcement of his peerage, which was to have been made in the Queen's Birthday Honours List, was not made, although the proposal was not withdrawn.

It is necessary at this point to consider Gordon's views on Home Rule. Although from the time the question had arisen he had favoured some form of self-government for the Irish, he was inconsistent in the degree of independence he would accord them. In this he did not differ remarkably from any of those who were at all willing to alter the Act of Union. When the first Home Rule Bill was introduced, he had been critical of Gladstone's method of raising the issue,[49] but he had favoured

---

[47]Gordon to Gladstone, 16 May 1893, Gladstone Papers, 44322.

[48]*Ibid.*, 25 May 1893.

[49]Gordon also criticized his nephew, Lord Aberdeen, Gladstone's lord-lieutenant of Ireland. Aberdeen had identified himself with the Home Rule cause and had thus been popular with the Irish. With (as it seemed to Gordon) "singular . . . want of taste and tact," he had announced to the large Dublin crowd that had gathered to see his departure and demonstrate in favour of Home Rule that he would inform the Queen of what, Gordon said, "was really meant as a declaration against her authority." Although Sir Arthur was fond of his nephew and pleased at his success, he could not resist composing for Lady Sophia Palmer's amusement an imaginary letter from Aberdeen to the Queen. He later heard that the actual letter Aberdeen had sent the Queen much resembled his own imaginary one, that the Queen had been furious and had complained bitterly of Aberdeen's betrayal of her and her position in making himself ostentatiously Gladstone's representative, not hers. (Gordon to Lady Sophia Palmer, 27 Aug. 1886; Stanmore Papers, 49222.)

the exclusion of the Irish from Westminster and the creation of an independent Irish parliament, at least so he told Gladstone in March 1886.[50] A few weeks later he wrote to Lady Sophia Palmer, "I do not think *an* Irish parliament inconsistent with the real unity of the Empire."[51] Of the two schemes for Ireland he preferred Gladstone's to Chamberlain's. The latter he felt to be the more revolutionary. "I had rather," he wrote, "see Ireland a separate state than England, Scotland and Wales under the rule of magnified vestries governing with all the jobbery proper to such bodies. I do not think the existence of a Parliament in Dublin is in itself at all incompatible with the maintenance of England's supremacy and Imperial Unity."[52] At the end of the year he was "not hostile to the restoration . . . of an Irish Legislative parliament.[53] Three months later he defined his position to Selborne as being in favour of giving Ireland "the status of a preresponsible-government colony like Canada before 1848,"[54] although a little earlier he had admitted, also to Selborne, that this was an "antiquarian's dream."[55] He made no more pronouncements on the question in his letters until September 1891. By then he felt determined to maintain the unity of the Empire although he was "desirous of according the largest degree of local self government which is compatible with the steady maintenance of that principle."[56]

Gordon, then, was not an opponent of local self-government for Ireland. He did, however, disagree with the particular schemes and the manner in which they had been put forward. Thus, had he entered either house of Parliament before the election of 1892, it would have been as an opponent of Home Rule.[57] He believed, however, that the recent campaign had so stirred the Irish as to make Home Rule inevitable and that unless Britain now came to an agreement with the Irish the latter would soon demand complete independence.[58] Shortly after the election, therefore, Gordon suggested to Gladstone that much might be done by executive action to establish Home Rule. There was, he thought, nothing to prevent the lord-lieutenant swearing in distinguished Irish members of Parliament as members of an Irish privy

[50]See p. 355, fn. 46.
[51]Gordon to Lady Sophia Palmer, 7 May 1886, Stanmore Papers, 49222.
[52]Gordon to Waterfield, 16 July 1886, Stanmore Papers, 49251.
[53]Gordon to Lady Sophia Palmer, 8 Nov. 1886, Stanmore Papers, 49222.
[54]Gordon to Selborne, 26 Feb. 1887, Stanmore Papers, 49219.
[55]*Ibid.*, 17 Dec. 1886.
[56]Gordon to Waterfield, 2 Sept. 1891, Stanmore Papers, 49252.
[57]Gordon to Selborne, 8 Sept. 1891, Stanmore Papers, 49220.
[58]Gordon to Sir Arthur Havelock, 11 March 1893, Stanmore Papers, 49207.

council or being guided in his executive actions by a committee of that privy council. The fact that such an Irish executive government had been established would make it easier to create an Irish legislature.[59] There would appear to have been merit in this suggestion—although Gladstone did not take it up. It may be doubted whether Parliament would have applauded such executive action, but once the step had been taken Parliament would have found it difficult to reverse.

The day after the Prime Minister introduced the second Home Rule Bill, Gordon wrote to him: "I think the new Bill in most respects better than the old one; but whatever may be the practical necessity for the change, my strong objection to the retention of the Irish members in the Imperial Parliament remains."[60] Gladstone had thus been informed before he made his offer of a peerage in May that Gordon supported Home Rule with reservations. Sir Arthur's statement in his letter of 16 May, that he "cordially accepted" Home Rule and thought he could "speak with some effect in its favour,"[61] meant in effect "I support Home Rule in the abstract and from my colonial experience I can speak on behalf of the principle." That Gordon's letter was worded so as not to discourage Gladstone from continuing with the peerage plan and, at the same time so as not to commit himself too far, can scarcely be doubted. He later spoke of it as "what in my conceit I thought a rather good letter."[62] He was, however, not altogether sure that he had retained his freedom and went to London to see Gladstone and make plain that his was a qualified support. To what extent he accomplished his purpose is not clear. He had another interview on 8 June and noted in his diary: "saw Gladstone about peerage. Some friends for it, some against. Myself doubtful."[63] On one of these occasions, or in a letter (missing), he evidently told the Prime Minister that if his (Gordon's) views did not lead Gladstone to reconsider his offer it would be gratifying to feel that his colonial service and personal friendship were being recognized and that Gladstone was not being moved by political considerations. Gordon, and Balfour and Wantage, whom he consulted, believed that this left the decision to Gladstone and that, since he did not reconsider the matter but proceeded with it, Gordon was within his rights to consider his peerage a free and not a political one.[64]

Lady Sophia, who had warned Gordon that whatever promises of

[59]Gordon to Gladstone, 18 July 1892, Gladstone Papers, 44322.
[60]*Ibid.*, 14 Feb. 1893.
[61]See above, p. 356.
[62]Gordon to Selborne, 4 Sept. 1893, Stanmore Papers, 49220.
[63]Gordon's diary, 8 June 1893, Stanmore Papers, 49266.
[64]Gordon to Lady Sophia Palmer, 19 June 1893, Stanmore Papers, 49223.

freedom he might receive from Gladstone would prove "hollow,"[65] was now satisfied that Sir Arthur had "won the day," especially after he had again consulted Balfour and Wantage, Argyll, the Buccleuchs, and the Abercorns. It is very probable that Gordon overplayed his opposition to Home Rule to those of his friends and relatives who opposed it, and that he underplayed his opposition to the Bill to Gladstone and others who approved it. In any event he agreed to accept the peerage apparently on the understanding that he was not to take his seat until the end of the session.[66] His barony was announced early in July.

Gordon was aware that his position at first would be difficult and painful. "It would," he wrote to Selborne, "be paying dearly for a seat in the House of Lords, to be cut by all one's Tory friends for taking a peerage from Gladstone at all, and by all one's liberal friends for voting against him after having done so."[67] The reference here to voting against Gladstone was to the other articles of the Newcastle programme, not to Home Rule. For the vote on the latter he would not be in the House, or so he thought. His confidence that, as a practical matter, he would not be concerned with the Home Rule Bill, and the dilatoriness of the officials in completing the formalities connected with his peerage induced in him a sense of security that led him to speak more favourably of the Bill to Gladstone than his beliefs warranted. Although he did write to the Prime Minister that, as he had always preferred the total exclusion of the Irish members from the Commons, he regretted the change in clause nine (an amendment which Gladstone accepted on 12 July), he also expressed his willingness to take his seat and even to speak in favour of Home Rule.[68] In mid-August he wrote to Gladstone concerning "the object I have at heart,—the formation of a bridge to render easier the transfer to the cause of Home Rule of the votes of men who profess to approve of Home Rule in the abstract, but object to the details of the measure." He thought his long removal from active political life might give him some advantage in making such an appeal.[69] What he probably planned was an appeal to the Lords to vote for the second reading as merely approving the principle of Home Rule on the understanding that the Bill would then be withdrawn and the question settled by conferences as the Reform Bill of 1884 had

[65]Lady Sophia recalled the shock she had felt in 1886 at the pressure that had been put upon her brother, Lord Wolmer.
[66]Gordon to Selborne (most private), 4 Sept. 1893, Stanmore Papers, 49220.
[67]Gordon to Selborne, 1 July 1893, Stanmore Papers, 49220.
[68]Gordon to Gladstone, 16 Aug. 1893, Gladstone Papers, 44322.
[69]*Ibid.*, 18 Aug. 1893.

been.[70] Both Gladstone and Kimberley approved of his speaking,[71] although it is not plain whether they knew what he intended to say.

It was now the end of August. Gordon had not yet taken his seat, the formalities connected with his peerage not having been completed. The debate in the Commons was coming to an abrupt end (the Bill passed third reading on the night of 1 September). When it became evident that the debate in the Lords would begin at once, Gordon suddenly shied away. He did not choose, he wrote to Gladstone, to take his seat "in the very midst of the Irish debate, nor yet immediately on its close, which might be open to much misconstruction, and I shall therefore postpone it till quite the end of this session, or the beginning of next."[72]

Gladstone replied immediately, requesting him, "in the most earnest manner," to reconsider his decision to stay out of the Lords until after the fate of the bill had been decided: "I wish I knew how to put into my words all the force with which I feel that I am entitled to make this request, and that your spontaneous declarations to me on this subject amount to engagements. . . . I feel that the matter is of the gravest order; nay more, that in writing thus I am writing in the sense of our old friendship and of all the obligations attaching to it, which includes the necessity of pointing out every danger appearing to touch duty and honour."[73] Gordon answered that he felt "the utmost repugnance to being hustled into the House immediately before the vote on this subject." Had he taken his seat a month ago, there would have been no question about the matter. He would go to London next day to see Gladstone.[74]

In London, Gordon found that the Prime Minister had taken notes of their conversations and was prepared to insist that he take his seat and vote for the second reading of the Bill. On his return home he went over Gladstone's letters and copies of such of his letters to Gladstone as he had retained and tried to recall the purport of their recent conversations. He did not think the Prime Minister "could fairly establish an honourable engagement with him." He could see, however, that Gladstone could make a very plausible case and that there would be grave difficulties for himself in contesting the point. He would have attempted resistance had his objections to voting for the second reading

[70]Gordon to Havelock, 11 March 1893 and 25 Dec. 1893, Stanmore Papers, 49207.
[71]Gladstone to Gordon, 22 Aug. 1893 and Gordon to Gladstone, 31 Aug. 1893, Gladstone Papers, 44322.   [72]Gordon to Gladstone, 31 Aug. 1893, ibid.
[73]Gladstone to Gordon, 1 Sept. 1893, ibid.
[74]Gordon to Gladstone, 1 Sept. 1893, ibid.

of the Bill been one of conscience, but this was not the case. The second reading committed him only to support the principle and not the Bill itself. He had long favoured the principle. He would have preferred to have abstained from voting partly because he objected to many of the Bill's provisions, but more because he did not wish to incur the disapproval of his right-wing friends, Selborne and his daughter, Argyll, the Abercorns, and others.[75] After a further unsuccessful appeal to Gladstone to spare him the necessity of voting, "which can serve no useful purpose except to add an unit to a minority. . . . ,"[76] Gordon capitulated. He took his seat as Baron Stanmore and was one of the minority of forty-one voting for the second reading.

In his reply to Gordon's final letter Gladstone had said, first, "that a position between the seat taken and the vote withheld is in itself thoroughly untenable," and, secondly, "that I have no power to release you from the effect of all you have said and written to us on political matters within the last twelve months. . . ."[77] The first statement indicates that Gladstone had not considered Gordon's peerage a reward for his colonial service and that to his mind all peerages were political. The second perhaps suggests two things: first, that Gladstone's powers of self-deception were still operative, because despite what Gordon had said and written in favour of Home Rule he had also written enough to indicate his strong objections to the Bill; and, secondly, that to the Prime Minister party came before friendship. Gordon had intimated that if Gladstone insisted on his vote it would mean an end to their friendship. Moreover, it must have been clear to Gladstone that whatever his interpretation of the "engagement" it was not Sir Arthur's. It is remarkable that Gladstone should have been so insistent on Gordon's vote in what was so obviously a lost cause.

Gordon felt that Gladstone had treated him badly and ceased corresponding with him until, on the occasion of the old man's retirement, he wrote congratulating him on obtaining at last the quiet and leisure he had so long desired.[78] An occasional exchange of mildly friendly letters followed, but they did not see each other until the summer of 1896 when Gordon, who was to write a life of Sidney Herbert, called upon Gladstone. He found him greatly changed: "Nothing could be more different than what he is now, and what he was when in office. Every trace of excitement, impatience, and violence, had

[75]Gordon to Selborne (most private), 4 Sept. 1893.
[76]Gordon to Gladstone, 3 Sept. 1893, Gladstone Papers, 44322.
[77]Gladstone to Gordon, 4 Sept. 1893, *ibid.*
[78]Stanmore to Gladstone, 5 March 1894, *ibid.*

disappeared. He was perfectly calm, perfectly rational, perfectly courteous. . . ."[79] They had an hour's agreeable conversation, mostly about Herbert. Then Gladstone asked him to see Mrs. Gladstone and shake hands with her. He agreed, and Gladstone left them alone. Mrs. Gladstone shook hands with him and immediately began berating him for deserting and "making a fool of William," who, she said, "had never the least taken in that I . . . meant more by my 'growls', and dissatisfaction, than many others did, who, nevertheless, 'stuck to William' when any party question arose."[80] Gordon did not know whether he was glad or sorry to have seen them again.

In addition to this cooling in his relations with the Gladstones after September 1893, Gordon found a change in the attitude of his friends on the right. Many of them doubtless shared the views of the Duke of Argyll, who, in a letter to Queen Victoria concerning the division in the Lords on the Home Rule Bill, wrote: "Among the small, factional minority of 41, there were several Peers notoriously opposed to the Bill in their hearts. The new Peer, Arthur Gordon is an example. What can have induced him to commit such an act as to vote for the Bill, is inconceivable to me. That he might avoid voting at all I thought probable. But to vote *for* the Bill seems to me very like telling a lie!"[81] The Abercorns ceased all communication with him, the Duke ending it by saying he would never respect him again. His relationship with Lord Selborne was strained for a time, but after a few months was on a normal footing. Lady Sophia was more difficult to conciliate than her father. It was two years before her friendship for him was fully restored although they began corresponding again sometime earlier. After learning that he intended to vote for the Bill she had begun a letter with these words: "I am bitterly disappointed and that is all I can say," and had then proceeded to say a great deal:

Almost everyone knows Mr. Gladstone by now and anything which he might have chosen to say or to impute would have been taken at its just value. Why because he behaves as if he were in the place of God and at the same time acts with the duplicity *either* of a bad man or a mad man, you or anyone else should act *contrary to intention* (and that *is* the truth), I cannot understand. Your letter to him is absolutely clear and I remember, so does my F[ather] and so no doubt do Willie[82] and hundreds of others y[ou]r strong clear expression absolutely against this most miserable, wicked bill. That you do not object to the abstract idea of a *subordinate* legislative

[79]Stanmore to Lady Sophia Palmer, 15 Aug. 1896, Stanmore Papers, 49223.
[80]*Ibid.*
[81]G. E. Buckle, ed., *The Letters of Queen Victoria*, 3rd ser., II, 314.
[82]Lady Sophia's brother, Lord Wolmer.

assembly in Ireland is no sort of reason for voting for a Bill—misbegotten, deformed in all its parts and which, if carried, could bring nothing but needless confusion, misery and weakness. . . .

You did not mean to vote for it . . . and no words, no cunning, no threats, nothing from Mr. G[ladstone] or anyone else would make *me* vote when I had intended not. You are free and to me it seems no sort of excuse that Mr. G. bullies or puts any amount of pressure. You knew what you meant— at most you might have to say "I have spoken unguardedly and loosely but I did not mean what you inferred and I expressly took the Peerage as a free man."

I have y[ou]r letters in which you wrote all this and you told me the Duke of Argyll, Lord Balfour, Lord Wantage, etc. all said it was plainly a *free* peerage. Why give in? Don't answer this. I would rather you did not.

In a postscript she added:

It is the giving in, in sacrificing to bullying when, if free (and everyone is who chooses to be) you know your opinions are or were the other way, which I cannot stand. And throwing yourself away for and at the feet of Mr. G. and throwing away the respect worth having of men like the Duke of Argyll and scores more. Truly Mr. G. has the power of witchcraft![83]

Gordon did not obey her injunction but replied the same day. There were several things he wished her to know: that he had intimated to Balfour and Wantage before any pressure had been brought on him by Gladstone that there was a possibility he might vote for the Bill (she could ask them if she liked); that Balfour did not share her opinion that he could have withstood Gladstone's denunciation had he refused to vote, but felt that he would not have been able to have made himself heard against it; that Lord Selborne was mainly but not entirely right concerning his [Gordon's] reasons for voting for the Bill.[84] "I am also influenced by a more selfish and vulgar feeling. As through my indiscretion it seems that misrepresentation and discredit are in any case inevitable, I had rather be supposed to have sold myself and paid the price rather than to have sold myself and evaded paying the price. . . ."[85]

The circumstances through which Sir Arthur Gordon emerged as a peer and voted for the first time in the Lords do not reflect credit upon him. He appears to have been less than candid with his friends on both sides of the Home Rule question. He was certainly foolish to think he could match the "Grand Old Man" in cunning. He talked too much, to too many, too indiscreetly. Nevertheless, much may be said to extenuate his conduct. He genuinely wished a peerage as an avenue to further useful work. He deserved a peerage for his long and successful colonial

[83]Lady Sophia Palmer to Gordon, 5 Sept. 1893, Stanmore Papers, 49223.
[84]The reference is undoubtedly to Gordon's long friendship for Gladstone.
[85]Stanmore to Lady Sophia Palmer, 5 Sept. 1893.

service and would have got one had it not been for the Queen. It appeared to Gordon that Gladstone's offer might be his last chance because by the time the Conservatives returned to power his claim on the basis of service could well be forgotten. Perhaps he was justified in exploiting his connection with Gladstone as far as he decently could. Gordon occupied the most difficult position possible in a political war. He did not believe fully in the cause of either antagonist and thus could not choose sides. Yet he was not a neutral. Agreeing in part with both, he could give partial support to both. He paid the price that all in such positions pay: he forfeited the regard of both sides. His only alternative would have been a retreat to the wilderness of private life and this, to him, would have been the same as suicide.

Only one event relieved Gordon's loneliness and unhappiness during his first weeks as a peer—his receipt of one of Fillingham Parr's (his old Fiji enemy) ridiculous letters. Parr wrote:

My Lord,
I see that your elevation to the peerage is gazetted today. I am not at all surprised that you should be anxious to hide the name of Sir Arthur Gordon, and to trust that under your new title it may never be remembered. The Colonists, in every one of your Governorships, had life long cause to remember you;—in New Brunswick (where you may remember the prayer for "Thy servant Arthur"),[86] Trinidad, Mauritius, Fiji—especially Fiji—New Zealand (Mr. Rusden, after the Bryce affair, will not, I imagine congratulate you) and lastly Ceylon. Now you will be remembered no more! How sad!! But, if you can allow a charitable thought to enter your mind, you may reflect with advantage that the word "Stanmore" will not arouse the worst of human passions in the thousands of breasts of those who have suffered under you, in the same way that the words "Arthur Gordon" do.
Having condemned yourself to oblivion you might surely give up your paternal interest in Fiji, & allow the Colony to be governed by a *man*, and not by a *thing*! It has a grand prospect before it if ever such a day should arrive, and no one knows better than yourself that since 1876 all its chances and opportunities have been cruelly stifled.
The Sigatoka executions I can never forget, but with "Arthur Gordon" gone, and a happier state of things existing in Fiji, I could more easily forget them than I can at present.[87]

II. LORD STANMORE

Gordon's career in the House of Lords, as Baron Stanmore, was not a remarkable one. At first he followed an independent line; but as the

[86]Egalitarian New Brunswick felt some shock and amusement at Gordon having the Bishop of Fredericton pray for the safety of "Thy Servant Arthur" immediately after the invocation for the Queen and members of the Royal Family.
[87]Parr to Gordon, 23 Aug. 1893, Stanmore Papers, 49242.

years passed he identified himself more and more with the unionist-conservative party in its resistance to the socio-political revolution taking place in the country. His transition was shared by many another whom time was passing by and whose emotional attachment to the constitution under which they had reached maturity obscured their clearness of vision.

Until the death of the Liberal government in 1895, Stanmore found his position an uncomfortable one. The friends of the government were "very naturally irritated," by what they rightly considered his "half-hearted support"; the Tories were "indignant at liberalism in any shape."[88] His position was not unlike the one which, after his father's retirement, he had occupied in the Commons forty years earlier: "desirous to support the government . . . but constantly repelled by its acting in contravention of principles which seem . . . to underly all true liberalism."[89] In August 1894 Lord Rosebery wrote that "no one can have attended the House of Lords this session without receiving the impression that your attitude to the ministry is one of more than common hostility" but that, although it was a "somewhat negative consolation," he was glad to learn that "ours was not the only party that had incurred your disapproval, but that all were involved in a general condemnation."[90] Stanmore replied that he always personally disliked voting against the government and was glad when he could vote for it.[91]

Although he rejected the accuracy of Rosebery's phrase "more than common hostility," there is evidence that Stanmore was uncommonly hostile to that group in the Liberal party which was, he thought, inclined to sacrifice individual liberty to the will of the majority.[92] He believed that that group had become dominant in the party and that the ministry was busily endeavouring "to promote Revolution and the abolition of the existing British Constitution." These efforts had not been successful as yet, but who could say "what may not be the result of constant pegging away, on the part of ministers turned agitators?"[93] Upon the fall of the Rosebery government, Stanmore wrote to Gladstone: "I hope I shall always be a liberal in [the] sense in which, a few years ago, both you and I equally understood the word, [but] I am afraid I must forego the name if those only are entitled to it who are prepared to substitute collectivist tyranny for individual liberty; to

[88]Stanmore to Gladstone, 21 June 1894, Gladstone Papers, 44322.
[89]Ibid.
[90]Rosebery to Stanmore, 11 Aug. 1894, Stanmore Papers, 49242.
[91]Stanmore to Rosebery, 12 Aug. 1894, ibid.
[92]Stanmore to Gladstone, 10 May 1894, Gladstone Papers, 44322.
[93]Stanmore to Sir Arthur Havelock, 12 Sept. 1894, Stanmore Papers, 49207.

divert to purely secular uses almost the whole mass of property now employed for religious purposes; and to 'annihilate' the House of Lords."[94] This letter was Stanmore's farewell to the Liberal party and to Gladstone. Two months earlier he had parted for the last time with Lord Selborne, who died in May. The loss of his closest friend left him very lonely. Lady Sophia wrote: "I am so sorry for you and your love was very precious to him."[95]

Stanmore's links with the past were being rapidly cut; but he found some consolation in two events, one private, one public. Lady Sophia Palmer now resumed her old familiar correspondence with him and the new government obtained a "marvellous majority." He believed the latter would mean that "the triumph of revolution" would be less rapid and less complete than he had expected.[96] He had only two regrets concerning the fall of the Liberals. He had prepared his first big speech for delivery in the Lords and it was now of no use, and he had lost his "uniform and most convenient answer to all applicants—that my relations with H[er] M[ajesty's] Gov[ernmen]t did not admit of my soliciting any favour from or making any recommendation to them."[97]

It is a little surprising to find Stanmore making the latter statement in the light of the use he himself had made, during the course of his career, of friends who were in a position to request favours of the government. Stanmore was, however, like Gladstone, capable of self-deception and was convinced that he had made his own way in life without benefit of patronage.[98] The available evidence is insufficient to determine the extent to which he refused to urge the claims of applicants for favours. It is clear, however, that he did try to secure appointment to Nyasaland for Sir Frederick Lugard, early in 1894, but without success.[99] And on 11 June, after talking with Lugard, Stanmore spoke briefly in the House of Lords on Uganda-Nyasaland affairs.

With the advent of the Conservative ten-year tenure of office in 1895, Stanmore did not become a thorough Liberal again—contrary to Gladstone's intimation of such to George Shaw-Lefevre. Doubtless his mind had an opposition cast and a minority had great attraction for him;[100] but he was generally in sympathy with the aims of the new government, and in 1896 he moved the address in reply to the speech from the

[94]Stanmore to Gladstone, 5 July 1895, Gladstone Papers, 44322.
[95]Lady Sophia Palmer to Stanmore, 8 May 1895, Stanmore Papers, 49223.
[96]Stanmore to Havelock, 13 Aug. 1895, Stanmore Papers, 49207.
[97]Ibid.
[98]See his letter to Lady Sophia Palmer, 20 Oct. 1886, quoted p. 347.
[99]Lugard to Stanmore, 6 June 1894 and 22 July 1894, Stanmore Papers, 49242.
[100]Stanmore to Gladstone, 5 July 1895, Gladstone Papers, 44322.

throne. Nevertheless, liberal traditions remained strong within him and general agreement did not preclude criticism. By the summer of 1896 he had come to believe that Lord Salisbury was "feeling the weight of his size and his years" and becoming "inert," that the government's foreign policy was "humiliating," and its domestic policy only that of "avoiding trouble." There were things, he wrote prophetically, which if not done by Lord Salisbury would not be done. Among them was the reform of the House of Lords; unless Salisbury undertook this work the House of Lords was "doomed."[101] There is, however, no record of the pattern or extent of the reform Stanmore had in mind.

It was to be expected that Gordon as Lord Stanmore would continue to interest himself in colonial affairs. Until the constitutional crisis between 1909 and 1911, most of his interventions in the debates of the Lords and many of his comments in letters to friends concerned colonial matters. He continued to intercede for the non-Europeans. One such opportunity occurred during the Jubilee of 1897. The celebration was designed to honour the self-governing colonies only, but Ceylon, despite its being told that no delegation was wanted, nevertheless sent one. The Colonial Office cold-shouldered it. Stanmore used some very plain language in Downing Street. The result was that the Colonial Office, although it did not officially recognize the Ceylon delegation, treated the members civilly and allowed them to see the procession from a window at the Colonial Office but—"incredible meanness"—charged them twelve shillings and six pence each for their seats.[102] He also managed to have the Ceylonese presented personally to the Queen. Without these attentions they would undoubtedly have returned home feeling more than a little insulted and shaken in their loyalty to Britain.

Stanmore's New Brunswick and New Zealand experiences left him feeling much less charitable towards the delegates from the self-governing colonies than to those from Ceylon. This is evident from his comment on the former and their behaviour:

The Colonial Premiers, (or Preemiers as they call themselves), must have had their heads completely turned, and I should think would all be kicked out of office when they go home, partly from the jealousy of less fortunate politicians and partly because they will be unbearable from the amount of conceit they have taken in. It was decidedly comic to see them in their royal carriages escorted by troops on their way to St. Paul's. They bowed and waved their hands and gesticulated graciously to the crowd as if they were the Queen herself. It was about time for them to be off, for they were beginning to commit *gaucheries.* One of them, Seddon of New Zealand,

[101]Stanmore to Lady Sophia Palmer, 15 Aug. 1896, Stanmore Papers, 49223.
[102]Stanmore to Havelock, 18 July 1897, Stanmore Papers, 49207.

while still the Queen's guest and driving in a royal coach with scarlet foot-
men, delivered a socialist address to the Fabian club![103]

Despite this "vulgarity and absurdity" Stanmore found the Jubilee "a
striking commemoration . . . imposing in its universality."[104]

Lord Stanmore felt that the next important imperial event, the Boer
War, might have been avoided, but that once Britain had engaged in it
she must fight it out to the end. This "unhappy war," he commented
sadly in 1902, "has been and is a miserable business,"[105] although it did
not produce any rift between him and the Liberal Unionist party. Two
years later, however, he found himself opposed to Joseph Chamberlain's
effort to unify the Empire by creating a tariff union. Stanmore had
always been a convinced free trader. He was therefore incensed when
Chamberlain proposed a British tariff and then, after its rejection by the
cabinet, appealed directly to the people. "Chamberlain," he wrote, "has
shattered to pieces the Liberal Unionist Party as completely as Mr.
Gladstone broke up the old Liberal party . . . and I cannot forgive him
for it."[106] Except on the Chinese coolie issue in the Transvaal, he
continued to support the government until its fall at the end of 1905.
Thereafter he occupied the Cross Benches, "the retreat of age and
neutrality."[107]

The treatment of the Chinese coolies in the mining areas of the
Transvaal was a matter which drew Stanmore's interest during the years
1904 to 1906 and upon which no one was better qualified to speak. In
August 1904, he protested against allowing the Governor of the Transvaal to break the prohibition, placed on him by the Royal Instructions
in 1902, to assent to ordinances which imposed restrictions on non-
Europeans but not on Europeans. The object of the restrictions on
Chinese labour in that colony, he pointed out, was not, as in Mauritius
or Fiji, to ensure performance of contract but, rather, to prevent all
association between Chinese and Europeans. A restriction with such a
motive was completely unprecedented. "The great principle . . . that
European and non-European residents in a country are to be treated
alike, is not one which it was intended to be dealt with in this way." He
noted that in the West Indies regulations which had formerly been
deemed essential to the protection of imported labour had gradually
been abandoned. He was led to fear, he said, that "the whole action,

103*Ibid.*
104*Ibid.*
105*Ibid.*, 27 March 1902.
106*Ibid.*, 6 Feb. 1904.
107Speech, 27 Feb. 1906, H. of L., *Debates*, CLII, cols. 959–61.

tone, and spirit of the Colonial Department of the present day show a grave and growing departure from the maxims which prevailed there some thirty or forty years ago."[108] In May of the following year and early in 1906, he again protested against the compound system employed to segregate the Chinese in the Transvaal. He warned of the danger of race hatred and of the bad effect of encouraging the white community to look down upon the immigrants as prisoners.[109] On this particular issue, Stanmore stood not only on the side of the angels, but also on that of the majority of Britons. On the two final issues of his life, the budget of 1909 and the Parliament Act of 1911, he was to stand with neither.

Stanmore was at first inclined to think that it would be dangerous for the Lords to reject the Lloyd George budget, although there was no doubt of their technical right to do so. He questioned whether it was "expedient to exercise a right which has been tacitly given up for centuries," and he stressed the "risk of playing our opponents' game and furnishing them with a plausible cry which might mislead the mob of ignorant voters who now elect our parliaments. . . ."[110]

After the Bill was published he abandoned that view although he continued to be cautious. If the land clauses of the Bill were to be dropped it would be best to let it pass. If they were not, then he believed the Lords were bound to divide it or reject it. If the Upper House were to assent to "the hardly veiled 'tacking' " involved in the first part of the Bill, it would proclaim its "utter impotence and incompetence" to play the part of a second chamber. "We shall forfeit our own self respect and the respect of the country, and we shall be swept away, as mere cumberers of the ground, with the common assent of all parties."[111] There were dangers in taking a bold course. The Lords might come to be considered "usurpers" and "unconstitutional tyrants"; but "at the worst we should end with dignity and not be branded by future generations as a set of mean spirited cowards who deserved our fate." He believed the "mass of intelligent opinion" was with the peers, but the question was whether intelligent opinion would be "overborne by the numerical force of an unintelligent mob." He considered that the Lords ought not simply to reject the Bill. Such action might be misrepresented. They should, rather, pass a resolution dividing it or affirming that that part of it which was not strictly financial should be relegated to another

[108]*Ibid.*, 11 Aug. 1904, CXL, cols. 196–202.
[109]*Ibid.*, 16 May 1905 and 27 Feb. 1906, CXLVI, cols. 444–47, and CLII, cols. 953–62.
[110]Stanmore to Viscount Halifax, 23 June 1909, Stanmore Papers, 49242.
[111]*Ibid.*

bill. As an alternative he suggested the rejection of those clauses which could be considered "tacks."[112]

Lord Halifax, to whom these suggestions were made, thought Stanmore's letter an excellent one and sent it to Lord Lansdowne, the official leader of the Opposition in the Lords. The latter considered it "very interesting and sensible."[113] At first Lansdowne had not intended to oppose the budget in the Lords, but as the Conservative and Unionist peers drew together in the face of the challenge to their privileges and to their constitutional rights, he changed his mind. So did Stanmore. He was among those who voted against the second reading on 30 November 1909. Entering the debate on the final day he said: "Since 1861 . . . the inclusion of all finance measures in one Bill has made it, as Mr. Gladstone said, most difficult [but] not impossible to reject them, and rejection would never have been resorted to had not Your Lordships perceived how powerful a weapon in the hands of an unscrupulous Government would be the admission that whatever they chose to cover with the sanctity of a Money Bill must pass without demur." He would, he concluded defiantly, "rather see this House destroyed than degraded."[114]

Stanmore made his last speech in the House of Lords on 3 July 1911, in the debate on the Parliament Bill. In it he moved that the House of Commons be not allowed to legislate upon the following matters unless it had a two-thirds majority of members of Parliament on third reading in each session in which a bill passed: the order of succession to the Crown, changes in the prerogatives of the Crown, disestablishment or disendowment of the Established Church of England or Scotland, creation of separate legislatures for any part of the United Kingdom, and any increase or diminution of the powers or privileges of either house of Parliament.[115] Such a motion was too reactionary to earn general support, and he withdrew it.

A week after Balfour and Lansdowne had been informed by Lloyd George of the King's pledge to create enough peers to pass the Parliament Bill, Stanmore, replying to a letter from Lansdowne, suggested how the fight might still be continued. He would agree with Lansdowne that, were further resistance impossible, it would be wiser to preserve the power of delaying legislation for two years than to throw it away. Yet he felt the peers might still win the battle. There were seventeenth-

[112]*Ibid.*
[113]Lansdowne to Halifax, 30 June 1909, Stanmore Papers, 49242, f. 302.
[114]Speech, 30 Nov. 1909, H. of L., *Debates*, IV, cols. 1309–10.
[115]*Ibid.*, 3 July 1911, IX, col. 55.

century precedents for the House of Lords dispensing with the attendance of members if it chose. Should the Committee on Privileges recommend, and the House resolve, that the peers who were created to pass the Parliament Bill be discharged from the service of the House for the remainder of the life of the present Parliament, there existed no authority or court which could override that decision. "We have," he wrote, "the same right to pronounce on our own privileges that the House of Commons has with regard to its privileges, and even if this were not so, there can be no appeal from a Superior Court to an inferior one."[116] This procedure had not been followed in 1832, but the case then was different. The Bill of 1832, while affecting the influence of the peers and the balance of the constitution, did not touch the existing rights of either house. Should his idea be seriously entertained, he told Lansdowne, he could furnish a whole budget of precedents and arguments. He had, he felt, some claim to be considered an historical expert, and the opinion he had formed on this matter was the result of years of reading. He denied being an extremist, but he noted that two hundred years ago a minister giving the advice which Asquith had given would have been impeached. Impeachments were now out of fashion, but he could see no reason why the Lords should not "arrest with a strong hand the attack on our independence, if we can do so."[117]

What Lansdowne's reaction to this letter was does not appear, but presumably he realized what Stanmore evidently did not: that were this advice to be adopted and to prove successful, the result would undoubtedly have been an Irish revolution and the eventual abolition of the House of Lords. The pressures for democratic advance had by now become irresistible and could no longer be overborne by legalisms however ingenious.

Arthur Hamilton Gordon, Baron Stanmore, had lived a few years too long. The times were "out of joint" for him. The Parliament Bill was his last controversy. He saw its passage but, fortunately, did not survive to see its results. His decline was rapid. He was well in the autumn of 1911 and his mind was clear and alert. By December he was "less well" and on 30 January 1912 he died "of old age"[118] in his eighty-third year. He had been the last survivor of Lord and Lady Aberdeen's families,[119] his brother Douglas, Canon of Salisbury, having died in December 1901.

[116]Stanmore to Lansdowne, 25 July 1911, Stanmore Papers, 49242.
[117]*Ibid.*
[118]Evidence of his son, the late George Arthur Maurice Hamilton Gordon, 2nd Baron Stanmore (d. Feb. 1957).
[119]Arthur Gordon's mother and father had both been twice married and both had had two families.

During the last twenty years of his life Stanmore had many interests not all of which were connected with the House of Lords. He was largely responsible for the revival in 1906 of the committee, called the Westminster Palace Committee, to decorate the houses of Parliament. At one time or another he was a member of the Ceylon Association, a member of the house committee and executive of the Gordon Boys' Home near Woking, a member of the standing committee of the Society for the Propagation of the Gospel, chairman of the Pacific Islands Company, and a director of the Bank of Mauritius and the Bank of New Zealand. He usually spent a part of the winter in Italy and Malta. He became an ardent, if not expert, photographer. "Photographed vigorously in the morning" is a typical diary entry during his visits abroad. The greater part of his time in England, however, was spent writing. In 1893 he published a biography of his father, and in 1906 a two-volume memoir of Sidney Herbert. In 1894 he produced the records of his administration of Mauritius in two privately printed volumes and between 1897 and 1912 his Fiji records in four volumes. During the same period he edited his father's letters and had them privately printed. He continued to carry on an extensive private correspondence.

Those with whom Stanmore corresponded most frequently during the last years of his life were Lady Sophia Palmer, Sir Arthur Havelock, and Sir William MacGregor. Sir William wrote what was probably the last letter Stanmore received. Even had MacGregor known that his great friend had come so near the end of his life, he could scarcely have written a more fitting tribute: "I do not think . . . that the founder of the present great prosperity of Suva and Fiji will ever be forgotten. It will all be remembered when you are gone. . . . It will go down to history that you made Fiji and saved Ceylon. I get much credit here [Brisbane] for my work in New Guinea. It should go to your address, not to mine.[120]

[120]MacGregor to Stanmore, 24 Nov. 1911, Stanmore Papers, 49203.

BIBLIOGRAPHY

❦

MANUSCRIPT SOURCES

I. MSS. of the Public Record Office

A. COLONIAL OFFICE—PUBLIC

Ceylon: CO 54, vols. 545–91; CO 58, vols. 80–94; CO 59, vols. 93–101.

Fiji: CO 83, vols. 5–31; CO 84, vols. 1, 2; CO 85, vols. 1–3; CO 86, vols. 1, 2A; CO 459, vols. 1A, 1B–6; CO 537, vol. 115.

Mauritius: CO 167, vols. 524–62; CO 172, vols. 95–107.

New Brunswick: CO 188, vols. 127, 131, 132, 137, 192; CO 189, vols. 8, 9.

New Zealand: CO 209, vols. 239–42.

Trinidad: CO 295, vols. 230–59; CO 298, vols. 34, 35; CO 300, vols. 76–81.

Western Pacific: CO 537, vol. 136.

B. COLONIAL OFFICE—PRIVATE

Cardwell Papers, Colonial Office Correspondence and Memoranda: (*a*) Correspondence with Hon. A. H. Gordon, 1864–1866, 30/48–6/39; (*b*) Correspondence with Rt. Hon. the Earl of Carnarvon and others, 30/48–6/40.

Carnarvon Papers: (*a*) Parliamentary and Colonial Office Papers, July 1866 to March 1867, 30–6/70; (*b*) Correspondence with the Governors of Fiji and New Zealand, GD 6/39.

C. FOREIGN OFFICE

Western Pacific: FO 58, vols. 168, 173, 177; FO 68, vol. 164.

II. MSS. of the British Museum

Aberdeen Papers: Correspondence of Lord Aberdeen with his youngest son, Arthur, . . . 1842–1859, vol. CLXXXVIII (Add. MSS. 43226).

Gladstone Papers: (*a*) Correspondence with 1st Earl of Kimberley, 1859–1872, vol. CXXXIX (Add. MSS. 44224); (*b*) Correspondence with the Hon. Sir Arthur Hamilton Gordon, 1851–1896, vols. CCXXXIV–CCXXXVII (Add. MSS. 44319–44322).

Layard Papers: Correspondence March, April 1865, vol. CLXXXIV (Add. MSS. 39114).

Stanmore Papers: Collection of private papers of Sir Arthur Hamilton Gordon, 1st Lord Stanmore (1829–1912), 1841–1912, vols. I–LXVII (Add. MSS. 49199–49276).

III. MSS. of the Bonar Law–Bennett Library at the University of New Brunswick

Stanmore Papers: Collection of private papers of Sir Arthur Hamilton Gordon pertaining to his administration of New Brunswick, 1861–1866, 3 vols. unfoliated.

OFFICIAL PRINTED MATERIAL

Parliamentary Papers: 1870, L (450); 1871, XX [C-393], XLVIII (269); 1875, XXXIV [C-1115], LIII [C-1188]; 1876, LIV [C-1404]; 1882, XLVI [C-3382]; 1883, XLVII [C-3641], [C-3689], [C-3691], [C-3814]; 1884, LV [C-3863], [C-3905].

Parliamentary Debates, House of Commons: 1882, CCLXX.

——— House of Lords: 1883, CCLXXXI; 1904, CXL; 1905, CXLVI; 1906, CLII; 1909, IV; 1911, IX.

Journal of the House of Assembly of New Brunswick, 1866.

Report of the Police Inquiry Commission [*in Mauritius*], 1872 (copy in Library, Royal Commonwealth Society).

PUBLISHED CORRESPONDENCE

BUCKLE, G. E., ed., *The Letters of Queen Victoria*, 3rd ser. (London, 1926–32).

GORDON, A. H., see Stanmore.

KNAPLUND, PAUL, "Gladstone-Gordon Correspondence, 1851–1896," *Transactions of the American Philosophical Society*, new ser., LI, p. 4 (Philadelphia, 1961).

MANNING, WILLIAM R., ed., *Diplomatic Correspondence of the United States: Canadian Relations 1784–1860*, IV (Washington, 1945).

MARINDIN, GEORGE EDEN, ed., *Letters of Frederic, Lord Blachford, Under Secretary of State for the Colonies 1860–1871* (London, 1896).

PALMER, ROUNDELL, see Selborne.

PHILLIPPS, L. M., and B. CHRISTIAN, *Some Hawarden Letters, 1878–1913* (n.p., 1917).

POPE, SIR JOSEPH, *Correspondence of Sir John Macdonald.* (Toronto, n.d.).

SELBORNE, ROUNDELL PALMER, EARL OF, *Memorials: Part I, Family and Personal, 1766–1865*, 2 vols. (London, 1896); Part II, *Personal and Political, 1865–1895*, 2 vols. (London, 1898).

STANMORE, ARTHUR HAMILTON GORDON, 1st Baron, *Mauritius: Records of Private and of Public Life, 1871–1874*, 2 vols. (Edinburgh, 1894), privately printed.

——— *Fiji: Records of Private and of Public Life, 1875–1880*, 4 vols. (Edinburgh, 1897–1912).

——— *Letters and Notes Written During the Disturbances in the Highlands (known as the "Devil Country") of Viti Levu, Fiji, 1876*, 2 vols. (Edinburgh, 1879).

NEWSPAPERS

Canada: *Evening News* (Toronto) 1894.

Mauritius: *Le Cernéen* (Port Louis) 1872, 1874; *Commercial Gazette* (Port Louis) 1867, 1871, 1872; *Overland Commercial Gazette* (Port Louis) 1873; *Progrès Colonial* (Port Louis) 1872; *Sentinelle de Maurice* (Port Louis) 1872.

New Brunswick: *Morning Freeman* (Saint John) 1867; *Morning Telegraph* (Saint John) 1865.

Trinidad: *Port of Spain Gazette*, 1868; *San Fernando Gazette*, 1867; *Trinidad Chronicle* (Port-of-Spain) 1867, 1868, 1870.

United Kingdom: *The Times* (London) 1875, 1881, 1883.

OTHER WORKS

BAILEY, ALFRED G., "The Basis and Persistence of Opposition to Confederation in New Brunswick," *Canadian Historical Review*, XXIII (1942).
———— "Railways and the Confederation Issue in New Brunswick, 1863–1865," *Canadian Historical Review*, XXI (1940).

BALFOUR, LADY FRANCES, *The Life of George, Fourth Earl of Aberdeen*, II (London, [1922]).

BARNWELL, P. J., *Visits and Despatches (Mauritius 1598–1948)* (Port Louis, 1948).

BODU, JOSE M., *Trinidadiana: Being a Chronological Review of Events which have occurred in the island from the Conquest to the Present Day, with brief notices of the Careers of some Eminent Colonists compiled from various sources* (Port-of-Spain, 1890).

BURNLEY, WILLIAM HARDIN, *Observations on the Present Condition of the Island of Trinidad and the Actual State of the Experiment of Negro Emancipation* (London, 1842).

CALDECOTT, ALFRED, *The Church in the West Indies* (London, 1898).

Cambridge History of the British Empire, vols. II, III, VII, pt. 2 (Cambridge, 1935–59).

CAMPBELL, G. G., *The History of Nova Scotia* (Toronto, 1948).

CHAPMAN, J. K., "The Mid-Nineteenth-Century Temperance Movement in New Brunswick and Maine," *Canadian Historical Review*, XXXV (1954).

CREIGHTON, DONALD G., *John A. Macdonald: The Young Politician* (Toronto, 1952).

[DE PLEVITZ, ADOLPHE], *Petition of the Old Immigrants of Mauritius presented on the 6th of June 1871, with observations by Adolphe de Plevitz* ([Port Louis], 1871) (copy in Library, Royal Commonwealth Society).

DERRICK, R. A., *A History of Fiji*, I (Suva, 1946).

DES VOEUX, SIR GEORGE WILLIAM, *My Colonial Service*, 2 vols. (London, 1903).

DE VERTEUIL, L. A. A., *Trinidad: Its Geography, Natural Resources, Administration, Present Condition, and Prospects*, 2nd ed. (London, 1884).

DRUS, E., "The Colonial Office and the Annexation of Fiji," *Transactions of the Royal Historical Society*, 4th ser., XXXII (1950).

ENSOR, R. C. K., *England, 1870–1914* (Oxford, 1936).

EVERSLEY, T. FITZ-EVAN, *The Trinidad Reviewer for the Year 1899* (London, 1899).

FIELDHOUSE, D. K., "Sir Arthur Gordon and the Parihaka Crisis, 1880–1882," *Historical Studies Australia and New Zealand*, X, no. 37 (Nov. 1961).

FROUDE, J. A., *The English in the West Indies or the Bow of Ulysses* (London, 1888).

GISBORNE, WILLIAM, *New Zealand Rulers and Statesmen, 1840–1897* (n.p., 1897).

GORDON, ARTHUR, "Wilderness Journeys in New Brunswick," *Vacation Tourists and Notes of Travel in 1862–1863*, ed. Francis Galton (London, 1864).

——— "Native Taxation in Fiji," *Proceedings of the Royal Colonial Institute*, X (1878–79).

——— "Native Councils in Fiji," *Contemporary Review*, XLIII (1883).

GWYNN, S., and G. M. TUCKWELL, *Life of Sir Charles Dilke*, I (London, 1917).

HALL, HENRY L., *The Colonial Office: A History* (London, 1937).

HANNAY, JAMES, *History of New Brunswick*, 2 vols. (Saint John, 1909).

——— *The Life and Times of Sir Leonard Tilley, Being a Political History of New Brunswick for the Past Seventy Years* (Saint John, 1897).

HARVEY, D. C., "The Maritime Provinces and Confederation," *Report of the Canadian Historical Association* (1927).

HAZAREESINGH, K., *A History of Indians in Mauritius* (n.p., 1950).

JACOBS, MARJORIE G., "Bismarck and the Annexation of New Guinea," *Historical Studies Australia and New Zealand*, V, no. 17 (Nov. 1952).

KNAPLUND, PAUL, *Gladstone and Britain's Imperial Policy* (London, 1927).

——— *Gladstone's Foreign Policy* (New York, 1935).

——— "Sir Arthur Gordon and Fiji: Some Gordon-Gladstone Letters," *Historical Studies Australia and New Zealand*, VIII, no. 31 (Nov. 1958).

——— "Sir Arthur Gordon and New Zealand, 1880–1882," *Pacific Historical Review*, XXVIII (1959).

——— "Sir Arthur Gordon on the New Guinea Question, 1883," *Historical Studies Australia and New Zealand*, VII, no. 27 (Nov. 1956).

LE BOURDAIS, D. M., *Nation of the North: Canada Since Confederation* (Toronto, 1953).

LEGGE, J. D., *Britain in Fiji, 1858–1880* (London, 1958).

MCINTRYE, W. D., "Disraeli's Colonial Policy: The Creation of the Western Pacific High Commission, 1874–1877," *Historical Studies Australia and New Zealand*, IX, no. 35 (Nov. 1960).

MCNAUGHTAN, I. D., "Colonial Liberalism, 1851–1892," *Australia: A Social and Political History*, ed. Gordon Greenwood (Sydney, 1955).

MAGNUS, SIR PHILIP, *Gladstone: A Biography* (London, 1954).

MALIM, MICHAEL, *Island of the Swan* (London, 1952).

MAUDSLAY, ALFRED P., *Life in the Pacific Fifty Years Ago* (London, 1930).

MILLIDGE, REV. J. W., "Events of the Decade 1860–1870," *Collections of the New Brunswick Historical Society*, IV (St. John, 1919).

MORRELL, W. P., *Britain in the Pacific Islands* (Oxford, 1960).

PARKIN, GEORGE R., *Sir John A. Macdonald* (London, 1909).

PARNABY, OWEN, "Aspects of British Policy in the Pacific: The 1872 Pacific Islanders Protection Act," *Historical Studies Australia and New Zealand*, VIII, no. 29 (Nov. 1957).

[PARR, W. F.], *Fiji in 1877: The First Three Years since Annexation under Governor Sir Arthur H. Gordon, K.C.M.G., or A Crown Colony of a Very Severe Type* (Levuka, 1877).

PENSON, L. M., "The Making of a Crown Colony: British Guiana 1803–33," *Transactions of the Royal Historical Society*, 4th ser., IX (1926).

POPE, SIR JOSEPH, *Memoirs of Rt. Hon. Sir John Alexander Macdonald* (Toronto, n.d.).

RUSDEN, G. W., *History of New Zealand*, III (London, 1883).

STOCK, EUGENE, *The History of the Church Missionary Society, Its Environment, Its Men and Its Work*, II (London, 1899).

WARD, J. M., *British Policy in the South Pacific, 1786–1893: A Study in British Policy prior to the Establishment of Governments in Pacific Islands by the Great Powers* (Sydney, 1948).

WHITELAW, WILLIAM MENZIES, *The Maritimes and Canada before Confederation* (Toronto, 1934).

WILBERFORCE, REGINALD D., *Life of the Right Reverend Samuel Wilberforce*, II (London, 1882).

WOODWARD, E. L., *The Age of Reform, 1815–1870* (Oxford, 1938).

INDEX